# Chaucer's Queer Nation

## Series Editors



Volumes in the series study the diversity of medieval cultural histories and practices, including such interrelated issues as gender, class, and social hierarchies; race and ethnicity; geographical relations; definitions of political space; discourses of authority and dissent; educational institutions; canonical and noncanonical literatures; and technologies of textual and visual literacies.

**Volume 34**
Glenn Burger
*Chaucer's Queer Nation*

**Volume 33**
D. Vance Smith
*Arts of Possession: The Middle English Household Imaginary*

**Volume 32**
Edited by Sharon Farmer and Carol Braun Pasternack
*Gender and Difference in the Middle Ages*

For more books in the series, see pages 265–67.

# Chaucer's Queer Nation

Glenn Burger

MINNESOTA

Medieval Cultures, Volume 34
University of Minnesota Press
Minneapolis
London

Several paragraphs of the Introduction are taken from "Queer Chaucer," *English Studies in Canada* 20 (1994): 153–69; reprinted by permission of *English Studies in Canada*. Earlier versions of chapter 1 appeared as "Shameful Pleasures: Up Close and Dirty with Chaucer, Flesh, and the Word," in *Queering the Middle Ages*, ed. Glenn Burger and Steven F. Kruger (Minneapolis: University of Minnesota Press, 2001), 213–35; and "Erotic Discipline . . . Or, 'Tee hee, I like my boys to be girls': Inventing with the Body in Chaucer's *Miller's Tale*," in *Becoming Male in the Middle Ages*, ed. Bonnie Wheeler and Jeffrey Jerome Cohen (New York: Garland Press, 1997), 245–60; reprinted by permission of the University of Minnesota Press and Palgrave/St. Martin's Press, respectively; the second essay copyright 1997 and also reproduced by permission of Routledge, Inc., part of The Taylor & Francis Group. Parts of chapter 4 are drawn from "Doing What Comes Naturally: The *Physician's Tale* and the Pardoner," in *Masculinities in Chaucer*, ed. Peter G. Beidler (Cambridge: D. S. Brewer, 1998), 117–30; and "Kissing the Pardoner," *PMLA* 107 (1992): 1143–56; reprinted by permission of D. S. Brewer Press and Boydell & Brewer Ltd., and the Modern Language Association of America, respectively. A portion of chapter 5 appeared in somewhat different form as "Mapping a History of Sexuality in Chaucer's *Melibee*," in *Chaucer and Language: Essays in Honour of Douglas Wurtele*, ed. Robert Myles and David Williams (Montreal: McGill–Queen's University Press, 2001), 53–62, 190–95; reprinted by permission of McGill–Queen's University Press.



Published by the University of Minnesota Press
111 Third Avenue South, Suite 290
Minneapolis, MN 55401-2520
http://www.upress.umn.edu

Library of Congress Cataloging-in-Publication Data

Burger, Glenn, 1954–
Chaucer's queer nation / Glenn Burger.
p. cm. — (Medieval cultures ; v. 34)
Includes bibliographical references (p. ) and index.
ISBN 0-8166-3805-5 (alk. paper) — ISBN 0-8166-3806-3 (pbk. : alk. paper)
1. Chaucer, Geoffrey, d. 1400—Views on sex. 2. Chaucer, Geoffrey, d. 1400—Views on homosexuality. 3. Homosexuality and literature—England—History—To 1500. 4. Chaucer, Geoffrey, d. 1400—Views on domestic relations. 5. Domestic relations in literature. 6. Body, Human, in literature. 7. Sex in literature. I. Title. II. Series.
PF1933.S35 B87 2003
821'.1—dc21 2002010195

Printed in the United States of America on acid-free paper

The University of Minnesota is an equal-opportunity educator and employer.

12 11 10 09 08 07 06 05 04 03 10 9 8 7 6 5 4 3 2 1

# Contents

# ACKNOWLEDGMENTS

This book has been a long time in the making, and its stages of conceptualization and development record my own transformation as a scholar and critic over the past decade. A talk by Teresa de Lauretis at the University of Alberta in 1990 on the multiple "homes" embodied in the lesbian experience first challenged me to rethink the possible intersections between private and public, sexuality and the academy, modern and medieval. My time with Dignity Edmonton and other gay/lesbian/queer community groups in the city was also instrumental in helping imagine myself and my work differently; Philip Knight in particular taught me much about how to be politically engaged, sharply critical, and absolutely human. I thank, too, my queer family during this time—Paul Harland, Brent Larson, Wayne McNamara, and Milton Schlosser—without whose support I would have foundered, as well as Anita Feth, Orval Henderson, and Thomas Slaymaker.

My thanks also go to the English department at Alberta for being a marvelously supportive and challenging environment in which to think through these transformations and to test out the ideas developed in this book. In particular, I want to thank the chairs of the department, especially Linda Woodbridge, Shirley Neuman, and Patricia Demers, for their generous support, individually and institutionally, for this project. Research release time funded by the university and the Social Sciences and Humanities Research Council of Canada was also crucial to the development of this project. My thanks go as well to the English department at Queens College and its chair, Nancy Comley, and the Ph.D. program in English at the Graduate Center and its executive officer, Joan Richardson, for providing a welcoming and supportive new environment in which to finish this book.

My own transformation as a critic coincided with one in the academy more generally, and in particular with a new openness to critical theory, cultural studies, and attention to gender and sexuality in medieval and Chaucer studies. This new historical and theoretical work has opened up wonderfully different possibilities for interaction and dialogue between pre- and postmodern, historian and literary critic, "traditional" and "cutting edge," and I have benefited enormously from it. I would especially like to thank Kathleen Biddick, John Bowers, Susan Crane, Judy Garber, Dianne Chisholm, Lesley Cormack, Carol Everest, Tom Hahn, Bruce Holsinger, Greg Hutcheson, Del Kolve, Rick Lee, Seth Lerer, John Plews, Daphne Read, Francesca Sautman, Susan Schibanoff, Stephen Slemon, Susan Smith, Sarah Stanbury, Michael Uebel, Nicholas Watson, John Weir, Scott Westrem, and Teresa Zackodnik for their enlivening conversation and helpful critique. Garrett Epp's ready wit and conviviality has been a source of steady encouragement throughout the writing of the book.

I would also like to thank my undergraduate and graduate students over the years, whose skepticism of and engagement with Chaucer, medieval sexuality, and queer theory has renewed me and kept me honest. My thanks go especially to my Ph.D. supervisees and research assistants in this project—Carolyn Ives, Lisa Ward, and Vivian Zenari.

Jeffrey Cohen has been a true friend and trusted critic throughout much of this process, without whose wise and creative support I would be much the poorer.

Sue Hamilton has stood by me through thick and thin, always superbly generous in her comments, smart and witty in her take on life and the academy, and just plain fun to be with at every turn.

Larry Scanlon was a discerning and careful reader of the manuscript for the University of Minnesota Press; David Wallace and Rita Copeland have been supportive and hands-on series editors for the book; Richard Morrison's tonic enthusiasm for the project has made him an absolute delight to work with while negotiating the Scylla and Charybdis of the academic publishing world; and Linda Lincoln has been an engaged and understanding copyeditor of the manuscript.

Last, to my parents goes my deep gratitude for their support. And to Steven Kruger—truest critic, fearless lover, ideal companion—go all my inexpressible feelings in the present and hope for the future.

# Introduction

Any book about a single author—especially one like this that treats the work of the first "great author" in the English literary tradition and whose critique situates itself within current sexual politics—raises particular and urgent theoretical questions. Why *Chaucer?* Why now? Why Chaucer's *queer nation?*

Contemporary gay/lesbian/queer readers are likely to ask why they should bother at all with a text and author at once premodern (and thus crucially outside current discourses of the body and nation) *and* foundational for many of the hegemonic discourses of modernity that have shaped who we are today. Those who would not self-identify in this way may wonder what their relationship could be to a *queer* nation, even Chaucer's. Traditional Chaucerians, and historicist medievalists more generally, may question what queer theory—a discourse arising out of modern regimes of sexuality—can offer to our analysis of the *Canterbury Tales,* emerging as it does within very different medieval medical and theological discourses of the body and desire. Queer theory, I can imagine them saying, might encourage modern gay, lesbian, queer readers of Chaucer to identify with perverse characters like the Wife of Bath or the Pardoner, but that hardly constitutes a "nation" and the process remains fundamentally a modern exercise anyway. What the *Canterbury Tales* means as a central text of the late English Middle Ages, and how Chaucer's authorship functions within an English literary tradition—such questions (and who decides them) must surely remain securely elsewhere.

Framing the critical questions in such a tendentiously identitarian fashion, while usefully underscoring both the potential conservatism in focusing a liberatory politics on the traditionally canonical and the potential presentism in bringing contemporary queer theory to bear on the medieval, also carries with it its own set of blindnesses. In particular, the comfortable historical divide maintained by keeping the postmodern antithetical to the premodern, or the canonical antithetical to the politically resistant in the case of queer theory and Chaucer, works to perpetuate "history" as we know it and to inscribe difference as otherness in stabilizing and narrowing ways. Yet surely one of queer theory's most useful interventions in modern sexuality studies—whether Michel Foucault's "invention" of the homosexual, Jonathan Dollimore's perverse dynamic, Judith Butler's queer performativity, or Eve Sedgwick's epistemology of the closet—has been its emphasis on the constructedness of modern regimes of sex/gender/sexuality and the identities founded on them.[1] And one of the most challenging features that a queer medievalism offers in turn is *its* ability to develop and insist on this historicizing impulse in queer theory itself, one that is often obscured by contemporary queer theorists' preoccupation with only modern and contemporary manifestations of the queer.[2]

My central argument throughout *Chaucer's Queer Nation,* then, is that under the pressure of producing a poetic vision for a new vernacular English audience in the *Canterbury Tales,* Chaucer reimagines late medieval relations between the body and the community. Even as the *Tales* respond to and attempt to represent a new symbolic order of modernity that is coming into being in late medieval England—organized around a new sense of individual and national identity—they incorporate the anxieties that such a departure from the past provokes. Attending to this performativity inherent in the *Tales'* construction of "Chaucer's queer nation" gives their readers (past and present) an opportunity to see the author and audience constructed with and by the *Tales* as subjects-in-process caught up in a conflicted moment of "becoming." In turn, such a historicization may help us as (post)modern readers understand that which has been left behind or not yet thought of in assuming modern identities, and so bring to present-day assumptions about identity the realization that social organizations of the body can be done differently. Analysis of the queer torsions present in the *Canterbury Tales* thus provides an exceptionally promising location to bring together the canonical and the marginal, the modern and the medieval, the historical and the theoretical, imagined not as stabilizing difference but as productive contiguity and rhizomatic connection.

The term *queer* has emerged in recent popular culture as an attempt to insist on alternative, more inclusive and less knowable, ways of self-identifying within a sometimes narrowing post-Stonewall identity politics. In doing so, this popular appropriation of the language of the oppressor sought, in the first instance, to exploit the absurdities of a proliferating set of post-Stonewall identity categories—lesbian/gay/straight/bisexual/transgendered/multigendered and so forth—to keep pushing beyond their conceptual limitations and resist their stable production. *Queer* as a term has thus tried to resist nominalization, functioning more often as an adjective, adverb, even verb, stressing epistemology rather than ontology. Equally important as such a deconstructive project around identity categories is *queer*'s articulation of a resistant politics in erotic rather than identitarian terms. The use of *queer* has thus become a way to signal a renewed and powerful "deviant" eroticism in opposition to a self-censoring, anti-eroticism that has emerged in some gay and lesbian circles as a result of the AIDS crisis and the mainstreaming of gay culture in many Western societies—an ascesis that often works to define present gay culture as somehow "grown up" and having progressed beyond the youthful and dangerous sexual exuberance of the 1970s.

Queer theory has had a similarly profound effect in academic culture, first in providing a crucial "third term" that allowed a different way to theorize the relationships between desire and politics than that offered by identitarian accounts of sexuality (often expressed in terms of a debate between social constructionist and essentialist positions). With queer theory, too, the privileging of erotic over identitarian politics has tended to turn it away from the delineation of the specificities of same-sex desire toward the articulation of a personal, political, and cultural praxis that remains as open as possible to the fullness of identifications that desire can excite. Thus queer theory has sought (1) to challenge the assumability of a biologically "real" body and a sex/gender system based on it; (2) to explore the crucial and disruptive role that perverse pleasure plays in the relationships between desire and power (both dominant and marginalized); (3) to historicize modern regimes of sex, gender, and sexuality, recognizing them as neither natural nor a progressivist supersession of previous epistemological frameworks; (4) to resist a separate spheres model for gender and sexuality that would define the relationship between feminist or gender studies and sexuality studies as "gender does *this* while sexuality does *that*."[3]

Queer theory is therefore intent on exploring the structuration and instantiation of sexuality (and homophobia/antihomophobia) rather than discovering some prior and stable "self" that will "explain" sexual activity. And by turning a term of the oppressor back on himself, queer theory chooses a very different form of resistance from that adopted by identity politics. The latter's attempt to substitute *gay* for previous terms of abuse or medicalization foregrounds a utopian intentionality. It registers the insistent hope that by such an act of metaphoric substitution, a historic misalignment of interior reality and exterior sign will be realigned so that the truth of this historically misidentified inner self can now be represented accurately. The *queer* of queer theory signals that such attempts at opposition are always already working within the coercive performances of sexuality and identity demanded by culture and that resistance is only very provisionally enacted (never absolutely secured) within circulations of power.

Emphasizing the performance of sexualities and identities and stressing the impossibility of "proving" sex, sexuality, and gender by recourse to a prior, foundational biological body, such theorizing attempts to map a more dynamic, less assured account of the body in motion within prevailing discourses of power. Queer theory's attention to the multiple axes of difference along which gendered, sexualized categories occur might thus provide a more nuanced account of the complex process by which "the other" constructs both the structures of hegemonic power and the means by which such power can be resisted. In this sense the deconstructive edge of queer theory, as opposed to the resistance of identity politics, emphasizes the oppositionality of *tactics* versus *strategy.* As Ross Chambers suggests:

> [O]pposition is always on the weaker side of any given power relationship, and consequently [it] tends to be improvisational and tactical rather than strategic, planned or calculated. It cannot rely on preformulated rules or preexisting positions of strength: it is always a matter of skill, adroitness, flair, of seizing the inspiration of the moment, of exploiting the specifics of a given here-and-now. . . . De Certeau . . . makes a useful distinction between *strategy,* which is the behavior of those in control of a given situation, and *tactics* as the art of existing in territory that is occupied by an other (what Deleuze and Guattari might call a "deterritorialized" situation); in those terms, oppositional behavior is a perpetual recourse to tactics, and it cannot become strategic without simultaneously losing its oppositional quality. It is that which eludes definition, the residue of all attempts at pinning it down.[4]

Queer theory, then, is useful in drawing attention to an author function composed of tactics and oppositional behavior, rather than the strategies of canonicity and hegemonic definition. It can thus reveal different modes of textual production in the *Tales,* ways of relating dominant authorities and the author function, author function and reader, that explore how the *Tales* might exist in territory occupied by another and might imagine a queer nation "which eludes definition, the residue of all attempts at pinning it down."

Like others working at the intersections of sexuality, race, religion, and nation in queer and postcolonial medievalist projects, in *Chaucer's Queer Nation* I attempt to bring postmodern and premodern, historicist and theoretical, marginal and hegemonic into a different, less knowable relationship with each other, to imagine a productive "middle" in which relationships between the past and present, marginal and dominant, canonical and noncanonical can proliferate. Here I have found methodological models developed by Gilles Deleuze and Félix Guattari to be particularly helpful.[5] Deleuze and Guattari argue in strongly convincing ways against the primacy of affiliation and heterosexist and determinist models for (re)production. Instead, their emphasis on mapping, machinic assemblages, bodies without organs, and rhizomatic connections encourages unpredictable and proliferative models for imagining agency and identification, a way of "becoming" rather than "being" in the world. Desire for Deleuze and Guattari is not controlled by a process of ascesis organized around lack, but is instead understood in terms of flows, lines of flight, plateaus of libidinal excitement. Similarly, their models for the circulation of power eschew stabilizing binaries and asymmetries, and emphasize dynamic flows between territorialization and deterritorialization, stratification and destratification, organ-ization and body without organs within machinic assemblages of desire and constraint. Their emphasis on the "middle" where things pick up speed, as opposed to the forced choice of one side of the binary of revolt and domination over another, as well as their resistance to a dependence on a modern Freudian/Lacanian psychosexual model for desire or a modernist historiography of supersession (as in certain impositions of a simplified Foucauldian paradigm), makes their work an especially valuable contribution to queer theory and queer medievalism.

Focusing on Chaucer's queer nation thus provides a particularly useful means to reorient the "subject" of investigation away from

"Chaucer"—that institutionalized authorial body so overwritten and overdetermined by critics and readers in order to be foundational for an English literary tradition—and in the process to resist the essentializing force of a Chaucerian identity and its intimate and intricate relationship with modern (hetero)sexuality. Again and again, Chaucer has been constructed as properly virile, masculine activity: enlarger of the English language and the person who made translation no longer necessary for his fifteenth-century "sons," proto-reformer/Protestant to the sixteenth century, the father of English poetry and encompasser of the whole English nation to Dryden, genial ironist and moralist to generations of modern critics and readers. Twentieth-century New Critics separated "Chaucer the man" from the bumbling, effeminate "persona" of his poetry precisely because it was Chaucer's ability masterfully to transcend his time and be one of "us" that continued to justify his originary place in the canon. The symbiotic relationship between the discovery of an essentially Chaucerian body of work and the embodiment of the great author figure that sustains it has thus been an important medium through which readerly desire is properly organized and manifested to produce whole, empowered, and properly socialized subjects. As this kind of potent "father," the Chaucerian body has become a foundational category for a longstanding essentialism at work in determining canonicity and authenticity in English studies and the social structures it subtends.[6]

Since 1980 different critical approaches have sought to reorient this desire in ways that would read against the tradition. Feminist critiques have questioned the "humanity" of this gendered body, focusing, for example, on Chaucer's trial for rape and the traffic in women that forms the basis of so much of his poetry.[7] Cultural materialist critics have emphasized the class interests that keep Chaucer as an author very much bound up in the expression of the desires of the ruling classes of the day, and hence not surprisingly a fitting foundation for an English tradition where "the literary" has provided the medium through which to form the "properly" socialized subject.[8] Historicist critics have attempted to reclaim Chaucer as really medieval or to properly situate his innovativeness within the early modern period.[9] These critiques have done much to reveal and question unexamined masculinist, classist, and presentist assumptions within the Chaucer tradition. But to the extent that they do so largely by reorganizing a desire we have been trained to feel for "Chaucer," substituting a different, "better" body for the canonical one, such critiques continue to essentialize the idea of "Chaucerian" embodiment and thus continue to limit how and what we desire when we read Chaucerian fictions. Even Carolyn Dinshaw's recent provocative attempt to "touch" the queerness of the Pardoner and the Wife of Bath, as well as "real" medieval queers like John/Eleanor Rykener, does so by distinguishing their queer voices from a "Chaucer" that *is* fundamentally and crucially heterosexual.[10]

What I am attempting to underscore here is the continuing power of *modern* identitarianism in Chaucer studies, its relationship to our investment in Chaucerian embodiment, and the "payoff" of that investment as a stabilizing set of foundational binaries (male/female, homo/hetero, masculinist/feminist, medieval/modern). How, then, do we queer our desire for the Chaucerian body itself and let go of our search for foundations and stability (in biology, history, authorial originals)? How can we bring medieval and modern sexualities (and their intimate relationship with a politics of representation) into nonheterosexualized, nonaffiliative contiguity and dialogue with each other without one colonizing or overdetermining the other? How do we as self-identified gendered and sexualized critics (gay, lesbian, bisexual, heterosexual) find the necessary tactics to queer a canonical body such as Chaucer's, and in the process also usefully "deterritorialize" our own overly secure modern identities? Here I think queer theory can help expose how the patterns of territorialization and deterritorialization that produce Chaucerian textualization—both pre- and postmodern—are neither solidly hegemonic nor purely countercultural, neither purely "medieval" nor "modern." Turning away from the Chaucerian body per se to a queering of our analysis of desire in the *Canterbury Tales* can in turn work to bring queer theory (and parallel theories of resistance in postcolonial and feminist studies) into a challenging and productive new engagement with canonicity and historicity.

For as queer Chaucerians and queer medievalists, we cannot simply reiterate the "answer" that Eve Sedgwick fantasizes a gay studies movement providing to the "keepers of a dead canon":

> From the keepers of a dead canon we hear a rhetorical question—that is to say, a question posed with the arrogant intent of maintaining ignorance. Is there, as Saul Bellow put it, a Tolstoi of the Zulus? . . . From the point of view of this relatively new and

> inchoate academic presence, then, the gay studies movement, what distinctive soundings are to be reached by posing the question our way—and staying for an answer? Let's see how it sounds.
>
> Has there ever been a gay Socrates?
> Has there ever been a gay Shakespeare?
> Has there ever been a gay Proust?
>
> Does the Pope wear a dress? If these questions startle, it is not least as tautologies. A short answer, though a very incomplete one, might be that not only have there been a gay Socrates, Shakespeare, and Proust but that their names are Socrates, Shakespeare, Proust.[11]

Sedgwick is not, of course, attempting to "find homosexuality" in the reductive sense of a transhistorical, anachronistic "gay sensibility," but rather highlighting and countering the willful ignorance of the "skeptical" critic who practices and perpetuates a presumptive and compulsory heterosexuality. Here "gay" resists the oppressive power of dominant culture to "other" dissident sexualities not by reproducing dominant culture's positivist historicism and stable identities, but by turning the categories of identity politics precisely against themselves. Sedgwick's reply contains a queer deconstructive edge precisely because we know the sexual practices of these three authors constitute a contemporary gay identity as much as they constitute a contemporary heterosexual one, which is to say probably not at all. Her use of "gay" thus insists on the provisionality of such identities by underscoring the presence of the supposed "other" within constructions of the dominant, and hence the "unnaturalness" of such constructions.

Posing Sedgwick's question in the same way with Chaucer does not, however, achieve a similarly queering effect. Applied to the Chaucerian body constructed by generations of "straight" Chaucer critics, gay more often than not forecloses on the kinds of questions Sedgwick's "answer" raises, and thus reinforces the very stability of the terms that an antihomophobic, antiheterosexist, postmodern analysis of Chaucerian fictions seeks to resist. After all, what little evidence exists about the historical Chaucer's own sexual activity—most notably and controversially the accusation of rape by Cecily Chaumpaigne—is clearly directed toward women.[12] If we cannot answer with Sedgwick's words, we can, I think, mount a similarly queer transgressive reinscription of the strategies of canonicity by attending to Chaucer's queer nation and the textual/sexual body it imagines.[13] Here the "Chaucerianness" of the text under consideration presents a problematic and potentially productive challenge to a queer historicism. We might reply that the very medium of textual and social reproduction attributed to "Father Chaucer," its particular attempt to represent subjectivity and agency by means of an individually "authored" sexed, gendered, sexualized, and classed embodiment, is itself queer. Situating Chaucer within his queer nation in the *Canterbury Tales* (as he himself does as narrator in Fragment VII or by his narrative interjection in the prologue to the *Miller's Tale,* and as the postmodern queer reader attempts to do in the present moment) can thus provide an even starker, stronger queer intervention into medieval and modern identity politics than Sedgwick's reply to the "keepers of the canon." In taking up these questions in terms of Chaucer's queer nation, I am attempting to resist both the stabilizing reproduction of a canonical "Father Chaucer" *and* the fiction of a pure path of resistance to canonicity (pursued either by constructing a "resistant" author figure or by simply rejecting an oppressive "traditional" author). Instead, I undertake a different kind of historicization of "Chaucer," encouraging readers to imagine a "Chaucer" before canonicity and thus to recognize—to borrow Jonathan Dollimore's term—the perverse dynamic at work within the *Canterbury Tales.*[14] For the more we can look beyond modern sexual identities, or the fantasy of their absence as "the medieval," the more we can begin to consider the complexity of premodern and postmodern subject positions.

My reading of Chaucer's queer nation is postmodern, not in the sense of coming after modernism (and hence self-defining as presentist), but rather in its resistance to a narrow historical teleology (premodern is superseded by modern, modern by postmodern, and so on) and desire to denaturalize and rehistoricize modern regimes of sexuality and the identities they define. We do not want to be "gay" or "lesbian" (to the extent that such terms, however intentionally resistant, reinscribe modern identity systems as inherent and natural), the queer theorist would say, and, more importantly, *we have never been heterosexual* (to adapt Bruno Latour's formulation).[15] That is, although we live within the inheritance of the modern West's formulation of sexuality (described so forcefully in Foucault's *History of Sexuality*) and the interiorized selves and liberal subjects it subtends, this inheritance remains haunted by the past it has sought to leave behind and remains unable to secure the future it so phantasmatically insists upon. To the extent that queer theory asks us to imagine outside the box of modern sexual identity politics and regimes of sexuality, then, it also asks us to rethink our relationships with temporality and the work of historicization. So, too, a queer medievalism asks us to think the temporal and conceptual "middle" differently, by resisting the stabilizing push of an absolutely other and distinct Middle Ages against which modernity can define itself and within which medievalists can isolate themselves.

If so, how can such readers do history differently so that new possibilities emerge from our study of the past without erasing its difference and so that such an engagement challenges us to think the present differently? Thinking queerly—that is, impurely but productively as both medieval and modern . . . and neither—provides a mode of analysis for thinking through, first, how there might be a sexual identity politics in the Middle Ages, and second, how one might become attuned to the differences *within* medieval identity politics and *between* medieval and modern identity politics. We can, I would argue, talk about a medieval identity politics organized around sexuality. But while this sexual politics can be seen as the ideological effect and justification of medieval social normativity, these medieval systems of sexuality and identity are historically distinct from those structuring modern heterosexuality, and are organized around supposedly foundational, biological categories of gender (masculine/feminine or effeminate or sodomitical) rather than modern categories of sex difference (male/female) and sexuality (homosexual/heterosexual). Bringing together the pre- and postmodern in this way can help us resist a simple incorporation of Chaucer within modern regimes of sexuality (presuming, for example, that the focus on marriage in the *Canterbury Tales* could simply *be* heterosexual in the modern sense). By working to disturb *medieval* regimes of sexuality even as it helps uncover their specificities, queer theory can also help us see and claim previously disallowed medieval sexual positions (disallowed both by our modern blindnesses and by the workings of medieval hegemonies) as both powerful and meaningful. For example, the bifurcation of sex/gender and sexuality that has taken place under the modern sex/gender/sexuality regime has at times worked to separate feminist and queer/

sexuality studies. A premodern without "the homosexual," but with sex/gender/sexual perversity aligned under categories such as "the sodomite" and "the feminine," presents a promising and challenging re-presentation of sex/gender/sexuality for the queer theorist working to think outside the box of modernity.[16]

A queering of medieval and modern identity positions as they relate to the *Canterbury Tales*—and along with this the related queering of a set of assumptions about history that has structured how we think about medieval and modern, pre- and postmodern, Chaucerian identity and canonicity—informs one trajectory of this book. A second trajectory attempts a similarly deconstructive take on what the reimagining of the relation between the body and community in Chaucer's queer nation might mean more specifically in social and political terms. Kathleen Biddick has recently described the creation of British and North American medieval studies as a particularly colonialist project.[17] But even before this general co-optation of "the medieval" to modern colonial self-definitions, "Chaucer" and a sense of "the literary" dependent on the originary power of the great author played an important role in the early modern construction and naturalization of a sense of "the English nation" and an incipient imperial identity. When in 1700 John Dryden in his "Preface to Fables Ancient and Modern" designates Chaucer "the father of English poetry," he also posits a relationship between Chaucer's depiction of a universal human nature and the ability of his poetry to transmit the history of the English nation: Chaucer "has taken into the compass of his *Canterbury Tales* the various manners and humours (as we now call them) of the whole English nation in his age. Not a single character has escaped him. . . . 'Tis sufficient to say, according to the proverb, that here is God's plenty. We have our forefathers and great-grand-dames all before us, as they were in Chaucer's days."[18] In different but contiguous ways, the Lancastrian cultivation of "Englishness" and a proper author for the ruling class, the Tudor and Elizabethan attempts to structure an English literary tradition beginning with Chaucer, and a tradition (beginning with Dryden but extending to E. T. Donaldson and after) linking "Father Chaucer" or "Chaucer the man" with "universal" bourgeois humanist values all colonize Chaucer and his characters in order to fit them into modernist narratives of progressive history and to mobilize them for the reproduction of hegemonic modern identities.

But like the Chaucer before canonicity and the sexualized body before modern heterosexuality that my project focuses on, the "nation" that the Canterbury project itself imagines must be understood as crucially *before* the modern nation-state. The *Tales'* organization of an imagined community of "gentils" anticipates the later centrality of a London-Canterbury axis that defines a national center founded on a national language, a national polity, and a national religious practice. But the *Tales* simultaneously reveal the complex set of material factors informing and often interfering with the creation of such a social imaginary. Here I draw on the immensely valuable historicist work—by such writers as Mark Jordan, Judith Bennett, Paul Strohm, Lee Patterson, Steven Justice, Christopher Cannon, Caroline Barron, David Wallace, Carl Lindahl, Anne Middleton, and others—that has emerged in recent years and that has complicated and developed how we think about the sodomite, the single woman, Chaucer's social situation, the relationship between town and country, parish and guild organization, vernacularity and lay power, the estates, and so forth. Thus, for example, "London" for Chaucer's pilgrims, rather than being the hegemonic focus of a national polity, is a set of interlinked and warring associations—the City (including guildsmen "citizens," English nonfreemen of the city, and foreign inhabitants) and Westminster (both court and parliamentary forces), as well as other, more amorphous groupings straddling both worlds (such as those Chaucer himself frequently inhabited). Moreover, since a "London" English is only just now in the process of being defined by such works as the *Canterbury Tales,* English is as likely at this time to signify a colonial history in relation to French and Latin and a fragmenting regionalism as it is a unified, imperially coherent identity.[19]

Here postcolonial theory provides, in a way analogous to how queer theory resists modern sexuality's naturalization and enforcement of its identity positions, a useful means by which we might, from within the inheritance of modern discourses of nation and empire, challenge their normative power. In the first instance, postcolonial theory can help us counter—as queer theory does in resisting the reading of a compulsory modern heterosexuality back onto the premodern—the imperial tendencies of canonical literary history to assimilate the "great author" and his work to narratives of empire or nation and the harnessing of the literary to the formation of hegemonic bourgeois subjects. Homi Bhabha's discussion of post-ality (post-feminism, post-modernism, post-colonialism) as an agential "middle," rather than a progressive historicist "after" or a revolutionary "against" suggests a different way of imagining the *middleness* of the social situation represented in the *Canterbury Tales*.[20] While Bhabha's "middle" is an attempt to resist the hegemony of modern social formations and to push us toward a postcolonial imaginary, it is suggestive for my similar attempt to resist the hegemony of modern social formations in always already "knowing" Chaucer's world (either as "medieval" or "proto-modern") and to push to imagine its premodernity otherwise. As with queer theory, it is postcolonial theory's efforts to think the effects of imperial history differently that are most helpful in my attempt to think about what actually constitutes the premodern and precolonial in the *Canterbury Tales*. As with queer theory, such a politics should help us claim previously disallowed social positions and desires as both powerful and meaningful.

Both postcolonial and queer theory, as well as historicist medieval and Chaucerian cultural studies, can therefore help us understand the complex imbrication of old and new at work in Chaucer's attempts to reimagine body and community in the *Canterbury Tales*. If the two dominant modes of medieval "imperial" subject reproduction are ecclesiastical and feudal aristocratic, both require the construction of "universal" identities that can circulate in a variety of local situations; at the same time, both must imagine a boundedness for those identities. That is, there can only be so much noble blood and only so much land; only a limited portion of the population can rise to clerical status and transubstantiate Christ's body and blood. Yet by Chaucer's time, both such modes of identity formation are integrated with a money economy and a model of capitalist growth and surplus production at work generally in the culture—both in the increasingly complex rural and village arena and in the growing number of urban centers (and especially in London). In these circumstances the hegemony of traditional ruling ideologies is under attack as new groups try to copy dominant subject positions to gain access to their systems of ideological reproduction and as subaltern voices try to gain agency from outside such systems.

Lying behind the *Tales'* focus on the middle strata of society, then, is a larger process at work in late medieval culture, that is, the construction of "bourgeois," lay models of identity as "copies" of clerical (especially monastic) and aristocratic "originals." Through the late medieval cult of death, and through guilds and lay parish organization, a new "middle" class of well-off laymen and laywomen gains increasing access to the ideological power of the body of Christ and thus to greater agency in defining their own identifications of community. A similar copying takes place in the secular sphere as, increasingly, "successful" nonaristocratic identities are being formed by translating markers of blood nobility (private space—like the private garden or the household—or romantic love) into more marketable and widely reproducible markers of "gentility." The most notable locations for such copying in the *Canterbury Tales* are the attempts to identify and ground a community of new "gentils," first in the domestic sphere—through the idea of companionate marriage—and second in the public sphere—through the idea of the pilgrimage body as the body of Christ. But this attempt to represent for a new social group a cohesive community identity based on existing medieval, imperial categories also brings with it, paradoxically, a necessary attention to the local factors involved in such an identity formation. In defining this new "gentil" identity, Chaucer's texts also reveal the temporally and spatially specific—and hence, contingent—nature of its middleness.

Chapter 1 continues the work begun here of theorizing the middle in Chaucer studies and in constructing new subject positions in the *Canterbury Tales*. The first part of the chapter brings into rhizomatic connection with each other John Preston's introduction to his collection of gay porn, *Flesh and the Word,* and the narrator's interjection on shame and pleasure in the prologue to the *Miller's Tale* in order to suggest new beginnings for a queer historicization of Chaucer, for the project of the *Tales,* and for the subjects created by such hermeneutical tactics. The second half of the chapter explores the masochistic contract at work in the *Miller's Tale* itself and the ways in which that contract constructs a subject who *is something* in experiencing shame.

In chapters 2 and 3 I consider the destabilizing effects of late medieval understandings of conjugality, noting their difference from other medieval models (for example, marriage as dynastic arrangement) and their crucial difference from modern heterosexuality. I suggest that a late medieval emphasis on conjugality made marriage "good to think with" for subjects of the "middle" order, like those self-defining as "gentils" in the *Tales.* Thus marriage in the tales of the so-called Marriage Group (in particular, the *Wife of Bath's Tale,* the *Merchant's Tale,* and the

*Franklin's Tale*) becomes a locus for inventing with the body in ways that are unpredictably both socially organizing and disorganizing.

Chapter 4 examines the queer performativity of Fragment VI in its re-presentation of the necessary, productive, and fearful encounters between male bodies and the feminine discussed in the first three chapters. In particular, this chapter focuses on the sodomitical and xenophobic panic occasioned by the excision of the female body in the *Physician's Tale* and the continued proximity of the perverse in the kiss that ends the *Pardoner's Tale*. I argue that in touching these bodies in this fragment, we encounter a body no longer simply emblematic of lack or absence, but rather constituting a point of experimentation in touch with the real. Fragment VI thus initiates and gestures toward a reading strategy that might increase and multiply in meaningful ways outside hierarchical models organized around sex/gender difference, heterosexual procreation, or celibate/lay distinctions.

In chapter 5, using Deleuze and Guattari's model of the book as machinic assemblage, capable of tilting toward both stratification and organization *and* a body without organs that is continually dismantling such organization, I consider how Fragment VII shows more explicitly than other fragments the queer torsions of the *Canterbury Tales* as a nonteleological, nonheterosexual, desiring machine. In particular, I focus on *The Melibee* as the most extreme example of this process, providing in its story of wifely counsel and domestic conjugality a reliable and safe medium through which to outline a newly sexualized and gendered individual identity for its "gentil" audience, while at the same time deterritorializing such an identification by situating the story within the hybridizing specificities of embodiment and desire that constitute Fragment VII as a whole.

Chapter 6 challenges attempts by the Host and the Parson, as well as subsequent continuators such as the author of the *Tale of Beryn*, to use the end of the *Tales* to fantasize an imagined "beyond" of the Canterbury project as its necessary point of completion, making, in the process, the *present* experience of the pilgrimage only a meaningful stage on the way to Canterbury and the knowable future it represents. I argue instead that the end-tales (Fragments VIII, IX, and X) continue to look "forward" in the manner of the Canterbury project, that is, to a productive "middle" state between London and Canterbury, between "middle" class and clerical orthodoxy, between national and penitential body. Such a disjunct and displaced "present" in the three fragments "ending" the *Tales* thus continues to explore the torsions produced in the *Tales'* attempts to map Chaucer's queer nation as it emerges into representability.

I have presented these summaries sequentially, and in a general fashion their order mimics that of the Ellesmere manuscript (generally taken as "authoritative" and as privileging the organism by virtue of its extensive marginal annotation and emphasis on the dramatic relationship between tale-teller and tale). Since the Ellesmere manuscript's order and sense of the *Tales* have become the basis both for current modern standard editions and for much twentieth-century understanding of what they mean, and thus the privileged medium for our reception of Chaucerian canonicity, there is a "rightness" to its haunting my own attempts to queer that canonicity. However, as should be clear, my purpose in the book is to encourage lines of flight and rhizomatic connections among the chapters and an appreciation of the *Tales* as much as a body without organs as a coherent organism. Such multiplicatory strategies, I would suggest, are in excess of the various external attempts to view the *Tales* as an organic body, embodied so forcefully in the Ellesmere manuscript's emphasis on *ordinatio* and its portraits of the pilgrims.

Thus, I have sought throughout my organization of the book to counter an inevitable tilt to an organic structure for the *Tales* with my own attempts at destratification. Chapter 1 encourages us to "begin" the Canterbury project not with the universalizing strategies of the General Prologue opening or the aristocratic/clerical compact of the Knight and Monk as "natural" first tale-tellers, but with the most abject and presentist of genres (fabliau) and class of speaker (drunken Miller), and with the deterritorializing effects of reading Chaucer through the achievements of gay porn and popular culture. Chapters 2 and 3 present marriage not as the heterosexualized endpoint of meaning production in the *Tales,* but as their dis-organized middle ground. So, too, these two chapters bring together as unpredictable lines of flight the medieval turn to conjugality, the in-betweenness of "gentil" self-identification, female masculinity, and bourgeois "men's concern." Chapter 4, unlike so many accounts of the Pardoner's "lack" as the end of critical inquiry, leading us naturally "back" to the eternal verities represented by proper masculinity, priestly authority, and right reading, instead foregrounds the centrality for the *Tales* of the Pardoner's wayward body and a sodomitical pleasure that cannot be divided into teleological sequence. And chapter 5 finds in Fragment VII's dizzying assemblage of disparate and often contradictory textual effects a model for the *Tales* more generally as a machinic assemblage. As such, chapter 4 (or 5) could in many ways be read just as fruitfully after chapter 1 as chapters 2 and 3. Similarly, *Chaucer's Queer Nation* "concludes" only in the sense of providing further permutations of the "middle" with its discussions of the *Melibee* and the end-tales as desiring machines, rather than as modes of properly socializing ascesis.

# 1

# Shameful Pleasures

## Queer Desire, Canonicity, History

Throughout their many disciplinary manifestations, Chaucer and Chaucerian fictions have played a preeminent role in defining, grounding, and maintaining "English Literature" and the discourses of heterosexuality and modernity that depend on it. As Elaine Tuttle Hansen succinctly puts it: "Chaucer has been known and valued differently in different ages, but he has always been read, talked about, and more often than not singled out for praise as the precursor to be emulated, the forebear to be revered, the Father of English poetry. . . . Present or absent, Chaucer matters."[1] What has been at stake here is the ability of the relationship between great author and reader to function as a faithful medium for proper social reproduction. Articulating a stable Chaucerian identity also reinforces a proper subject position for its readers—whether that is attained by giving up an individual "modern" self in order to understand medieval otherness or by becoming "like" Chaucer the universal man and hence a full liberal subject.

This is a reading history whose effects have been, and remain, punitive and dangerously reductive for a variety of contemporary politically engaged projects of cultural study—notably feminist, antihomophobic, queer, and postcolonial ones. I want to begin thinking through the relationships between such contemporary cultural studies and Chaucerian texts by situating the question in terms of contemporary queer subjects and their desire to dream the present differently. By "queer" here I mean in the first instance those subjects self-identifying as gay, lesbian, bi, transgendered, or otherwise, and in the second, those engaged in current struggles to denaturalize modern identity systems and the oppressive hegemonies founded on them. Would such queer subjects, then, be better off without Chaucer altogether, looking instead for other forefathers or foremothers, or focusing on an immediate past that more clearly can be *ours*? Is Chaucer, perhaps, the limit case for our ability to queer the literary and the past tradition it has been made to embody? If not, what improperly productive relationships might there be between Chaucer's queer nation in the *Canterbury Tales* and the contemporary queer subject?

However attractive the fantasy of a complete break with canonicity might be, I think it remains just that, a fantasy. The belief that by purging ourselves of all the "dead white males" we will purge ourselves of the effects of canonicity risks naturalizing a relationship with history as ascetic and renunciative as that demanded by a hegemonic "tradition." Without question, the recuperation of queer subjects, texts, and their history has been a powerfully transformative process for recent cultural and historical study, developing alternative and resistant accounts of who "we" are and affirming past presences too often erased or marginalized in official accounts. But recuperation, in and of itself, does not address what is problematic in those assumptions (about the literary, about history, about queer studies) that are embedded in the questions I have been asking. Certainly one of the most crucial benefits made possible by the success of modern antihomophobic movements has been the opening up of history for queer subjects: the personal histories of individual gay/lesbian/bi/transgendered/queer subjects have been able to come into representation in provocative new ways, and in equally profound ways, queer subjects in the past have become more visible on their own terms. Rich as this work of recuperation has been, its limitations have also been felt in recent years: a growing body of queer cultural studies remains almost obsessively presentist in its focus. The work of historicization in gay/lesbian/queer history and literary studies continues to be focused on the eighteenth, nineteenth, and twentieth centuries. In medieval studies we seem too often and "naturally" to run up against the blank wall of historical "evidence," so that medieval queerness emerges as primarily a set of isolated voices drowned out by the noise of heteronormativity. Addressing this problem is not a simple matter of rejecting the so-called Foucauldian divide—before such-and-such a date we have sodomites, after, homosexuals—or moving the great divide back into the early modern period. Nor will it be addressed by substituting queer for homosexual or gay/lesbian, or whatever other identity category we may want to subscribe to. Certainly the complicating of an essentializing identity politics, an increase in awareness of the complexity of identifications circulating within modern regimes of sex, gender, and sexuality, as well as the tonic effect of reemphasizing the power of erotics within queer theory have all been helpful in opening up room to maneuver for contemporary queer subjects and cultural critics. And with that has come at least the desire to attend to the complexities of historicizing queerness. But in crucial ways, it seems, queer subjectivities and much contemporary queer theory and cultural analysis continue to reproduce prevailing narratives of modernity and its teleological historicity, in the process uncannily tracing the effects of heterosexuality and canonicity back into the history of sexuality.

Yet, if queer theory has taught us anything, it is the constructed nature of this modern regime of sex, gender, and sexuality. Surely the queer subject we desire to become, the queer subject we desire to discover in our past has, in Bruno Latour's trenchant formulation, *never been modern.* Although Latour's analysis originates in the history of science, his insights into the distorting effects of modernity are equally relevant to historians of sexuality and to medievalists. According to Latour, modernity has managed, at least from the seventeenth century, both to proliferate hybridizations—between nonhuman and human, nature and culture, the scientific realm and the philosophic/political/discursive realm—and to deny them absolutely through a mode of purification that keeps the realm of nature (whose "facts" scientists merely observe and articulate) forever and absolutely distinct from the social and discursive realms. To sustain this system, modernity defines itself in terms of a radical rupture with its premodern past and understands *that* premodern still to exist in so-called primitive cultures today. Current critiques of modernity are doomed to failure, according to Latour, because both "antimoderns" (in their desire to believe in the recovery of an absolutely different pastness) and "postmoderns" (by whom Latour rather narrowly means Baudrillard and Lyotard) are unable to step outside of modernity's own definitions of the playing field. However, the very success of modernity in proliferating hybridizations has in recent years made these hybridizations impossible to ignore, and thus worked to denaturalize the mechanisms of modernity, exposing its own historicity. This allows us to witness modernity not as some irreversible process of nature and march of progress, but as a "modality of historical action": "When we see them as networks, Western innovations remain recognizable and important, but they no longer suffice as the stuff of saga, a vast saga of radical rupture, fatal destiny, irreversible good or bad fortune. . . . Another field—much broader, much less polemical—has opened up before us: the field of nonmodern worlds. It is the Middle Kingdom, as vast as China and as little known."[2]

This does not mean that modernity is simply the false consciousness of moderns; Latour is instead careful to grant the idea its own effectiveness, its own historicity. But he does want to insist that the modernist revolution and arch of progress are not history itself: "The events of 1789 [i.e., the French Revolution] were no more revolutionary than the modern world has been modern," and thus "[t]ime is not a general framework but a provisional result of the connection among entities."[3] As a result, Latour is able to suggest different spatial and conceptual models for imagining temporal relationships and our relationships to history:

> Let us suppose, for example, that we are going to regroup the contemporary elements along a spiral rather than a line. We do have a future and a past, but the future takes the form of a circle expanding in all directions, and the past is not surpassed but revisited, repeated, surrounded, proliferated, recombined, reinterpreted, and reshuffled. . . . In such a framework, our actions are recognized at last as polytemporal.

And he goes on to suggest that "[i]t is the sorting that makes the times, not the times that make the sorting."[4] A less polemical, a-modernity, then, might allow more of us to regain the capacity to do our own sorting of the elements that belong to our time, in the process rediscovering the freedom of movement that modernism denied us—a freedom, in fact, that we have never really lost (since we have never really been modern). Such an a-modern sorting calls us to a different kind of historicization in order to better resist the normativizing influences of a hegemonic past. We need, in short, to engage queer desire in more fully nonteleological ways with the workings of history and canonicity, recognizing its polytemporality. Mapping sexuality's long and varied history in this way could help us see not only the queer torsions within the past, including the premodern past, but also those within present narratives of liberation and resistance.

Perhaps that is the point, too, to begin to think about why contemporary queer readers might *desire* to read Chaucerian fictions at this moment in history and how they might go about creating a space to do so. Such an endeavor is not likely to, nor should it, naturalize some kind of "Queer Chaucer" to counter "Father Chaucer" or "Chaucer, the protomodern Man"—in other words to continue to operate within the confines of a simplifying identity politics. Instead this work of historicization should help us better understand why Chaucer's queer nation in the *Canterbury Tales* and the author/reader functions it inscribes have never been modern (or medieval in the circumscribed and stabilizing way that a modernist literary tradition or historiography might want to overdetermine "the medieval" and "the Chaucerian"). Rather than seeking a stabilizing Chaucerian identity, as the forces producing canonicity traditionally desire, and by that the reproduction of proper identities for a succession of properly socialized subjects, the queer historicization I am suggesting would proliferate our possible identifications with and through the past. Queering Chaucerian fictions—past and present—may thus be helpful in engaging with, and furthering, the growing desire of postmodern queer subjects to historicize their present locations in the fullest possible way.[5]

As a kind of case study for such a different engagement of past and present, marginal and canonical, I want to bring into queer contiguity with each other the introductions to two of the first gay anthologies to be published by mainstream presses—David Leavitt's *Penguin Book of Gay Short Stories* (1994) and John Preston's *Flesh and the Word*—and the narrator's "blameth not me" interjection in the prologue to the *Miller's Tale*.[6] My intent here is to counter the "natural" tendency to read the three texts through the fiction of modern authorship and its great tradition of the liberal subject, and the fiction of the great divide between "the literary" and popular culture (or heterosexual and homosexual or medieval and modern). Instead, I want to uncover the rhizomatic rather than affiliative connections between these very different (and uncannily similar) moments in history and subjectivity, and thus to ask what intensification of desire, what new dreaming of the present and the past, might occur by reading a moment of new beginning in the Canterbury project, not retrospectively through the lens of "Father Chaucer" and the modernity he originates, but *pro*spectively through the lens of contemporary queer desire unleashed in pornography.

In the first instance I would like to think about how a queer Chaucerianism might help unpack the effects of canonicity within the project of modernist gay liberation, for traditional categories of "the literary" and "the author," as well as the modernity they inscribe, can haunt attempts to build a resistant hermeneutics for contemporary gay/lesbian/queer studies, as much as for current queer medieval studies. In his introduction to the *Penguin Book of Gay Short Stories,* one of the first mainstream attempts to collect and define an emergent "gay literature," David Leavitt notes:

> Unlike our heterosexual counterparts, for whom history, rituals of courtship, models for behavior, and codes of decorum are handed out daily in the classroom, we must seek out, furtively, some sense of our connection to official history, not to mention some sense of our own history, which by definition is discontinuous, a series of stops and starts that begins again each time a young gay man or lesbian sneaks his or her way to the gay section at a bookstore—if indeed there is a gay section; if indeed there is a bookstore.[7]

Leavitt begins in a familiar place, with the problems that gay and lesbian subjects face in extending their "history" beyond the confines of the personal and contemporary because of their perverse location on the private/public divide. But the effect of Leavitt's introduction (and indeed the structure of the anthology itself) is to efface any such discontinuity by articulating a liberatory relationship between proper reading and the development of a whole self, able at last to inhabit history fully. He outlines his own reading history as a "coming out" from isolation to integration: beginning with the unsatisfactory representations of gay experience he found in his first forays into the gay section of the bookstore (Gordon Merrick's *The Lord Won't Mind* and Andrew Holleran's *Dancer from the Dance*), followed by the discovery of gay novels like Robert Ferro's *The Family of Max Desir* ("that rarity" among gay literature of the period, "a novel in which a gay man plays an integral role in the unfolding drama of family life"), and leading to the successes of more recent gay literature "that, rather than fawning over angels made flesh, transformed homosexual experience into human drama; a gay literature that was literature first and gay second."[8]

Two trajectories emerge in this narrative push to a "new level of liberation . . . that would allow gay men and lesbians to celebrate their identities without having to move into a gulag."[9] The first is backward. Having emptied the gay past by emphasizing its lack of a proper sense of "the literary," Leavitt can then fill it with "proper history" by inserting a gay canon always already there, but invisible in the subcultural ethos of the gay lit section of his Palo Alto bookstore in the seventies. And what should have been in that bookstore and available to the young gay subject?

> For starters, *The Folded Leaf,* William Maxwell's seminal tale of love between teenage boys, published in the late forties. J. R. Ackerley's agonizingly honest autobiography, *My Father and Myself;* Sanford Friedman's *Totempole;* perhaps some of Forster's posthumously published gay stories. I knew about none of these books back then. . . . It took years more to dig out the other books I could have read when I was sixteen, instead of *The Lord Won't Mind* and *Dancer from the Dance.* Not that these books prettified or idealized gay experience—we are talking about nothing so simple as "positive role models"; but they told the truth. The men who inhabited them were recognizably human.[10]

The other trajectory of Leavitt's narrative is forward, with "gay" functioning as the fulfillment of a modernist narrative of progress. Leavitt concludes his introduction with the story of a performance at a benefit to fight attempts by the American Right to use the National Endowment for the Arts as a weapon against sexual self-expression. A young man and woman, identifying themselves as "a fag" and "a dyke," ask everyone who is gay to stand up. A quarter of the audience does so. Then they remind the audience that the king of Denmark wore a yellow star when he heard that his Jewish subjects would be required by the Nazis to wear one. Once again, all gay members of the audience are asked to stand up. Now three quarters stand up; the rest remain in their seats, "eyes grim and steadfast, clutching their armrests as if for their dear life."[11] In Leavitt's account, the "present" already signifies its own "pastness," as current identity politics—in which "gay" is a resistant minoritizing term in opposition to "straight" heterosexuality—is represented in the process of being superseded by the inevitable progress of history. Thus, however privileged a place he claims for gay writing and reading practices, they remain bound up in hegemonic reproductory formulations of "the literary," a "great tradition," and the progress of history. And for Leavitt, the most positive achievements of his collection's stories are their establishment of a gay "tradition," their exploration of "the dilemma of living as part of a minority," their presentation of "the problem of sexual identity in all its individualistic complexity," and most especially, their success in having nongay writers agree to be included in a gay anthology. The effect of his historicizing, then, is the fantasy of the end of sexuality itself. But in contradistinction to Foucault's call for an "end" to identitarian politics in order to stress "becoming" rather than "being," in order "to invent with the body, with its elements, its surfaces, its volumes, its depths, a nondisciplinary eroticism: that of the body plunged into a volatile and diffused state through chance encounters and incalculable pleasures,"[12] Leavitt's formulation enacts a stabilizing fulfillment (and hence perpetuation in the present) of modern gender and sexuality identity categories. For while Leavitt may be trying to resist the minoritizing and stultifying effects of a rigid identity politics, his reconfiguration of "gay" as a universalizing category works to reinscribe many of the foundational assumptions of modernism and the universal liberal subject.

If Leavitt reconfigures "gay" as the fulfillment of the very tradition and canon that a dominant heterosexuality purports to advance, he does so to avoid the delimiting of gay identity that a heterosexist ideology attempts when it marginalizes gay as other to itself. What becomes problematic in this historicization of gay reading and subjectivity, however, is its enunciation of "proper" gay desire in terms of a tradition of renunciation of self—traditional, that is, from the point of view of dominant culture—in order to become "recognizably human." In the process, there is a disavowal of the proliferative, unpredictable identifications produced in the individualized "improper" pleasures of that countercultural gay erotics that Leavitt represents as merely delusional "fawning over angels made flesh" and thus now properly left behind in the past. What is especially disturbing to the queer Chaucerian here is the ease with which a very familiar double bind of modernity emerges. The renunciation of the pleasures of an "uncontrollable" fleshliness constructs not only a properly disciplined subject, but a subject that is only made fully modern by defining *improperly* gay pleasure as locked within an absolutely other, primitivizing pastness. These are the workings of canonicity and modernity that have succeeded so effectively in marginalizing and containing premodern difference, often by defining a Chaucer defiantly and magnificently other to the pastness, the "medievalness," of his contemporary moment.

Yet as Louise Fradenburg and Carla Freccero have so usefully emphasized in their reflections on the processes and paradoxes of queer historicization,

> Scholars and activists have reminded us not only that sex has a history, but also that history has its pleasures. Queer theory, the history of sexuality, and gay and lesbian studies pursue a fraught but ebullient rethinking of the ethics of pleasure. While recent studies in sexuality make clear that we ought to know the past, they also affirm that we want to. . . . We do not, then, pursue the history of sexuality just because we think we must; we study it because we know that what we must or ought to do is intimately related to what we want to do. . . . History—and not just family history—is an erogenous zone.[13]

And I want now to turn to two "fraught but ebullient rethinkings of the ethics of pleasure"—John Preston's introduction to his anthology of gay porn, *Flesh and the Word,* and the narrator's address to the reader in the prologue to the *Miller's Tale*—to disturb established relationships between past and present. Such queer contiguity, I will argue, can help us theorize new models of subjectivity and readerly practice, in the process resisting previously installed relationships between "the literary" and modern identities, and between such identities and hegemonic social reproduction.

Preston's first volume of *Flesh and the Word,* published two years before Leavitt's *Penguin Book of Gay Short Stories,* also arises out of and responds to the successes of gay identity politics in the 1970s and 1980s. Preston's title, however, with its queerly performative play on "the Word made flesh," embraces the scandalously contaminating power that comes from linking pleasure in fleshliness with the incarnational discourses of Christianity.[14] And his anthology encourages the very rhizomatic, unpredictable, and "improper" identifications on the part of the queer desiring subject with "angels made flesh," history, and tradition that Leavitt sought to occlude and erase.

In his introduction to his collection, Preston, like Leavitt, attempts to historicize the relationships between reading and identity, fictional/textual production and agency, desire and history. He does so by means of a personal narrative that begins in the primal scene of many gay narratives—before coming out, before Stonewall, before true adult identity has been achieved:

> When I was a teenager in the sixties I used to find every excuse possible to travel, alone, through Harvard Square. There for sale at a kiosk that specialized in foreign and exotic publications were small, digest-sized, black-and-white photo magazines, many of them from Britain, that featured pages of nearly naked men. The magazines were almost hidden in a corner of the booth with their titles—names like *Physique Pictorial*—hardly visible. Their existence took my breath away. Getting from the stand to the cash register with an obliquely titled, pocket-sized magazine took all my adolescent courage, and then I could never look the clerk in the eye. I most often wouldn't dare take the books home after I bought them—something might be discovered there—but I'd find some private place to sit (usually a library) and study the images, a young boy's erection painful in my pants. I would memorize the faces and the bodies and keep them in my mind, my private reserve of sensual delight.[15]

Read through the lens of Leavitt's definition of gay literature (or, for that matter, of much of mainstream society's definition of culture generally), Preston's narrative constitutes a debilitating lack of identity, an empty past that inscribes the writing present as its progressive fulfillment. Unlike "then," now "we" can have a gay identity, gay authors, a gay literature; now we can begin to move toward being fully in charge of our own representation.

Yet I am drawn to the "young boy's erection painful in my pants," and the memorization of faces and bodies kept "in my mind, my private reserve of sensual delight." What is so interesting about this moment is the clarity with which Preston reproduces the lack of a "proper place" for such deviant desire, its absence of identity, even as he outlines—de Certeau-like—an alternative walking through the city and the various spaces and identifications in and through which subjectivities find expression. And it is precisely the absence of a "proper" reading position and authorship—in all their bourgeois, mystified naturalizations—that makes this moment an enabling one for Preston. In this way it provides a resistance to the "forgetting" that de Certeau describes as the basis for authorship and the fiction of a proper place: "In 'forgetting' the collective inquiry in which he is inscribed, in isolating the object of his discourse from its historical genesis, an 'author' in effect denies his real situation. He creates the fiction of a place of his own *(une place propre)*."[16]

For Preston, absence of authorship and absence of the fiction of a place of his own do not necessarily signify "lack," and he distinguishes these early encounters with pornography from a resistant sexualization of "innocent" heterosexual representations of masculinity and the male body:

> It wasn't that there weren't other images that I could make sexual. . . . I had those same experiences with such seemingly innocent media as the Sears Roebuck mail-order catalog, with its pages and pages of underwear models. What made *Physique Pictorial* and its peers so devastatingly powerful was their sexual purpose. . . . These were nearly naked men whose photographers obviously knew they were creating erotic images as they emphasized the lines of barely draped genitals with lighting and pose. . . . It was both safer and more pleasurable to look at images of men who were straightforwardly posing for me. . . . It also felt more realistic, whether or not it was true, to think of myself in a relationship with one of the models. Whatever else that model was doing, I could believe he was posing for me. I didn't find him in undress by mistake, the way I felt I did with my Sears models.[17]

Moreover, such pornographic encounters differ in intensity, not in kind, from the excited but painful reading against the grain that is necessary in a queer encounter with the classically "literary." As a queer reader, Preston finds himself forced to read out of the absence of a place of one's own an author without a place of *his* own: "No matter how much my high school English teacher insisted that Walt Whitman was only talking about friendship—and she did insist on that—I knew better as soon as I read *Leaves of Grass*." Even in the case of a contemporary writer representing homosexuality, a similar situation occurred, since he could only pass as an "author" to the extent that he would not create the fiction of a place of his own as a gay man. Thus, "Reading anything that was homosexually oriented was exciting in the sixties. A simple passage of a Nelson Algren novel that acknowledged a gay character's sexuality, no matter how sordid the context, was important to me."[18] What Preston describes in all these cases is the opposite of an economy of the proper place. Instead, it is in the *privacy* of the *public* library that he finds a space to "study the images" of *Physique Pictorial;* the powerful effects of that study reorient and empower his different reading of the literary. Distinguishing differences of private versus public, popular versus literary, consumption versus appreciation, proper versus improper are crossed and recrossed in enabling ways for the queer reader. As Preston remembers it: "I wasn't simply consuming those images. I was beginning to conceive of myself as one of them."[19]

Integral to the process Preston describes is a recognition of its queer performativity. Eve Kosofsky Sedgwick, responding to the "weird centrality of the marriage example" for J. L. Austin's articulation of performativity in speech act theory, has begun instead to speculate

> about a performative elaboration that might begin with the example, not "I do," but, let us say, "Shame on you." . . . [T]he very grammatical truncation of "Shame on you" marks it as the product of a history out of which an I, now withdrawn, is *projecting* shame—toward another I, an I deferred, that has yet and with difficulty to come into being, if at all, in the place of the shamed second person. The verblessness of this particular performative, then, implies a first person whose singular/plural status, whose past/present/future status, and indeed whose agency/passivity can only be questioned rather than presumed.[20]

Clearly the young Preston conforms to such a place of the shamed second person in a performative moment of "Shame on you": "I could never look the clerk in the eye. I most often wouldn't dare take the books home after I bought them—something might be discovered there—but I'd find some private place to sit (usually a library) and study the images, a young boy's erection painful in my pants." What is interesting, though, is that such conformity manifests the in-betweenness of what Sedgwick has called "shame's threshold between sociability and introversion. . . .

Shame, as opposed to guilt, is a bad feeling that does not attach to what one does, but to what one is. . . . [O]ne therefore *is something,* in experiencing shame."[21]

The young Preston's choice of the *Physique* pictorials over the catalog pictures can thus become a recognition of that *being something* in experiencing shame: "Whatever else that model was doing, I could believe he was posing for me. I didn't find him in undress by mistake, the way I felt I did with my Sears models." The young Preston also chooses such a shameful identity when he chooses the queer readings of the classics in spite of the "Shame on you" directives of his teachers and the tradition of reading they invoke and represent. So, too, does the adult Preston when he returns to his younger self and is drawn to that young boy's erection or when he anthologizes and writes gay porn (instead of pursuing the more "adult" literary interests a Leavitt would wish for a contemporary gay man). In desiring the questionable identities and identifications of shame, Preston is moved to choose the verblessness of a particular performative that implies an "I" "whose singular/plural status, whose past/present/future status, and indeed whose agency/passivity can only be questioned rather than presumed."[22] It is not that the adult Preston, as a gay man, has somehow found a place to leave that earlier shame behind, to excise it as a toxic presence. The intimate relationships of porn, shame, interest, and identity that he outlines in his preface make it clear that that is exactly what he does not want.[23] Preston thus invites his reader into an experience of the queer performativity of "Shame on you" and the transformative identifications it makes possible.[24] For it is not porn per se, but the particular location in which porn places the queer subject in relation to identity, shame, and interest in the world, that fascinates Preston, and that makes its queer performativity so necessary.[25]

Rather than the mastery of "the gaze," or the subjection of mass consumption, the move to the apparent margins, the choice of "superficial" pleasures (as opposed to the depths of bourgeois selfhood), and the excitement of "a young boy's erection," provoke identifications for Preston that lead to the excesses of postponed identity, a subject-in-process neither strictly cultural, nor countercultural: "One of the excitements—and confusions—of being gay was understanding that I could be, in so many different ways, both the active and the passive partner. Sexologists might use those terms only in relation to who performs what physiological acts, but I was quickly aware that there was a whole range of possibilities, emotional as well as sexual."[26] Rather than some utopian free space that pornography inhabits, Preston inscribes the possibility that pornography's non-"literariness" might work to constitute that impure space in which the imposition of hegemonic identities can be deferred and in which alternative communications and identifications become possible.

Obviously the workings of ideology are not absent from this process. On the one hand, dominant ideologies determine where and how such pornographic material is produced and distributed, attempting to control how individuals can encounter the material and how it fits into "representation." On the other hand, the identifications of pornography in turn shape subjectivities as they come into consciousness. Such identifications can become powerful ideologies within countercultures shaped by such readings, and can therefore determine what is "properly gay" sexuality and practice. In de Certeau's terms, space is always threatening to be overtaken by place, the improper to become an economy of the proper place. Nonetheless, says Preston, "For myself and for many other gay men, pornographic writings were how we learned the parameters of our sexual life. We could have more than a simple ejaculation with a nameless partner. Pornography was how we developed our fantasies, both sexual and emotional. The eponymous Phil Andros was a hustler and a porn star who was not only showing us how to come with some literary flair, he was pointing out how life worked, where the decent folk were, and who should be avoided." Preston also points out that *Gay Whore,* a porno book from 1967 containing a climax scene in which the two men end satisfied and happy, provided a representation unavailable either in mainstream writing or in early "homosexual literature."[27]

In turn, Preston's anthologies of gay porn now function in a similar fashion to resist the canonization of gay writing, which has succeeded in carving out a "proper place" within the literary for its production and in creating the fiction of a place of its own. In part this resistance occurs by refusing the illusion of authorship and the proprietary rights it makes possible: "I make no claim that the writing here is anything but pornography.... People would try to say that my sexual writing—or Samuel Steward's or someone else's—was 'too good' to be discarded as pornography. I disown that distinction completely. Pornography and erotica are the same thing. The only difference is that erotica is the stuff bought by rich people; pornography is what the rest of us buy."[28] Thus Preston insists on remembering the collective inquiry in which he is inscribed, on connecting the object of his discourse with its historical genesis, on foregrounding the material conditions producing his desire: "I suppose that some people will say that what I'm doing is taking a lot of work that would be labeled pornographic and making it into erotica by presenting it in this volume, brought to you by a division of one of the largest publishers in the world. It's an amusing thought."[29]

Translating gay porn into a high-end format—the published hardcover anthology—cannot erase its "proper place" in the low-end marketplace. Preston's recognition of the rhizomatic connections between "literature" and nonliterary "ephemera" disrupts the usual hierarchies established by the literary/nonliterary binary, suggesting instead the complex imbrication of both as commodities in a common marketplace. By mobilizing the circulation of identities original to the porn magazine setting against the inevitable attempt by literary ideologists to rearrange the waywardness of porn into erotica, Preston resists assuming the stilled affiliative identities of a literary tradition as the "proper" gay identity. In re-presenting gay porn the way he does, Preston puts the tracings made by traditional handlings of desire back onto the multiplicity of the map (to use Deleuze and Guattari's terms).[30]

Several features of his anthologies are noteworthy in this regard. Preston includes "history," but not in any straightforward teleological or identity-affirming way. Pre-Stonewall examples, along with post-AIDS material, suggest not some inevitable march to freedom, but the difficult and liberatory process of creation in the middle of adversity, ideology, chance, and unstable desire. In a similar fashion, Preston's choice of material challenges distinctions of genre and gender. Writing about pornography and descriptions of "real" gay cruising grounds mix with pornography "proper." The relationship between pornography as trainer of desire and desire as shaper of the pornographic medium is constantly blurred as readers are encouraged to wander at will through the anthology and in turn are seduced by desire into fantasizing the unthinkable. Some of the hottest stories are written by women about gay male sex (frequently s/m) for a supposedly gay male reading audience. Throughout, Preston's inclusion of woman-authored gay male porn, of nonfiction, of mainstream "literary" writing such as Edmund White's or Alan Hollinghurst's, and most notably of "hard core," "violent" s/m porn, such as Aaron Travis's "Slave" or Pat Califia's "Belonging," insists on the power of fantasy and resists any notion that porn (and writing/imagining generally) constitutes the mimicry of a binary logic. Preston's anthologies resist the pull of the sexologist's manual (whether cultural or countercultural); they never seek to tell us who "we" are. Instead, like Deleuze and Guattari's middle, the space they inhabit is that of the *and . . . and . . . and,* a place of the subject in process, of a multiplicity of rhizomatic identifications that imitate nothing, reproduce nothing, but are instead their "becoming world."[31]

What I have been trying to suggest, then, are some of the ways that Preston embraces the gay anthology as "deformative," that is, in Sedgwick's words, "versions of performativity (okay, go ahead and call them 'perversions'—or 'deformatives') that might begin by placing some different kinds of utterance in the position of the exemplary."[32] In contrast, Leavitt's turn to the literary as an attempt to secure a privileged place for "gay" within the modernist project enacts its own reproduction of social and epistemological stratification. In making this contrast, however, I do not want to produce "true" gay culture out of yet another hierarchizing binary of plenitude and lack, good and bad, liberatory and repressive. Instead, Deleuze and Guattari's idea of machinic assemblage, I think, provides a different textual and hermeneutical structure for exploring the mutually constitutive processes of desire we see at work in these two projects:

> In a book, as in all things, there are lines of articulation or segmentarity, strata and territories; but also lines of flight, movements of deterritorialization and destratification. . . . All this, lines and measurable speeds, constitutes an *assemblage.* One side of a machinic assemblage faces the strata, which doubtless make it a kind of organism, or signifying totality, or determination attributable to a subject; it also has a side facing a *body without organs,* which is continually dismantling the organism, causing asignifying particles or pure intensities to pass or circulate, and attributing to itself subjects that it leaves with nothing more than a name as the trace of an intensity.[33]

The anthologizing projects of Preston and Leavitt, then, taken together work powerfully to demonstrate how the category of "gay literature" functions as a kind of machinic assemblage in the present moment, capable of tilting the previously marginal and repressed either toward stratification and assimilation into existing modes of production and power or toward deformative dis-organization and proliferation that risk placing different kinds of utterance in the position of the exemplary. In turn, the projects of Preston and Leavitt provide a different take on the anthologizing project of the *Canterbury Tales.* Might we think of its performative inscription of "gentil" identity through storytelling in similar terms? That is, as a machinic assemblage tilting toward an organization of lay, secular experience in ways that so anticipate modern regimes of sexuality and the liberal subject as to make the *Tales* readily accessible to assimilation to that modernist narrative, while at the same time evincing a queer performativity that puts different kinds of utterance into the position of the exemplary?

Certainly there is much in the *Tales* that seems preoccupied with telling us who *we* are. A succession of authorized readings (beginning with the Ellesmere scribe) have made the delineation of identity foundational to what and how the *Tales* mean. Not only does the Ellesmere scribe make the relationship between tale-teller and tale the crucial *ordinatio* structuring the confusing proliferation of genres and versions of authority on the road to Canterbury, but the portraits further this process by condensing the *General Prologue*'s tendency to ground meaning and agency in the individual embodied and socialized subject (rather than in a simple universal moral type or secular estate). Alongside this penchant for organizing the *Tales*' incitement of desire for fleshliness is the repeated and privileged emphasis on marriage and sexualized male/female relationships as the core of much of this work of anthologization. We shall discuss the significance of this focus on marriage in detail in chapters 2 and 3. For now we shall simply note that the first lines of the *General Prologue* begin the *Tales* with the familiar linkage of human love and the generative cycle of nature and that the marriage example begins and ends the first, commissioned tale of the collection. The *Knight's Tale* inscribes at its opening and closing the marriages of Hippolyta and Theseus, Palamon and Emily, as performatives that make vividly intelligible the relationships between heterosexuality and social reproduction.[34]

But if we place a different kind of utterance—other than the well-polished lens of modernity and heterosexuality—in the position of the exemplary here, say that of Preston's deformative desire precisely to fawn over the angels made flesh that a too easy assimilation of the *Tales* into modernity might deny as active in them, what might we see? As Lee

Patterson has noted, "In an important sense, the *Canterbury Tales* really begin with the *Miller's Tale*—although even this is something of a false start."[35] Patterson is, of course, situating his remarks within the context of an argument that in the *Tales* Chaucer is intent on stepping out from under the oppressive weight of a courtly tradition of "making" to develop new modes of expression and representation. And the *Miller's Tale* will indeed seem a "false start" if we remain locked within traditional models of domination/revolt and of progress and modernity as the defining terms for the *Tales*. Situating this supposed "false start" in the context of Sedgwick's "deformative," however, we see instead how the emergence of the (problematized) first person at this moment in the *Tales* becomes a richly productive question rather than a stabilizing presumption.

For, like Preston's backward glance, the narrator's interjection at the beginning of the *Miller's Tale* foregrounds a performativity quite different from the normativizing power of the marriage example as it is presented in the narrator's and Knight's sanctioned openings to the *Tales*. The dramatic moment to which the narrator draws our attention stages both the drunken, churlish resistance of the Miller to the silencing power of shame, and the projection of shame that establishes identity for the withdrawn subject uttering the deformative "Shame on you"—that is, the moral and social suasion of the Miller's betters (represented in this instance by the narrator, the Knight, and the Reeve):

> What sholde I moore seyn, but this Millere
> He nolde his wordes for no man forbere,
> But tolde his cherles tale in his manere.
> M'athynketh that I shal reherce it heere.
> And therfore every gentil wight I preye,
> For Goddes love, demeth nat that I seye
> Of yvel entente, but for I moot reherce
> Hir tales alle, be they bettre or werse,
> Or elles falsen som of my mateere.
> And therfore, whoso list it nat yheere,
> Turne over the leef and chese another tale;
> For he shal fynde ynowe, grete and smale,
> Of storial thyng that toucheth gentillesse,
> And eek moralitee and hoolynesse.
> Blameth nat me if that ye chese amys.[36]

This narrative interjection evokes a similar moment of projected blame near the end of the *General Prologue*. There, the narrator asks his readers out of "curteisye" not to attribute any "rudeliche and large" speech in the forthcoming tales to *his* "vileynye" because "Whoso shal telle a tale after a man, / He moot reherce as ny as evere he kan / Everich a word" (I.725–26, 734, 731–33). But the project of disavowal that results from this appeal to the demands of verisimilitude keeps any potential shame accruing to certain "low" tales and forms of speech at a safe distance from the narrator and the reader. Like Leavitt's literary transformation of subcultural homosexual experience—"fawning over angels made flesh"—into human drama, the narrator's emphasis on words being cousin to the deed is necessary to avoid turning his anthologizing project into some "untrewe / Or feyne thinge" (735–36). Potential "vileynye" is thus transformed by the mediation of a hermeneutics of linguistic and social propriety into an empowering truthfulness of human drama.

Here, on the other hand, the narrator's interjection in the prologue to the *Miller's Tale* places both himself and his readers in a much more dynamic relationship with shame, flesh, and the word that explores how one *can be something* in experiencing shame. The narrator's comments here appear to place him in a renunciatory identity position similar to the *General Prologue:* "M'athynketh that I shal reherce it heere" (I.3170), that is, "It displeases me, I regret, that I shall repeat it here." In proving that he knows better than the Miller, however, the narrator also foregrounds that shame the Miller himself does not feel, or that is occluded by his drunken state. At the same time, the narrator's emphasis on his own and his reader's self-consciousness around shame curiously works to incite a desire for what he is intent on renouncing. In performing the shame the Miller cannot or will not on his own, the narrator also performs his own identification with it and by it. So too, the narrator's private/public address to the now clearly textualized reader—"Turne over the leef and chese another tale"—offers the reader the choice of being placed *with* the Miller by choosing to read his tale, even as the narrator explicitly projects shame onto such an identification.[37] In doing so, the narrator and reader can *choose* to identify as subjects in process, performing at times contradictory public and private functions. "Blameth nat me if that ye chese amys" thus acknowledges the queer performativity inherent in the unstable and unpredictable set of relationships necessary to establish identity here. The narrator's insertion of the effects of such textuality thereby resists the universalizing "now" of traditional medieval representations, even as the moral tenor of his comments would appear to assert it.

We can get a distance on this material, but only by disavowing our own mobility and involvement within its pluralistic universe. This is, then, a profoundly "deformative" moment of identification for the reader of the *Tales,* placing "Shame on you" in the position of the exemplary. For the queering of the stability of the very estate identities being inscribed by the generic and social organization of the first fragment disturbs the pattern of domination and revolt that Fragment I assures us is normative. The narrator raises in its extremity the ability of the performative "Shame on you" to shut down interest and communication. But he does so only to stress the unlikelihood of such an event taking place in the way intended; indeed, the performance of "Shame on you" works as much to excite desire, to maintain interest in the Miller and his tale, to explore an "I" identifiable in and emerging from the shadows of that performative. And this "I" is also a reader in the process of being constructed, arising out of a secondary position vis-à-vis the traditional medieval clerical "right reader" (born from allegorizing, transcendent patterns of reading).

The recent work of Lee Patterson, Paul Strohm, and David Wallace in different ways provides a context for this new reader in the newness of Chaucer's social condition.[38] I shall take up this question in more detailed ways in subsequent chapters, but we might note for now that the "turn to the social world of contemporary England" that Patterson finds in the *Tales* accentuates for him the newness of this collection as textual artifact: "The presence of the *Tales* is for the modern reader so unavoidable, their achievements so undeniable, that we approach them with a sense of inevitability that assumes their permanent existence. But there was a time when they had not been written, and their coming into existence was not preordained. If something rather than nothing, then why this thing rather than another?"[39] The queer performativity of the *Miller's Tale,* then, constitutes a fraught moment where this set of newnesses coalesces and comes to consciousness: the fabliau as a new Chaucerian genre and the body of the tale-teller as foundational for the tale (and the pilgrimage body for the *Canterbury Tales*). But in both cases their instantiation as *the* Miller's tale in a performative relationship with a set of received assumptions about how such a tale and tale-teller signify (to which the narrator's interjection draws our attention) inscribes the deformative as speaking voice. As such, it foregrounds the dangerous centrality of an authorial voice in relation to the shift taking place in the constitution and transmission of cultural capital. The medieval monastic and university clerical culture had little need for the category of literature outside of allegory. Yet at the same time, from the late twelfth century on, there is, in the development of a vernacular literature, the development of a category of fiction with truth value, neither sacred scripture nor strictly allegorical veil surrounding transcendent truth.

Fabliau, pilgrimage storytelling as carnivalesque release, drunken interruptions from social inferiors can be seen, then, as constituting the pedagogic lie that proves the truth of hegemonic authority. But which hegemonic authority? The successful use of the *Canterbury Tales* by its early readers to canonize the category of the literary and to constitute a new bourgeois subject and idiolect suggests that the "newness" the *Tales* represents is a potent social force. It would be overly simplifying and stabilizing, though, to see the moment of the *Tales* simply as the formation of a new soon-to-be dominant identity (which, for lack of a better term, we might call "gentry") displacing the old high medieval ones of the noble/clerical compact. Instead, the narrator's interjection at the opening of the *Miller's Tale,* precisely at that moment where a "new" order interposes itself among the old (the Miller's interruption, after all, disrupts the old aristocratic/clerical compact by replacing the Monk as second tale-teller), explores the processes of identification that produce and reproduce power in the world.[40] In doing so, this deformative moment explores the desire for "newness" itself (and with it, that which will come to be called modernity), even as the forces already installed call that a deforming experience. It is this dynamic that makes this moment as exciting for the postmodern, queer reader as it clearly was for the late medieval reader. For the narrator's comments here reveal the opening of the *Tales* as a moment of libidinal excitement, a fever pitch of intensity in a process of organization not yet climaxed.

Like Preston's moment at the kiosk in Harvard Square, which inscribes a set of identifications as yet polymorphously desiring but on the verge of "becoming" identifiable (i.e., homosexual/gay, with a public forum for such an identity being constructed alongside a counterdiscourse that linked private/public in new ways), so, too, Chaucer's narrator inscribes in the scene of the Miller's interruption a similarly preoriginary moment where we see a new reader being born out of the valorization of individuality and a proper space for the author, yet desiring so much more.[41] Such an interest in the world, such a push to associational identifications rather than communitarian identities and ideologies is, of course, at the heart of the desire to represent new bourgeois ways of being in the world, those new identities and ideologies that we have come to call modern. What makes the *Canterbury Tales* so appropriable for the new class of late medieval readers (and so serviceable to successive generations in their attempts to define and reproduce hegemonic identities) is its ability to fantasize as "the real" that new symbolic order of modernity that is coming into being—one organized around individualized and nationalized identities.

The narrator's interjection frames the frame, as it were, and highlights its perverse use in the *Canterbury Tales*. The frame here does not act as the stabilizing commentary that brings out the core meaning of a text, as it would in the glossed Bibles; nor does it simply act as a carnivalesque, regulated space for the personal, such as one might find in the margins of illuminated manuscripts,[42] or in the "upsadoun" world of medieval festival or pilgrimage.[43] Rather what we have here is the fictional frame as erogenous zone, functioning as the space where desire is valorized to the extent that it can be represented, but represented under the sign of shame. Thus, we witness the construction of a mechanism to allow a sense of modern history, but because it is done under the sign of shame, this mechanism cannot unproblematically achieve the status of exemplary utterance. It is instead experienced as a deformative that continues to incite desire even after its alleged "work" of inscribing "bourgeois" desire for representation is done. Our attention is, one might say, directed back to a young boy's erection painful in his pants. The postmodern queer reader, then, might very well embrace that blush of shame with which the narrator "opens" the *Miller's Tale* as a productive middle, an afterimage resonant with possibilities too often forgotten in communitarian and identitarian visions of the pilgrimage body. And in the remainder of this chapter, I want to take up this question of shame in relation to the sadism constructing dominant medieval accounts of masculinity as they are presented in the *Miller's Tale* itself. In particular, I am concerned with how the masochistic contract established by the *Miller's Tale* with its readers resists such sadism by desiring instead a "desexualized" body operating within, yet not completely controlled by, the ideological structures of desire.

## INVENTING WITH THE BODY IN THE *MILLER'S TALE*

Despite the very best efforts of the Host to forge an orderly and homogeneous pilgrimage body, the unexpected intervention of the Miller irrevocably alters the nature of the Canterbury game. Fabulously excessive, the *Miller's Tale* remains one of Chaucer's best known and most popular stories, not least because of its brilliantly layered and doubled plot, which parodies both the courtly love stories of the *Knight's Tale* and the biblical stories of the Flood and the Annunciation. Moreover, the drunken Miller and his parodic fabliau are insistently and volubly iconoclastic in their attempts to "quite" the refined nobility and transcendent assurance of the sober Knight and his courtly epic. Set in the now of late medieval domestic life and reproducing the flavor of day-to-day life and conversation, his tale asserts a natural order and bodiliness almost asphyxiated by the Knight's excessively symbolic and institutionalized ordering of existence. However churlish, the Miller seems to offer a breath of fresh air by providing a moment of fictional verisimilitude more directly mirroring the present of the Canterbury pilgrims.

But the *Miller's Tale,* for all its carnivalesque bawdy, ends with a vision of chastened masculinity and restored social control that in many ways reproduces the *moralitas* of the *Knight's Tale,* albeit in starker colors and bolder strokes. In the tale's climactic moment, with one thrust of the hot "kultour" Absalon finally behaves like a proper man, Nicholas's excess heat is dissipated, and John's overweening social pride—that a carpenter could know God's "pryvetee"—is brought down to earth by his ignominious fall. Directed at the female body as punishment for the shame that Absalon has undergone because of the misguided kiss, the branding actually punishes Nicholas's wayward male body. The physical violence represented in the branding thus works to "remasculinize" the potentially effeminate behavior of the men in the tale, correcting a humoral imbalance that has resulted from a male loss of bodily control. According to medieval medical theories, the combination of Absalon's lack of virile heat and lovesickness without relief should actually make him the most likely candidate for cauterization. One cure for that lovesickness was cauterization, either potential (performed by caustics applied to the inflicted area) or actual (performed by fire on the afflicted area). Absalon, then, applies a version of the former to his lips and mouth after the misguided kiss, and the latter to Nicholas's buttocks with the hot "kultour." Nicholas's problem, of course, is not a lack of virile heat, as his night of lovemaking and flatulence indicates. But a nonsexual release of this excess heat—via the branding—would restore a humoral balance more appropriate for a single clerk and perhaps make a lively female mate sexually available once more to her chastened husband.[44]

But more important for the tale's fabliau moral, the symbolic violence in the laughter that follows generalizes and institutionalizes this process of remasculinization. As a result, John's delusions of special favor above his station, Alison's lack of governance as wife, Nicholas's and Absalon's inattention to professional duty, indeed the general lack of good governance represented by the Miller's hijacking of the Canterbury game, are all "corrected," and communal order reasserted, by the tale's disciplining of the body.[45] To the extent, then, that the laughter of the *Miller's Tale* works to restore proper masculinity, the tale "quites" the *Knight's Tale* only so far as it translates the Knight's message onto another discursive terrain. The generic difference of the *Miller's Tale,* rather than absolutely distinguishing it from the *Knight's Tale,* instead allows it to bring to the surface, with all the obscenity and immediacy of the fabliau medium, the erotic violence animating the Knight's encounter with the body and power in his tale. In the process, the *Miller's Tale* foregrounds the bodily signifiers and first rank of signification and understanding that the *Knight's Tale* takes for granted in its absolutist, transcendent account of the formation of masculine subjectivity. The severity of such attempts to rebalance the male body at the end of the *Miller's Tale,* and consequently to restore the hegemony of a "proper" masculinity and heteronormativity, thus reproduces *in extremis* the sadism of the *Knight's Tale* and its impositions of institutionalized masculine power and knowledge.

In describing the project of these tales as sadistic, I want to point to the larger representational questions posed by their attention to physical domination and the eroticization of violence. What we find in both tales is pornology rather than pornography; that is, a literature "aimed above all at confronting language with its own limits, with what is in a sense a 'non-language' (violence that does not speak, eroticism that remains unspoken)."[46] For as Deleuze reminds us: "With Sade and Masoch the function of literature is not to describe the world, since this has already been done, but to define a counterpart of the world capable of containing its violence and excesses." Paralleling the symbolic violence that takes place in these tales with the disciplinary regulation of Sade's fictions, will, I hope, draw attention to the ways the eroticism of both tales "is able to act as a mirror to the world by reflecting its excesses, drawing out its violence and even conferring a 'spiritual' quality on these phenomena by the very fact that it puts them at the service of the senses."[47]

The *Knight's Tale* underscores again and again the need to discipline "the body." Emilye's desire for unproductive virginity gives way to marriage; Palamon's solipsistic devotion to love is replaced by a dutiful attention to the institutions that further the common good; Arcite's productive activity as loyal retainer to Theseus and knightly advocate for Emilye allows his heroic stellification in death. At another level, the actions of Theseus (and the tale's fictionalized relationship with tale-teller and audience) inscribe the necessity for the personal to turn by reflection upon itself into the impersonal and institutional. The *Knight's Tale* thus emphasizes its own apparently inevitable enactment of a series of increasingly schematic substitutions. The chaotic desire of Palamon and Arcite is organized by the restraint of the Knight as tale-teller directing our attention to Theseus as embodiment of properly ordered masculine desire. In turn, the magisterial artistry of Theseus and the tale as a whole allows desire to be directed even higher to the purified order of Egeus's Boethian mastery of individual desire.

Yet, as Deleuze notes, following Georges Bataille, "the language of Sade is paradoxical *because it is essentially that of a victim.* Only the victim can describe torture; the torturer necessarily uses the hypocritical language of established order and power."[48] While for some readers of the tale, both Theseus and the Knight might seem to fit the bill of "torturer," such an obfuscatory use of violence better describes the interventions of the Reeve in his tale.[49] The Knight, as victim of that very order he seeks to embody absolutely, instead maps out the kinds of systemic and systematic disciplining of the individual and social body necessary to achieve that perfect institutionalization. In Sade's fictions the spiritual and the obscene, symbolic violence and literal physical violence, are fused; in Fragment I of the *Canterbury Tales* these functions are split between the *Knight's Tale* and the *Miller's Tale*. Both, however, enact the turn to the purely demonstrative that Deleuze underscores as essential to the project of sadism:

> With Sade we witness an astonishing development of the demonstrative use of language. . . . The libertine may put on an act of trying to convince and persuade. . . . But the intention to convince is merely apparent, for nothing is in fact more alien to the sadist than the wish to convince, to persuade, in short to educate. He is interested in something quite different, namely to demonstrate that reasoning itself is a form of violence, and that he is on the side of violence, however calm and logical he may be. He is not even attempting to prove anything to anyone, but to perform a demonstration related essentially to the solitude and omnipotence of its author. The point of the exercise is to show that the demonstration is identical to violence.[50]

For in different but mutually constitutive ways, the eroticism of the first two Canterbury tales forces the participants and readers to conform to an institutionalized hegemonic view of the body—whether individual or social—as organic hierarchy. The lower regions of the body are ruled by its head, just as the individual is ruled by the stars and matter by the transcendent will of God. This universal hierarchical principle in turn produces and naturalizes a series of interlinked binaries and essentialisms. In the social sphere, the noble is naturally going to rule the baser elements of society just as (and because) the head rules the baser elements of the body and as spirit takes precedence over matter. In terms of gender, the masculine is to the head and nobility as the feminine is to the lower limbs (especially the genitalia) and baseborn churls.[51] In the *Knight's Tale* these "truths" are read back into biological sex in an essentializing and stabilizing fashion that creates a chilling memorialization of that medieval masculinist hegemony in which, as Will Sayer has stated,

> Women passively carry a sex identity while men are actively engaged in gender. Male sex is the 'default' . . . in that its possession is not a matter of concern since attention is turned to the

> more important issue of gender realization. Women are marked, not least by the Church, with the sign of the deviant sex (non-male and variously virginal, reproductive, maternal, socially destabilizing, voracious) and this marking limits the types and degree of gender realization that are possible. Gender is then contained by the female sex and the force is centripetal. For the man, male sex, like superior physical strength, is the given, the point of departure is the elaboration of gender; movement is centrifugal.[52]

Thus, in the *Knight's Tale* "good" femininity (i.e., the [female] body seeking the guidance and control of a properly masculine will) acts as a frame that throws into relief true masculinity (generally arising out of noble and heroic [male] activity). And in the *Miller's Tale* "bad" femininity (whether the female body left untended or male bodies sliding into effeminate confusion because of improper desire) finds the rod of correction it so achingly needs to take on proper desire and true masculine agency.

Let us return again to the branding scene. If Absalon's original intention for the hot "kultour" had been successful, his action would have scored a violently misogynistic blow against the female body that humiliated him. The action of the tale's plot, however, substitutes Nicholas for Alison. With one stroke, as it were, the focus shifts to the male body and Absalon's cauterization of it. The branding thus reproduces that sealing off of the male body that Absalon attempted earlier when he tried to purify his lips, abandon lovemaking, and rededicate his body to the proper pursuits for which it is intended. However much Absalon's unreasoning desire for revenge may want to destroy the (female) body, the tale's plot rearranges that desire into a more constructive, disciplinary, and hierarchized relationship of reason and body. We laugh at both men because they are apparently getting what they deserve, and what they deserve is the necessary disciplining of the body that will restore the mind-body balance that constructs proper masculinity and the social and cosmic order that depends on it. Implicitly, then, the tale reassures its readers that the truly masculine subject position lies outside the tale, accessible via the distantiating laughter of the community: a masculinity that will put everything in its place and conform to a preexistent transcendent order of things. In short, we return to the hegemonic masculine subject position outlined by the *Knight's Tale,* but now imagined as always already present within the present moment—that is, discoverable within the moment of pilgrimage dialogue as much as in the transcendence of "olde stories," and available to the wider category of "gentils" rather than limited to an aristocracy of blood.

For this reason, the apparent otherness of fabliau carnival to courtly restraint can be seen as the disguise necessary to mask its complicity in articulating for the masculine an erotics of domination and power as knowledge. And Foucault's ambivalence about Sade's apparently subversive sexuality is also applicable to the drunken Miller's "quiting" of the Knight. According to Foucault, the body as Sade sees it is still strongly organic and anchored in hierarchy, the difference being that the hierarchy is not organized—as in old fable (the *Knight's Tale*)—starting from the head, but starting from the genitalia. Thus Sade formulated an "eroticism appropriate to a disciplinary society: a regulated society, anatomical, hierarchized, with its carefully allotted times, its controlled spaces, its duties, and surveillance."[53] The Miller may restore "the body" that the Knight so often occluded, but he restores that body to remasculinize it and incorporate it within the gender politics that the *Knight's Tale* initiated.

Although the "end" of the *Miller's Tale*—its trajectory of desire as fabliau—may be erotic discipline, the activity unleashed in achieving such control also works to resist a "pure" demonstration of the sadism I've just outlined. Let us return to the branding scene once more. As I have said, in the first instance this is the sadistic moment that "makes sense" of the tale . . . if we accept it as effective substitution for the earlier kiss, if we substitute proper masculinity in place of the effeminate activity of Nicholas, John, and Absalon, if we leave behind any desire for contact with the female body. In short, if we accept its "end" as teleological and absolutely necessary, we will not be lost irrevocably to the world of the Knight and its disciplined, heteronormative epistemology. The tale "works" in this way, however, only if we can leave behind the story and its characters. Even by the end, though, can it really only be said that Alison passively carries a sex identity or that the tale has succeeded in containing gender by the female sex in a force that is reassuringly centripetal? Could the layering of the tale, its redoubling of plot events within the tale (and by placement within the *Canterbury Tales* in relationship to the *Knight's Tale*), also work to keep us close to its parts in ways less easily normalized and hierarchized than the ending's substitutions would like?

Peter Beidler has pointed out that in all the European analogues "it is the male lover who presents his buttocks out the window for the kiss, while the woman stays in the shadows. Chaucer is unique among early tellers of the story in having the woman execute the trick."[54] And as countless readers of the tale have commented, Alison is the one character not explicitly forced to undergo a comic fabliau comeuppance in the climactic moments of the tale. For even as the branding successfully reaches the wayward male body, the female body that it has intentionally aimed for steps back into the safety of the tale's margins. This might seem yet another oppressive illustration of the female and the feminine being marginalized and pushed into the background. Certainly in the first instance Alison's marginality appears to signify only that the (female) body has served its purpose. The marginality of her body thus forms an outline that brings into view the sealing off of male bodies and the construction of a secure hegemonic masculine subject position outside the tale that the tale's plot strives to effect. Although set up in this way as a binary that will authorize the production of masculinity, such a marginalization of the female body also works to keep us in touch with the tale as tale, with character as developing, unknowable in any final sense, the production of all identity as performative.

For margins also tell their own story. They mark the embodied facticity of text and can mark a textual excess that, although "unknown" or "forgotten" by the ideological directive as to what a text means, may yet excite its own peculiar curiosity within the reader or author. A textual reader who chooses such a wayward position might thus contract for a different engagement with the story than the submissive posture of the tale's "conclusion" demands. In the case of the *Miller's Tale,* female marginality can serve as a reminder that the "ending" of the tale is itself a kind of margin. Dominant masculinity tries to declare that margin as "end" in a way that seals off what the tale means, bounding it as if it were the property of "properly" masculine subjects. A reader of the margins, however, might question the stability and "trothe" of such a hierarchized version of masculinist binaries such as surface and depth, center and margin. Of course, as V. A. Kolve reminds us, "the baring of an arse has, in fact, its own humble area of provenance within medieval art—the borders of illuminated manuscripts."[55]

Moreover, Absalon's mistake in branding Nicholas rather than Alison parallels an earlier, similar moment of comic displacement for Absalon's desire, his kissing of Alison's "naked ers / Ful savourly" instead of his "sweete cynamome's" lips (I.3734–35, 3699). Alison's mocking

"Teehee" (I.3740) underscores the hapless Absalon's unexpected relationship to the female body and the consequent disruption of male knowledge/control that ensues from his misguided kiss. Absalon's return, and the tale's attempt to substitute his "meaningful" encounter with Nicholas for the earlier kiss, depend on and can never leave behind that earlier encounter with Alison's bottom. Branding and kiss remain contiguous and mutually constitutive, however much the tale's ending attempts to hierarchize and substitute one for the other—just as the meaning of the *Knight's Tale* is (re)constructed by its generic encounters with the world of the *Miller's Tale,* even as the *Knight's Tale* attempts to leave that world behind. Alison's "Teehee" is thus an instance of category confusion that reverberates throughout and in spite of the tale's ending—much like the "nether ey" (I.3852) that Absalon kisses and then attempts to see from the panoptic position of masculinity. Although her "Teehee" cannot constitute "voice," in the sense that it is not ascribed meaning within the dominant culture of the tale, Alison's marginal notation of masculinity in the tale does "speak," to the extent that it marks the physicality of the feminine as that "other" without which masculine identity could not "be" and that place of shame and humiliation that the *Miller's Tale* keeps returning us to as readers.

Such a countermovement of signification within the tale challenges its final imposition of disciplinary order, blurs the "difference" between "hende Nicholas" (I.3199) and this "Fair yonge wyf" (I.3234), and suggests that both sex and gender are slippery and sliding signifiers, as much multiply contested sites of meaning as regulatory fictions. If we were to think about the possible relationships between the inscribed male reader for the tale and those men associated with the king's affinity, who form at least one of Chaucer's actual audiences, what would make the *Miller's Tale* useful to such men is precisely its attention to the politics of representation: that under the guise of generic and social difference—a churl's tale in opposition to the nobility of the Knight's—it can take into account the fluid and ambiguous status of gentility in the later Middle Ages, as well as their own contradictory position as "new men" within nobility. Paul Strohm, for example, has discussed the contradictions and anxieties inherent in the position of late medieval "gentils," contradictions exacerbated in the new class of "esquires en service" to which Chaucer and much of this male audience belong:

> As a preliminary observation, then, we may say that every knight and esquire of the late fourteenth century, including Chaucer himself, was subject to two conflicting social evaluations: each shared with the great lords of the kingdom a common assessment of gentility, even as each shared with his fellow merchants, citizens, and burgesses of the middle strata the fact of nonaristocratic status or social rank.... But Chaucer's stratum of gentlepersons "*en service*" eludes confident characterization. Though inserted in a social hierarchy between knights and other *gentils gentz,* they lack the traditional support of lands and rents. Though aligned by their work with the growing body of clerks, scribes, lawyers, and literate tradespeople, they are separated from that body by their gentility.[56]

On the one hand, such an enlargement of hegemonic subjectivities takes place on the backs of "others" by writing a more mobile masculinity through the exclusion of "churls" and "women." On the other hand, to achieve such representational flexibility, the reader must be aware of the advantages of activity for individual gain and the need to keep "the body" in motion. To that extent, the reader remains "with" Alison as much as or more so than with the men of the tale. And the tale explores and gives voice to the instabilities of any identity such "new men" might find for themselves, ready at any moment to slide into abjection. This kind of activity thus works to inscribe the body and the feminine as necessary, useful, even privileged, in ways that the explicitly masculinist trajectory of the tale's plot and "moral" would choose to obscure or deny.[57]

Such a loosening of gender within the *Miller's Tale* is necessary to mobilize a fabliau masculinity that will authorize a "lower" part of society and the social body as having as much access to knowledge and power as the higher. To allow—if only as fantasy—that a churl might have access to knowledge that a knight does not have makes possible the creation of an inscribed reader that is male and properly masculine (in the sense that he, unlike Nicholas, Absalon, or John, comes out on top and with controlling knowledge), but not limited to the static univocal subject position of the *Knight's Tale* and its presumptive nobility. This new reader is authorized to turn the leaf based on the wider-ranging, more mobile "trothefulness" of his judgment. In doing so, the *Miller's*

*Tale* can represent change and movement within stable categories in ways the *Knight's Tale* was unable to.[58]

To accomplish this degree of representational movement within hegemonic masculinity, the *Miller's Tale* must therefore bring us into contact with the feminine and the body in ways that disorganize the stable heteronormativity of the *Knight's Tale.* The latter fantasizes a static spectacular moment *sub specie aeternitatis,* and the *Miller's Tale* (with its various distantiation techniques) also aims for its own kind of cold theatricality. But its continued contact with the feminine represents a far more mobile, provisional masculine subject—embroiled with the material in disconcerting and unsuitable ways, but because of that, accessible to a far wider variety of individuals. By allowing the body its place, the *Miller's Tale* makes possible a more open understanding of who warrants access to masculine agency, yet only by foregrounding even more systematically than the *Knight's Tale* the need to regulate that masculine body. The abjection of Nicholas, Absalon, and John because of their excessive, effeminate physicality becomes the necessary fulcrum that will turn desire away from the (fe)male body toward that "proper" masculinity happening at the outer boundaries of the tale—in the laughter of John's neighbors and in the projected laughter and superiority of the inscribed audience (fictional Canterbury pilgrims and textualized reader). Proper masculinity then finds articulation as that which welcomes such violent disciplining of the body, whether imagined as the doer or the receiver.[59]

Yet there is also a second, "forgotten" abjection that lingers within this instantiation of fabliau and marks the political work of the Canterbury game: that is, Alison as the putative recipient of Absalon's hot "kultour," and with it, the projected, but forgotten, abjection of Alison within the tale. The branding is ostensibly directed at Alison, fantasizing the impossible as possible: banish the feminine, seal up the body, and secure a transcendent masculine identity. Yet as we have seen, part of the project of the *Miller's Tale*—as a specific textual moment in the here and now—is to "open up" a hegemonic masculine identity supposedly securely anchored in transcendent notions of class and blood in order to admit "new men" like Chaucer and his immediate audience. And such a move requires fantasizing the male body as abject, open, and effeminate.

That the turn from physicality and the feminine constructed by the ending of the tale might itself be a fantasy therefore becomes a threatening by-product of this process of abjection/remasculinization. Such a mediated recognizing and forgetting of gender instability and the riskiness of identification constitutes that excess produced by the politics of representation that marks its production of an individual identity within and outside generic and social discipline. The same male reader who "necessarily" submits to the discipline of masculinity must also choose "necessarily" to take on Alison's part in order to learn the truth of the tale. In other words, the generic sadism of fabliau—as it is experienced within the specific textual moment that is the *Miller's Tale*—constructs an alternative masochistic trajectory of desire: back toward a (humiliating) acknowledgment of the bodily, a *masochistic contract,* as it were, toward persuasion rather than instruction, contract rather than demonstration.[60]

By way of illustration, consider the reverberant energy of Alison's tonic laugh within the tale and its difference from the disciplinary laughter of John's neighbors and the Canterbury pilgrims that ends the tale. Alison's "Teehee" focuses our attention—and Absalon's—on her "nether ey." In highlighting the misguided kiss, her laughter makes explicit a masochistic contract already initiated by Absalon's desire. That is, Absalon has chosen the humiliating position of the courtly lover, not as the way to discipline and masculinize its subject (as the sadistic pattern of the *Knight's Tale* would suggest), but instead as a pleasurable escape from masculine activity itself. Absalon, as fabliau structure demands, may later reject this masochistic contract for the pure demonstrative of proper masculinity (represented by his hot "kultour"). But can such a substitution of an instructive, pure demonstrative for the persuasions of the masochistic contract ever be completely secure within the dynamic relationship this tale constructs with its audience? Alison's reverberant presence/absence in the tale suggests otherwise. So, too, does the Miller's embrace of his humiliating position in opposition to the Knight.

The *Miller's Tale* reorients the Host's stabilizing plans for the Canterbury game almost before it gets started: both by its presentation of Alison as female body outside masculine control and by its (re)presentation of that threatening possibility in the Canterbury frame itself, by means of a drunken Miller who refuses to accept his place. In this way, the tale challenges its audience to "see" via the nether eye; that is, to learn through a feminine, queer touch as much as a masculinist, dominating gaze.[61] The reader who embraces the full potential of the queer contiguities in the textual moment offered "him" by the *Miller's Tale* (whether in reading on or in turning the leaf) to some extent at least enters into a contractual agreement to choose the "humiliation" of the tale's category confusion and thereby choose contact with the unnameable "hole" (I.3732) that Alison's characterization offers as mediation/margin/boundary between individual desire and ideological mastery.[62] Such a reader, choosing pleasurable excess, seeks to defer the closure of disciplinary control for the present inventiveness and mobility of fiction. While the panoptic masculine gaze shapes fabliau by casting it as nobility's fantasized "other," the *Miller's Tale* as feminine/effeminate nether eye also works to bring its reader up close to the liberatory potential of fantasizing what isn't known.

Thus the *Miller's Tale,* even as it reproduces the turn to discipline the *Knight's Tale* so adamantly insisted on, also resists the sadism constructing dominant medieval masculinities. In doing so, the tale queers the heteronormative sexual politics of the *Knight's Tale* and *Reeve's Tale* by desiring instead a "desexualized" body operating within, yet not completely controlled by, the ideological structures of desire. The *Miller's Tale* strives, as Foucault puts it, "to invent with the body, with its elements, its surfaces, its volumes, its depths, a nondisciplinary eroticism: that of the body plunged into a volatile and diffused state through chance encounters and incalculable pleasures."[63] This strategy serves an immediate political end of multiplying subject positions that confer masculine agency, opening up discursive space for new social groups and recognizing the new uses possible for fiction as fiction. But to do so, it must also necessarily disorganize sex, gender, and sexuality so that masculinity and femininity, male and female difference, heteronormative and effeminate/sodomitical as regulatory fictions become multiply contested sites of meaning in the spaces that open up between reader/frame/story and desire/knowledge/power.

Leo Bersani, in "Is the Rectum a Grave?" has noted a similarly disorganizing potential for power-filled masculine subjectivities inherent in a similar modern conceptual "black hole," male/male anal sex:

> A reflection on the fantasmatic potential of the human body—the fantasies engendered by its sexual anatomy and the specific moves it makes in taking sexual pleasure—is not the same thing as an a priori, ideologically motivated and prescriptive description of the essence of sexuality. Rather, I am saying that those effects of power which, as Foucault has argued, are inherent in

> the relational itself... can perhaps most easily be exacerbated, and polarized into relations of mastery and subordination, in sex, and that this potential may be grounded in the shifting experience that every human being has of his or her body's capacity, or failure, to control and to manipulate the world beyond the self. Needless to say, the ideological exploitations of this fantasmatic potential have a long and inglorious history. It is mainly a history of male power, and by now it has been richly documented by others. I want to approach this subject from a quite different angle, and to argue that a gravely dysfunctional aspect of what is, after all, the healthy pleasure we take in the operation of a coordinated and strong physical organism is the temptation to deny the perhaps equally strong appeal of powerlessness, of the loss of control. Phallocentrism is exactly that: not primarily the denial of power to women (although it has obviously also led to that, everywhere and at all times), but above all the denial of the value of powerlessness in both men and women. I don't mean the value of gentleness, or nonaggressiveness, or even of passivity, but rather of a more radical disintegration and humiliation of the self.[64]

If, as Karma Lochrie has recently asserted, sodomy in the Middle Ages was primarily conceived as a gender disorder, then the modern homo/hetero binary cannot simply reproduce itself on a quite different medieval sex/gender system. The sodomitical thus becomes a continuum of activities (not necessarily sexual) that includes many that to modern eyes would seem "normal" and "heterosexual":

> The fear of same-sex sexual activity cannot be separated from this prevailing agenda of ensuring the separation, difference, and hierarchy of masculine and feminine. The concern for procreation is of secondary importance, since it was still possible to procreate (or desire to procreate) and still commit a crime against nature. Or, to put it another way, because the only reason for gender differences in the first place, according to Albert and Aquinas, was for the purpose of procreation, there is no threat to procreation that is not also already a threat to gender difference and divinely order asymmetry. When desire is detached

> from procreation, the whole reason for gender difference itself disappears, along with the difference itself.[65]

The kind of masculine play with powerlessness that I have been describing as active in the *Miller's Tale* can be seen as constantly threatening to slide into such a sodomitical pleasure, and hence into something like the far more radical disintegration and humiliation of the self that Bersani discusses. The *Miller's Tale* probes the effects of powerlessness and nonteleological pleasure in provocative and unpredictable ways that will continue to reverberate well beyond the organizing power of Fragment I's attempts at generic or social order, as we will see in following chapters.

# 2

# Medieval Conjugality and the *Canterbury Tales*

In chapter 1 I argued that the *Miller's Tale* "begins" the Canterbury project by foregrounding subjectivity and identity as richly productive questions, rather than as stabilizing presumptions. In particular, the *Miller's Tale* "loosens" the class and gender hierarchies anchoring the body in the *Knight's Tale* enough to imagine through its masochistic contract a body in motion, fluid and powerfully unpredictable in its representational flexibility. The identity positions offered by such an embodiment, however, bring with them both the reassuring prospect of participation in the construction of a properly dominant masculinity and the uneasy recognition of the instabilities that such an encounter with newness unleashes. Not surprisingly, therefore, it is the feminizing power of such a perversely dynamic activity—especially as linked back to the female body—to which the *Miller's Tale* keeps returning its readers as a place of potential shame and humiliation. Such a vexed and vexing appearance of the feminine at precisely the moment that the *Miller's Tale* challenges its inscribed readers—largely male, bourgeois, and lay—to invent with the body suggests that whatever new beginning it provides for the *Canterbury Tales* will be bound up in a larger attempt to reconfigure medieval sex/gender relationships in unpredictable and provocative ways. This chapter explores that question by considering the larger relationships between the *Tales'* definition of an emerging modernizing elite, the so-called gentils, and a new emphasis on conjugality in late medieval marriage. Chapter 3 will then focus on the particular inventions with the body such conjugality makes possible in the *Wife of Bath's Tale,* the *Merchant's Tale,* and the *Franklin's Tale.*

## Mapping the History of (Hetero)Sexuality in the *Canterbury Tales*

The eruption of the Wife of Bath into the Canterbury project so soon after the *Miller's Tale* foregrounds its concerns ever more forcefully and explicitly in terms of "the matter of woman," so that a succession of male narrators fixate on this issue with a frequency and urgency that is hard to ignore. Indeed, the "woman question," especially as it is naturally and necessarily linked with the married estate, becomes *the* privileged site for exploring and resolving those difficult questions posed by the kinds of uneasy relationships between sexualized bodies and gender identifications found in the *Miller's Tale.* At least half of the *Canterbury Tales* situate themselves within a network of relationships established by marriage, and a significant number focus directly on individually chosen conjugality and the couple-centered household it establishes. In contrast, only three tales—the *Man of Law's Tale,* the *Second Nun's Tale,* and the *Physician's Tale*—represent forms of female chastity, whether chaste marriage, consecrated virginity, or pure maidenhood. Another, the *Prioress's Tale,* might be seen as representing female virginity indirectly through the innocence of the "litel clergeon."

The apparent success of the Wife of Bath in forcing the question of woman and marriage to the forefront of everyone's attention in the *Tales* led George Lyman Kittredge in 1912 to argue that a self-contained and ordered marriage debate runs through the *Canterbury Tales.*[1] As Kittredge envisaged it, the *Wife of Bath's Tale* began a marriage debate that ran through the *Clerk's Tale,* the *Merchant's Tale,* and the *Franklin's Tale* and constituted one of the conceptual unities of the Canterbury project itself:

> The Marriage Group of Tales begins with the Wife of Bath's Prologue and ends with the Franklin's Tale. There is no connection between the Wife's Prologue and the group of stories that precedes: there is no connection between the Franklin's Tale and the group that follows. Within the Marriage Group, on the con-

> trary, there is a close connection throughout. That act is a finished act. It begins and ends an elaborate debate.[2]

Since each tale so clearly represents the personal experience and character of its teller, the existence of the marriage group also bears witness to the "vital importance of considering the *Canterbury Tales* as a connected Human Comedy."[3] The Wife's provocative manner and false doctrines regarding women and marriage cannot but scandalize the Clerk and bring his attempt at retribution; the Clerk's ironical tribute to the Wife and her dogmas in the so-called Lenvoy de Chaucer, "with complete dramatic inevitability, calls out the Merchant's *cri de coeur*"; and so on.[4] Moreover, the fact that the Clerk does not reply immediately, with the separate estate rivalry between the Summoner and the Friar intervening, becomes for Kittredge a mark of Chaucer's artistry: "The drama of the Pilgrimage is too natural and unforced in its development under the master's hand to admit of anything so frigidly schematic."[5] Equally important, Kittredge's belief that autonomous individuals are debating the value of their experience within an ordered group structure sets up a progressivist teleology for these tales where the *Franklin's Tale* not only comes last, but "ends" the debate by resolving the mistakes of earlier tales and fulfilling their incomplete understanding of what true marriage really is:

> It was the regular theory of the Middle Ages that the highest type of chivalric love was incompatible with marriage, since marriage brings in mastery, and mastery and love cannot abide together. This view the Franklin boldly challenges. Love *can* be consistent with marriage, he declares. Indeed without love (and perfect *gentle* love) marriage is sure to be a failure. The difficulty about mastery vanishes when mutual love and forbearance are made the guiding principles of the relation between husband and wife. . . . We need not hesitate, therefore, to accept the solution which the Franklin offers as that which Geoffrey Chaucer the man accepted for his own part. Certainly it is a solution that does him infinite credit. A better has never been devised or imagined.[6]

Kittredge's "discovery" of marriage at the heart of the Canterbury project provokes a series of linked assertions about what is "natural," both in the *Tales* and in life. If the dramatic nature of the *Tales* exposes the true nature of each pilgrim, this discovery in turn produces the marriage debate and its structured delineation of the truth about marriage. The supposed natural order represented by the Marriage Group in turn allows Kittredge to uncover modern conjugality, and the modern liberal, heterosexual subject it subtends, as the inevitable endpoint of Chaucer's project for the *Canterbury Tales:* "The Franklin's Tale is a gentleman's story and he tells it like a gentleman."[7]

The enormous contribution of feminist and gender medieval studies since 1980 has, of course, made it impossible to ignore the gendered assumptions lying behind Kittredge's belief that the Chaucerian discussion of marriage reaches its fulfillment in a "gentleman's story told like a gentleman."[8] Similarly, the class politics producing not just a man but a *gentle*man as the desideratum of the *Tales* has been explored by a variety of cultural materialist analyses of Chaucer's social situation—of the social contest represented in the pilgrimage frame and animating late medieval English social organization—as well as of the class politics operating in the construction of a great author and a literary tradition.[9] But in many ways, the presumptive heterosexuality that characterizes Kittredge's discussion has remained unchallenged, or in some cases has been categorically affirmed as Chaucerian, and thus continues—implicitly or explicitly—"naturally" to structure the current debate about these tales and their subject matter.[10]

How, then, do we resist reading the representational strategies of the *Tales* as simply participating in and reproducing what we already "know," so that the "medievalness" or "modernness" of their inscriptions of a sex/gender system are not conveniently and safely implicated retrospectively within the triumphant history of modern (hetero)sexuality? To discern the singularity of representations of conjugality in the *Tales,* we need at once to acknowledge their (retrospective) place within a now dominant modernist history of sexuality, their anxious and engaged position with relation to medieval sex/gender systems, and their ability to dream sexuality differently. The distinctions made by Deleuze and Guattari between the twin impulses of "mapping" and "tracing" are especially useful here in stressing not a simple dualism of right and wrong, but inter-implicated methods of describing our encounters with the world and culture: "What distinguishes the map from the tracing is that it is entirely oriented toward an experimentation in contact with the real. . . . What the tracing reproduces of the map . . . are only the impasses, blockages, incipient taproots, points of structuration."[11] For Deleuze and Guattari the work of historicization thus moves in two directions simultaneously. Tracing describes the work of selection and hierarchization of what counts as important, allowing for the naturalization of past hegemonic constructions by fitting events of the past into stabilizing *grands récits* or progressivist teleologies that delimit who we are and who we can be. Mapping, on the other hand, attempts a process of description that would delineate what constitutes a moment of libidinal excitement for a culture. These are moments where dominant representational systems are in dialogue, competition, and conflict with a desire to "say more" in representational terms. This, for Deleuze and Guattari, marks "an experimentation in contact with the real," a "plateau" in their terms, where the organizing power of hegemonic representations (whether "old" and established or "new" and about to be established) is unable to exert its full force over the unrepresentability, and thus possibility, of "the real." Historicization as mapping, then, seeks to put the present moment in touch with that which in the past constitutes those moments of plateau so that the present, too, can pick up speed, intensifying its elements of libidinal excitement.[12]

Marriage in the *Tales,* I would argue, marks just such a moment of libidinal excitement and the potential for a mapping of power relations for those involved in it, rather than simply a tracing of hierarchizing power relations that would mark stable points of separation between inside and outside, top and bottom. If we are to avoid reproducing a stabilizing dualism between medieval and modern, hegemony and resistance, heterosexual and queer, masculine and feminine, male and female, in our historicizing of the marriage tales, we must also avoid simply tracing modern heterosexuality back onto the map of the history of sexuality. To discover the enabling, empowering otherness of the present, as well as the past, we need instead to understand how current regimes of (hetero)sexuality are not some inevitable fulfillment of the march of history, but rather its narrowing modernization, its impasse, blockage, and point of structuration. What this demands of our investigation of conjugality in the *Tales* is threefold: (1) a recognition of a retrospective "narrowing modernization" of the *Tales* as (inevitably) part of the march of history toward modern heterosexuality; (2) a recognition of the modernizing forces at work within the *Tales* to construct a new and proleptically hegemonic present heteronormative masculinity; and (3) a mapping of sexuality in the Tales that remains in excess of either endeavor, not least because it is a necessary product of such attempts to imagine present hegemonic forms differently. Historicizing marriage in the *Tales* without recourse to a modernist historiography begins by recognizing how Chaucer's treatment of conjugality, rather than grounding heterosexual subjects in either stable, hierarchized "medieval" or "modern" social relations, actually represents a site for mapping those potentially unstable fluid social relations involved in "gentil" self-definition. It thus attends to the "perverse presentism" bound up in these tales' attempts to use lay conjugality to think through the new intersections of economic, political, and estate interests necessary for successfully negotiating late medieval culture and society.

Judith Halberstam, writing in the context of early modern relations between women, has recently argued for a "perverse presentism" that is "not only a denaturalization of the present but also an application of what we do not know in the present to what we cannot know about the past."[13] Building on Michel Foucault's call in *Discipline and Punish* for a "history of the present" that refuses conventional models of history and their presentist insistence on narratives of progress and supersession, and on Eve Sedgwick's suggestion in axiom five in *Epistemology of the Closet* that "the historical search for a great paradigm shift may obscure the present conditions of sexual identity," Halberstam argues for a "perversely presentist model of historical analysis": "If, as I suggest throughout this book, there are multiple forms of female masculinity within our present culture, only some of which are annexed indisputably to lesbianism, might it not also be the case that historically, female masculinity takes on a huge variety of forms? In other words, what we do not know for sure today about the relationship between masculinity and lesbianism, we cannot know for sure about historical relations between same-sex desire and female masculinities."[14] Similarly, I would argue that today's urgent debate about what constitutes "marriage," as well as the enormous variety of human and household relationships that are grouped together under the supposedly known and homogeneous category of *heterosexual* marriage, suggests that what we do not know about the present should be applied to what we cannot know about the past. Thus, as I argue here and in the following chapters, to think we can "know" late medieval marriage by simply projecting contemporary understandings of heterosexuality or marriage back onto the medieval moment, or equally subsuming this moment into present understandings by seeing it *only* as proto-early modern heterosexual marriage, is to render this past (in Eve Sedgwick's formulation) "destructively presumable."[15]

In this chapter and the next, I want to consider both why marriage—almost from the moment the tale-telling project begins—emerges as the representational category of choice for so many tale-tellers and how the *Tales'* emphasis on conjugality resists inscription in either medievalist or modernist histories of (hetero)sexuality. I will begin by asserting two statements that may seem counterintuitive: first, that "the matter of woman" as it is represented in these tales does not simply reproduce some transhistorical category of "woman" or the truth about medieval female experience, and second, that the emphasis on domestic conjugality in so many of the *Tales* cannot simply be read retrospectively through the lens of modern heterosexuality.[16] The problems these statements raise cannot simply be resolved by recourse to an alternative historicism focused on proving the alterity of the *Tales'* representation of marriage in order to resist such an "anachronistic" reinscription of modern heterosexuality back onto the *Tales'* purely "medieval" subject positions. For both "medieval" and "modern" sex/gender systems can exert their own normalizing power over our readings of the *Tales*. Clearly it is true that sex and gender questions in the *Canterbury Tales* are not organized simply along modern binarisms of masculine/feminine and homo/hetero, but instead are located within the larger field of a complex sex/gender system articulating personal and social relations by means of premodern identity categories (such as virginity, celibacy, marriage, and sodomy). As I have noted already, though, supposedly dominant and natural medieval categories—clerical, aristocratic, virginal—are rarely the central concerns of the "real time" of the *Tales*. However much the *Man of Law's Tale* may attempt to "reorient" the focus of the pilgrimage back to such orthodoxies—with its emphasis on Custance as quasi-virginal, quasi-saintly wife—the *Wife of Bath's Prologue and Tale* (the first tale told by a female narrator) forces attention back to "the question of woman" in terms that foreground the concerns of a sexually active, economically vigorous, socially mobile middle estate.

For these reasons, I would argue that the tales of the so-called Marriage Group take up the risky object lesson of the *Miller's Tale*—that hegemonic subject positions previously presented as transcendent and fixed are discoverable within the present moment and thus written on the body in empowering and provocatively unstable ways. Marriage in these tales, therefore, becomes a locus for "inventing with the body," whether as an organizing or disorganizing principle. Tales told by the male narrators (including the pilgrim Chaucer) take up these questions in ways that explore how to deal with the concerns that such a position engenders, with how to shape and stabilize the loosening of gender and social class that the *Miller's Tale* began. The *Wife of Bath's Tale* focuses instead on the variety and unpredictability of the presentism that such inventing with the body brings. In either case, conjugality in these tales is clearly a category that has become "good to think with" for the late medieval laity, a representational category with which new social interests can assert themselves within and against the hegemonic power of established categories like the clerisy and the nobility.

Of course, as Kathleen Biddick has pointed out, one hegemonic medieval category that was "good to think with," and one traditionally undergirding the precedence of celibacy over marriage, was the Eucharist: "[I]t guaranteed the symbolic order of medieval Europe.... It is as if the host functioned in the way in which the 'phallus' does today in contemporary psychoanalytic debate."[17] In my adaptation of Biddick's phrase, the equivalent unit of thought to the host or phallus is that of "wife" used as a conceptual marker conceived as an extension or embodiment of husbandly authority, of lay male self-identification, and as ground for an authoritative household identity. That is, I wish to draw attention to the "weird centrality" of bourgeois marriage in late medieval society (at least as represented in texts like Chaucer's *Canterbury Tales*), its innovativeness within a sex/gender system established at the time of the Gregorian Reform and its representational force in configuring a new hegemonic sex/gender system that we associate with early modern society. In other words, an emphasis on the representational power of conjugality by certain lay groups within late medieval society as a way of identifying their "gentil" identity makes the married estate in the period an unstable "middle" category within traditional medieval modes of social organization. Hence conjugality becomes an important category for thinking through the complex and contradictory desire of a newly emerging late medieval/early modern "middle" class. Historicizing marriage in the *Tales* in this way can, I hope, mark the middleness of this moment—neither the medieval absolute other against which modernity defines itself, nor an early modern antecedent to modern heterosexuality (where either works to stabilize modernist narratives of progress and supersession)—but instead as an enabling place of hybridization for late fourteenth-century and early twenty-first-century subjects.

Hybridity is an especially useful term for thinking through the complexities of medieval conjugality's linguistic and social relationships, not least because of its own complex and conflicted place within modern sexual, racial, and colonial/postcolonial discourses. Robert Young has recently explored the term's genesis in eighteenth- and nineteenth-century concern with the results of linguistic and sexual contact as they threaten racial and cultural (im)purity.[18] The increased linguistic and sexual contact brought about by European imperialism in this period produces not only new hybrid forms (such as creole and pidgin languages or miscegenated children), but a growing preoccupation in the late nineteenth century with the larger cultural consequences of such hybridity. By mid-century a term originally applied to "an animal or plant, produced from the mixture of two species" (Webster, 1828) is used to denote the crossing of people of different races to produce the "half-breed" (OED, 1861). And hybridity becomes a key issue in a cultural debate about whether the different races were one species or many, whether hybrid issue of different races marked a fertile amalgamation of different races or a degenerative miscegenation, whether certain races were superior by process of natural selection, and so forth. In a general sense, medieval conjugality also disturbs medieval understandings of linguistic and social norms to the extent that it marks a new kind of contact between the sexes (bringing male and female together in one body), a hybrid "superior" role for the laity in relation to the clerisy, and a noble estate available as much to a merchant as to a knight.

Hybridity as it has been theorized by Mikhail Bakhtin and Homi Bhabha also provides a useful model for thinking through the complex ways that medieval conjugality provides a conduit through which power relations flow, change, and crystallize in hegemonic ways, working to resist and subvert authority. For Bakhtin hybridization occurs at the boundaries between the linguistic and the social: "It is a mixture of two social languages within the limits of a single utterance, an encounter, within the arena of an utterance, between two different linguistic consciousnesses, separated from one another by an epoch, by social differentiation or by some other factor."[19] And Bakhtin distinguishes between two different types of hybridization. The first is that unconscious and organic hybridization always at work in language formation, the "mixing of various 'languages' co-existing within the boundaries of a single dialect, a single national language, a single branch, a single group of different branches, or different groups of such branches, in the historical as well as paleontological past of languages."[20] The second is a conscious and intentional hybridization where two individualized language consciousnesses and two points of view are not simply mixed, but set against each other dialogically.[21] In the first instance, we can think of the conjugality that develops in the later Middle Ages as constituting an unconscious, organic hybridization of secular and clerical discourses concerning individual, gender, and estate relationships in marriage. But as Bakhtin notes, "while it is true the mixture of linguistic world views in organic hybrids remains mute and opaque, such unconscious hybrids have been at the same time profoundly productive historically: they are pregnant with potential for new world views, with new 'internal forms' for perceiving the world in words."[22] At the same time, we can see that the *Tales'* impersonated artistry, to use H. Marshall Leicester Jr.'s phrase, encourages a more intentional hybridity that is inevitably internally dialogic.[23] Thus, as Robert Young puts it, "Bakhtin's doubled form of hybridity therefore offers a particularly significant dialectical model for cultural interaction: an organic hybridity, which will tend toward fusion, in conflict with intentional hybridity, which enables a contestatory activity, a politicized setting of cultural differences against each other dialogically. Hybridity therefore . . . involves an antithetical movement of coalescence and antagonism, with the unconscious set against the intentional, the organic against the divisive, the generative against the undermining."[24]

Homi Bhabha focuses Bakhtin's discussion of hybridity and dialogic imagination specifically in terms of the structures of colonial identification and dis-identification. Thus for Bhabha, hybridization is

> the name for the strategic reversal of the process of domination through disavowal (that is, the production of discriminatory identities that secures the 'pure' and original identity of authority). Hybridity is the revaluation of the assumption of colonial identity through the repetition of discriminatory identity effects. It displays the necessary deformation and displacement of all sites of discrimination and domination. It unsettles the

> mimetic or narcissistic demands of colonial power but reimplicates its identifications in strategies of subversion that turn the gaze of the discriminated back upon the eye of power. For the colonial hybrid is the articulation of the ambivalent space where the rite of power is enacted on the site of desire, making its objects at once disciplinary and disseminatory—or, in my mixed metaphor, a negative transparency.[25]

Or as Young puts it, "Hybridity becomes the moment in which the discourse of colonial authority loses its univocal grip on meaning and finds itself open to the trace of the language of the other, enabling the critic to trace complex movements of disarming alterity in the colonial text."[26] What I am interested in here is how the *Tales* might push the representational possibilities of this newly defined category of marriage in directions not intended by a clerical, colonizing pattern of disavowal with regard to sex and marriage. Both in this chapter and in chapter 3 I will pursue this line of thinking to suggest a colonizing dimension to the sacrament of marriage and a hybridity in the ways that the sacrament was taken up by the laity it was addressed to. Although in important ways the church was "ours," an integral part of the identity of the late medieval English laity, it was also a "foreign" (at times literally so) bureaucratic system centered on Rome: its "real" subjects were a clerisy whose allegiances were to the institutional apparatuses of the church and whose education and "foreign" language separated them in important ways from the laity they represented and from whom they were drawn. While the sacrament of marriage (and the individual choice it allowed) provided a use value to lay sexual activity, its articulation after the Gregorian Reform also provided a new way to maintain an old essentialism distinguishing clerical and lay identities in absolute ways, now by distinguishing a celibate clerisy from a necessarily noncelibate laity through the supervaluation of complete celibacy over a (marginally) enhanced marital discipline of sexuality.

## The *Canterbury Tales'* Modernizing Elite

The Wife of Bath's famous invocation of experience at the beginning of her *Prologue*—"Experience, though noon auctoritee / Were in this world, is right ynogh for me / To speke of wo that is in mariage" (III.1–3)—has usually focused attention more on the "female woe" that results from medieval sexual politics than on the category of marriage itself. In chapter 3 I explore how the Wife of Bath's manifestation of a "female masculinity," rather than functioning as the improper ground against which a naturally hegemonic male body can assert its identity, provides a kind of masculinity that is most informative about gender relations and most generative of social change. In the remainder of this chapter I want first to consider how "experience" must also necessarily and dangerously be "right ynogh for me" for a new group of "middle"-class (largely male) subjects coming into representation in the *Tales*. I want then to ask how and to what extent a newly defined conjugality in marriage could provide an important discursive location for such a new group of subjects to gain control of the representational means of production and thus to gain access to the power that self-identification can bring.

The *Canterbury Tales*' attempts at social organization obviously work within traditional medieval feudal and ecclesiastical conceptual categories. They cannot but reflect, therefore, the complex nexus of differential binaries established by means of such categories—cleric/lay, noble/churl, celibate/noncelibate, virgin/wife, Christian/Jew, masculine/feminine, masculine/sodomite, and so forth—that, operating in a mutually constitutive if sometimes confused relationship with each other, together form a dominant "medieval" discursive terrain and social imaginary. Yet the "subject" matter of the *Canterbury Tales,* especially in those tales focused on the matter of woman and marriage, often seems to be demanding more than this conceptual inheritance can provide. As Jill Mann has demonstrated, a rich tradition of estates satire underlies the narrator's apparently dramatic, lifelike depictions of the pilgrims in the *General Prologue* and throughout the frame of the *Canterbury Tales*. Nonetheless, she argues, Chaucer's characters are not abstract, timeless figures, but are represented as bound up in a realistic spatial and temporal existence; they are not simply acting out a role, but expressing their consciousness of doing so.[27] And Lee Patterson has gone on to point out:

> To an extraordinary degree, Chaucer allows the members of the various estates to define themselves, a procedure that in effect undermines their definition as estates. Rather than being representatives of social functions, in other words, the pilgrims be-

> come individuals who have been assigned those functions, men and women enacting externally imposed roles toward which each has his or her own kind of relationship. They become, in short, subjects.[28]

More specifically, they become subjects of a particular kind, part of that emerging "middle" class of people whose experience cannot really be expressed through any of the traditional medieval socioeconomic discourses. The high medieval feudal order traditionally saw itself dividing into three discrete and stable estates: the clergy, the chivalry, and the peasantry; or "those who pray," "those who fight," and "those who labor."[29] In Chaucer's pilgrimage audience, as Strohm has emphasized, one knight stands in for the traditionally influential group of landholding aristocrats and knights; a single plowman stands in for the 90 to 95 percent of the population who were free or bonded agricultural laborers. "Present in vast disproportion," Strohm says, "are people from the 'middle strata.'"[30]

Even when such "middle"-class individuals, difficult to discern within traditional estates divisions, come into visibility as subjects in the Canterbury game they fail to cohere as a stable, homogenous group and remain notoriously resistant to organization. Technically, such pilgrims still fall within the third estate of "those who labor." Yet these characters often and explicitly fulfill their estates functions in ways outside the norms of proper/improper labor generated by the feudal economy. Patricia Eberle, for example, notes how much a bourgeois commercial language and outlook animate the value system of the *General Prologue,* at times in opposition to older, authoritative clerical or feudal classifications of good and bad characteristics.[31] Carl Lindahl's more recent attempt to "rank" the Canterbury pilgrims according to the criteria outlined in the protocol lists of noble households has produced mixed results: "The composite result of this classification shows that no more than five of the pilgrims would fit into categories outside the stratum I identify as the middle class. The middle world is almost equally divided into two sub-groups, which represent the *gentils* and churls among the free and less-than-noble medieval population." However, while the dividing line is clear between those who would dine at the knight's table—only the Knight, Monk, Prioress, and perhaps the Squire—it is far more difficult to draw a line between those clearly distinguishable as "gentils" and those absolutely marked as "churls." Only the Sergeant at Law, Merchant, Host, Franklin, Guildsmen, and Nun's Priest are unequivocably among the upper middle class, and only the Reeve, Manciple, Miller, Canon's Yeoman, and Cook are clearly among the lower middle class (and in this latter group, the first three would be closer to the higher group in many respects than to the near servitude of the Cook).[32]

The instabilities of any attempt to characterize the pilgrims as a group offers at least the potential for mobility in the kinds of associations such membership in the "felaweshipe" of pilgrims makes possible. Both Carl Lindahl and David Wallace have proposed parish guilds—those religious and fraternal organizations popular in late fourteenth-century England—as the everyday models for the unpredictable social interaction represented in the *Canterbury Tales*.[33] Furthermore, Caroline M. Barron has suggested that, although parish guilds in London lacked the governing role in city life that they had at York or Coventry, London guilds "were more spontaneous, and more voluntary, than elsewhere. It was not necessary to join them to get to the top or to exercise power."[34] In the process of being distinguished from craft guilds, such religious guilds differed in intent from confraternities organized by religious houses to raise money from lay people for spiritual ends. According to Barron, parish fraternities, especially in the late fourteenth century, "were essentially communal chantries. Those who were not rich enough to endow a personal chantry could, nevertheless, contribute to the costs of a fraternity chaplain who would pray for all the members, both living and dead."[35] The bulk of guild income seemed to be directed toward the hiring of a fraternity priest and clerk, and to materials necessary to maintain a guild chapel and to mount decent funerals for guild members.[36] Moreover, the majority of members of the London guilds came not from members of the great mercantile companies (who could probably afford to endow private chantries for themselves and their families), but from members of the artisan crafts in the city: brewers, butchers, dyers, carpenters, smiths, and tailors (precisely the guildsmen we find included in Chaucer's Canterbury pilgrims). "[T]he parish fraternity movement," says Barron, "was, predominantly, a 'middle class' artisan movement and to such men the parish fraternity was often the center of their social and spiritual world." Finally, membership in London parish fraternities, Barron notes, was "not only predominantly artisan, it was also markedly feminine. All the guild ordinances which have survived specify sisters as well as brothers . . . [and] it is clear that women joined the fraternities on equal terms with men; they did not join solely in their capacity as wives."[37] In addition, because most fraternity priests were maintained on a yearly ad hoc basis and depended on the ability of wardens or masters of the guild to collect the funds necessary for their salaries, "more than most of the clergy within the late medieval church, their livelihood depended upon the whim of lay people. If the brotherhood failed to hold together, or if its members disliked their chaplain, then his salary might not be forthcoming. May it not be that this element of control was attractive to lay men and women?"[38]

But what different kind of political engagement might such an attempt to represent social crossing and heterogeneity signal? David Wallace has argued that the pilgrim *compagnye* of the *General Prologue* instantiates an English version of the kind of new "associational ideology" developed in Trecento Florence, which "suggested that all inhabitants of the city-state share equal footing on a lateral plane. Such communal ideology may be developed in cell-like local structures (such as parish guilds) and reproduced through larger ones, such as city-oligarchies, city-states, and (ultimately) nations. . . . This process of group formation [in the *General Prologue*], where the right to exist *as* a group is simply assumed from within rather than conferred from without, represents a singular moment of political confidence that will not be repeated on English territory. Nothing like it is conceivable on the Shakespearean stage."[39] It is also possible to see parallels to such "political confidence" closer to home, in the sense of national community some have seen articulated in fourteenth-century parliamentary innovation and in the idea of a "community of the realm" represented in the commons.

Judith Ferster has noted that a "community of the realm" rhetoric was common currency in thirteenth- and fourteenth-century England for some very concrete reasons: "Medieval England was remarkably unified—not in the sense that all its inhabitants across the spectrum of wealth, power, and status had similar material interests or agreed on issues, but in that they were aware of the country they lived in, their relations to the various parts of government, and the parts' relations to each other."[40] Moreover, by the time of the Good Parliament in 1376, "in which the commons took the lead in attacking the king's ministers, the 'community of the realm' was represented not by the magnates [as it had been at the time of Magna Carta in the early thirteenth century], the great land-owning aristocrats, but by the parliamentary commons, minor land-owners who represented the localities." If, as Ferster maintains, "[t]he central government reached across geographical and class lines to help foster 'the political nation,'" it did so in part because this exchange of gentry for magnates as articulators of the "community of the realm" made possible a broader sense of involvement of the general population.[41] Both knights and freemen of ungentle blood worked together in determining who represented the shire at parliament, and the activity of the house of commons promulgated a different concept of representation, one where its members derived authority from the fact that, in theory at least, they spoke for the whole community rather than their own individual or class interests.[42] Equally important was the exchange of information and news—from the regions to London, and from London back to the regions—that this sense of community demanded and in turn made possible.[43]

Clearly the very real associational possibilities in such a system of exchange are productive of the kind of "sharing equal footing on a lateral plane" that might make the leap from "cell-like" local structures (such as parish guilds or parliament as the creature of the king or particular aristocratic oligarchy) to national ones (the commons as the embodiment of the community of the realm, an English nation made up of localities knit together through a common system of exchange emanating out of Westminster or London). But as John Bowers has recently reminded us, England in the late medieval period, "like the United Kingdom today, was not really a nation but a state," and it is important to note the deep fissures of geographic, linguistic, economic, class, and cultural difference an associational ideology must cross or occlude. Recent work on the Rising of 1381, for example, has challenged and complicated how we might understand the "gentry" as "speaking for" the larger community of the realm or the idea of reciprocity in the exchanges between localities and the center.[44] And Bowers has drawn attention to the imperialist possibilities inherent in the systems of exchange knitting together late medieval English society. Citing Ranulf Higden's "repeated commonplace observations on the linguistic differences within the British Isles as well as the temperamental dispositions of its peoples—southerners quiet and gentle, northerners restless and fierce,"[45] Bowers argues that because of this lack of a sense of *national* homogeneity, the process of state making required centralization to enforce uniform practices, demanding the ascendancy of London/Westminster over the provinces, especially those of the north: "[C]ommonality is achieved only when the center is able to assert its superiority over the rest of the country.... Only the ascendancy of a single regional dialect would spell success."[46] Thus Bowers sees the *Canterbury Tales* as instrumental in this process, as

> an official corpus of vernacular writings such as Chaucer's would become essential for the cultural construction of nationhood as a form of social and textual affiliation. A native-language literature, created in such political circumstances, fictionalizes the national identity by ignoring, effacing, ridiculing, or domesticating ethnic and provincial differences, especially linguistic ones.... It [the *Canterbury Tales*] objectifies the nation's *composite* nature as a hodgepodge of different classes, a jumble of regional representatives, and a mixture of the jargons of gender, religion, and professional class—but *not* a mixture of regional dialects.... Chaucer's pilgrims derive from many regions of England—the Wife of Bath, the Clerk of Oxford, the Shipman of Dartmouth, the Reeve of Norfolk—but they gather in a London suburb and are represented as speaking the London dialect of the poet himself. One of the narrator's unstated duties is to translate provincial dialects into 'Londonese.'"[47]

Chaucer's Canterbury pilgrims (and the class and "national" identity they represent), I would argue, are thus caught within an empowering but also contradictory situation—one with the possibility of new associations and articulations along a lateral plane, but also bound up in a process of "internal colonization" (as Bowers calls it) that could co-opt those reimagined communities to the needs of a developing centralizing state apparatus. The very elasticity of a term like "gentils" as it is employed in the *Tales,* stretching to incorporate the upper echelons of the "middle strata" as well as many whose social situation is far less securely "upper" middle, may thus be its defining characteristic and chief attraction for a group such as the Canterbury pilgrims. It gestures toward exclusivity, while giving participants a sense of equal footing on a lateral plane. Similarly, although this group forms the majority of the pilgrims, it constitutes a minority of the general population and is largely confined to southeast England. As a group, then, the "gentils" are focused on London as center—economic (in the city), governmental (in the royal court and bureaucracy, and in Parliament at Westminster), and ecclesiastical (in the Archbishop of Canterbury's physical presence at Lambeth Palace and his precedence over the whole English church)—in ways that encourage a certain exclusivity and hegemonic centrality for themselves. However, what "gentils" defines is anything but stable and authoritative, since membership in this group requires a constant labor of self-definition that cannot be secured by recourse to foundational categories such as noble birth or clerical ordination.

Thus it is especially the experience of this labor of self-definition that the *Tales* foreground. The Pardoner's estate, for example, should ensure his inclusion as a "gentil," yet his supposedly "vicious" status brands him as necessarily other to the "gentils."[48] The Wife of Bath, on the other hand, claims access to this group by dint of hard labor and material rewards, and she achieves a certain success in this regard—to the extent that her claim to equality rouses a great deal of "men's concern" about what that might mean for the identity politics of the day. The Reeve's careful distinction of himself from the churlish activity of the Miller asserts a virtual "gentil"-ness or proximate likeness based on the labor of emulation. Yet the term "gentil" is elitist in its ability to communicate the desire of its members to self-identify "middle" as "upper." As such, the ability of "gentil" to designate a middle stratum functions in a charged relationship of identification/disidentification with preexisting groups above and below it. "Gentil" occludes the labor involved in generating its surplus production so that this group can represent its "difference" from "those who labor" as feudal laborers. "Gentil" also identifies a "nobility" that diligent emulation of one's "betters" can produce, but that is, nonetheless, loosened from "natural" associations with the aristocratic or clerical estates.

The attempt by various parts of the pilgrimage company to self-identify as "gentil," then, defines *as a group* a modernizing elite that is finding the means of its self-representation within the present moment, and thus signaling a certain disidentification from past representational models that no longer seem open or descriptive enough, even as it desires access to the elitist power that traditional forms of representation can confer. In this regard, the asymmetrical relationship between the pilgrims' self-presentation and the social practice of late fourteenth-century England may have suggestive parallels with that between Chaucer and his probable audience. According to Paul Strohm, the pilgrims represented in the *Tales* come from different parts of these middle strata than those probably occupied by Chaucer's actual audience:

> The pilgrims' tilt away from Chaucer's circle is most vividly revealed in the four categories of the 1379 poll tax, the first of which consists entirely of *gentils* down through the rank of esquires "en service" and the other three of which include sergeants at law, attorneys, aldermen, merchants, sergeants, franklins, pardoners, summoners, and others. Chaucer's actual audience would have been concentrated largely in the first of these four groups; the pilgrims are drawn mainly from social and occupational groups described in the other three.[49]

Yet Chaucer's own class relationship to his actual audience is also anomalous. Lee Patterson rightly emphasizes both the degree of difference between the situations of those chamber knights at the top of the scale of royal service and Chaucer's, near the bottom, and the differences between him and those near him in rank and service to the king:

> The chamber knights were thus both intimate royal servants with free access to the king and fully fledged members of the "international chivalrous class." Chaucer, as the brevity of his military service, his modest financial means, his undistinguished position as an *armiger regis,* and his political obscurity all testify, was not. . . . Chaucer was thus very much on the margins of the chivalric community of honor, the small group of rich and powerful men who comprised the ruling class of fourteenth-century England and who were bound together by a shared set of values and a common life-style. Nor is it easy to find an alternative place within the social structure where he naturally fits. On the one hand, his status as *armiger regis,* his military service, and his diplomatic and political responsibilities were consistent, as Hulbert has demonstrated, with the career patterns of other of his rank. On the other hand, he was set apart from men of similar background and rank by his predominantly urban residence, his lack of significant landed wealth, and, above all, by his role—first as controller of the customs from 1374 to 1387, and then,

> after his return to the king's service in 1389, as clerk of the king's works until 1391—in the civil service.[50]

In his involvement with a "civil service," Patterson sees Chaucer as representing "a new and somewhat anomalous phenomenon, the 'gentleman-bureaucrat' who was gradually taking over the administration of government from the clerics who had traditionally filled these positions. This process, as R. L. Storey has shown, took place largely in the first decades of the fifteenth century, which indicates the extent to which Chaucer was in the vanguard of a social movement that would not become widespread until his death."[51]

It would be easy here to enact a process of tracing, defining a narrowing point of structuration that would establish Chaucerian "originality" in anticipating the new "reality" of early modern subjectivity. But the situation that Strohm and Patterson outline would indicate instead just how much the *Tales* makes possible a process of mapping, as much a threatening delineation of an experimentation in contact with the real as a reassuring tracing of knowledge and power. The pilgrimage audience gains representational force from its capacity to fill in the space of the narrative frame, to inhabit it as fully its own, even as the newness of its representational strategies draws attention back to the necessity to be in some truthful relationship to the "real" of the everyday (a social terrain, however, where they constitute only a minority of participants). Similarly, the *Tales*' representation of such a modernizing elite maps the complex relationships of desire between Chaucer and his "actual" audience, rather than tracing hegemonic identity and agency for the "new men" of the early modern state and its originary "great author."

The flexibility and newness of a term like "gentils," the sense in which inhabitants of any group it designates share a kind of equal footing on a lateral plane, should highlight its significant differences from terms that may appear near synonyms, such as "middle strata" or upper middle class. As such, "gentils" shares as a representational category a certain necessary undecidability and "middleness" with Chaucer's own social situation. But "gentils" as a term also, I think, foregrounds a similar sense of being in the vanguard of a social movement that would not become widespread until a later period. Chaucer is not simply some proto-Lancastrian or Tudor bureaucrat in the making, nor are the "gentils" of the *Tales* simply prototypes of the early modern gentry that will follow with the likes of Thomas Chaucer in the fifteenth century or the Boleyns in the sixteenth. The "middleness" the term attempts to represent may gesture toward the forces that will be realized in such a way, but it also represents the coming into representation of subjects-in-process, a "becoming historical" that embodies a moment of libidinal excitement at the social level that cannot be contained by future narrowings of what such subjects can mean.

What I want to underscore in this discussion is the uncertain blending of "experience" and "auctoritee" that marks the path by which the "gentils" come to dominate the landscape of the *Canterbury Tales.* By virtue of their majoritarian articulation, their individual "realities" fill the representational space of the pilgrimage, yet their minoritarian position in terms of conventional estate classifications and the practices of everyday life in late medieval England emphasizes the unpredictability and vulnerability of such a representational politics. Not surprisingly, then, the process of subjectification taking place in the tales of the so-called marriage group to a great extent remains obstinately focused on the identification of those emerging "middle" groups beginning to coalesce around a new set of differences and (to use Partha Chatterjee's formulation in relation to a different social/historical "plateau") their own "vital zone of belief and practice that straddles the domains of the individual and the collective, the private and the public, the home and the world, where the new disciplinary culture of a modernizing elite has to turn itself into an exercise in self-discipline."[52]

Chatterjee's discussion, of course, is located in a very different cultural and temporal moment. But there are a number of similarities between the role played by the new Bengali middle class in nineteenth-century colonial India, as he describes it, and that played by the "gentils" of the *Canterbury Tales.* The name the Bengali class gave to itself was *bhadralok,* "respectable folk": "[I]t was this class that constructed through a modern vernacular the new forms of public discourse, laid down new criteria of social respectability, set new aesthetic and moral standards of judgement, and, suffused with its spirit of nationalism, fashioned the new forms of political mobilization that were to have such a decisive impact on the political history of the province in the twentieth century." Since Chatterjee's project is to consider the question of social agency with this class, he is particularly concerned with mediation, "in the sense of the subject who stands 'in the middle,' working upon and transforming one term of a relation into the other. It is more than simply a problem of 'leadership,' for I will be talking about social agents who are preoccupied not only with leading their followers but who are also conscious of doing so as a 'middle term' in a social relationship.... The colonial middle class, in Calcutta no less than in other centers of colonial power, was simultaneously placed in a position of subordination in one relation and a position of dominance in another."[53] As a means of exploring and problematizing this 'middleness' and the consciousness of middleness on the part of the Calcutta middle class, Chatterjee concentrates on the *Rāmkṛṣṇa kathāmṛta,* looking "specifically at the construction there of a new religion for urban domestic life.... The *Kāthamṛta,* it seems to me, is a document of the fears and anxieties of a class aspiring to hegemony. It is, if I may put this in a somewhat paradoxical form, a text that reveals to us the subalternity of an elite."[54]

Chaucer's "gentils" also form a new class of vernacular, English subjects focused on London and its centralized power bases, "respectably" distanced from any "churlish" ancestry and no longer needing to articulate themselves as a transnational feudal ruling class (whether secular or clerical). Yet, of course, as inheritors of French and Latin, aristocratic and clerical, traditions defining what the common heritage of medieval culture ought to be, but increasingly aware of these traditions as distinctly "other" and undergirding national (French) and international (church) institutions, these "gentils" too are placed simultaneously in a position of subordination in one relation and dominance in another. As we will see in this and subsequent chapters, conjugality—as it is articulated in late medieval redefinitions of the estate of marriage—empowers many of marriage's "middling" lay participants as equal to or better than previously superior clerical and aristocratic elites. To understand the full performativity of marriage in the *Tales,* then, we first need to explore how and why conjugality within the estate of marriage might provide an appropriate discipline through which a new modernizing elite can "translate" established identities and forms for articulating such identities—romantic love and a lay aristocratic identity, or Latin school culture and a celibate clerical identity—onto a new social and cultural terrain, thereby creating surplus value for a "modern" identity. Such a new disciplinary culture has to turn itself into an exercise in self-discipline, where the most valued understanding can come from within (that is, from the experience of the lay subjects it is attempting to define) rather than from outside (that is, from the definitions of marriage assigned by celibate clerical commentators). The new "middle experience" defined (though lacking the established authority of externally defined nobility acquired through bloodline or clerical celibacy acquired through vows and school culture) can still become, in Chatterjee's words, a "vital zone of belief and practice that straddles the domains of the individual and the collective, the private and the public, the home and the world," and one might add, husband and wife, masculine and feminine.[55] This is a disciplinary regime that many can participate in and thus one that draws its zone of practice and belief widely across a variety of class and estate lines. Although it is a regime that favors "those who labor," it also clearly finds it crucial both to define and exclude as a group those who are "below" such a modernizing elite and to claim kinship with those groups traditionally seen as "above" it.

By adopting Chatterjee's term, "modernizing elite," for what the "gentils" try to represent about themselves in the *Canterbury Tales,* I want to underscore their status as a group less coherently definable than early modern "gentry" or the modern liberal subject, even though elements of those who would define themselves as "gentil" in the *Tales* or by means of constituting themselves as the intended audience for the *Tales* can be linked genealogically with such groups that cohere in the fifteenth and sixteenth centuries. I do not want to limit this modernizing elite to the late fourteenth-century English urban merchant patriciate, or to some collusive compact of "new men" linking the king's affinity (especially established *esquires de service*), merchant patriciate, and aristocracy in a new, modern version of the high medieval ruling compact between aristocracy and clerisy. Clearly, there are trajectories within the tale-telling politics, and certainly in fifteenth-century (and later) understandings of what the *Tales* mean, that would tilt in the direction of such a point of structuration and sedimentation. But the undecidability of "gentils" in the *Tales* themselves would indicate the possibility of a more experimental mapping at work here.

As we will see below, since marriage, as an institution, underwent a radical redefinition in the twelfth and thirteenth centuries, it provides a zone of hybridization conducive for such a modernizing elite to assert its agency and self-definition. This project of identity formation, however, must deal with the anxieties that such a departure from the past and its attendant misidentifications necessarily bring as this new social group comes up against the transcendent inherited identities shoring up the high medieval clerical/aristocratic compact.[56]

## MAKING MARRIAGE NEW

Until the mid-eleventh century and the time of the Gregorian Reform, church authority and doctrine remained of far less importance than local custom and law in defining and controlling the institution of marriage. In Roman and Germanic law, marriage was a relatively private matter, and parental or other kinship authority was often paramount. Christianity did contain the seeds of a different and more detailed regulation of marriage, but throughout the late antique and early medieval period, the church's attempts to exert control over such matters as divorce, concubinage, and relationships within forbidden degrees of consanguinity, for example, were sporadic and inconsistent. The role of the church in shaping the institution of marriage thus remained a largely pastoral one, with the authority of the bishop or priest matched by lay traditions of family, tribal, or local custom, and to a lesser extent, Roman and Germanic civil law. Michael M. Sheehan has characterized these first thousand years of the church's life

> as a period during which Christian doctrine, confronted by a bewildering profusion of marriage customs, concentrated its efforts on defending and enhancing the moral value of matrimony. Steady insistence on the permanence and sanctity of the relationship of husband and wife, and on the limitation of erotic sexuality to that relationship, gained significant acceptance by society, even though individual practice and the different civil customs and laws lagged well behind. The Church's position was often locally stated, was not always consistent, nor was it organized and complete.[57]

R. H. Helmholz puts the matter somewhat differently, stating that "[p]eople retained a control over their matrimonial affairs which was compatible only with the notion that marriage was a personal matter, one which could not be absolutely regulated by Church or State."[58] As we shall see, this tension between marriage as a personal matter and marriage as an arena to be absolutely regulated by church or state takes different forms as a result of changes in the institution of marriage throughout the high and late medieval periods, but this tension between personal and public remains a complicating factor that affects how such changes are taken up and put into practice.

The general reorganization of Western European life taking place by the latter half of the eleventh century and heralded by the Gregorian Reform movement of the period not only begins to separate very clearly a celibate clergy from married laity, but also radically reconceptualizes the institution of marriage. As part of that widespread attempt by the church to regulate more generally all aspects of Christian moral and spiritual life, marriage undergoes a detailed examination by canonists and theologians during the late eleventh and twelfth centuries so that, as Sheehan notes, "between the beginning of the twelfth century revival and the end of the thirteenth century, in an intellectual effort that has probably had no equal in western tradition except possibly today, marriage was examined at all levels of thought ranging from theology, through moral guidance and law, to confessional practices."[59] Moreover, the new ecclesiastical definition of marriage that develops is then promulgated throughout the West with a consistency and universality not envisaged or attempted by earlier church interventions into the practices of everyday life associated with the married estate. The new definition stipulated the following:

> 1) The matrimonial bond was created by consent; neither consummation nor formality of any kind was required for validity. 2) It was the consent of the couple that created the marriage bond. Whatever the role of the family or the lord may have been, it was secondary and dispensable. 3) It was preferred that the marriage bond be created in a public setting; but, inasmuch as external formalities were developed and imposed, they were located within neither familial nor seigniorial structures but in the local community considered in its religious or parochial capacity. 4) There was a desire to internalize the marriage relationship. Theologians emphasized the bond of charity between the spouses and the possibility of its growth as a reason for their choice of each other. 5) Throughout the discussion by both canonists and theologians the point of view was one that focused on the couple: by and large, lordship was ignored; the wider family

circle and even the children born to the couple received little attention.[60]

The initial focus of canonists and theologians in the twelfth century was on formulating a clear definition of what constituted an indissoluble, true marriage.[61] Two schools of thought developed, both of which made individual consent central to their definitions of marriage, thereby differing substantially from longstanding lay practices that emphasized family, financial, and feudal concerns at the expense of personal choice on the part of bride and groom. The first and older theory, supported by Gratian and the Bolognese school, held that the consent of the two parties *(desponsatio)* only initiated marriage and required the proof of subsequent sexual union *(commixtio sexuum)* to render it indissoluble. The second view, developed by Peter Lombard and the school of Paris, distinguished between two types of *desponsatio,* one by words of present consent *(verba de presenti),* the other by words of future consent *(verba de futuro)*. Guided by the perfect example of the marriage between Joseph and the Virgin Mary, Peter Lombard thus insisted that present consent alone created a perfect marriage and an indissoluble bond. Future consent, on the other hand, initiated a true marriage only when completed by sexual relations. Peter Lombard's more emphatically consensual model for marriage was the one adopted by Pope Alexander III (1159–81) and thus became the basis for future articulations of church policy regarding marriage.[62]

The church's designation of consent as the cornerstone of what made a marriage licit had a number of important ramifications for ecclesiastical policy, marriage law, and the representation and practice of the institution itself in medieval society. By the thirteenth century the church had successfully promulgated a new view of marriage where the need for consent meant that in theory, at least, the rights of the individuals involved took legal precedence over the wishes of parents, extended family, and feudal lord. And ecclesiastical authority thereby extended its earlier established claim to control all aspects of clerical life and the disposition of church property (by its recent campaigns against simony and clerical marriage) into new and pervasive aspects of lay private and public life. The church's emphasis on individual consent, however, also meant that in theory the church reaffirmed marriage as fundamentally a private matter that did not require the involvement of ecclesiastical authorities to make it valid.[63] Thus the church had to accept the legality even of so-called clandestine marriages—that is, marriages occurring in private with the words of present consent uttered in the presence of lay witnesses, and not in public in front of a priest and the parish community. In practice, though, the church also stressed the value of, and increasingly the necessity for, legitimate marriages being preceded by the publication of banns and being celebrated *in facie ecclesie* (that is, at the church door in the presence of the local community and under the jurisdiction of the local parish priest). Otherwise, the difficulty of distinguishing between words of present and future consent, or of discovering possible impediments to a legal marriage (such as relation within a forbidden degree of consanguinity or the presence of a living partner from a previous marriage) could result in grounds for legal dispute of the validity of a marriage at an ecclesiastical court.[64] Thus, says Sheehan, the years between the advent of Pope Alexander III in 1159 and the death of Innocent III in 1216, when papal judgments in marriage cases gradually reduced the teaching of the schools to consistency and applied it throughout the Western Church,

> saw the growing demand that marriage take place publicly within a religious ceremony. This was in accord with the growing emphasis on the sacred aspect of matrimony, but it was also seen as a protection of the rights of the couple. The private exchange of consent, inasmuch as it was without witness, was difficult of defense before the courts. Furthermore, as the law of impediments was developed by canonists, it became clear that it was necessary to go beyond the information available to the couple, or admitted by them, to establish their freedom to marry. Early in the thirteenth century, the system of banns, a public announcement of the intention to marry made at mass in the parish church for several weeks before the event, was developed in northern France and England. This method of control was adopted by the Fourth Lateran Council [1215] and applied throughout the Church. It obliged parishioners to provide information to the parish priest if there were any reason to prevent the proposed marriage from going forward.[65]

But if, early in the twelfth century, the secular rite of marriage began to become an ecclesiastical ritual of which the nuptial mass and blessing were part, this new two-stage system involving announcement of intent (banns) followed by public exchange of consent (church marriage ceremony) required the concerted teaching activity of conciliar and synodal legislation, pastoral manuals, sermons, liturgy, and drama over the next two hundred years to instantiate it completely as the actual practice of the whole church. As Sheehan notes, by the fourth quarter of the fourteenth century, "[t]he records of cases that appeared before bishops' officials reveal a general understanding of the necessity of consent by the spouses for the validity of a marriage, the successful defense of a union against the prohibition of parents, the frequency of clandestine marriage, and the clear evidence of young people making preliminary arrangements for marriage without parental involvement."[66] Thus, even as the church was claiming exclusive competence over marriage at the expense of longstanding customary practice favoring secular authorities like parents and feudal lords, its own emphasis on individual consent could work against its gaining complete disciplinary control over a longstanding lay belief that marriage was a private, personal matter.

The new emphasis in canon law and theology on individual consent as the basis for marriage proceeded out of its revaluation as a sacrament by Peter Lombard and others in the twelfth century. This sacramental function for marriage in turn encouraged a much greater emphasis on the value of the personal relations it established between a man and woman. Not only was marriage now conceived as a consensual relationship between two people that should be exclusive and permanent, but such a relationship, properly imagined and practiced, clerics thought, should also promote a growth in love and reciprocity.[67] This is seen, first of all, in the way that an appreciation of the intrinsic goodness of the married state led to the articulation of a so-called conjugal debt in canon law, stipulating that each spouse owed the other right of access to proper marital coitus. The right of spouses to their marital due could therefore be abrogated only by mutual consent.[68] But canon law also calls for the desirability of growth in marital or conjugal affection *(maritalis affectio)*. As Pedersen notes, in Roman law the term was used to establish the existence of marriage, to distinguish marriage from concubinage, and to establish the right of offspring to inherit. Thus "the meaning of *affectio* was virtually synonymous with *affectu*, indicating the will of both parties to transfer ownership of lands and goods. As such, the word was most often used to emphasize that a spouse had displayed a willingness to allow the legal effects of marriage to come into effect and thus to indicate the quality of will needed to enter into marriage."[69] However, in later canon law the term took on a larger signification. Gratian's *Decretum* of around 1140 emphasized the emotional content of *affectio maritalis* and separated this from marital consent. The decretals of Pope Alexander III (1159–81) sketched out the meaning of the term in more detail, making marital affection not only a requirement for the establishment of marriage, but also a required part of married life that endured during the entire marriage. Sheehan, commenting on the abundant evidence in papal decretals and in local ecclesiastical courts that both men and women often demanded the enforced society of their spouse, notes that this is "an important indication of what some spouses expected of marriage, of what made it desirable and worth defending in court: a sexual partner even though another was preferred, a place in society, shelter and sustenance, etc." Thus the concept of marital affection seems to have been often used to describe external aspects of an ideal "employed against a certain type of behavior (excessive correction of a spouse, mistreatment of a spouse, etc.). More positively, husbands were ordered to provide suitable dress for their wives, to see to their proper nourishment, etc., as required by marital affection."[70] In the cases from York analyzed by Pedersen, the original Roman legal sense of *affectio* as the simple intention of creating a marriage coexists ambiguously and at times uneasily with a newer, developing, more emotional understanding of the term.[71] Pedersen cites the deposition given by an Emma Munkton regarding the marriage of Simon Munkton and Agnes Huntington. "Emma Munkton describes the marriage," he says, "as a process consisting of a series of steps, from the initial *traductio* of the woman into the man's household, through the solemnization of the marriage at the church in front of witnesses to the birth of their son. The information on marital affection—which she volunteered to the court without being asked—shows that she saw it as the external expression of an internal reality. Her use of the phrase 'in so far as this witness could make out' makes it clear that she was aware that she could not be sure that the external signs of affection actually covered the inner reality of the emotion. In other words, in her use of the term, marital affection consisted of two parts, an inner reality and an outer expression."[72]

There is further evidence of the capacity for this understanding of marriage as sacrament to articulate a kind of conjugal love that goes beyond either the external aspects of marital affection or the contractual obligations of equal sexual rights. Sheehan notes that the Judeo-Christian scriptures provide "a remarkably developed reflection" on the relations between spouses: "There is a description of the creation of mankind and an explanation of the difference of genders in terms of the purpose of their relationship. Furthermore, that relationship had a history—a history in which there were two principal moments, namely the fall of Adam and Eve and the coming of Christ, after each of which sexuality and marriage and the relationship of spouses within marriage took on new meanings and new possibilities."[73] In addition, the now sacramentalized estate of marriage based on mutual consent can, in the twelfth and thirteenth centuries, be incorporated into a developing discourse of friendship that draws on the classical tradition of Aristotle and Cicero. Thus, Thomas Aquinas, discussing the indissolubility of marriage, writes: "Furthermore, the greater that friendship, the more solid and long lasting it will be. Now, there seems to be the greatest friendship between husband and wife, for they are united not only in the act of fleshly union, which produces a certain gentle association even among beasts, but also in the partnership of the whole range of domestic activity."[74]

In the first half of the twelfth century, Hugh of St. Victor in the *De sacramentis* develops, at least as an idea, the near equality that the friendly association within domestic conjugality should bring:

> For since [woman] was given as a companion *[socia]*, not a servant or a mistress, she was to be produced not from the highest or from the lowest part but from the middle.... She was made from the middle, that she might be proved to have been made for equality of association. Yet in a certain way she was inferior to him, in that she was made from him, so that she might always look to him as to her beginning and cleaving to him indivisibly might not separate herself from that association which ought to have been established reciprocally.[75]

And in the third quarter of the thirteenth century, while a university professor of theology in Paris, Robert de Sorbon provides the following exegesis to Genesis 2.18 as part of a sermon on marriage:

> "It is not good for man to be alone; let us make him a help like unto himself." ... Indeed he said 'like unto himself'; this corre-

> sponds to equivalence. By this is indicated that the woman must be the equal of the man, or his companion, not under him and not above him.
>
> Also, woman was made from man's rib, not from the upper part or from the lower, but from the middle, that by it might be designated that woman must be man's equal.[76]

This correlation between Eve's origins and the status of the woman's position in marriage is also featured in the *Parson's Tale* and its discussion of marriage as a remedy against *luxuria* (X.925ff.). There the fact that she was not formed from Adam's head provides an argument against a wife having sovereignty in marriage, and the fact that she was not formed from the foot an argument against her being "holden to lowe; for she kan nat paciently suffre" (X.927). For the Parson, Eve's middle position in relation to Adam's body results in the more neutral and conventional admonishment that "[m]an sholde bere hym to his wyf in feith, in trouthe, and in love, as seith Seint Paul, that a man sholde loven his wyf as Crist loved hooly chirche, that loved it so wel that he dyde for it. So sholde a man for his wyf, if it were need" (X.928). Subsequent comments focus in far more detail on the many ways in which a wife should be subject to her husband and serve his needs and desires.

But it is in those sermons directed at those in the estate of marriage itself (a subset of a popular genre of sermons directed *ad status,* i.e., to the various estates), that we find outlined in the strongest form a kind of love between partners and equals that had heretofore been imaginable only between male friends. In their analysis of two minor and three major thirteenth-century collections of *ad status* marriage sermons, D'Avray and Tausche reach the following conclusions:

> Behind the individual features of the marriage sermons of these different authors one may discern a strong family resemblance. These writers all belong to a common tradition of doctrine, and we repeatedly meet the same ideas and topoi: the essential goodness of marriage, which was founded in Paradise and honored by the Lord's presence at the wedding feast of Cana; the faith binding husband and wife to each other, the begetting of children, the sacramental character of marriage, and its function as a remedy for incontinence; the consequent duty of each

> partner to agree to have intercourse at the other's request; the heinousness of adultery and the many crimes it involves; the obligation to abstain from intercourse at certain times; woman as temptress; the obligation of the husband to treat his wife with respect, as his 'socia' ['partner'], and of the wife to obey her husband; the responsibility of parents for the moral education of children; the duty to get married properly in public, not clandestinely.[77]

And Andrew Galloway notes that, while it is common in sermons on the marriage at Cana to assert that marriage is authoritative because it was instituted by God, an early fourteenth-century German preacher, Peregrinus of Oppeln, "begins with a commendation of marriage as a divinely instituted *ordo* superior to the other religious orders: unlike the Benedictines, the Cistercians, and the other religious *ordines,* 'the order of marriage alone has been instituted by God; happy indeed are those who have such an abbot.'"[78]

Guibert de Tournai provides a particularly interesting example of these new definitions of conjugal love, distinguishing between two kinds of love possible within marriage: the first, *dilectio carnalis,* he deals with in the first half of his sermon, covering such questions as when sexual intercourse is permitted; the second, *dilectio socialis,* takes up the second part. Guibert begins this section thus: "There is also a kind of love founded on partnership *[dilectio socialis],* and this is the love which husband and wife owe to each other, because they are equal *[pares]* and partners *[socii].*"[79] And when discussing the motives for marriage, Guibert goes on to argue: "[T]his love [i.e., love founded on partnership] ought to be formed in such a way that the motives for it are pure, so that the husband and wife should not love each other or be joined in marriage for the sake of some temporal gain, or a beautiful figure *[forme],* or to gratify their lust, but so that they may live together [*vivant simul* (!)] happily and decently, so that God may receive honour, and the marriage yield fruit for the service of God. . . . For when they are equal *(pares),* then they live in peace; but when they have got married for the sake of a dowry or for something temporal they always quarrel. So if you want to get married, marry an equal."[80] Or as David D'Avray puts it, writing more generally about twelfth- and thirteenth-century preachers on marriage, "[L]ove is for them a feeling which belongs to the domain of free will and choice. . . . In their view married love was a moral obligation and one which married people could be persuaded by arguments to fulfil."[81]

The revaluation of the marriage estate, and of the procreative sex occurring within this new sacrament, marks the response of orthodox Christianity to the challenges posed by the antimaterialism of the Cathar heresy. But these new definitions of marriage also validate the new "separate spheres" delineation of sex (male/female) and estate (clerical/lay) difference after the Gregorian Reform: that is, a separate celibate male clergy placed over a married laity, but within that lay sphere, a dominant masculinity (husband and father) directing and controlling a carefully circumscribed femininity (wife and mother).[82] If marriage is a sacramental means to grace, then, as the church maintained, it must also involve a personal act of will. Thus, individual consent becomes *the* defining act constituting a binding marriage in the eyes of canon law and ecclesiastical courts (and arbitration of marriage disputes is indisputably under the jurisdiction of such courts). The record of the period, however, also shows repeated attempts by the church to gain as much control as possible over lay marriage, particularly by discouraging (and in countries remaining Catholic after the Reformation, by the end of the sixteenth century, outlawing) clandestine marriages. Church officials thus increasingly emphasized the need for proper publication of the banns in local parishes and for a marriage ceremony conducted by the parish priest at the parish church door under the watchful eye of the local community (to ensure that the two participants were free to choose marriage to this partner).

In this way, church practice gradually worked to bring an institution initially theorized as fundamentally individual and private back under the controlling gaze of ecclesiastical and civic authority.[83] Despite this movement to disciplinary control, laws on consanguinity that moved away from agnatic lineage and the kind of extended family of the feudal regime to the at least theoretical primacy of individual consent and the installation of local community and priest (rather than extended family) as guarantors of marital propriety, all work to emphasize the symbolic importance of the freely established, single-family (male-ruled) household as the foundational model for imagining the properly functioning social body. Moreover, while this debate initially takes place at the rarified level of clerical theological and canon law discourses, throughout the period activity at the local level (for example, in ecclesiastical courts and parish sermons) effectively works to spread this new understanding of marriage to every level of society, so that "[b]y the fourth quarter of the fourteenth century, there is ample evidence from local ecclesiastical courts to show that the revolutionary ideas touching matrimonial consent that began to assume consistent form in the *Decretum* [of Gratian in the mid-twelfth century] were known even by the young."[84]

The essential role assigned to individual consent, the importance of sexual consummation of the marriage vows as a sign of their fulfillment, and the sacramental role assigned to procreative sex and a personal relationship are all powerful signifiers of an embodied, personally chosen yet authoritative identity, one distanced in important ways from traditional ideologies of kinship and estate. In emphasizing individual choice I am not suggesting that late medieval marriage was some utopic place of free choice, nor that the church of this period was an institutional force dedicated to lay empowerment. Such an opportunity for personal agency is always in tension with larger social forces, as the concerted efforts of the church from the Fourth Lateran Council (1215) to the Council of Trent (1545–63) to bring marriage vows within the purview of ecclesiastical and community authority demonstrate. Both rural and urban single men and women increasingly tried to build up land and movable goods in their own right before marriage, economic factors that would encourage their having a greater voice in the disposal of such economic resources in marriage.[85] Nor did the desire and power of parents and family members to influence marriage choice—sometimes in an extremely coercive, even violent fashion—disappear just because theology and canon law defined the essence of the true marriage as resting on the free choice of the individuals to be married. But I do want to counter any modern, heterosexist presumption on our part that marriage as we currently understand it is some transhistorical "fact," or its corollary presumption, that the late medieval married estate was a simple matter of dynastic, arranged marriage. Instead, I want to stress how an emphasis on conjugality in late medieval marriage makes it something of a "new" creation with an ambiguous but increasingly important role to play in the representational politics of the day.

What I am interested in exploring here is how the married estate, clerically defined as "inferior" to celibacy, nonetheless comes to be redefined in a way that allows it to structure an empowering identity for individuals and groups not previously given representational force. At the private level, it allows individual men and women to assert their right of choice, although clearly family and economic factors still worked to constrain individual choice. Mary Carruthers, for example, notes that the sale by parents of their children's rights to marry was prevalent among both the gentry and the bourgeoisie of the late Middle Ages. She cites the example of Stephen Scrope, writing around 1440: "For very need I was fain to sell a little daughter I have for much less than I should have done by possibility." This same Scrope, says Carruthers, at fifty and "'disfigured in my person [by illness]' was considered a fine match for twenty-year-old Elizabeth Paston."[86] And Pedersen points out that the threat of force had to be very severe indeed—usually that weapons had been drawn—before a court would pass a sentence annulling a marriage for force and fear.[87] Another Paston example, however, illustrates the continuing power of individual desire in the face of an often contradictory parental will and the complex familial terrain on which individual consent in marriage was played out. In a Valentine's Day letter in 1477, Margery Paston writes to her would-be husband, John Paston III:

> Ryght reu*er*ent and wurschypfull and my right welebeloued Voluntyne, I reco*m*mande me vn-to yowe full heretely, desyring to her*e* of yowr welefare, which I beseche Almyghty God long for to p*reser*ve vn-to hys plesur*e* and [y]owr herty*s* desire. And yf it please [y]owe to her*e* of my welefar*e*, I am not in good heele of body ner of herete, nor schall be tyll I her*e* from yowe;
>
> > For [th]*er* wottys no creatur*e* what peyn [th]*at* endur*e*,
> > And for to be deede I dar*e* it not dyscur*e*.
>
> And my lady my mod*er* hath labored [th]e mat*er* to my fadur*e* full delygently, but sche can no mor*e* gete [th]en [y]e knowe of, for [th]e which God knowyth I am full sory.
>
> But yf that [y]e loffe me, as I tryste verily that [y]e do, [y]e will not leffe me [th]*er*for; for if [th]*at* [y]e hade not halfe [th]e lyvelode [th]*at* [y]e hafe, for to do [th]e grettyst labure [th]*at* any woma*n* on lyve might, I wold not forsake [y]owe.[88]

Pedersen also cites the intriguing example of William Aungier, who in 1357 sought the help of the archbishop's court in York to have his marriage to Johanna Malcake annulled, despite having slept with her once after marriage, because "she does not prize an affection that is upheld. And therefore, for sure, I intend never to consent to her that she be my wife, nor to cohabit with her."[89]

More broadly, at a symbolic level, the newly sacramentalized married state substitutes local community (either those assembled at the parish church door or those persons vouching for private marriages in ecclesiastical courts) for a larger feudal kinship (of lord or extended family) as its authorizing witness. Additionally, such a "personal," "companionate" view of marriage allows the representation of "proper" identities organized around the individual household for a new group of "bourgeois" subjectivities. Deportment books, such as that of the Knight of La Tour Landry or the *Menagier de Paris,* directed at marriageable daughters or young wives, write on the bodies of these women a "gentle" identity for the feminine, and via that ground, a new, potentially dominant form of masculinity for their male authors.[90] Marriage, then, is something "good to think with" for a variety of new lay forces in the later Middle Ages, in the process of being reincorporated within the disciplinary gaze of hegemonic forces in late medieval society even as (or perhaps because) it assumes a growing importance in asserting new forms of lay identity.[91] And in this restructuring of lay gender relations within conjugality, the feminine is given its place, even revalued upward, while at the same time contained by the masculine control of a properly husbanded household.

The estate of marriage in the later Middle Ages thus acts as a nexus for complex and at times contradictory individual and institutional desires. As such, conjugality provides a medium in which to voice a larger gender anxiety exercising late fourteenth- and fifteenth-century society that in crucial ways parallels an earlier gender anxiety Jo Ann McNamara has identified as arising out of the Gregorian clerical reforms of the twelfth century. As McNamara has pointed out, "We are so accustomed to thinking of the medieval clergy as violently abusive toward women that we have missed a chronological subtlety. Clerical misogyny reached a crescendo between the mid-eleventh and mid-twelfth centuries."[92] This crescendo of clerical misogyny has its roots, McNamara maintains, in a gender crisis attendant on the Gregorian Reform's insistence on priestly celibacy. For one consequence of the Gregorian Reform's imposition of a monastic model of celibacy for the secular clergy was a revaluation of celibacy more generally among the laity as well as the clerisy.

According to McNamara, this revaluation of celibacy allowed a blurring of traditional gender assignments as both women and men gained authority and personal agency by living an apostolic life of chastity and poverty:

> The ideology that had long been associated with the renunciation of sexual activity pointed strongly toward the inclusion of women among the "people" rising to the top of the medieval hierarchy. . . . Many men saw abstinence as a means to drop out of the whole power system. Instead of using celibacy to control society, they renounced the burdens and corruptions of governance. These latter-day apostles began to experiment with a syneisactic life. . . . The renunciation of sex without separating women from men narrowed the definitional grounds between the genders.[93]

As McNamara notes, the reaction to this threat of gender minimalism and consequent social fluidity took two forms as the twelfth century progressed. The first was the separation of male celibate clerics (and the power linked to this new form of dominant masculinity) from women. Not only was celibacy no longer a route for women to access masculinity and its authority, an increasingly anxious male clerisy sought to protect itself from the evils of women in every arena (and in turn to protect women from themselves by claustration for the celibate and marriage for the secular female).[94] The second was the reassertion of the worth of lay marriage and the validity of its controlled sexual union. This new definition of woman and her proper relationship to man required the feminizing of the female (as Aristotelian body and receptacle, mother, helpmeet, needing male protection and regulation) and the masculinizing of the male (as possessing the vital seed in procreation, head of the household, agent of outward action) in the newly sacramentalized partnership of marriage:

> The body politic was increasingly womanless as university-trained administrators began to develop outside the kindred-based feudal system. . . . Women were securely tied to a nature defined by sexual and reproductive functions and thus disqualified for participation in the new public spheres. . . . By midcentury [i.e.,

> mid-twelfth century], the marital crisis was winding down. The decrees on clerical celibacy were definitively reinforced in 1148. Gratian divided the social world into celibate clergy and married laymen, thus securely defining manhood in conjunction with activity in the public world. Bernard of Clairvaux, among others, re-visioned the social order as a new binarity, with the celibate clergy placed over the married laity.[95]

As McNamara notes, this clerical articulation of separate (and unequal) spheres for male/female and clerical/lay "natures" succeeds for a time in stabilizing the transgressive power of celibacy to diminish the importance of sex and estate difference for social relations.

Inscribing sex and estate difference in this way provides a privileged and stable identity for the male clerisy, but in the process creates an ambivalent and unstable identity position for the married layman, a subject at once in a position of dominance as man vis-à-vis woman, and subordination as lay vis-à-vis the cleric. By the fourteenth and fifteenth centuries, at the level of practical consciousness, many of the distinctions between "lered" and "lewed," cleric, i.e. "clerical," and lay, activity are becoming increasingly blurred, as lay state bureaucracies become important locations for the employment and advancement of clerics, as a lay male intelligentsia takes on many of the functions previously reserved for the literate clerisy (book production, bureaucratic administration, and other activities associated with literacy), and as the institutional demands arising out of church property absorb the clerisy into the activities of late medieval capitalism. Mary Carruthers, for example, notes that

> [t]he conclusion that many who entered Oxford did so without expecting to pursue clerical careers is supported from a number of sources. A count based on Emden's *Register* of students and masters between 1350 and 1410 reveals a steady thirty percent who did not proceed to orders; this percentage is undoubtedly too low. . . . Sylvia Thrupp points out that London merchants of the fourteenth and fifteenth centuries were ambitious to achieve educational polish through university training. . . . The paternal concern of Clement Paston (d. 1419) is typical: a 'good pleyn husband' himself. . . . he sent his son William (b. 1378) to university, thereby starting his family's fortunate rise,

> and succeeding generations of Pastons followed his example. One of Richard FitzRalph's charges against the friars...was that 'very many of the common people' feared that the friars at Oxford were taking advantage of youthful students and pressing them too soon into orders. . . . The concern of the common people in 1357 is echoed a century later by Margaret Paston, who cautions her son Walter, a clerk at Oxford, 'that he benot to hasty of taking of orderes [th]at schuld bynd hum till [th]at he be of xxiiij yere of agee or more. . . . I will loue hym bettere to be a good seculare man [th]an to be a lewit prest.'[96]

In a different context, Fiona Somerset, discussing the politics of "lewed translacion" in the *Summoner's Tale,* notes the late fourteenth- and early fifteenth-century clerical uneasiness about potential lay judgment and argumentation in writings against Wycliffite polemic: "All these writers implicitly appeal to a common model of what 'proper' lay/clerical interaction would consist in: it posits 1) that the clergy and laity are entirely distinct and have their own separate spheres, 2) that each can be viewed as a seamless, consistent, unified whole, 3) that clerical governance, administration, judgment, and so on should be reserved to the clergy alone, and, crucially, 4) that the Latin literacy, competence in argumentation, and information the clergy have as a consequence of the kind of education they receive are equally their own particular reserved province."[97]

Increasingly, then, the dominant public discourses of the later Middle Ages are those of married laymen as much as those of a celibate clerisy, something Patricia Eberle underscores when she notes that many of the religious in the *General Prologue* manifest a commercial outlook indistinguishable from that of the Merchant or Host, or that the Narrator rushes to account for the Knight's poor garb in order to defend his "worthiness" not just in traditional feudal terms, but in those of the newer market-driven sense of worth.[98] Increasingly, too, within dominant masculinity, lay and clerical interests are coming together in common cause, and the old division between celibate clergy and married laymen outlined by McNamara becomes in many practical respects an outdated binary. The gender crisis of the later Middle Ages thus arises out of the need to destabilize the social order created by Bernard's binary of celibate clergy placed over married laity enough to make room for a new class of married laymen standing on a more equal footing with the celibate cleric as exemplary of hegemonic masculinity.[99] As a result, it is necessary, first, to draw new boundaries around a superior masculinity that can contain certain laymen and clerics rather than simply trace old distinctions between celibate cleric and married layman. Equally important, ways must be found to separate newly authorized lay males from their "inferior" lay subjects, both male and female, that will work more broadly than previous noble/nonnoble categories.[100] Conjugality within the lay married estate, itself a new representational mode arising out of the Gregorian Reform, provides precisely that complex nexus of sex, gender, sexuality, class, and community identifications needed to map this more inclusive, yet still privileging, masculine "gentil" identity.[101]

It is thus crucial when viewing the newly emerging representational category of "gentils" in the *Tales* to factor in the unstable presentism that the attempts to represent bourgeois conjugality in marriage must involve. Such a presentism opens up room to maneuver for a new group of subjects seeking access to hegemonic forms of self-representation, but in doing so, their desire risks a potentially shaming and dangerous deformation of traditional "universals" as it attempts to articulate a modernity that will historicize such traditions enough to permit their supersession by new forms of representation. Such a desire on the part of these "new men" also risks exposing the arbitrariness of such a "modern" system of representation: how its supposed universals are rooted in the accidents of a changing historical moment and how such universals can thus never truly or fully "know" the "real" they supposedly describe and contain.

In the following chapter, then, I explore further how conjugality figures as a "deformative" in the representational politics of the *Tales,* necessarily engaging and playing with the potential for change within the present moment, rather than tracing an always already existing "nature."[102] In doing so, I want to emphasize that I am not intent on reinstalling the idea of a marriage *group,* but rather am attempting to stress the push toward such organization *and* the disorganizing potential inherent in such a discussion. We can see assembled in these tales the raw material for what will come to be organized as heterosexuality and modern companionate marriage (and with that the making of the modern liberal subject and autonomous self on such embodied foundations). But that dominant order is not always already present and it is not already formed here in the *Tales,* however much they, and the originary "great author" they have been used to establish, might participate in such a formation of modern heterosexuality. Rather, we see a representational system in the *Tales* that is more concerned with exploring the fullness of possibility that the present moment has to offer. That some of the reasons for this are hegemonic cannot be denied, but that is not the whole story.

# 3

# Modernity and Marriage in the *Canterbury Tales*

Although the Wife is not the first pilgrim to deal with marriage, or to focus on the importance of marriage in representing and deciding proper sex/gender relations and the social orders that rest on them, her tale does make visible a new desire to bring modernity, conjugality, and a new elite's self-definition into some kind of proper alignment. Both the *Knight's Tale* and the *Man of Law's Tale* use marriage to stabilize sex/gender relations in important ways, yet both also present a false consciousness about marriage that occludes crucial but troubling changes in medieval approaches to the institution and its signifying power for social and political relations.[1] Both tales attempt to tie manhood and masculinity back onto the male body in powerful ways that will ground gender difference in biological sex difference and reinscribe the naturalness of the noble lay male body. In the case of the *Knight's Tale* what is occluded is the sacramental understanding of a marriage whose essence is individual consent; in the *Man of Law's Tale,* it is both the matter of consent and the changing relationship between dominant lay and clerical masculinity in the later Middle Ages (and the changing definition of what constitutes the dominant "noble male body"). The Wife of Bath calls these accommodations into question both by focusing attention on marriage as their "forgotten" category and by decentering the hegemony of the male body as it is represented in these earlier tales. To understand how this happens we need to understand how in her *Prologue* she is able to exploit that perverse presentism bound up in conjugality, and thus to exploit to her own ends how marriage had become both "good to think with" for a number of competing interests within late medieval culture and, perhaps because of that, a confused and overdetermined category.

I begin by focusing on the challenges to heteronormativity produced by the Wife of Bath's queer repositioning of "female masculinity" within medieval understandings of gender and marriage relationships. Subsequently, I turn to the *Merchant's Tale* and the *Franklin's Tale,* both told by lay male narrators reacting to the Wife of Bath who in their different ways attempt to normalize and contain the Wife's claim to present on its own terms what is often rendered the abject or inferior category by traditional medieval discourses.

## Female Masculinity and the Wife of Bath

Like any good preacher, the Wife of Bath knows the value of repetition. "Biology is destiny," she tells us again and again in her prologue; therefore let us make the most of what nature has given us. And since as wise a maker as made our sexual organs surely meant them to be used for the purpose of sex, the Wife logically concludes: "In wyfhod I wol use myn instrument / As freely as my Makere hath it sent" (III.149–50). In this way the Wife demonstrates how she supposedly finds room to maneuver in a discursive framework that presents as a fact of nature not only clerical misogyny and its celibate-dominated imaginary, but also the absolutist, binarist sex/gender system these produce. Equally explicit here is the fraught relationship between the celibate clerisy that undergirds such a hierarchized sex/gender system and the women and feminine energy that threaten it. By embracing and valuing her unpromising, "barly-breed" nature, the Wife tries to make the female body visible in ways that will forcefully reimagine the abject status assigned to it by an antifeminist clerical tradition *and* find a new use value for the feminine in lay culture's equation of female with wife. To do so, her prologue, while genuflecting in the direction of medieval gender verities, also foregrounds, even revels in, the feminine—that hermeneutically marginal and ephemeral matter that dominant medieval culture insists must be put aside if any movement toward proper masculine understanding is to take place.

In grounding her argument in the authority of personal experience and physical presence, the Wife's mode of self-presentation also suggests an engagement with the present that is significantly different from the masculinist clerical hermeneutic she argues with. Rather than simply pointing "back" to a transcendent, originary moment in the past or "outside" to the frame of some hegemonic authority, the Wife claims to occupy a present that is its own moment. Her emphasis on "experience," then, to the extent that its examination of the present generates its own authority, marks by such autonomy a liberatory rupture from past traditions and threatens to "historicize" both the past and present in unpredictable ways. How much, though, does the prolonged "argument" between the sexes that dominates the foreground of the *Wife of Bath's Tale* really help "dream the present" differently?[2] What kind of liberatory analysis is initiated by the Wife's explicit turn to "the feminine" (and consequent chastening of dominant masculinity) or by her reliance on authentic presence as the foundation for experiential authority—and for whom might such an analysis be effective?

To answer such questions, it is important both to acknowledge the indelible presence of the female body that the Wife's biological determinism insists on and to resist the stabilizing turn to the feminine that her "nature" presupposes and supports. Doing so exposes the tale's actual preoccupation with a female body engaged in what would "normally" be seen as dominant masculine activity, that is, with a kind of *female masculinity* that, as Judith Halberstam has recently suggested in the context of nineteenth- and twentieth-century representational systems, "far from being an imitation of maleness, actually affords us a glimpse of how masculinity is constructed as masculinity."[3] If, on the one hand, in her prologue the Wife vociferously and absolutely accepts the definitional status quo established after the Gregorian Reform—asymmetry between male/female, masculine/feminine, cleric/lay—on the other hand, the bodily presence established in the same prologue engages with a masculinity particularized in a unique here and now, and is therefore implicitly more complex than the discursive gender framework—assuming the universality of its own categories—would allow.

In the process of embracing the delineation of "natural" and universal gender roles and the social asymmetries that arise out of and depend on them, the Wife exposes the fluidity of such roles, especially the crossing of definitional boundaries that must occur for "middle"-class laymen to gain access to masculine power and agency by means of the married estate, and the fullness of possibility in the present moment that this potentially wayward activity creates. That the Wife forces her audience to attend to *her* experience, and through it to the authority of personal experience itself, thus inscribes in her embodiedness the ambiguities and contradictions of "gentil" identity that we have already discussed as central to the Canterbury project. In this respect, what can easily be taken as personal idiosyncrasy emerges as crucial to the larger identity politics of the *Tales,* reinforcing a reality effect created by the apparently contradictory interaction of conventional estates satire and individual self-presentation, and the dogged insistence that the experience of the married estate is as good to think with as any clerical discourse.

Certainly the liveliness of the Wife's self-presentation in her prologue and tale is hard to resist, and it is extraordinarily difficult, even for a hardened postmodern reader, to avoid responding to the Wife as if she were a "real" person.[4] Not only is there an unusual congruence between the portrait of the Wife in the *General Prologue* and the subject that emerges in the prologue to her tale, as well as between the tale-teller and kind of tale told, but the Wife's "autobiographical" prologue—longer than the tale proper—sets the tone for both the subject matter and the mode of understanding for the tale. Like the Wife's self-portrayal in her prologue, the *General Prologue*'s description emphasizes her status as Wife (married five times at the church door) and as bourgeois success story (pushing her way forward to give the collection in church first, excessively and expensively costumed in fine materials, able to afford pilgrimages to every major shrine in Christendom). Several of her facial features (gat-toothed, red-faced) anticipate the Wife's equation of her amatory proclivities to biological determinism, and her deafness in the *General Prologue* would appear to "prove" the narrative she outlines in her prologue, notably Jankin's blow to the head when she tears a leaf out of his antifeminist book.

Moreover, this "self" that insists on voice and visibility (within the social moment of the Canterbury tale-telling but also more fundamentally within the systems of representation that make up the social imaginary of that moment), seems to be synonymous with newness, contemporaneity, and presentism, and thus to be perpetually at odds with and refusing to be silenced by universals, tradition, the conceptual dominance of the past and its transcendent values. As already noted, this point is made by the Wife's explicit insistence on her own "experience" over against universal "authorities." But it is also brought home by her implicit validation of a series of accidentals that make up this experience—sex, gender, economic clout, outward display, a vernacular "popular culture," gossip, "marginal" social differentiation within estates and across sex/gender divides—as capable of "speaking" the subject within a variety of constantly mobile performative displays of identity. Even while expressing herself in often quite traditional terms, then, the Wife's self-presentation and fictional account of *her* unique experience still seem quintessentially "modern," and the strong "reality effect" created by her characterization encourages us to assume that her uniqueness points straight back to "real life."

Strangely, though, the Wife's emphasis on the authenticity of her strong presence tends to produce masculinist and feminist responses that reinscribe the very rigidity of the binaristic sex/gender system she finds so coercive and supposedly seeks to resist. By encouraging a gender analysis that is so stabilized by sexual certainty and biological "fact" that it can represent experience only as an either/or, both masculinist and feminist reading strategies can insist that the Wife *must* mean something final about woman and "the feminine." Because of their stabilizing and mutually constitutive "natures," such gendered reactions work to maintain a dangerous conflation of sex and gender, discursivity and materiality. The set of differences constructed upon such supposedly secure biological foundations—medieval/modern, past/present, male/female, masculine/feminine—thus constitutes a kind of massive red herring that encourages audiences to accept the fictional as the real and ideology as nature. Both masculinist and feminist reactions treat the Wife's claim to being as a fact of nature, rather than as a performative. Her claim to biological certitude, therefore, can too easily become the ground for a similarly stable understanding of gender if the Wife's presence points the way to the truth about "the feminine," and with that ontological certitude, the truth about how and what the present means. Such a "buying into" the discourse of presence that the Wife's argument establishes works to reinstall the very obfuscatory power of ideologies that her example would appear to resist. Masculinist responses will therefore often stress what she is *not*—whether in relation to other women and femininity (not Alceste the faithful wife, nor Custance the noble mother, nor Prudence the good helpmeet) or to men and masculinity (not those dominant forms of clerical, noble, or bourgeois masculinity that we see in the Clerk, Knight, Franklin, or Merchant). Feminist responses will often focus on her truth value as a manifestation of the reality of medieval women's lives.

The Wife's claim to material presence, read through the lens of a masculinist medieval clerical hermeneutic, for example, signifies the *un*-Real, that is, the present moment's lapse from universally held and true values. Therefore the Wife's wayward presence, by demanding the supersession of female mastery by proper male husbandry, would posit exactly the sort of natural ground on which to present a chaotic, threatening presentness necessarily eliciting its supersession by the transcendent order of a universal, timeless presence. And a set of universal identities—clerical and noble—can thus be built on the foundations of the Wife's "kind" and its imperfect "nature." Such identities depend on their limits and boundedness being seen as natural (and not as limitation in terms of the categories themselves). That is, the limit for priest is the natural category of maleness, for noble, the natural category of blood. Despite the necessity for such categories to find expression in a variety of different temporal and local situations, despite the material and contingent factors affecting such expression, the categories maintain the fiction of "natural" boundaries by imagining a universal, transcendent history.[5]

Thus, the Wife's insistence that *she* is her tale (and that *her* experience can therefore record the fullness of women's experience) has often elicited a correspondingly strong and "naturally" masculinist response from male audiences. To those like the Friar or Jankyn, her fifth husband, those trying to embody that antifeminist, clerical tradition the Wife cites at the beginning of her prologue, this false "Wife" is living proof that "woman" can never rise above the natural limitations of her sex and can only embody a monstrous femininity; she therefore cannot be allowed access to masculine power. To pilgrims like the Clerk, the Merchant, and the Franklin, the Wife signals the deformative power of the feminine when it is not properly husbanded by a dominant masculinity, and her argument therefore demands the refutation provided by their delineations of proper, "real" femininity in the so-called Marriage Group.

These male reactions reinscribe ever more forcibly the Wife's explicit argument that biology is destiny, insisting that in the Wife's case authenticity and presence can register only marginality and disempowerment. The more strenuously she speaks, the less she "matters" and the more she registers as merely "feminine," albeit noisy, background to this (masculine) audience's conversation. And a succession of male critics, medieval and modern, have looked at the Wife and seen only the need to reinstall themselves (i.e., as properly masculine and heteronormative) and their desire (for hierarchized gender relations, the beautiful, docile woman, and so forth). In such a hermeneutic, feminine matter "naturally" forces a turn to the authority of the past. The very presentness of the tale's emphasis on experience works to ground and "prove" the naturalness of a universalizing, transcendent historiography—whether medieval hegemony disguised as God's plan or, in a later modern critical tradition, dominant male subjectivity disguised as "the universal man."

But the Wife's claim to function as the true voice of "woman" for the pilgrimage group also posits the possibility and legitimacy of an alternative "feminist" reading of the matter of woman, one that would look for its authority not to the "past" of dominant masculinity, but to a "future" of feminine autonomy, not to the stabilizing force of "what has been," but to the empowering speculation about "what can be." Implicit in the Wife's self-presentation, then, is the articulation of a desire to resist or even step outside the controlling lens of an authoritative, masculinist clerical tradition and view sex/gender relations otherwise. Such a "feminist" reaction embedded in the Wife's rhetorical strategy provokes a historicization of the feminine, foregrounding by means of the Wife's presence the actual lack of representation of an authentic women's experience. The pattern created by such a hermeneutical strategy is one of looking to a future (or for modern critics, an alternative Middle Ages discernible only to the modern reader), where the female voice can have a presence and authority denied in the medieval present.[6]

However much the Wife inscribes the fiction of presence, though, we will look in vain for certainty and truth in the various types of foundationalism practiced by such a "bodily presence." Instead we need to question both the naturalness and the authenticity of her "identity" as "*the* Wife of Bath" within the *Canterbury Tales*. The Wife may *say* she is revealing her true self by exposing her absolutely female body, but what we actually see is an excessively clothed, occluded body, and with that the impossibility of getting past the social construction of sex and gender difference.[7] The Wife's self-presentation, rather than providing a secure foundation for an authentic self, points to a discrepancy between activity in the present-day world and how such activity reaches representation, forms recognizable identities, and gains agency and power. The

Wife presents a vision of herself as quintessentially female and feminine (a picture authorized by prevailing masculinist ideologies). The consistency of this picture, however, disguises the significant ways in which this "authentic" self-presentation departs from how other accounts document the medieval practice of marriage and women's work among that wide group of people medieval social theory categorizes as "those who labor." To respond as fully as possible to the ways that the *Wife of Bath's Prologue and Tale* dream the present differently, then, we need to understand more fully their interruption of the kind of straight journey between male and female, masculine and feminine, past and present that patterns of reading constrained by hegemonic (and antihegemonic) ideologies have traditionally demanded.

There are several odd features that make this a complex and contradictory narrative, despite its apparent directness. The most striking is the Wife's claim that she was both married at the age of twelve and married three times (apparently in rapid succession) to men much older than herself. According to the Wife, the marriage market, for all its materialism, conceives of sex and gender in a socially decontextualized way: a woman's sole possession is her body (and later, her good name), and the only innate skills she can labor with are those of sexual play and feminine argument. Thus, the Wife marries at twelve, the earliest age possible because the point at which medieval authorities deemed the female body to be fully formed for sexual reproduction. And her first three marriages are contracted with rich old husbands, that is, with those men who in popular opinion are most able to pay top dollar for, and most likely to value, the female body as body. Both facts emphasize the successful "sale" of her beauty and sexual favor on the market. Her subsequent attempts to master these three old husbands by titillating rather than properly fulfilling male desire to produce a material surplus for herself are presented as the feminine out of control. In this way she becomes a monstrously flawed mirror image to that masculine (self) control that should be (according to hegemonic values) at work in the world she presents, but is not.

As with so much else in her self-portrait, the Wife implies that she differs from other women not in kind, but in the degree to which she embraces and exploits a conventional situation. But when we examine what we know about late medieval English marriage practice, we see that the Wife's self-presentation is in several ways outside the norm.

The demographic evidence for the period would seem to bear out John Hajnal's contention that the "Northwestern European Marriage Pattern" was generally quite different from the Wife's example.[8] The Wife's narrative would fit far more closely with the practice that seems to have prevailed in the Mediterranean south of Europe throughout the late medieval and early modern period, where marriage was almost universal and usually contracted between a young woman and an older man, and where the average age of the woman at marriage was mid-teens. In northwestern Europe, on the other hand, a later age of first marriage for both sexes appears to have prevailed, significant numbers of adults (including women) never married, and women in their first marriages generally married men close to their own age. Marriage at the earliest possible childbearing age, as the Wife suggests happened to her, would seem to have been more likely in northwest Europe with daughters of the very rich—nobles and members of the urban merchant patriciate—because of their value in cementing political and business alliances and in order to ensure their sexual purity. Even in such cases, however, the average age for these women to marry during the later Middle Ages was more likely to be the mid- to late teens, although arrangements for marriage and betrothal may have started in the early teens.[9]

In contrast, for nonelite women in northwest Europe in the later Middle Ages, the pattern was dramatically different from that described by the Wife. It would seem that for a broad band of subjects, both in village and town, from better-off peasant to artisan and merchant, the more material resources a family had at its disposal, the more likely a girl would marry later—in her late teens to mid-twenties. Indeed, the better the material situation of a young single woman, the more likely she would be to try (and be able to) defer marriage as long as possible.[10] In the first instance, such deferral allowed the accumulation of private property—whether land or movable goods—for single men and women to bring to marriage and to ensure their financial independence from their respective families. But in the case of women, deferral of marriage was an important, indeed perhaps the crucial, means by which they could assert and maintain a public as well as a private subject position for themselves.[11] As Judith Bennett has pointed out for women in the medieval countryside, conjugality defined gender by creating expectations that males would be publicly active householders and females passive dependents. Thus, for wives, an important public/private divide was established by marriage, so that it was primarily adolescent daughters and widows who had access to public forms of representation. Household status can often be more significant than gender in negotiating the private/public divides structuring the economic, social, and legal economies of village life. The significant difference between men/husbands and women/wives is that the former are always capable of adult public, active functions, whether married or not, while the latter are capable of "adult" public functions only if widowed or unmarried.[12]

The Wife's account also inscribes a presumptive marriageability by erasing the possibility of singleness—whether as a life-cycle single woman postponing marriage until her twenties or as a lifelong single woman. According to Maryanne Kowaleski, "estimates strongly suggest that singlewomen were almost as numerous in some medieval regions and cities as they were in the better-documented early modern period. Our firmest medieval data comes from late fourteenth-century England, where poll-tax data suggest that roughly 30 percent of all women aged 14 or older were single, although significant variations were evident, with towns hosting the highest percentage of singlewomen."[13] In contrast, in Italy in the same period, only fifteen percent of adult women were single. In this regard, the "wifeness" of the Wife of Bath's self-presentation mirrors the blinkered viewpoint of a medieval clerical tradition with regard to representing women. Commenting on the ways that thirteenth-century clerics categorized the social order in their sermon literature, Sharon Farmer notes:

> In their ad status sermons—sermons, that is, that were addressed to people of various walks of life—these authors usually categorized men according to their occupations or social status, and women according to their sexual or married status: nuns and virgins (either consecrated virgins or young girls), widow, and married women. Moreover, despite the fact that married women were considered the lowest of the three categories because they did not practice chastity, marriage, in this system of classification, was the prism through which all women were viewed.

Nuns were "married" to Christ and increasingly by the late medieval period under the control of male clerics. As Farmer has demonstrated, "unattached women in thirteenth- and early fourteenth-century Paris received institutional support only if they fit the prism of marriage—as widows did—or were willing to submit to male clerical authority" (as an equivalent to husbandly authority) by living in sanctioned quarters.[14]

The Wife does not mention lands or movable goods provided by her family as dowry, nor indeed anything at all about the social situation of her family. Her autobiography would insist instead that *she* is able only to draw on what is "natural" to her as woman, that is, her body, as her equivalent to family name, movable goods, or land in the marriage business. Her marketplace is the marriage bed; her wares, the desirability of her female body and whatever sexual favors she can "sell." In representing her situation this way, she reiterates the naturalness of the conventional equation of woman/wife and the private domain. Yet for all this emphasis on *her* body as *the female* body trapped in a marginalized femininity, the Wife of Bath also claims to present a highly individualistic account of a female body that has achieved a certain level of material success and public freedom within marriage. Her audience cannot but identify her as *the Wife of Bath,* noting in spite of themselves that she also represents the possibility of a female body successful *in her own right* without male protection and leadership (whether in the form of a husband, father, uncle, or priestly mentor). A corollary to this can be found in the habit of certain modern (mostly male) critics of addressing the Wife more intimately as "Alison," a similar recognition of her success in achieving "modern" autonomy in terms of a coherent individuality and selfhood. Here it seems particularly noteworthy that the character developed in the *Prologue* "succeeds" as *Wife* not widow, and moreover, as a wife who behaves *like a man* in assuming an active public function whether married or not.[15]

In doing so, I would argue, the representation of the Wife resists easy assimilation into the model of wife as *femme coverte de baron*—literally a woman "covered" by her husband—that defined her status under English common law. In doing so, the Wife also disrupts the patterns of male self-identification that depend on such a female nonidentity and the consequent linking of maleness and masculine hegemony that it makes possible.[16] The Wife's narrative *un*-covers, forces into the open, that which should be secret. Moreover, the polemical force of her argument seeks to establish her own success in converting marriage from hiding place to staging ground for her self-identification. Her repeated claim that she is working *in her own right* establishes a certain kind of female masculinity as the central issue in her representational strategies. In turn, what the Wife's account foregrounds, despite the supposed biological determinism of her "nature," is the crucial significance of individual and class *labor,* and its generation of a surplus production that provides the means for individual agency.[17]

This focus on the importance of labor and surplus production in the Wife's account suggests that "the real" that the Wife's presence represents is neither the biological determinism supposedly undergirding a dominant sex/gender system, nor the actual life experience of a particular class of medieval women, but rather the labor and surplus production of a new class of subjects in late medieval English society. The Wife thus presents the female body "clothed" in many of the appurtenances of "masculine" activity and its claim to power.[18] This more wayward intersection of sex (female) and gender (masculinity) taking place in the Wife's inscription of female presence in the *Tales* poses (to use Judith Halberstam's formulation) in fractal terms the gender geometries that map the relations between body and community.[19] If the *Wife of Bath's Tale* provides a strong, politicized critique of dominant masculinity, it is not by presenting the Wife as a simple either/or choice within a transhistorical, "natural" sex/gender binary—monstrous femininity or laughable imitation of real masculinity—but instead as an example of a performative "female masculinity" that interrupts the kind of straight journey between male and female, masculine and feminine that would allow us comfortably to "end" in a dominant and heternormative masculinity and its productive circulations of male power.

Such a view leads us in different directions from the stabilizing approaches taken to gender by both Carolyn Dinshaw in *Chaucer's Sexual Poetics* and Lee Patterson in *Chaucer and the Subject of History*. For Dinshaw, the Wife of Bath's autobiographical narrative starkly sets her "joly body" up against the oppressive teaching and glossing of a patriarchal tradition.[20] Patterson, on the other hand, sees the Wife's countering of the social authority of the Man of Law as moving "from the political opposition generated by the class inequality of Fragment I to an ideological antithesis determined by gender," one that necessarily links the Wife with the woman's realm of the asocial and thus with a politics of individualism rather than class-determined dissent.[21] I would argue instead that the "middle" role opened up for women in the conjugality of the marriage sacrament, and its openness to thinking the unequal equal, as well as the importance of such conjugality in articulating the individual household as a place where individuals might share equal footing on a lateral plane and where their right to exist *as* an entity is assumed from within rather than conferred from without, keeps the sexual politics here political in the widest possible sense. The Wife's claim to be "wife" and "gentil" in her own right embodies a middleness that does not admit the kinds of containment or decontextualization that Patterson describes. The Wife's exploration of marriage in her prologue and tale articulates that location as one of hybridity, where clerical definitions of marriage can be turned against attempts at outside control. Marital conjugality maps both social responsibility and private life, career and character, a regulatory system and a place where its participants might imagine sharing equal footing on a lateral plane. The Wife's exploration of marriage imagines that location as a place where its subjectivities can be assumed from within, rather than simply conferred from without. Late medieval "gentil" marriage—neither the early modern bourgeois household where fathers ruled, nor the feudal/Catholic hierarchy writ small—as it is articulated by the Wife has within it an unstable mobility crossing both Wallace's absolutist lineages and associational forms.[22]

What is so easily glossed over in the Wife's feminist/antifeminist account of female marital activity is the room for maneuver made possible by the conflicting legal and social definitions of "wife" and "middle" class during this period. As Mary Carruthers notes:

> The customs of the bourgeoisie, customs that had the effect of law, gave propertied married women rights that were denied them by both the common law (which affected the rights of women whose property was held in manorial fiefs) and the canon law. Among the burgesses, married women retained the ownership and control of their property and could enter into contracts in their own name, their husbands having neither legal liability nor power of consent in such matters. . . . When custom conflicted with common law, the Court of Common Pleas tended to rule in favor of the custom.[23]

Carruthers further situates the Wife as an active agent within a vital late medieval English wool trade, not as a simple weaver, but rather as "a capitalist clothier, one of those persons who oversaw the whole process of cloth manufacture—buying the cloth, contracting the labor of the various artisans involved in manufacture, and sending bales of finished broadcloths off to Bristol and London for export."[24] And Julia Bolton Holloway, Joan Bechtold, and Constance S. Wright have pointed out that "Bath city records, for instance, show us women as prosperous property owners as a result of their textile labors—as we see with the Wife of Bath."[25] D. W. Robertson Jr. argues more specifically and tendentiously that "[o]ne of the most striking features of this rising cloth industry was its rural character" and cites, among others, R. E. Glasscock's statement that during the fourteenth century "cloth-making was spreading rapidly in the rural areas made possible by the spread of the fulling mill, and encouraged by urban entrepreneurs who, free from the restrictions of town gilds, could produce cloth more cheaply in rural areas."[26] Robertson provides as a model for the Wife a bondwoman, Margery Haynes, who in 1435 at Castle Combe in Wiltshire inherited from her first husband chattels including a fulling mill and a gig mill for teaseling cloth, maintaining control over her holdings throughout her second marriage: "Margery was a singularly wealthy woman, in spite of being a bondwoman. Her mills undoubtedly supplied a generous income, and the fulling mill and gig mill must have been especially profitable, since they would serve the needs of some of her fellow clothiers as well as her own. . . . A 'milling-place' might be small in area, but the cash flow to be expected from it would have been far greater than that from many acres of agricultural land, or from a large number of borough tenements."[27] Beryl Rowland, on the other hand, finds the textual and historical evidence to be against any elevation of the Wife from artisan weaver to capitalist entrepreneur.[28] And Heather Swanson notes that medieval artisans did not easily form a coherent, self-conscious group, and ranged from the wealthy and prestigious to the indigent and even destitute. She points out that for most of the fourteenth and fifteenth centuries, the greatest generator of wealth was not industrial production or investment, but the control of trade. In larger towns and cities, therefore, a merchant class was able to emerge and form a closed elite, creating the means by which to define a clear separate artisan class. In smaller towns, however, individual artisans were able to rise to positions of leadership in the local community, a situation inconceivable in larger centers.[29]

The Wife of Bath, of course, is *not* a historical figure. Nor is it reasonable to assume that we will somehow find *one* true historical model that will capture her essence. What is more important to note is the particular resonance that both "clothmaker" and a West Country location might have in late fourteenth-century England, as well as the great variety and potential contradiction within supposedly unified categories such as "Wife" and "bourgeois," since it is this instability that the Wife's self-representation both obscures and foregrounds. Much critical ink, for example, has been spilled over the Wife of Bath's signing control of her lands and possessions to Jankyn, her fifth husband. Yet it was not uncommon for an older, propertied wife married to a younger husband to sign over control of her business interests as a public sign of trust that would provide the younger man with the necessary authority within the local community to better manage the household business interests. If this were the case with the Wife of Bath and Jankyn, her signing over control of her property could be viewed as signifying not so much venereal besottedness as good business practice. Jankyn's supposedly "masculine" display, reading clerical exhortations against the dangers of wayward wives, would then emphasize instead Jankyn's own lack of business acumen and blindness to the bourgeois success that commitment to his wife can bring. Similarly, the Wife's associations with clothmaking at this particular moment in late fourteenth-century England and the West Country, far from proving female abjection and provincial inferiority, place her at the center of recent English economic achievement and of an economy moving rapidly beyond past feudal social and economic models. Even such acts as her pushing forward at the offering in her parish service or her marriages at the church door present us with a subject fully involved in local parish life in a way consistent with a successful bourgeois subject. Her self-presentation as an old bawd and sexual predator, then, is ideological obfuscation of this Wife's participation and success in *public* masculine enterprise and commitment to an orthodox conjugality in marriage.

The Wife of Bath's portrayal of female masculinity and its paradoxes thus opens up the question of politics in the *Wife of Bath's Tale* in two ways. The first works to disturb hegemonic modes of gender representation and the circulation of power that depends on the stability of dominant masculinity. The second reveals the contradictions and discoherences occasioned by the kind of economic and political change happening in late medieval English society. In both instances, the Wife's foregrounding and re-presenting of marriage acts as a medium for a strong engagement with late medieval/early modern representational politics. Her request to the pilgrimage "compaignye" that they not get annoyed "If that I speke after my fantasye," since her "entente nys but for to pleye" (III.189–94), needs to be understood at two levels. In acknowledging no "auctoritee" for her "self" in the traditional hegemonic medieval epistemologies, the Wife echoes the position of that group of people motoring the economy of late medieval England (and accounting for the dramatic change in production that within a hundred years turned the English wool trade from one exporting raw materials to Flemish processors to one producing its own cloth for internal consumption and export) and its surplus production in the countryside and provincial towns. This is a class situation capable of moving her into some kind of "rightful" association with "the gentils," a regional equivalent of the lesser guildsmen, but one whose mixing of urban and rural, artisan and merchant, whose provincial vernacularity in short, also keeps the Wife embarrassingly proximate to "churls" like the Miller or the Reeve. The Wife's social situatedness, like her sexual politics, registers as hybridity and carries with it a political volatility that cannot be completely contained.

The Wife's emphasis on "pleye," then, participates in a discursive system that would interpellate her and her kind as inferior, yet at the same time insists via its subtext on the very real labor such subjectivities perform and thus the crucial way in which they must have put in play successful and necessary identities. We tend to think of the Wife's emphasis on play as necessarily leading to abjection at the hands of hegemonic authority (emphasizing as it does an untenable autonomous female body and a monstrously uncontrolled feminine). But the Wife's play also reprises the Miller's intervention into the Canterbury social order, this time from a more elevated social and economic position that cannot neatly be labeled "churlish." As Carruthers has noted, "The *MED [Middle English Dictionary]* glosses of 'maistrye,' 'maister,' and 'maistress(e)' make it clear that in Middle English 'mastery' connotes skill and the authority or control deriving from superior ability, rather than the idea of simple dominance devoid of merit or skill."[30] And while the Wife, like the Miller, makes a similarly "personal" argument for disgracefully uncontrolled play (now not low-class drunkenness but a biological female imperative), for such an argument really to be persuasive for her audience, that audience would have to remain dangerously superficial in its reasoning and pompously obtuse in its hermeneutic. The

Wife, therefore, seems to be playing with the way "estate" describes something both contingent and open to individual manipulation—that is, referring to the different kinds of vocation-related positions both men and women could occupy in late medieval society—and supposedly "natural" and fixed—that is, reconfiguring the "asocial" position the estate of woman occupied.[31]

The Wife's association with marriage is often interpreted as placing her in a private, individual "woman's" realm, one of those factors linking her with the sphere of "the feminine." This association is reinforced by the fact that her stagings of marriage—notably her argument with the first three old husbands, her fight with Jankyn, and the loathly hag's lecture to her new husband in the tale proper—all take place in the privacy of the bedchamber. But clearly marriage for the Wife and her society can never be simply women's business, nor a truly private matter. The joys and woes of marriage that she makes the material of her narrative condense complex social, political, and economic structures governing late medieval society.[32] One of the main differences between this tale and the *Miller's Tale* is precisely this sense of the necessary intersection of "public" discourses with the supposedly "private," and with that, a historicization of marriage, dominant masculinity, and social change. In each of the three linked stagings of "the wo that is in marriage" that take place in the prologue and tale, the wife's combination of female body and "masculine" behavior provokes a reconsideration of dominant masculinity, the gender question, and the social hierarchies that depend on such distinctions.

Thinking through the Wife's attempts at agency as *female masculinity* rather than opposition or subversive reinscription of the feminine can help focus attention on her engagement with the new, fourteenth-century attempt to think dominant masculinity differently. In the face of bourgeois activity in the world, social mobility, a quest for precedence, and an emphasis on work and meritocracy, can the Wife's predilection for mastery, her pridefulness, her emphasis on material success earned by her own efforts appear only as a monstrous femininity? In important ways, the Wife's performance is as successfully "masculine" as that practiced by dominant masculinity in the world of the here and now; and equally importantly, we see this masculinity represented in the tale via the "wayward" female body. The Wife, as she makes clear, is no heretic. She makes no attempt to chart the marginalized, innovative path. She vociferously accepts the roles assigned by the state apparatuses structuring dominant gender ideologies. As a result, it is easy for her audience to assume that they know in some absolute sense who she is and what her "natural" place should be—female, wife, working person. But is such knowledge ever so securely knowable? Her articulation of her estate is not in feminine terms only, however much her male audience might like to fix it so. Instead her estate—woman, wife, "bourgeoise"—is articulated "like masculinity," as she constantly seeks to be on top by making the most of her situation in terms of material success and power. She is that conundrum: the wife who is not content to order the household, to provide a feminine ballast to her husband, to make procreation and mothering her first business. Instead she uses the forms of another's institutional power to further her own ends (rather like an upwardly mobile "gentil" man who will act like his betters to further his own ends), marrying at the church door but getting what she wants, recognizing that success depends on the ostentatious show of success. Nor do we see proper male masculinity at work in her prologue or tale. Men are present, but the Wife's narrative insists superficially ("wrongly" in hegemonic terms) and in the deep structures of its narrative (a way much harder to argue against) that masculinity is "up for grabs," a floating signifier with "woman" as its commodity fetish. Thus the Wife's is a female masculinity that shows us the construction of dominant masculinity without reinscribing the male bodies in which such masculine power traditionally inheres.

As noted in chapter 2, Jo Ann McNamara suggests that in the twelfth and thirteenth centuries, the primacy of celibacy and the reaction to unhusbanded women led to a linking of women with the feminine and a claustration of such bodies either literally within monasteries under the control of celibate male clergy or legally and metaphorically in marriage. She notes in this regard that "[t]he imagery associated with celibate women as brides of Christ was revived in male rhetoric, where it firmly placed even the most resolute virgin in the gender system as a structural wife."[33] The example of Margery Kempe and the work of Caroline Walker Bynum and others would suggest that, by the later Middle Ages, marriage and the necessarily positive (if unequal) valence assigned to the feminine within it encouraged some women to find agency and authority through the conceptual freedom that the wifely and maternal estate afforded when translated onto a spiritual discursive terrain. Through the concept of spiritual marriage, the femininity of Christ, and so forth, these women were able to carve out an authoritative space within a gender binarism favoring dominant masculinity.[34]

It is particularly interesting in this regard that the Wife and her tale make no attempt to invigorate the conceptual power of the feminine; rather her prologue and tale appear to embrace an excessively and violently gendered world in which masculinity is naturally dominant. Notable here is the fact that within the confines of the tale, *men* want marriage; moreover, what they really want—even when they don't know it and when their estate ideologies would say otherwise (both Jankyn as could-have-been cleric and the rapist in the tale as aristocratic knight)—are the benefits of a companionate conjugality. The Wife lives in a world far removed from Fontevraud Abbey in the twelfth century as described by McNamara, where men and women living together in apostolic poverty and chastity dressed alike, worked together, and generally blurred distinctions of class and gender. In the Wife's world, estate, sex, and place in the gender hierarchy are written very clearly on the body and in one's costume and actions. What the Wife does do, however, is to present two of the master narratives shoring up the old order, where control of the world is divided between a celibate clergy and a married lay aristocracy: clerical antifeminist satire and courtly romance. But in the process she emphasizes the pastness of both such narratives and the gender hierarchies they inscribe; instead she presents us with a present in which old styles of domination are not the crucial issue.

In this way, her self-presentation in the *Tale* gestures toward a "dropping out" of traditional gendered power structures. That is, in the first instance, the Wife foregrounds a masculinity separated from its "natural" foundations. (Later in this chapter we will see how, paradoxically, elsewhere in the *Canterbury Tales* other narratives work to secure this floating masculinity for new male subject positions.) In the second instance, the Wife's foregrounding of such an alternative masculinity allows not just ideologically conservative but also unpredictable associations—a less organized body and a more gender-confused "Wife" and "marriage." The *Wife of Bath's Prologue and Tale* thus condenses in its account of marriage how a new group of men imagine themselves at the center of male power and dominant masculinity, or rather how marriage allows this identification of a wider group of people as ruling caste subjects. The Wife's rhetorical relish in announcing *her* centrality in her household and community—in the marriage bed, in parish life, in local commerce, in the Canterbury pilgrimage group—acts as a vocal re-presentation of a group of secular men (i.e., those "gentil" men dominating the pilgrimage group) and their insistence on their place at the table in the aftermath of the twelfth-century masculinist compact. Spanning the urban/rural, peasant/bourgeois, male/female divides of the late fourteenth century, the unseemliness of the Wife and her individualistic and uncategorizable energy "represents" this middle of late medieval economic, political, and social activity. Compare her, for example, to the Guildsmen and their wives—the wives do what the Wife does, but via their husbands, and the Wife does what the Guildsmen do, but without their institutional guarantees of a properly bourgeois masculinity. The Wife of Bath's emphasis on the value of labor and on the "middleness" of her socioeconomic position (securely connected neither to a rural landed gentry nor to an urban merchant patriciate) thus foregrounds a moment akin to that which McNamara talks about for the twelfth century. There, it was a transgressive by-product of the Gregorian Reform's emphasis on celibacy; here, it is a by-product of that same reform's necessary (and protracted) revaluation of the feminine and marriage. And the *Wife of Bath's Tale* postulates a similar gender parity in relationships between men and women (and also between classes of people). This is the move that the deportment books, such as the *Menagier de Paris* or that of the Knight of La Tour Landry, would work against, as they attempt to reinstall gentility along with (and by means of) a domesticated femininity.

Let us look at the incident with Jankyn and his book at the end of the prologue. Here we need to note the movement from a universalizing "they say" and a disembodied authority that the Wife so unsuccessfully reacts against at the opening of the prologue to the inscription of the voice of dominant masculinity in the book that Jankyn reads from and in the context of a marriage between the Wife and a clerk. This materialization and commodification of dominant masculinity and the hegemonic power of celibacy and the clerisy work to place such power within a particularized present, within a "modern" moment open to change and reconfiguration:

> But now to purpos, why I tolde thee
> That I was beten for a book, pardee! . . .
> And whan I saugh he wolde nevere fyne

> To reden on this cursed book al nyght,
> Al sodeynly thre leves have I plyght
> Out of his book right as he radde, and eke
> I with my fest so took him on the cheke
> That in oure fyr he fil bakward adoun. (III.711–12, 788–93)

This moment of clerical citation by Jankeyn re-presents the opening "They say" citation of clerical antifeminism by the Wife at the beginning of the *Prologue*. Now, however, such citation registers clearly as a performative that inscribes the construction of dominant masculinity. But more importantly, this citation is historicized differently from the universalizing historicizing of the opening or from a modernist sequential historiography. The Wife reacts in terms of a female masculinity—neither a monstrous feminine seeking dominance over the male, nor the husbanded and controlled feminine of bourgeois companionate marriage. Although we are encouraged to see this concluding altercation simply as a repetition of the Wife's relationships with her first three husbands (but now with the older Wife taking the place of the three old husbands), its manifestation under the sign of the Wife's female masculinity changes how it signifies. For the Wife now also calls on Jankyn to recognize identifications in excess of the univocality offered by his clerical authorities. That is, his situation as husband and local agent inserts class markers that are potentially at odds with traditional clerical discourses; his current wife, for example, could be of material benefit in furthering his career. In a curious way, the Wife's intervention with the book also underscores that the book is getting in the way of her being a helpmeet to her mate. If she is to provide an interlocutory relationship that can help Jankyn articulate subject positions that will let him navigate the complexity of the present, he must first be able to hear what she is saying (and in a larger sense see and hear the full range of possibility that she can bring to the relationship). This will necessarily demand her behaving in a "masculine" fashion. What the Wife is encouraging here is the possibility not of "they say/you are," but an I/you relationship fluid and mobile in its set of identifications and its interrelationships with ideologies.

Compare this to the misguided kiss of the *Miller's Tale* and the uses of the female body there. What makes the latter moment staged by the Wife poignant and powerful is its shrewd reading of current circulations of power and manipulations of a representational system along with its representation of a desire for difference, change, and productivity. Therefore, it is not just a cynical grab for power (whether through the overt search for female "maistrie" on the part of the Wife, or representationally, as a means of containing the feminine in order to further the inscription of dominant masculinity for a new class of male readers). Nor is it simply the articulation of a future desire (i.e., a feminine reality that will be fully voiced by modern readers). Instead this is a desire to make the most of the *present* based on a clear-sighted, multiple understanding of that present moment. It is the masochist's desire to push the body beyond its limits, as it were. Thus, when the Wife rips the offending pages from Jankyn's book of wicked wives and shoves him into the fire, Jankyn retaliates by boxing her ears (leading, we are told, to her deafness). But in the end, the Wife maintains, Jankyn is forced into an apology by her verbal and physical abuse of him. Here symbolic violence (the sadism of clerical antifeminism) leads to physical violence (the Wife's tearing a leaf out of Jankyn's book) and then to a different kind of violence (the Wife's subsequently hitting Jankyn on the cheek and his agreement to her mastery) that marks a masochistic contract assumed by the male. This signals an interesting replay of the "Shame on you" of the *Miller's Tale*. Here a potentially shameful acceptance of the Wife's mastery (and her female masculinity) is actually the means for doing things differently. This action makes clear the dominant processes of male masculinity's sadistic mastery (learning the profession) even as it suggests an alternative self-professing in Jankyn's imagined adoption of the Wife's masochistic contract and a different kind of "maistrie." Understanding the gender geometries of these exchanges in fractal terms thus resists stabilizing views of the feminine as some momentary "escape" or position of unknowability whose only purpose ultimately is to enable a move to dominant masculinity's order.[35]

The *Wife of Bath's Prologue*, then, historicizes dominant masculinity not as some monolithic universal (as a citational method of clerical antifeminism would encourage) but as located in a particular present moment. More importantly, via female masculinity, the *Prologue* reveals the construction of dominant masculinity and encourages the desire for something other. It underscores that what we are seeing is *not* directly relatable back to "real" life or to a transcendent, universal "real." The

Wife does not tell us something real about late medieval women; indeed, in important ways, her difference from reality is underscored. What she and her story "represent" are the desires for dominance (seen most clearly with the group of "new men") of a section of contemporary society. Because this is not yet "real" this desire is potentially nomadic and capable of appropriation. Thus the Wife comes in for condemnation because she is too successfully "modern."[36] She at once embodies the fearfulness of a society in which change and presentism could feminize and disorganize male power and also the concomitant but antithetical desire for exactly enough change and fluidity so that a group of men could enter the center of dominant masculinity and male power. Resisting established and hegemonic linkages between sex and gender in this way helps us attend to how the *Wife of Bath's Tale* focuses on "becoming" rather than "being," functioning as a mapping rather than a tracing of sex, gender, and sexuality, and encouraging thinking about identity as a process with multiple sites for becoming and being.[37] And in doing so the *Tale* thus interrupts the naturalization of a universalizing historiography at work in maintaining the male in dominant masculinity.

## Boy Talk and Conjugality under Control: Two Case Studies

I close my discussion of the so-called marriage debate with the two tales told by lay male narrators reacting to the Wife of Bath because each in different ways attempts to normalize and contain the Wife's claim to present the usually abjected terms of medieval debate on her own terms. Both the *Merchant's Tale* and the *Franklin's Tale* attempt to organize gender and social relations within conjugality in order to stabilize their potentially uncertain middle social situation. Bringing conjugality under the control of its own subjects in this way—as opposed to organizing it from above by a celibate clerisy—potentially establishes it as a vital zone of belief and practice that straddles the domains of the individual and the collective, the private and the public, the household and the world, so that it can become exactly that place where the new disciplinary culture of a modernizing elite can spectacularly turn itself into an exercise in self-discipline.

## PRESENT PANIC IN THE *MERCHANT'S TALE*

Modern criticism of the *Merchant's Tale* has remained curiously preoccupied with two related questions: first, how much the character of the newly wed and supposedly bitter Merchant in the tale's prologue affects the tale, and second, the tale's "apparent failure of decorum, its mixing of genres, styles, voices, and tones, of pagan and Christian elements, even of narrative levels."[38] Originating with Kittredge and J. S. P. Tatlock and followed by G. G. Sedgewick, E. T. Donaldson, Norman T. Harrington, and others, the prevailing critical tradition has seen the tale as a darkly reductive satire of marriage dominated by the bitterness and cynicism of the Merchant.[39] This view has also led many readers of the tale to see the so-called marriage encomium (IV.1267–1392) at its beginning not as January's voice, but as a direct intervention by the disgruntled Merchant into the marriage debate.[40] Dissenting opinions have challenged a too-close identification of Merchant and January and focused instead on the tale's comic features as a lighthearted satire of the "old lover" figure in the tradition of fabliau and folktale.[41] More recently, Lee Patterson has attempted to cut across this critical divide by attending to the complexities of the Merchant's class position as they relate to subjectivity in the tale and account for the many apparent contradictions of the Merchant's presentation of himself and his tale.[42] For Patterson, "The point is not that the Merchant nihilistically believes nothing but rather than [sic] he simultaneously does and does not believe everything. Teller of an almost perfectly self-canceling *Tale,* the Merchant is revealed as searching for but unable to find a system of values, beliefs, and meanings—an ideology—by which to endow his world with meaning.... Moreover, and most brilliantly, he [Chaucer] shows us that what this instability of social identity precipitates is an ideology of the subject. Lacking a secure social identity, the Merchant is overwhelmed by an inner selfhood, what he calls at the outset the 'soory herte' (1244) that his *Tale* seeks to silence but everywhere expresses."[43] For Patterson the Merchant's lack of a social identity and thus a secure prospect on the world drives him to focus "with obsessive attention upon the inner landscape of unsatisfied desire that is staged in his own failed marriage."[44] And this deflection of the animating psychological dynamic of the tale, from his social identity as merchant to his failed marriage, accounts for the contradictions that the tale harbors.

Patterson makes, I think, an extremely valuable intervention into the critical stalemate that has so often characterized critical approaches to this tale, especially in foregrounding the importance of ideology in the tale's complex narrative strategies around identity and interiority. But the separation Patterson establishes between the Merchant's social identity (as a potential location for a representational politics) and marriage (as the location of an isolated inner selfhood unable to articulate a confident class ideology) sets up an overly stabilizing binary, one that misses the agential possibilities that the tale's treatment of marriage provides for its male author and audience. Rather than constructing an ahistorical, isolated inner self that reflects the Merchant's sense of lack within the present social imaginary, the tale's focus on marriage and interiority provides the means by which such "new" subjects learn the necessary self-discipline through which they can both fit into and articulate a new disciplinary order.

The Merchant's outburst after the *Clerk's Tale* seems as oddly untypical in estate terms as the so-called Lenvoy de Chaucer with which the Clerk ends his tale. So successful was the business caution displayed by the Merchant in the *General Prologue,* where his "resons he spak ful solempnely, / Sownyng alwey th'encrees of his wynnyng"—and where "So estatly [he] was . . . of his governaunce" that "Ther wiste no wighte that he was in dette"—that the narrator could not even learn his name (I.274–75, 280–81). Yet this same Merchant, now simply as a result of hearing the *Clerk's Tale,* appears willing to self-identify in ways that seem as dangerously transparent, personal, and domestic as the Wife of Bath. The Merchant here characterizes himself solely as a henpecked husband unable to stop himself from breaking into a highly personal and unflattering account of the "wepyng and waylyng, care and oother sorwe" (IV.1213) he has known in his two months of marriage to a tyrannical and shrewish wife. The dramatic effect created by the Merchant's outburst thus threatens to provoke a series of potentially debilitating self-identifications reminiscent of the Wife of Bath. The structure of the *Merchant's Tale* itself also continues this parallel between Merchant and Wife by encouraging readers to see it as a darkly comic realization of the Wife's insights about the "woe that is in marriage," but now from the husband's point of view. The overt action of the *Merchant's Tale* duplicates the masculinist antifeminism that structures the Wife's argument in her prologue: that the female body is all desire, that a young wife wants mastery of the old husband's fortune, that women are inveterate liars, and so forth. At the level of the tale's deep structure, January's excessive self-indulgence produces a male effeminacy that acts as a mirror image of the Wife's female masculinity. This characterization of January also curiously parallels the Wife's excessive "wifeliness" (with her multiple marriages and embrace of her "barley bread" status) and its disturbance of the heteronormative power of traditional marriage discourses. January, as much as the Wife of Bath, constitutes a kind of unimaginable limit case for medieval practice and theory concerning lay sexuality—a prosperous layman who insists on absolute freedom of choice about marriage and individual fulfillment and who, inversely to the Wife, postpones marriage till the last possible moment. Like the Wife, his method of self-presentation emphasizes unbridled desire and self-gratification. Like her, too, he "accedes" to hegemonic authority by marrying, but in such a way that rhetorically he can persuade himself that he has evaded such institutional control.

The initial effect of the Merchant's outburst—intended or not—would thus appear to bracket the tale with an autobiographical frame that clearly encourages its audience to draw parallels between the experience of the newly married (and thus henpecked) Merchant-narrator and the old husband January in the tale, deceived and cuckolded by his libidinous young wife and squire. The Merchant comes to visibility in the pilgrimage moment framing his tale, like the Wife of Bath, apparently shaped by the exigencies of embodiment, and thus claiming to speak with an experiential authority whose very basis in personal felt experience denies it "real" authority. However, the Merchant's autobiographical outburst also clearly works to secure him agency at a crucial point in the pilgrimage; for the Host, sensing an interesting story, asks him to tell a tale following the Clerk. The apparently spontaneous turn to autobiography that prefaces the *Merchant's Tale* might therefore be read as a staged interruption intent on securing the very agency that it gets. Unlike the Wife of Bath, the Merchant's appeal to the personal carries no threat of hijacking the Canterbury project from other male participants, but instead gains him agency by underscoring his access to a public community of fellow men by assuming the husband's voice in a way that the Clerk—as celibate—could not (a shortcoming that ensures that the Clerk ends up speaking, in part, from the place of Griselda rather than Walter). We might in fact read the Merchant here not as engaged in an uncontrolled outburst, but instead as carefully controlling his release of "personal" information. This control actually stands in stark contrast to the performance of the Wife of Bath, especially when he makes very clear that *his* experience will not and cannot be the subject of his tale—"of myn owene soore, / For soory herte, I telle may namoore" (IV.1243–44).

The Merchant seems intent, then, on re-forming that very masculine control and self-definition abrogated by the Wife's rhetoric. To do so, he restages in as complex and calculating a fashion as possible the masochistic contract we saw laid out in the deep structures of the fabliau form of the *Miller's Tale*. But the Merchant here focuses such an inventing with the body clearly in terms of the problematic hybridity of the married estate: capable of bringing the secular man on par with the cleric, but also putting masculine and feminine, public and private, transcendent and material, in an intimate and mutually constitutive relationship as "one body." Precisely because there is nothing purely one thing or the other, nothing absolutely stable or given about this estate, it provides the ideal situation in which to work out how a properly masculine subject goes about disciplining the body in relation to his community. Marriage in the *Merchant's Tale,* then, stands in for a broader social and political experience that cannot be represented or talked about directly by the Merchant and his sect (here, too, he clearly marks himself off from the Wife and her mode of self-representation). If the tale that follows arises out of his experience, its presentation makes sure that any personal message is conveyed indirectly and safely. The supposedly personal, domestic revelation of the Merchant's marital state thus constitutes a similarly indirect pattern of speech. Its focus on the tyranny of a shrewish wife marks not a simple condemnation of marriage per se, but a carefully framed comment on the dangerously destabilizing account of "wife" by the Wife of Bath and the overly accommodating presentation of a tyrannical ruling class's right to rule by the Clerk.

In this regard, the Merchant's new condition and the dangers it poses—the private loss of household control to a shrewish wife threatening the kind of stable, public reputation necessary for mercantile success in uncontrollable and unpredictable ways—can be read as shorthand for the dangerous middle ground this new class of male subjects inhabits. Unlike the Clerk (or the husband in the *Menagier de Paris,* who uses the tale of Griselda to shape a young wife's feminine nature), the Merchant does *not* focus his tale on the reformation of the feminine by means of a masculine male will disciplining the female body. Rather, the Merchant in his attempt to reform masculinity risks taking up the Wife's focus on a male body abjected by its relations with the female, indeed now focusing attention on the (ef)feminizing power of male desire in such a situation. If the *Clerk's Tale* moves its audience from one naturalized identity (where *gentillesse* equals noble birth) to another (where *gentillesse* equals noble behavior), it also naturalizes a new kind of feminine (one akin to that outlined in the deportment books) as the anchor of such a masculine identity. Thus Griselda's innate and rocklike goodness is the ultimate signifier of Walter's inherent goodness, borne out in his initial discernment in choosing her. The *Merchant's Tale,* on the contrary, exposes the contradictions inherent in such a view and explores the performativity of such identities and the masculine/feminine, ruler/ruled, noble/churl binaries on which they are founded. This may be why he is at such pains to respond to, and underscore, the claim in the *envoy* to the *Clerk's Tale* that the Griseldas of the world are long gone and that his present (and ours) has a different, more difficult system of identifications through which identity is claimed, (re)produced, and maintained.

The Merchant is, like the Wife of Bath, hyperaware of hegemonic forces that would interpellate present selves, deciding who we are and what we signify. But he is also intent on establishing common ground with such forces, reassuring his access to their power by virtue of his gendered/sexualized status as husband (and a thrifty husbandman of the resources given to him).[45] The Merchant is also intent on *not* being seen as embodying, as the Wife of Bath did, either the fearfulness of a society in which change and presentism could feminize and disorganize male power or the concomitant but antithetical desire for exactly enough change and fluidity so that a group of men could enter the center of dominant masculinity and male power. The *Merchant's Tale* focuses such potential anxiety in two directions, both embodying a potentially shameful identification of merchants and their class, but also both in crucial ways clearly "other" to this merchant narrator: first, on the inherent waywardness of the female body of May, who like the Wife of Bath embodies a certain bourgeois energy and upward mobility, and, second, on the feminized body of January, whose unhusbanded desire is here associated with the excess of a foreign knightly class. If the *Merchant's Tale* functions structurally as a mirror image of the *Wife of Bath's Prologue and Tale,* then, it is to contain the latter's unpredictable energy in appropriate disciplinary forms and thereby resolve the very problems it raised. The Wife brought home her story, literally in her autobiographical prologue and metaphorically in her English Arthurian tale. The Merchant resolutely "others" his material by emphasizing its distance from his life story and by "exoticizing" it with an Italian knightly setting.[46] We could go on with a series of such comparisons: the Wife emphasizing the control of biological nature, gender, ideology, female masculinity, a wandering "middle" methodology; the Merchant emphasizing the self-control of an individual perversity, the rule of the law, male effeminacy, a teleological methodology. In this way, the dangerous proliferation of pleasure, mixing of past and present, generic and gender confusion that the Wife's storytelling emphasized becomes in the hands of the Merchant a supposedly contained object lesson safely "out there." Male effeminacy is confined to the solipsistic self-regard of an entrenched nobility, and the wayward class and gender confusion that results from such lack of self-control in one's "betters" is inscribed on "lower-order" bodies in January's household. More generally, this kind of perversity and potential insurgency is carefully contained within that which is authoritatively "story" (not the confusing autobiography of the Wife) and within the debased location of extreme presentism (not noble "old story," but one set within the confines of a foreign, Italian mercantilism and its blurring of traditional class distinctions). The kinds of potential economic, social, and epistemological divisions raised by the Wife within the "home"—English society, the ideal household—can thus be occluded in the circumlocutions of the Merchant.

Unlike the Wife, then, the Merchant's "thick description" of a present moment is not intent on dreaming the present differently. Rather he attempts to insert himself at the center of a conservative enterprise that would re-form that dominant masculine control and self-definition abrogated by the Wife's rhetoric (and at a deeper level threatened by her valorization of individual desire). In articulating such a reformation of masculine self-control, the Merchant must also acknowledge (and attempt to contain) powerful threats to it—one from "above," that is, from an unthrifty (self)-consumption of an entrenched aristocracy and a lack of excess production of the clerisy *and* the other from "below," from a potentially uncontrollable category confusion provoked by the desire for change of the "lower" estates (wives, feminized others, an undefined about-to-become gentry group of people). The Merchant thus attempts to reconstitute that disciplined and disciplinary masculine gaze of an authoritative past within the complexity of the present moment. But the internal contradictions occasioned by his possible identification with the very male protagonist he is satirizing, his mixing of fabliau and the romance genre, the alternating sexed and gendered perspectives the tale provides on its action, all are indicative of the tale's inscription of the impossibility of securing the very stable, unitary satiric perspective it appears to desire. For if the end of the *Merchant's Tale* is to set the Wife (and husbands and wives generally) straight about marriage and sex/gender relations, this is an enterprise that the Merchant must acknowledge still needs to value change positively, that must value the circulation and increase of capital. How, then, can one reform the present (and future?) in a traditional satiric mode when one remains oriented to present change and the progressive futurity change makes possible? This is the double bind that the *Merchant's Tale* both acknowledges and attempts to occlude: to build on the kind of personal profit that the Wife so unembarrassedly embodied and that motors the discursive economy of the Merchant, his estate, and the hegemonic social forces they are part of, and yet to maintain the natural predominance of stable identities and the stable social order they undergird. The Merchant is thus intent on ensuring that "one" will control one's household and oneself (with this "one" being self-consciously a socially entitled male subject masquerading as the universal category). But the tale remains imbricated in the very category confusion it seeks to resist and ultimately can do no more than proffer its brand of masculine hegemony as one alternative among many.

The tale's location in Italy is especially noteworthy in this regard, for January epitomizes that society's amalgamation of the old-style feudal model for aristocratic male identity with the practices of late medieval proto-capitalism. As a character, then, January embodies both a fantasy of merchant patriciate *practice* successfully wedded to the hegemonic *forms* of chivalric identity and an anxiety over the perverse slippages that such a pursuit of modernity might make possible. January is characterized repeatedly by his desire to embrace the new, a process condensed in his decision to marry May. Despite January's knightly status, we see little evidence of the old feudal order or its ideological modes. There is no evidence of the extended kinship ties that would characterize a social model organized around agnatic lineage and multiple family name associations. January does not manifest his "self" through knightly display—prowess in arms, courtly lovemaking, or political activity and patronage. Nor is it his ownership of land and association with a title or locale that grounds his and others' sense of who he is. Rather, it is January's ownership of his household "movables" (such as squire, hangers-on, garden, wife, and so forth) that matters. January's ability to display surplus production, notably in his ownership of privacy (the garden, the household, the bedchamber, May's body, his imagination), determines and projects his sense of self into the world. And that self looks much more like the "new" merchant patriciate than like "old" representations of chivalric knighthood.

This makes the tale's focus on January's old age and impotence all the more telling and problematic. January's decrepit physical state provides a material ground for his metaphoric impotence as a sign, and thus the basis for the tale's satiric undercutting of his self-delusion and failure as a proper model for dominant masculinity. January may appear to embrace the new possibilities offered by the sacrament of marriage and its emphasis on individual choice and conjugality. But the narrator's sneering approach to the forms of the sacrament, as well January's glib use of the forms to fulfill a desire at odds with the sacrament's intent, draws attention to the persistence of an unrepentantly "old" class identity in this story. At bottom January's mode of self-expression remains that of the medieval knight: focused on exterior action and domination and directed always outward to public display and activity at all costs.[47] But the *Merchant's Tale* has a very different relationship to January's conspicuous consumption and display than might be evinced in a traditional romance. Here there is a very real fear that January's behavior may bankrupt the self by not attending to the means of production of the surplus January claims as his right. This seems different from an old-style aristocratic phantasm that such excess is an inalienable right that comes naturally with one's body (that is, with the title, lands, and noble blood that one inherits as a result of who one is and who one's family has been); moreover, without such a continued display, that performative identity will be in danger. This is perhaps why January is represented in ways both like and unlike the Merchant: like in that he marries late in life at the peak of his success, and unlike in that he buys into the surface of prevailing ideologies (of courtly and sacramental marriage, for example). Moreover, the Merchant might just as likely identify with May to the extent that May's marriage is thrifty in bringing her immediate "enfeofment" in January's lands.[48] No mention is made of May's family or dowry; instead she seems a free agent, or one made a free agent by January's self-involvement and ability to see only the image of her that he has created. In addition, the tale delineates the ways that January's marriage leads away from feudal obligations and aristocratic success. Marriage brings May land, yet May provides neither feudal liege loyalty nor legitimate reproduction of January's bloodline. January's marriage so late in life offers little possibility for issue and presents his decision as the culmination of a life of excessive self-indulgence rather than social responsibility. Damian's courtly love-longing puts him at odds with his feudal and contractual obligations to January (as his squire and a member of the personal household); so much so that by the end of the tale not only has he cuckolded his knight, but there remains the strong presumption that Damian's blood will flow in January's heir's veins (since January's old age makes him far less likely than his squire to have successfully impregnated May).

What, then, is the role of the masculine in this tale? January links masculinity with sexual potency and with the ability to have one's way. If this is the case (and it might be linked with knightly behavior and chivalric excess), then to be successful one should be young, for masculinity seems to be all about the exercise of raw power. Much of the tale's cynicism comes from such a reductive association, for various transcendent ideologies (Christian, classical/literary, chivalric) are introduced only to have them presented as so much window dressing on the fact of entrenched (i.e., old and tyrannical) power. Knightly action, as represented in the character of January, is presented as "every man for himself," rather than in its traditional form as the noblest part of the body politic, capable of speaking for the whole. Both May and Damian are forced into a similar set of moves. As a result, by the end of the tale the outward forms of dominant masculine authority may appear to have found a successful mode of reproduction (literally, if May is indeed pregnant by Damian, thus providing January with an heir he and society will authorize as "legitimate"). But at the same time, the tale would seem to function as a warning to the knightly class to learn to behave differently if its members are not to become sterile and to be weeded out of the new social order. Perhaps, also, the tale provides a similar warning to that enlarged "gentil" class coming into power; they are at risk from the misdemeanors of the old ruling class, but are also unable to do away with it. Instead this group must appeal for nobility's reformation, and hope that eventually thriftiness and gentry-class values will win out (a position, simultaneously empowered and passive, that is similar in certain crucial ways to that articulated by Griselda and the Clerk). To this extent the *Merchant's Tale* stages the divisions within dominant masculinity (or would-be dominant masculinity). The "enemy" is both the social underclass welling up (as potentially unleashed in the wayward rhetoric of the *Wife of Bath's Tale*) *and* the previously hegemonic ruling class (nobility and clerisy). If we all desire access to the private garden, how do "we" get there? "I" might be mistaken for the "other" that hegemonic power defines itself against, and hence this would-be hegemonic "I" might be rendered an object of the gaze, colonized and objectified into a shameful abjection. To fight that possibility, the Merchant "stares back" as it were. But he must do so *while* shoring up the very institutional forms whose power he seeks to contain insofar as they might limit his potential movement. Thus, rather than the institutional critique the Merchant at one level desires, his form must remain that of satire and *individual* reformation—hence the generic confusion and contradiction within the *Merchant's Tale*.[49]

The only way around this problem, it seems, is to exercise duplicity and a contained raw power of one's own (often associated with the feminine via May and Proserpine's speech). Yet in a curious way, these feminized and feminine characters find power only to the extent that they inscribe a perverse dynamic back into the exercise of dominant power. For example, the actual reproduction signaled at the end comes from the exchange of potent semen coming from Damian's penis and May's presumable orgasm. This reproduction is clearly more powerful than the assertions of ownership expressed by January. Yet their desire finds expression only in a moment and an action severely circumscribed and one that ultimately will reproduce the authority of January and his kind. The perversity of the production of authority is made absolutely clear, even as the advantages of willful ignorance are made abundantly clear. All will benefit from this arrangement. It is in this sense a brilliant replaying of the concerns of the *Clerk's Tale* from the point of view of an insider, a grumbling May (i.e., the merchant class) in a marriage of convenience with the inherited and inheriting January (i.e., the aristocratic class). If this is the case, the Merchant as May may acknowledge the necessity for marriages of convenience with an essentially impotent aristocratic class and its empty forms in order to gain access to the garden.

But two qualifications to this position are also posed by the *Merchant's Tale*. The first is suggested by January's loss of vision. This might be a way of talking about the limitations of a sovereign subject constructed on an outmoded model of masculinity and agency. January surveys the town (colonizing it in his mind), he reconstitutes May in his mind as the willing wax on which he can imprint and reproduce his form, he prefers young women (i.e., refusing to grant maturity to the feminine, the mercantile, the other) because they can be shaped like warm wax, he is his household and they are him, his wife is a chattel like his other goods, his garden is absolutely his. January's "surveillance" certainly has parallels with scopophilia and colonization (although it is expressed as aristocratic right and as tyranny). But January's is also an impossible identity to maintain; January is not potent enough and what he thinks of as naturally his, as extensions of his self—Damian and May—have wills of their own. Moreover, the fact that January has imprinted his dominating image of May so completely in his mind means that he cannot do without that "thoght"; he thus loses power, becomes vulnerable. The second qualification is suggested by the wax and key metaphor. Damian counterfeits January's key, which May has passed to him via her skillful impression of it. Therefore, May, rather than being wax shaped completely by January, remaining the dominated, abject incorporated into his fantasy, becomes the medium for counterfeiting January's key/penis, opening the garden space (January's "private" self) and her own body to Damian's more potent "thronging." This suggests the desire to pass on January's phallic power to Damian. While that does not clearly happen in the tale—and thus the agency of the Mays and Damians of this world is always already contained—the *Tale* itself becomes the means to represent, reproduce, and stage that desire as successful in the future. If indeed May is pregnant at the end of the tale, May and Damian/May's child will inherit January's estate. Even if not, the tale invites its readers to imagine fully what January does in the garden with May and thus to enter at will into January's supposedly secure, private space.

The Merchant is intent on showing how no one can be a free agent, despite the aristocracy's traditional presumption to such freedom or the fantasy by the Wife and her sect (which is not, of course, simply women) of its general availability. As a result, both private and public identities come under an extraordinary disciplinary scrutiny in the *Merchant's Tale*, one that underscores the difficulty of ever keeping both in balance in such an improperly husbanded world. Hence the tale's satire of January's excessive emphasis on his complete privacy, of his vaunting ambition in presuming his freedom to marry or not, of his scopophilic autonomous eye/I; or of the ineffectual tyranny of "rulers" like Pluto and Prosperine; or of the institutional control of subjects by the ecclesiastical and communal spheres in January's world. If there is the possibility of a disciplinary culture emerging that will be able to turn itself into an exercise of proper self-discipline, it comes from the success of the narrator in remaining secreted within his story and the middleness of the textual eye/I it establishes. The *Merchant's Tale* is at once intensely aware of how authorities construct value from outside (and intent on holding them in a certain abeyance) and also intent on constructing its own (masculine) safe vantage point of self-valuation. This is a properly disciplined subject that is nonetheless now (newly) installed as part of that very disciplinary regime that has traditionally interpellated that subject. Such a subject becomes an integral part of the machinery of surveillance itself, yet remains aware of the need for the very individual desire it surveys and consequently works under continual threat of effeminization. Thus, there is necessarily a certain level of panic involved in such a process of identification; one can never be absolutely sure, never get it absolutely right.[50]

The *Merchant's Tale* focuses its readers' attention on a proliferation of subject positions at work within the supposedly stable and secure "privacy" of January's household. The tale provides multiple perspectives on its plot and characters, multiple forms available to contain what they might mean, multiple cultural locations and ideologies governing them in which to discern their value. Yet despite the tale's multiple desiring subjects and its frank acknowledgment of the surplus production arising out of such desire, these same individuals and their actions remain curiously isolated and contained. The overall effect is to lock the tale's readers within a present experience that is our ultimate guide, yet is also in excess of any of the authoritative ideologies invoked. Curiously the satiric structure of the tale here does not, as might be expected, send us "back" to the secure hermeneutics of a golden past, nor "outside" to a present embodiment of transcendent social authority (whether in the form of clerical school culture, ecclesiastical juridical authority, or a hegemonic lay authority based on established bloodlines). Instead, the tale takes us "within" the hegemonic masculine subject (represented by January's household, and especially his garden of personal delight). The tale's action encourages us to focus on the would-be autonomous, private, domestic sphere of individual desire and subjectivity it represents as the place to learn how to shape a properly masculine hegemonic point of view. In this regard, the *Merchant's Tale* provides a sophisticated exploration and reworking of that same masochistic contract we saw at work in the fabliau structure of the *Miller's Tale*. But here the very disorganization of sexed and gendered social relationships that January's effeminate, self-indulgent desire makes possible and even encourages also works to "educate" the inscribed (male) reader into a properly sadistic hegemonic position. Whatever else happens, this reader must not be blind to anything taking place (and hence is not likely to be blindsided by unexpected action or its consequences). What separates this readerly activity from earlier ones is the privileged position given to the unpredictability of the present moment and its hermeneutic as productive of value. If "I" am going to participate in the creation of this kind of surplus, I must "labor" to make the present productive of a surplus that can be harnessed for the "common profit" and, equally important, I must construct a present moment and common profit that will include "me" as its empowered subject.

## "Fre" Subjects: Discipline and Difference in the *Franklin's Tale*

The *Franklin's Tale,* much more directly than the *Merchant's Tale,* attempts to represent as something positive social difference and the destabilizing effect it appears to have on supposedly stable signifiers. The tale reveals the potential divisions *within* dominant masculinity that the social and economic changes of the late medieval period are producing. But rather than figuring such change as the sign of present social confusion and opprobrious diminishment from a past golden ideal, the tale represents change as a sign of a progression that we might read as "modernist." The patterns of modernity structuring the *Franklin's Tale,* not surprisingly, have made it for Kittredge, and for many subsequent critics, the natural point of fulfillment for the Marriage Group and its debate about social relationships. For Kittredge, the *Franklin's Tale* provides that ideal balance of mutuality in marriage and other social relations that characterizes true gentility. Its successful articulation of the wholeness of the modern (heterosexual) subject is thus foundational for any understanding of the completeness of Chaucer's "Human Comedy" in the *Canterbury*

*Tales* and of the underlying organic unity knitting the work together in spite of superficial fragmentation. "Arveragus the man" (or Aurelius or the Clerk of Orleans) provides an essential background that figures "Chaucer the man," and that substitution in turn makes possible the production of "Chaucer the great author" and thus grounds, ultimately, the universality of the proper (modern) reader of the *Canterbury Tales*. What seems crucial for Kittredge, and for those arguing that the *Franklin's Tale* represents some kind of social balance and resolution, is the way that the would-be modernity of the tale encourages a retrospective reading back onto it of a hitherto dominant modernist hegemony, installing its progressivist historiography and its autonomous, liberal (heterosexual male) subject as universals.

An approach like Kittredge's thus poses a fundamental problem in trying to read back onto the tales as truth the very structures of modernity it is performatively trying to install (and for which it has been used by later readers). Only if viewed through the narrowing lens of retrospection could the *Franklin's Tale* be seen as an *end* point for a marriage debate that clearly continues in later tales such as the *Shipman's Tale* or the *Tale of Melibee*. I would argue instead that the *Franklin's Tale* occupies a crucial middle position in the Canterbury project (according to the Ellesmere order, twelfth in the twenty-four tales actually told, or twelfth out of twenty-three tale-tellers) without insisting on the "natural" validity or conceptual centrality of its arguments for the Canterbury project as a whole. Instead, it seems more accurate to think of the tale as trying to re-present marriage's hybridization as organic. This requires a new kind of historicity and a revaluing of the worth and reliability of female constancy and of the feminine more generally.[51]

To achieve this representational flexibility, the tale reconfigures potentially destabilizing differences among characters (based on behavior, estate, blood, and so forth) as marginal to a deeper, integral "freedom" these subjects are capable of realizing. To fuel this new discursive economy, the tale emphasizes the liberatory power of the cultural capital brought about by "gentility," a nature envisaged as somehow separate from and foundational to both "old" forms of feudal capital produced by bloodline and the school and "new" forms produced by the money economy and surplus production of late medieval capitalism. Access to the cultural capital of gentility allows subjects to be "fre" in the old sense of giving of their worth (without risk of bankrupting themselves or the larger social institutions they maintain) while manifesting freedom in the modern sense of individual autonomy. In short, the tale is intent on establishing a new disciplinary culture of the middle, modernizing elite *as* culture. Thus, it brings together characters whose natural estates traditionally represent the dominant ideologies of high medieval hegemonic culture (the noble by birth, the noble by clerical schooling, the noble by courtly love schooling). But the inability of each character to fulfill his estate in traditional ways, rather than marking some essential difference among groups of men or between present action and past perfection, instead functions to inscribe a positive valence for widening the definition of what constitutes the ground for hegemonic subjectivity, with a new universal subject of "gentil" providing an empowering, "progressive" redefinition of "noble."[52]

To achieve this positive valence for change, the *Franklin's Tale* inscribes in its plot the inevitability of moving toward a sense of "modern" progressivist history: Phebus gives way to magic, magic to the efficacy of scientific charts. By implication there may be different ways to think "Christian" and "chivalric," limitations to (and goings beyond) the effects of their traditional ideologies. With such a historical way of thinking would also come a certain urgency in reconciling the necessary contradictions such diversity produces, a need to show that such superficial contradiction is not really constitutive of epistemological or ontological difference and thus capable of giving way to a deeper set of unities. It therefore becomes urgent to establish the primacy of the interiorized, individualized self as foundational for this set of underlying unities. Thus the *Franklin's Tale* insists on a necessary individual autonomy, for it is personal restraint and action that generate the surplus cultural capital that enables each character to demonstrate that he or she is "fre." This is not a simple mimicry of aristocratic "franchise" (that is, "nobility of character or generosity of spirit"), but rather a new articulation that seeks to fuse "fre" in its traditional sense of "franchise" with "fre" in its newer meaning of "free." The *private* and personal marriage vows that Arveragus and Dorigen make, which are represented as the culmination of clerical and courtly discourses of love and marriage, therefore really move the discussion into new and uncharted (and potentially dangerous) territory—as the action of the tale explores. Without Arveragus, is there a Dorigen, so much is her subjectivity articulated in terms of this private, individualized domestic relationship? So, too, Arveragus's real "honor" in the tale comes through the behavior of his wife and his behavior in relationship to her, not through his martial exploits (which emerge in the tale as almost too long a wandering in the world of courtly play). The tale seems to hold out the possibility that each character has the potential for individual autonomy by exercising his freedom to make the kinds of crucial decisions that will give each character "reality." Such autonomy is imagined as the achievement of a full sense of oneself via the realization of a sense of interiority and the rhetorical ability to articulate that inside against the outside world of church, court, and economy.

The tale also explores, however, the instabilities and difficulties of representing this new sense of self, and the body it is grounded on, by means of the rhetoric at one's disposal (which reflects the desires of an other—another class, another gender, another age, another language). The courtly rhetoric of the tale's language, plot, and setting may be organized around aristocratic otiosity. Yet the tale's characters must employ such rhetoric to their own "thrifty" ends to articulate an individualist epistemology and ontology in certain crucial ways cut loose from the moorings of fixed aristocratic bloodlines, hierarchized and stable estate identities, and so forth. Thus the various "problems" that the tale exposes may look like conventional courtly love dilemmas about which one can talk forever without any necessary closure: How can Dorigen remain in conversation with her true, *fin amor,* Arveragus in his absence? How can Aurelius attract Dorigen's attention enough for her to constitute a true interlocutor for his love-longing? How can Dorigen remain faithful to her true love and her promise to Aurelius? But each in its own way demands a kind of thrifty closure foreign to conventional courtly discourse. Thus Dorigen's apparently excessive response to the black rocks, which she worries will keep Arveragus from returning safely to her, cannot be resolved by public play in the garden of courtly love because it is a marker of their uniquely private and modern conjugality.[53] So, too, Aurelius interprets her concern about the rocks literally to reframe the problem in ways that can be negotiated scientifically and legalistically and thereby turned to his advantage. Indeed, at no point is it really possible to fix exactly what the black rocks themselves really are because our understanding of how their disappearance is being effected is constantly changing—sometimes the result of pagan prayer, sometimes astrological science, sometimes scientific observation of tides, sometimes a "magic" indistinguishable from the play of rhetorical colors or an after-dinner dramatic spectacle.

The rocks, and Dorigen's response to them, provoke a set of differences that in the end only appear to threaten (but never deliver) fragmentation or conflict. Instead, the apparent differences of the tale—between aristocrat and clerk, old and new, courtly and bourgeois, universal and particular, French and English—are productively crossed and recrossed by the action of the tale's plot. In doing so, the tale creates space for a mode of hybridization that looks and sounds unconscious and organic rather than dialogic. Squire and knight, clerk and squire, masculine and feminine, could be irreconcilably divided, reducing rather than augmenting a "fredom" that must be limited to a narrow class of persons. Similarly, for the Franklin to choose an old Breton lai might look like colonial mimicry, and its hybrid English manifestation here as simple diminishment from a purer original. But such a dialogic hybridity is also downplayed by the tale's success in presenting its "fredom" as natural, an unconscious and organic crossing of difference. In this way the middleness of this Franklin's Brittany—neither French nor English, neither purely aristocratic nor purely bourgeois, neither hegemonically old nor frighteningly modern—creates an intensely local space in which to imagine a new sovereign subject.

However, there is no similarly "fre" place for Dorigen and the female body in such a new order. While the tale would maintain that each person can be "fre" (although what constitutes such a person is still clearly limited in class terms), the action of the tale inscribes a crucial difference between Dorigen and the men in the tale that runs deeper than any class difference could. Quite substantial differences of birth, education, and control of goods among the men can be acknowledged and surmounted by the action of "fredom" in the tale. In crucial ways, however, Dorigen's access to this new selfhood is never a real possibility. For the men in the tale, trading her means "giving her up" to secure the ideal of domestic stability that she represents and the consequent "freedom" it can provide for them as male subjects. It is not the body of woman that the men *really* want, the tale seems to say, but rather the ownership of the ideal of female constancy. Woman's constancy is more profitable to think with in this new discourse than a simple dynastic marriage or courtly love conquest. It secures true capital in that it grounds a sovereign subject, making commodifiable the aristocratic and clerical values that were previously the preserve of a particular caste. Such a "marriage" and the domestic unit it represents look as much forward to the reformed garden of Milton's *Paradise Lost* as back to the ephemeral and enclosed courtly garden of the *Romance of the Rose*. The tale must thus stabilize Arveragus (as the originary of courtly value) to make possible the potentially destabilizing reproduction of "freedom" in the other universal autonomous subjects of the tale. Dorigen is the medium for this reproduction, which is necessarily *not* one of physical reproduction (aristocratic bloodline), nor of an incarnate Word made flesh (clerical), but a sovereign (male) subject reproducing itself by its ability to package and circulate a newly commodified gentility.

# 4

# Queer Performativity in Fragment VI

## Doing What Comes Naturally

In *The Idea of the Canterbury Tales*—still one of the most richly provocative readings of the Pardoner and his place in the *Tales*—Donald Howard focuses on the perversity of Fragment VI as a whole: a fragment apparently uniquely isolated within the Canterbury project and curiously alienated from (or by) its ordering principles. Other tales and fragments fit together in spite of an admittedly unfinished "big picture" for the *Tales* as a whole. Characters introduce themselves and their tales from the frame (as with the Wife of Bath), tales are commissioned by the Host, estate and personal rivalries prompt revenge narratives, references to the progress of the pilgrims help order individual fragments' relationships with the whole, or thematic links like the marriage debate cross-link individual tales and fragments. But the *Physician's* and *Pardoner's Tales,* says Howard,

> belong to no group, have no link with another tale, contain no reference to time or place. The "alestake" mentioned in line 321 might be anywhere: it is a place abstracted from topography, probably a symbol. Nor do the manuscripts give the fragment any consistent place in the order of the tales. . . . You can put the fragment in any of the gaps in the existing structure (between Fragments I and II, II and III, V and VII, or VII and VIII) and manufacture a literary or thematic relationship, but none asserts

> itself. I mean to suggest that it belongs in the no-man's land where it is, "floating" on the periphery of the interlaced structure.[1]

According to Howard, there is a *conventional rightness* to the place of Fragment VI on the periphery of any ordered structure for the *Tales* that arises out of the "estranged world" conjured up by this fragment—its avaricious and cold narrators, grisly morality and grim tales, and generally "grotesque" elements whose proper place can only be on the periphery of medieval meaning systems. And convention would seem the crucial factor distinguishing the reception of this fragment from that of numerous other fragments and tales that actually do have radically different places in the various early orderings of tales. Notable in this regard is Fragment VIII (placed—in manuscripts groups with orders different from the Ellesmere—before Fragment VI) and those tales associated with the marriage debate (e.g., the *Franklin's Tale,* the *Merchant's Tale,* and the *Clerk's Tale,* as well as Fragment III containing the *Wife of Bath's Tale*). In none of these cases, however, has an inconsistent place in the order of the *Tales* made them seem to "float" on the periphery of the *Tales'* structures of meaning. On the contrary, the very inconsistency of their place in early orderings of the *Tales* could be seen as bearing witness to just how much they "fit in"—how easily they move within the overall frame—and mark what is properly central in their material to emerging fifteenth-century understandings of what Chaucer's Canterbury project is all about.[2]

In the first instance, the "pariah-like" nature that Howard sees as integral to Fragment VI, and in particular sees crystallized in the "feminoid" Pardoner, clearly emerges out of the intensity with which this fragment foregrounds questions of perversity and the clarity with which it appears to frame such questions within stable, purely "medieval" universals. And to that extent, Fragment VI reproduces a familiar set of binaries—proper/improper, orthodox/perverse, natural/unnatural—that regularly works to establish the supposed hegemony of a (largely clerically articulated) medieval imaginary. But this perversely floating fragment also poses the question, "Who fits in, and how?" in the starkest way possible. And in presenting the oppressive force of the essentialized gender system lying behind medieval identity politics without many of the usual mediating devices, the fragment functions as a kind of limit case for the sustainability of the modes of production of hegemonic medieval identities. Thus, the *Physician's Tale* may parallel the *Second Nun's Tale* in its attempt to make the virginal body a sure defense against perversity and a speaking picture of the divine (masculine) will. But in the end, masculine authority in the *Physician's Tale* is claimed not through the reformed female body and the consequent surmounting of an ineffectual violent perversity, but rather through the destruction of the female body and the isolation of proper masculinity within a no-longer-reproductive male body. In the *Physician's Tale,* representation becomes literally a matter of life and death for Virginia, and the excision of *any* female presence in the *Pardoner's Tale* even more effectively "kills off" the matter of woman that has so dominated previous Chaucerian fictions. Moreover, the repeated symbolic violence practiced by the Host and other pilgrims against the Pardoner constitutes a kind of queerbashing, that, while not technically misogynist, does arise out of a similar fear of the feminine. And the kinds of connections made between the two tales and tale-tellers by the activities of the Host and Pardoner in the fictional frame bring the male body into view to an extent not seen elsewhere in the *Canterbury Tales.*[3]

Few other sets of tales, then, so explicitly and anxiously bear out Elaine Tuttle Hansen's contention that "in Chaucerian fictions, we cannot directly hear women's voices . . . but we can hear 'men's concern.'"[4] And I would question, therefore, whether the grotesqueness of this fragment really can lie only in its stark outline of a perverse identity that is other to traditionally dominant medieval norms—that is, a sodomitical *cupiditas* in opposition to redemptive charity and chastity. Surely what is grotesque in this fragment is precisely its bringing into view the gaps, fissures, and contradictions in medieval meaning systems caused by competing and not always reconcilable medieval identity politics. And it is this queer valence implicit in Howard's emphasis on the unplaceability and estrangement of the grotesque in this fragment, and in particular his choice of "feminoid" to describe the perversity of the Pardoner's "nature," that I want to make explicit and intensify. For the grotesqueness of Fragment VI that Howard so forcefully highlights, rather than simply reinstituting a familiar pattern for the co-construction of dominant and marginalized identities through a process of disavowal of the perverse other by the properly central, instead works to disrupt and discohere "normal" homosocial structures. Attending to the queer torsions produced by the production of hegemonic masculinities in the *Tales* can thus bring into view a more dynamic and threatening role for this fragment's "floating on the periphery," one that underscores its unexpected abutments, queer contiguities, and dangerous proximity with the proper.

The delicate "balancing" of differences that marriage made possible in earlier tales is here an impossibility, as a more clerical and "medieval" privileging of virginity excises the feminine (and the female body). In consequence, Fragment VI represents a certain dismissal of lay desire, and its necessary emphasis on the value of embodiment, in its return to high medieval clerical values. Thus, however negative the reaction of other pilgrims to the Wife of Bath, it is nothing as intense as the reaction to perversity in the *Physician's Tale* or the disgust shown by the "gentils" and Host to the Pardoner. Bereft of such mediating points of similarity as the Wife's Englishness or her estate as bourgeois wife, the sexually ambiguous, foreign Pardoner registers now not as perverse presentism, but as starkly "alien."

If we are to explore the extent of the "men's concern" at work in this fragment (i.e., in the phobic purificatory moves of the *Physician's Tale* or in the phobic othering of the Pardoner by the "gentils" in the pilgrimage frame) we cannot simply read this fragment through the self-serving lens of a supposedly unitary and authoritative medieval Christian nature, nor simply reproduce the limiting structures of a modern sex/gender system. We need, instead, to historicize as fully as possible the gendered and sexualized hermeneutics "subjecting" readers and writers in Fragment VI. And in doing so, it would seem more useful to focus on the *processes* of differentiation establishing identity rather than, as is so often the case, to focus on the supposedly secure identities—male/female, homo/hetero, sodomite/Christian—such processes say they establish. What, for example, might it look like to loosen "the feminine" from its "normally" essentialized sex/gender systems—both medieval and modern—and track it along the axis of sexuality? Are there potentially enabling and destabilizing *dis*-identifications that might occur as a result? Reading this way, we can see more clearly how Fragment VI challenges the processes by which the *Canterbury Tales* attempts to loosen late medieval readers from a celibate/noble sex/gender system by foregrounding the anxieties that such a process of loosening produces, especially around identity categories based on new articulations of vernacularity, social estate, and gender. For the masochistic contract so masterfully visible and veiled in the action of the *Miller's Tale,* the homosocial bonds so strenuously maintained within the controlled access to women's bodies fantasized by the male-authored tales of marriage, the powerful materiality of a distinctly English and present bourgeois voice imagined more generally in the marriage debate instigated by the *Wife of Bath's Tale,* all such necessary, productive, and fearful encounters between male bodies and the feminine, Fragment VI represents in the context of a sodomitical and xenophobic panic.[5]

If gender and sexuality come together under the sign of "the feminine" in this fragment, and in the process work to trouble both past and present understandings of the relationships between sex, gender, and sexuality, they do so, I would suggest, because Fragment VI crystallizes a process of *femme-graphesis* that we have seen operating more covertly elsewhere in the *Canterbury Tales* (especially the *Miller's Tale* and the *Merchant's Tale*) in such a way as to produce a kind of *sodomitical panic* for its characters and readers. I am, of course, here both drawing on and somewhat resistantly adapting Lee Edelman's concept of *homographesis* and Eve Sedgwick's discussion of *homosexual panic.* Both terms arise out of and engage primarily with modern discursive practices organized specifically around the homo/hetero binary. They are thus, as I will attempt to show, at once highly suggestive in highlighting difference within the "medieval" discursive terrain that goes unacknowledged in traditional medieval and medievalist discussions and limited by the occlusions engendered by their locations within modernism. Translating Sedgwick's notion of "homosexual panic" as "sodomitical panic" helps move us away from the simple question of whether the Pardoner is a sodomite or not. But the term also notes how this sodomitical panic differs from that described by Sedgwick by focusing less on modernity's obsession with the problematics of male/male desire per se, and more on the Middle Ages' concern with emasculation. Here the construction of "femme-graphesis" by analogy to Edelman's "homographesis" is helpful in highlighting such medieval difference in sex/gender categories. But so, too, does the medieval mix of gender and sexuality in its construction of queerness expose the masculinist potential inhering in Edelman's dependence on homosexuality as the defining feature of *homo*graphesis. The argument of modern queer theorists, then, illuminates the medieval, but the complexity and difference of the medieval situation in turn can usefully complicate the arguments of these modern theorists. In particular, taking the medieval into account in this way can reinforce connections between queer theory and feminism that contemporary antihomophobic analyses are explicitly striving for and yet have implicitly obscured at times by the shadow of modernity. Such a productive hybridity between post- and pre-modern, gender and sexuality, gay and queer, can, I think, better describe the complexity of the late medieval sex/gender system represented in this fragment, as well as the complexity of "medieval"/"modern" interactions taking place in our attempts to read this fragment as a "present" situation (i.e., in the fullness of its medieval presentness and in the fullness of its ability to speak to our present).

In *Epistemology of the Closet,* Sedgwick suggests that, with the development of a "crystallized male homosexual role and male homosexual culture [before the end of the eighteenth-century], a much sharper-eyed and acutely psychologized secular homophobia was current. . . . this development was important not only for the persecutory regulation of a nascent minority population of distinctly homosexual men but also for the regulation of the male homosocial bonds that structure *all* culture—at any rate, all public or heterosexual culture." She then goes on to argue that "the historically shifting, and precisely the arbitrary and self-contradictory, nature of the way *homosexuality* (along with its predecessor terms) has been defined in relation to the rest of the male homosocial spectrum has been an exceedingly potent and embattled locus of power over the entire range of male bonds, and perhaps especially over those that define themselves, not *as* homosexual, but *as against* the homosexual. Because the paths of male entitlement, especially in the nineteenth century, required certain intense male bonds that were not readily distinguishable from the most reprobated bonds, an endemic and ineradicable state of what I am calling male homosexual panic became the normal condition of male heterosexual entitlement."[6]

What, then, is the force of transposing Sedgwick's term, so precisely located in a particular modern moment of the definition (via a legal, medical, and psychological discourse) of same-sex (male) relations, into the very different "medieval" moment of "sodomitical panic" I am attempting to describe for Fragment VI? One effect, perhaps, is to shift attention away from a modern sexuality's preoccupation with the hetero/homo divide toward a broader discursive terrain. Put more specifically in terms of Fragment VI, the effect would be to shift attention away from such questions as whether the Pardoner "really" is a homosexual, eunuch, or unrepentant sinner. As Mark Jordan has so brilliantly demonstrated, sodomy as an abstract name (with a concomitant identity, "the sodomite") is an "invention" of medieval clerical Christian culture.[7] Sodomy at times marks a set of prohibited acts (both autoerotic, same-sex and non-reproductive acts by men, between men, and between men and women) that all Christians might be capable of—here a Christian taking up and narrowing of the classical *luxuria* so that it becomes focused primarily in terms of genital sex acts. At other times sodomy delineates a "people" with a distinct point of origin—Sodom—and hence a minority always already present within Christian history. Or it signals a biological predisposition to certain actions, a "natural" untreatable phenomenon—a sinful identity particularly to be found in the clerical ranks. Sodomy is thus a category to which anxiety about the erotic is displaced in a clerically dominated culture that would maintain that the most natural man is the celibate, and in which the erotic needs to be suppressed to make allowances for the human weakness in the majority of lay married people. As Jordan puts it, "[t]he place of the erotic in Christian love is no more settled for other-sex couples than for same-sex couples.... The irrational force of the Christian condemnation of Sodomy is the remainder of Christian theology's failure to think through the problem of the erotic."[8] Thus, in a larger sense, the very attempt to wipe out the sin, also, paradoxically, constitutes sodomy as "a pleasure that cannot be divided without remainder into teleological sequences." It becomes the discursive marker of an erotics, of a sexuality itself, erased from dominant accounts of "nature" organized as a reproductive teleology and superseded by the higher celibate, "masculine," Christian perfected body.[9]

Sodomy as a category and identity, then, is *not* translatable by the modern terms *homosexuality* and *homosexual*. Thus, according to Jordan, however much the invention of sodomy as an abstract name modeled on blasphemy may have allowed for the creation of an identity, "the sodomite," which has its own name, geography, topography, and history, that identity remains distinct from the modern homosexual.[10] On the other hand, the creation by medieval clerics of such a mythical "tribe," and a term that is both minoritizing and universalizing in turn, may have created the conceptual ground on which to birth the modern homosexual. Jordan goes on to point out that the development of the medieval term, "the Sodomite," means that in the Western tradition,

> [t]he idea of an identity built around the genital configuration of one's sexual partners is, in our tradition, the product of Christian theology. The rapid acceptance of the term 'homosexual' as a term of identity was prepared, long before, by a double mistake in medieval theology. Because Latin theologians thought in terms of Sodomites, we have found it so easy to think of ourselves as *being* homosexuals, as having a lesbian or gay *identity.* When we lesbians and gays think of ourselves as members of a tribe, as a separate people or race, we echo medieval theology's preoccupation with the Sodomites. Perhaps there is some room for gratitude to Peter Damian even here. And room for correcting some pages in the first volume of Foucault's *History of Sexuality.*[11]

Certainly there are analogies between medieval sodomite and modern homosexual as subject categories constituted as negatives by dominant culture; it may even be possible to discern the occasional utopic resistance to such representations anticipating modern "gay" liberation, as James Miller has argued for the newcomers who have no name for themselves in Dante's *Purgatorio.*[12] But at the same time, neither "the homosexual," nor his more optimistic "gay" younger brother will likely be found reproduced exactly in medieval systems of representation because such categories are "born" out of modern, not premodern, axes of difference. What these absences indicate is not that it is impossible or irrelevant to talk about sexuality (in the sense of an identity organized around a bodily reading of sex, gender, or sexual practice difference), only that it should not be the modern hetero/homo axis of sexuality we are presuming or blindly reproducing.[13]

Sodomitical panic is suggestive for the *Canterbury Tales* in at least three ways that have similarities to Sedgwick's discussion of a "homosexual panic" arising out of the paths of entitlement required of certain male bonds. Certainly the position of a medieval celibate male clerisy also requires "certain intense male bonds that were not readily distinguishable from the most reprobated bonds."[14] In a different way, the situation of laymen, whose homosocial interactions so necessarily involved the traffic in women, is always placed in a necessarily vexed and unstable relationship with *luxuria* and the threat of a slide into a debilitating unmasculine femininity. In a larger sense, sodomy stands for the possibility of a positive valence for an erotics based on a "pleasure that cannot be divided without remainder into teleological sequences," a pleasure that might be seen as a discursive motor of the Canterbury project itself.[15] To focus on the *sodomitical* panic of this fragment is to focus in the first instance on its medieval otherness to the modern in a way that challenges both the knowability of the medieval on its own terms (i.e., only in terms of the clerical culture "inventing" the abased term as a way of defining its own hegemony) and the universality of the modern and its sexualized identities. The sodomitical, in this way, also leads us back to a different imbrication of sex and gender in the medieval sex/gender system, one requiring a defamiliarization of gender for our consideration of the moment of "becoming" that multiplies the identifications provoked by Fragment VI.[16]

In the title chapter of his book, Lee Edelman proposes a project of "homographesis" to critique the current cultural conceptualizations of gay identity. For Edelman, the term *homographesis* maps simultaneous processes of oppression and resistance inherent in modern reading strategies. In the first instance, homographesis signifies the process by which dominant ideological strategies assign to gay bodies a visible "difference." Thus as Edelman describes it, "the construction of homosexuality as a subject of discourse, as a cultural category about which one can think or speak or write, coincides... with the process whereby the homosexual subject is represented as being, even more than inhabiting, a body that always demands to be read, a body on which his 'sexuality' is always inscribed." But Edelman also outlines another, resistant homographesis, a reading and writing practice that counters the labor of disciplinary inscription by resisting categorization, that is "intent on de-scribing the identities that [a conservative social] order has so oppressively inscribed."[17] Edelman's analysis thus helps him, as a product of that modern regime, variously constructed as homosexual/gay man/queer, to disconnect from and destabilize current oppressive modes of representation and to think otherwise about his own place within the present. In taking up Edelman's discussion of difference to outline a reading and writing practice that could counter the labor of both modern and medieval disciplinary inscription and to explore how Fragment VI describes the identities that a conservative social order (whether clerical or lay) has so oppressively inscribed, we might usefully substitute medieval gender for modern sexuality categories—that is, "the feminine" for "the homosexual"—and retheorize the relations between gender, sex, and sexuality. Thus, to paraphrase Edelman for my own project: we can think how "the construction of the feminine as a subject of medieval discourse, as a cultural category about which one can think or speak or write, coincides . . . with the process whereby the feminine/feminized subject is represented as being, even more than inhabiting, a body that always demands to be read, a body on which his/her gender/sexuality is always inscribed."[18]

The work of Joan Cadden, Thomas Laqueur, and others has highlighted the instabilities and slippages inherent in medieval models of sexual difference.[19] Whether presenting a one-sex model that views the female body as an inferior male body turned in on itself or a humoral model organized around differences in vital heat, medieval views of biological sex and the difference they inscribe on the body seem far less stable and absolutist than the modern two-sex model, and less likely to be effective foundations for medieval cultural meaning. As Laqueur reminds us, in classical and medieval medicine, the body

> was not the biological bedrock upon which a host of other characteristics were supposedly based. Indeed, the paradox of the one-sex model is that pairs of ordered contrarieties played off a single flesh in which they did not themselves inhere. Fatherhood/motherhood, male/female, man/woman, culture/nature, masculine/feminine, honorable/dishonorable, legitimate/illegitimate, hot/cold, right/left, and many other such pairs were read into a body that did not itself mark these distinctions clearly. Order and hierarchy were imposed upon it from the outside.[20]

In such a scenario, obviously, neither gender, nor sex, nor sexuality can be securely founded on or fixed by a biological body, nor are sex and sexuality the crucial axes of difference in determining identity that they are in modern society. Instead the body registers the shifting variables of a socially defined set of distinctions around masculinity and femininity that determine successful identification and care of the self. Thus the process of identification that happens in modern discursive regimes along parallel essentializing axes of sex (male/female), sexuality (homo/hetero), and race (white/black), might more likely take place in medieval practice along the axis of gender (masculine/feminine). Essentialized gender difference provides the stabilizing foundation by which medieval dominant culture regulates "the natural." In doing so, the suppressed/oppressed category of the feminine inscribes and identifies a greater variety of othered bodies—women's, heretics', Jews', Saracens', effeminates', sodomites'—than is the case in modern Western regimes of representation.

Moreover, the connection made throughout the Middle Ages between an essentialist gender system and a coercive narrative frame provides one of the controlling fantasies by which medieval dominant culture constitutes and maintains its identity.[21] Such a model of "the natural" presupposes for the male or female body, or by analogy the sexualized textual body, a structuring gendered frame that either authorizes its inherent truthfulness as "the natural" or condemns its lack as perversity. Just as an unstable sexual body needs to be framed by a hierarchized and essentialist account of gender difference, so too with the analogous sexualized textual body. Rather than text or author providing the foundational moment for cultural production,[22] the instabilities occasioned by their dependence on material, and thus ephemeral and contingent, media demand the stabilizing frame of a "higher" authority to make manifest an essential truthfulness and "masculine" will. Virginity (and its lesser cousin, chaste procreation) delineates the true nature of the "masculine" will for the sexes, just as the citation of authorities, allegorical explication, or sententious kernels of wisdom do for the text. The frame of gender and narrative authority then becomes the controlling presence that warrants the body's continued existence and usefulness as signifier.

In this conceptual model the feminine can signify only as a ventriloquized voice and a dummy's body, registering as everything the masculine is not.[23] As such, the feminine must be fantasized as Other to be absolutely transformed into speaking pictures of the truly masculine: as with female saints like Saint Cecilia, or Saracen and Jewish converts, who all surmounted their natural bodily weakness by manifesting a higher, "masculine" will. Or the feminine must be absolutely expunged (as with heretics and disobedient Jews or the effeminate Appius in the *Physician's Tale*), or exiled beyond the margins (as in Saracen kingdoms of the East), or hermetically sealed (as in the Jewish ghettos of European Christendom).[24] If this essentializing connection between gender and narrative frame constitutes the coercive phantasmatic ideal of medieval dominant culture, however, the performativity inherent in its actual cultural instantiation guarantees that both masculine will and narrative authority remain far more anxious and unstable sites of meaning than their "nature" would appear to allow (especially as new sources of power circulate by means of a more "modern" lay-based masculinity organized around the traffic in women).

Fragment VI, then, constitutes one of Chaucer's most complex and provocative explorations of the relationship among gender, sexuality, and power, for it inscribes as *crisis* a representational strategy at the heart of the Canterbury project, that is, the desire to write on the gendered, sexualized body a new "bourgeois" identity often at odds with a previously clerically defined transcendent self. In doing so, the fragment gestures toward, but fails to achieve, an autonomous subjectivity and authorial stability that, according to Hansen, has made Chaucer paradigmatic for an English literary tradition: for, as she reminds us, "reading Chaucer... enables us to study... the alleged birth or infancy perhaps of 'the author'—recognized from the beginning, paradoxically, as already a father figure—as an individual and a personality who seeks to enjoy all the material and symbolic privileges of maleness while transcending the constraints of 'the body writing' to grasp the otherwise unavailable, to take a neutral or universally human position."[25] In Fragment VI, on the contrary, such a "modern" authoring of an autonomous self can be found only in the disturbingly "unnatural" activities of the Host and the Pardoner. And it is instead the "medieval" identity politics of the *Physician's Tale* that appear to inscribe a masculine subject position, successfully transcending the constraints of "the body writing" by defining its activity as "natural." I put both "medieval" and "modern" here in quotation marks because the performative inscription of both kinds of identity politics in Fragment VI keeps them at play with each other as part of the specificities of *this* present moment (of tale-telling in the frame, of authorial production, of textualized reading practice within the context of manuscript culture, of a reading practice anticipated in the future). Neither response can be "safely" historicized—either in "traditional" medieval allegorizing messianic time, or in "early modern" sequential historical time—and the resulting admixture is precisely at the heart of the "grotesque" of this fragment and its "floating" nature. What makes this moment especially interesting is that in it we can see the set of forces that will be harnessed to produce "Chaucerian" authorship and the "modern" autonomous subject (that is, a universalized category founded on sexed and sexualized bodies). But such a naturalization has not yet taken place, and as a result, what this fragment records instead is the *tension* of attempting to write oneself via another. Its attention to tactics forestalls the stable authorship, selfhood, and masculinity that are *later* written into Chaucerian texts, showing instead the need to attend to movement and process, rather than to stability and teleology. This fragment's performative framing of medieval identity politics as practice rather than nature brings to consciousness the internal contradictions and paths of resistance possible within such a representational system, even as it reproduces that system's hegemonic turn to stability and order.

In the rest of this chapter, then, I want to focus on the processes of femme-graphesis inscribed in the *Physician's Tale* and the *Pardoner's Tale* to understand their incitement of a male sodomitical panic. In the case of the *Physician's Tale,* attending to gender in this way helps resist a presumptive "knowing" of what the tale means—whether through the lens of medieval clerical culture and a "natural" originary purity that can be endlessly reproduced without perversion, or through the lens of a modern sex/gender system that would see the tale as necessarily being readable as about "woman." In the case of the *Pardoner's Tale,* while the tale may not be about sexuality in the modern sense, attending to the queerness of the "feminoid" Pardoner and the sodomitical panic that he engenders—and that the final "kiss of peace" with the Host cannot successfully resolve—helps us see the activity of medieval sexuality while also forestalling the imposition of either a medieval or modern identity politics as a simple strategy to fill the Pardoner's emptiness with a stabilizing definition of "us" (whether medieval "gentil" self-fashioning, modern dominant culture's identities, or an alternative modern gay culture's counteridentities).

## The *Physician's Tale* and the Bodies That Matter

The *Physician's Tale* is particularly interesting in its attempts to harmonize an inherited classical medical/social model of the body with the demands of Augustinian Christianity. As Laqueur points out, the advent of Christianity both rendered classical harmonies of bodily humors more problematic and perpetuated their usefulness. For example,

> in its advocacy of virginity, [Christianity] proclaimed the possibility of a relationship to society and the body that most ancient doctors . . . would have found injurious to the health. . . . One's intimate experiences of sex, in this new dispensation, were the result not of an ineluctable heating of the body but of the fall and of the estrangement of will that the fall brought. . . . But Augustine's images for how "impregnation and conception" might be "an act of will, instead of by lustful cravings," were very much still of the old one-sex body found in the classical doctors. . . . Augustine did not envisage the modern body in which ovulation, conception, and even male ejaculation are known to be independent of whatever subjective feelings might accompany them. Heat and pleasure remained an ineradicable part of generation.[26]

Throughout, the *Physician's Tale* focuses on the care of masculinity needed to secure the proper reproduction of masculine identity and authority. To accomplish this end, the tale enacts a series of transcendental metaphoric substitutions: Virginia stands in for Virginius, Virginius for Nature, Nature for "my lord" God, copy for original. Stabilizing and securing Virginius's name thus secures not only his individual authority as potent patriarch, but the originary status of all patriarchal authority and control. Curiously, then, the sex of Virginia's body is at once central and irrelevant. For the tale seems concerned less with the inscription of sex difference than with proving the natural ability of an active and essential masculine will to frame and control the perversity of a passive and accidental feminine carnality. Any distinction between Virginius and Virginia ought to signal only accidental, rather than essential, difference.

The focus on the lay father's masculine will, the complete excision of the female body and male femininity, as well as the attempt to harmonize medical and clerical discourses of the body in the tale are especially interesting in light of the late medieval gender crisis discussed in chapter 2. The new hegemonic masculinity outlined there demanded some elision or occlusion of previously fixed distinctions between a superior clerical, celibate subject position and a lay, married one. Since in this older model of sex/gender difference, the lay estate in clerical discourses is "naturally" associated with a greater degree of bodiliness, it slides more easily into a feminine lack of mastery. The *Physician's Tale* resolves the question of lay and clerical difference by fantasizing a limit-case lay male subjectivity freed of the "problem" of bodiliness by being able, in quasi-clerical fashion, to purge itself altogether of the female body and femininity. In this case, the tale responds to the late medieval gender crisis by trying to reinscribe the kinds of binaries that resolved the previous twelfth-century crisis outlined by McNamara, the difference being, of course, that the tale does so to imagine the possibility of parity between lay male and clerical positions.

In the *Physician's Tale,* then, conformity of the (wo)man's body to the inherent, "masculine" will of Nature brings about the rule of the universal transcendent will of God. Good sexual order guarantees good social order. And the Physician, as a manipulator of the humors and a harmonizer of the individual body with the natural order, can have a profoundly important role in knitting together nature—whether physical, social, or theological. For the essence of masculine power is its definition of subjectivity as activity. Only the properly masculine subject carries the vital energy for procreation; thus it is crucial that the effects of embodiment—in the sense of mere materiality without such power—be carried by the category of the feminine. What gives biological "women" like Nature and Virginia instrumentality in the *Physician's Tale* is their ability to stand in for and give voice to the will of the Father. And to do that and be properly masculine, their bodies must signal away from irrelevant material accidents of sexed and sexualized bodies ("the feminine"), back to some always already present original ("the masculine"). The "a" ending of Virginia's name therefore indicates carefully gendered grammatical control; for as subject it should point only to a virginal rootedness in the antecedent will of the Father. Conformity of the (wo)man's body to the inherent, "masculine" will of Nature thus brings about the rule of the universal transcendent will of God.

When the perverse gaze of Appius threatens to sully first the body of purity (Virginia) and then its essence (Virginius's reputation), the "natural" order must be inscribed on the physical and social body in ever more extreme ways. At whatever cost, true masculinity must maintain itself as subject, not object, of the gaze of the other. And for that stable subject position to be maintained, no residue of the masculine body can be left to view for potential appropriation or reconfiguration. Because the distinction Virginius/Virginia should signal only accidental, not essential, difference, when Appius desires Virginia's female body rather than her signification as emblem of Virginius's power, he sexualizes and feminizes both Virginia's and Virginius's body, disrupting the normal homosocial exchanges within proper masculinity. Appius thereby feminizes his own signifying power as a proper man, foreclosing on his own agency as his actions objectify and bring into view his own excessive materiality. Such gender slippage, moreover, threatens the hierarchized binaries of accident/essence, lying/truth, perversity/naturalness that gender essentialism maintains, and exposes as proximate a feminizing, cupidinous perversity that proper masculinity insists must always be outside itself. One might think of Appius's actions as potentially provoking a kind of sodomitical panic, which is only averted by the drastic action Virginius takes in cutting off his daughter's head. This is a pattern that is then repeated in a less controlled and more productive fashion in the frame by the actions of the Host and pilgrims vis-à-vis the Pardoner.

To deny such perversity, it seems, the tale must excise the accidental altogether—whether in cutting off Virginia's head, in hanging Appius, or in denying its own embodied state as fable—all to maintain the active subject position defined as proper masculinity. In particular, the tale asserts its status as authoritative text by emphasizing the absence of narrative play: "this is no fable. . . . The sentence of it sooth is, out of doute" (VI.155–57). The textual body, like Virginia's, is dispensable. Only masculine substance matters in this foundational myth of purity. At every level, materiality is rendered unproblematic by a series of metaphoric substitutions that obscure the activities of the various sexual/textual bodies encountered in the tale. In this world, it would seem, there is no time to complain, no allowance for individual desire, for accidents of time and place. The truth will out no matter what.

Only by extreme, coercive activity on the part of Virginius, the Physician, and the other successful men who follow their example in framing and controlling what the tale means, can the individual and the ideological be aligned as one and the same activity. For the supposedly "natural" boundaries separating Virginius from Appius, masculine from feminine, essential truth from perverting falsity, are themselves constructions requiring the continuing "work" that (1) Virginius does to maintain intact what Virginia means, notably by cutting off her head; that (2) the Physician does to the *materia* of his text by attempting to excise its materiality as fable; and that (3) the tale's audience (Host and "gentils") do by announcing their "proper" reception of the tale in their rejection of the Pardoner.

This perverse dynamic at work within the masculine "body" of the *Physician's Tale* is further exposed to view in two additions of the Physician to his otherwise pared down version of Livy's tale.[27] In the twenty lines given to Nature near the beginning of the tale, she appears to speak directly to us as "I," literally enacting the kind of reproduction she is describing, where a subjectivity is naturally present and voicing the will of an anterior, superior "lord." But the last line of the speech—"Thus semeth me..." (VI.29)—introduces the voice of the Physician as an artist figure, who, Pygmalion-like, paints the "I" that has spoken by refracting it through his own subjective desire. Similarly, the Physician later breaks his narrative to advise "ye maistresses" hired to govern "lordes doghtres" (VI.72–73), and "ye fadres and ye modres" in "charge of al hir surveiaunce" (VI.93, 95), that they should make sure that their children "ne perisse" "by ensample of youre lyvynge, / Or by your necligence in chastisynge" (VI.97–98). In creating and then closing these gaps in his narrative, the Physician emphasizes the permeability of supposedly secure boundaries, the ever-present possibility of perversion, and the need for vigilant surveillance to keep the relationship between original and copy intact. Yet only at such a fraught moment does it become possible to talk about "the Physician" as a "real" character in his tale.

The ostensible text of the Physician may be that the true social body inheres in proper masculine activity and that one naturally chooses such masculinity. For example, Appius's "sentence" is false because he chooses the feminizing material body. By choosing Virginia's accidental body (i.e., sexy woman) rather than her signification as emblem of Virginius's power (i.e., chaste daughter and worthy wife), Appius objectifies himself and ceases to have proper agency as a man. But the subtext of the *Physician's Tale* says something else. There remains a residue of the personal and rhetorical, even in such a simplifying, pared-down account. To that extent, the body of the Physician inheres in his tale, exposing a "me"—objectifiable and appropriable—to view. His is a subjectivity hard at work to subsume itself without a trace within the ideologies of dominant culture by proclaiming such ideological configurations as "natural" and invariably active and in control. Yet the manipulations necessary to maintain such a "natural" authority, as well as the personal and present gains from such service to dominant culture, help us "see" the masculine body more clearly, and in doing so, open it to potential appropriation and reconfiguration.

The Host's subsequent efforts to appropriate the Physician's "sothe" more actively and remuneratively for his own ends in the present Canterbury game foreground this residue of the personal even more explicitly. And the very sexual/textual boundaries that the *Physician's Tale* sought to efface by representing them as transparent and irrelevant emerge ever more clearly. The "sentence" of the *Physician's Tale* would have us focus on Virginia's inner beauty and nobility, that is, on that "original" nobility in Virginius, and ultimately, in God. The Host's response, however, foregrounds the exterior vessel. His assessment that "too dear she bought beauty" (VI.293) and "her beauty was her death" (VI.297) stresses a material, gendered body; the feminine supplement of the tale—story as story; fable's affect rather than effect. And the Host concludes, "This is a pitous tale for to heere / But nathelees, passe over; is no fors" (VI.302–3), even though the Physician has been absolutely explicit that his "historial thing" *is* "fors" and cannot be passed over.

What the Host so clearly admires is not simply how the Physician as tale-teller was subsumed within a "higher" masculinity and will—as the tale would demand—but rather how, in doing so, the Physician also expressed his own agency and power in shaping and regulating feminine lack and perversity. The Host responds as one man to another. He acknowledges the presence of the Physician in his tale as an embodied, desiring individual constructing a "nature" that demands constant vigilant surveillance of that body to avert perversity and loss of control. The Host's comments recognize and seek to reproduce the homosocial packaging of identity taking place in the Physician's tale, thereby providing an insightful account of how the Physician secures agency as a true man within the masculinist economy of language and power outlined by his tale.

Thus the Host not only sets himself up as a mock Physician to the pilgrimage body, he also seeks to reproduce a set of metaphoric substitutions similar to those enacted by the Physician in his tale. Just as the Physician's identification with Virginius provided the Physician with a means of putting the body "out there" in a supposedly safe way that would be masculine and active, so too, the Host's identification with the

Physician will give the Host authority and instrumentality in shaping the pilgrimage body. The Physician inscribed the masculine, first in terms of control of a potentially dangerous female "lack" in the person of Virginia, and then in the even more dangerous feminization of masculine will in the perverse desire of Appius. Similarly, the Host attempts to write *his* masculine will, first by selecting "Thou beel amy, thou Pardoner" (VI.318) to tell the next tale, and then by excising the Pardoner's feminized body and perverse desire after he has told his tale. The Physician's account suggested a potentially useful slippage between the "natural" desire of "the people" for the truth about Appius's actions and that of the tale's implied audience that allows both to represent their "natural" recognition of the "truth" through a necessary othering of perverse desire onto Appius/Claudius.

This perverse dynamic in the *Physician's Tale* is echoed in the "gentils'" later, supposedly "instinctive" recognition of the Pardoner's perversity and in their subsequent attempts to excise such perversity from the pilgrimage body. Cut off potentially feminizing cupidity, tell us some moral thing, behave like a true man, and "we" will speak the will of God. The more "we"—Host and "gentils"—fix the Pardoner as naturally absolutely other and subordinate (i.e., passively nonmale, perversely sodomitical, excessive), the more "our nature" is guaranteed as central and dominant (i.e., actively "masculine," straight, "sotheful"). But the Host's stress on the Physician's potent "tools of the trade," his emphasis on his own potency by denying a proper "tool" to the Pardoner, and even his more general allusions to the medical benefits of recreative play (including storytelling), underscore the material bodies so perfunctorily "killed off" in the *Physician's Tale*. And in bringing the *materia* excised by the *Physician's Tale* back into play in this way, the Host comes dangerously close to destabilizing the Physician's absolutist account of the natural, on which dominant culture relies for its hegemonic power.

Moreover, any intended smooth transition from one articulation of the natural to the next is disturbed by the Pardoner's reenactment of the ambiguous "sentence" of the *Physician's Tale* as refracted and vulgarized by the Host:

> First I pronounce whennes that I come,
> And thanne my bulles shewe I, alle and some.

Our lige lordes seel on my patente
That shewe I first, my body to warente. (VI.335–38)

That is, the Pardoner, too, begins with the assumption that the sign of an originary authority (here papal) will naturally subsume any potentially perverse materiality by overwriting its masculine will on that body. The Host did something similar when he assumed the Physician's role (e.g., his choice of the Pardoner as the next tale-teller in order to provide "solas" after the melancholic affect of the Physician's story). The Pardoner's comments here foreground the gaps in the seamless garment of masculinity that the Host's bodily/bawdy appropriation of the Physician's story made visible. The *Physician's Tale* proclaims itself a "historial thing" (VI.156) that will necessarily impose its unifying will on all who listen to it; body will "naturally" give way to "sentence." Yet ironically, it is just this absolutist claim, to produce the same effect no matter what the context, that makes the tale such a useful commodity for the Physician and the Host, that allows them to use the story of Virginia to gain agency within the existing configurations of ideology. And an awkwardly similar absolutism and commodification of desire characterizes the commerce between the Pardoner and his "lewed" audience. The Pardoner underscores just such a perverse dynamic with his reminder that he uses Latin merely to "saffron" (VI.345) his preaching and stir "lewed" folk to devotion.[28]

The Pardoner therefore makes explicit what the Physician and Host dare not acknowledge: the activity of the objectifying desire of his audience being written on him and the body of his text even as he stands in for "the father" and existing ideological configurations. The Physician purported to tell one "true" storial thing that repeats the originary name over and over without alteration, even at the risk of killing off the body itself; whereas the Pardoner regularly tells a hundred or more "false japes" (VI.394) in his preaching and chooses "olde stories" (VI.436), not because they will transmit an anterior, primal will, but because they're what his audience wants to hear. And he does the same thing now for the pilgrimage audience by situating the exemplary tale they have demanded within a dizzying series of frames that emphasize duplication and dissemination without a controlling originary subject, the copying of copies rather than a "truly masculine" procreative reproduction. Thus, when we reach the Pardoner's story "proper," the kinds of foundational binaries emphasized in the Physician's story have collapsed. Is it "false jape" or some honest thing, made up or historial, ephemeral or essential, the Pardoner's or our own? The Pardoner's excessive reproduction of the constructions of proper masculinity and the natural taking place within medieval identity politics thus "spoils identity" to the extent that it de-scribes the identities that a conservative social order has so oppressively in-scribed by means of essentialized gender difference.

If the question of how we work upon the world and constitute it as a social entity emerges as a crucial one in this fragment, equally pressing by the end of the *Pardoner's Tale* is our recognition of the socially and linguistically constructed "bodies that matter" that enable this representational work to take place, and that are themselves always already subjects and objects of desire. The Pardoner's queer re-presentation of the feminine, to adapt Sedgwick, "far from being capable of being detached from the originary scene of shame, cleaves to that scene as a near-inexhaustible source of transformational energy."[29] As such it constitutes that queer performativity Butler has described as

> this relation of being implicated in that which one opposes, this turning of power against itself to produce alternative modalities of power, to establish a kind of political contestation that is not a "pure" opposition, a "transcendence" of contemporary relations of power, but a difficult labor of forging a future from resources inevitably impure.[30]

The perspective of a dominant masculinity may seek to read in the Pardoner only the sodomitical horrors of feminine nonidentity, a hermeneutical dead-end that writes true identity as someone else's and elsewhere. But the Pardoner's troubling body—ceaselessly performing gender and sexuality but never getting it "right"—can also provide an important point of entry back into the perversities of a medieval politics of representation that the Physician's story of Virginia and its fictional frame both enacted and attempted to disguise. Similarly, the representational flux occasioned by our own attempt to de-scribe the complexities of such a "medieval" moment can also bring into view the modern body in different ways and help queer *its* claim to naturalness. Such a double process of historicization might thereby open up room to maneuver for postmodern bodies (and subjectivities) as more than that which is already known and represented.

## KISSING THE PARDONER

From Kittredge on, with his delineation of the Pardoner as "the most abandoned character among the Canterbury Pilgrims," the queerness of the Pardoner's character has been a driving force in Chaucer criticism.[31] Walter Clyde Curry began speculation about the Pardoner's deviant "identity" long ago with his suggestion that the Pardoner was a congenital eunuch, and this viewpoint, with qualifications, remains a deep-seated one.[32] Others have suggested different abnormalities—for example, Monica E. McAlpine's "homosexual," Beryl Rowland's "testicular pseudohermaphrodite of the feminine type," and Eric W. Stockton's "manic depressive with traces of anal eroticism"—but have continued to locate the Pardoner's identity in some essential physical "nature."[33] Richard Firth Green has argued instead that the Pardoner is an effeminate heterosexual womanizer.[34] Whatever form it may take for these different critics, the readily apparent perversity of the Pardoner's body provides convincing proof of his true identity. Thus Melvin Storm, for example, states categorically that "[w]hether the Pardoner is a gelding, a mare, or both, his physical nature mirrors his performance as a churchman."[35]

An equation between properly active masculinity and right reading and writing is, of course, a commonplace of medieval hermeneutical theory, epitomized in Alain de Lille's vision of a Nature who, "in order to insure genealogical succession, endowed her handmaiden Venus with two instruments of rectitude—*ortho*graphy, or straight writing, and *ortho*dox coition, or straight sexuality."[36] The continuing power of this approach as a structuring principle for the *Pardoner's Tale* is evident in Eugene Vance's semiotic analysis:

> [T]he Pardoner conspires [to set] *himself* up as a moveable shrine endowed with relics unsurpassed by those of anyone else in England.... What is more, the kneeling posture to which the Pardoner summons the pilgrims would place their noses right before his deficient crotch. Thus, the Pardoner compels the lurid trajectory of his self-dramatization to converge on the very locus of his own false powers, both physical *and* spiritual.

The Pardoner's invitation to kneel and kiss his relics therefore elicits a retort from the "virile Harry Bailly" that is "not just *ad hominem*" but "a revolt of proper language in the low style—of terms *in proprio nomine*—against the adulterous eloquence of the Pardoner when the Host invokes his fear of Christ and the cross and then performs his verbal surgery." And the act of charity that "is now called for in order to turn the laughter of derision into the laughter of play" appropriately comes from the Christlike, regenerative actions of the Knight, "himself a master of the high style, and the teller of a noble tale whose hero, Duke Theseus, the Knight himself will now emulate as he heals the divided social order by summoning forth the kiss of peace."[37]

In terms of the masculinist heterosexual language underpinning most medieval hermeneutical models and persisting in readings like Vance's, the Pardoner's unmanly body neatly constructs a series of reassuring binaries: impotent Pardoner/virile Host, sterile Pardoner/vigorous "gentils," morally bankrupt Pardoner/spiritually worthy Knight, blind Pardoner/clear-sighted critical audience. Only a truly "lewed" audience, characterized by a feminizing cupidity and a love of material ornament equal to the Pardoner's, would be rendered sterile by his presence. The masculine "gentil" reader will "naturally" erase the Pardoner's false presence and substitute his own virility for the Pardoner's absent testicles, Christ's pardoning words for the Pardoner's fake relics and materialism. The redeemed reader's "circumcised" tongue will thus speak with precisely the authority denied the Pardoner by an "unnatural" body.[38]

But by essentializing the Pardoner in this way, the binaries structuring such medieval and modern hermeneutical models preclude a full analysis of the viewing subject's implication in the Pardoner's sexual dissidence.[39] Neither some unnatural monster absolutely other to us, nor some symbolic entity of nonmeaning, "he," the Pardoner, is both of these things and more, a nexus of intermingling discourses about the subject and its meaning that cannot settle into a reassuring ordered hierarchy, but must work in conjunction, even in competition, with one another. Donald Howard's characterization of the Pardoner as "feminoid" crystallizes this radical unknowability about the Pardoner's body—"he is a mystery, an enigma"—and begins to articulate the sodomitical panic its strangeness so often induces—"He has a magnetic power of attraction partly because he is frightening and loathsome."[40] And Steven Kruger has powerfully and provocatively explored the homophobia inhering within constructions of the Pardoner's otherness as well as the difficult and conflicted process by which the modern queer reader might claim him as one of our own.[41] What I want to focus on in the rest of this chapter is that moment at the end of the tale when "we" as the Pardoner's audience are brought up close and personal with the very body we have acknowledged as essentially perverse and different.

For the Pardoner's exhortation to kiss his relics at the end of his tale suddenly pushes his quotation of authority, powerfully present throughout the tale, to an absurd extreme. And if the language of the Host's reply turns the Pardoner into a theological sodomite or hermeneutical eunuch, the Knight's initiation of the kiss between "Sire Pardoner" and "Sire Host" (VI.963, 964) addresses the Pardoner as one occupying a necessary place within the homosocial dialogue governing the day-to-day activity of church and society.[42] For the diplomatic and chivalric courtesy kiss of greeting; the feudal homage kiss; the kiss sealing a betrothal, marriage, or other contract or marking the end of a personal or family feud—all were important social rituals that stressed common class, political, and economic interests. The liturgical kiss of peace, moreover, signaled the exchange of the Holy Spirit that fused individual believers into the common Body of Christ.[43] And by the high Middle Ages, when church seating tended to be separated on gender lines, that kiss would have been exchanged between members of the same sex. After the thirteenth century, especially in England, a cleric distributed the rite to lay members of the congregation, who kissed a wooden or metal board (the pax or paxboard) that resembled the host and often contained a picture of Christ crucified.[44] Given that seating in congregational churches followed social precedence and that family pews and household chapels were increasingly prevalent, the late medieval liturgical kiss of peace, whether bestowed on another person or on a paxboard, would have stressed external social and economic similarities or an interior, personal involvement in the eucharistic sacrifice more than it would any traditional reconciliation of difference.[45]

The different kinds of kisses imagined by the Host and the Knight, and especially the conceptual dissonances they embody, draw attention to themselves as socially constructed performances. Such brushes with the Pardoner thus help bring to consciousness *this* discursive moment—neither sermon nor riotous nonmeaning—as a point of metaphoric dissonance that forces the Pardoner and his audience together in unauthorized yet meaningful ways. For example, when the Host is initially asked to kiss the Pardoner's relics, the request could be viewed as a call for a kiss of peace (if the relic is seen as a paxboard). Such a call would not only give the Pardoner authority over the Host, but would do so by granting the Host the precedence he clearly desires—precedence, however, as sinner rather than as social leader. The Host, who rightly imagines the Pardoner's request as a perversion of the feudal kiss of homage, stresses his absolute difference from the Pardoner by presenting the counterimage of the theological pervert or sodomite kissing the devil's anus. The repulsion he feels at the idea of touching the Pardoner reminds us of the ability of the kiss both to establish and to cross crucial boundaries. For touch is the lowest of the senses, precisely because it is the most embodied. Not surprisingly, the kiss also functioned in the Middle Ages as an icon of carnal desire, of *luxuria* and *cupiditas,* as much as of the Holy Spirit and *caritas.*[46] While the Knight's initiative can be read as an attempt to substitute for the Pardoner's false relics, or for the Host's image of debased carnality, an "official" image of the Pardoner as a kind of paxboard that the Host can kiss with impunity, such a kiss nonetheless conjoins like and unlike in a way that cannot easily be contained.

The play of the *Pardoner's Tale,* by inverting or perverting the hegemonic activity of the fertilizing penis/pen, runs counter to the repressive binaries of a hermeneutical model based on heterosexual reproduction. Even though the Host and the Pardoner's kiss ostensibly functions as the endpoint in a series of attempts to define the Pardoner as absolute other, it also underscores the continuing proximity of the Pardoner and shows how his efforts to assert identity—his transgressive desire—mirror ours. The final framing gestures of the Host and the Knight can never completely erase the Pardoner's presence and effect a reassuring metaphoric substitution. Instead, the kiss—that moment when we are forced to "touch" the Pardoner—extends the resistance to categorization and control initiated by the Pardoner's body, holding up for analysis the constructions of masculinity and meaning that are taking place within this time and place.

If for a moment the supposed unity of the dominant male gaze is disrupted by the kiss—with attention turned away from the imperfections of the Pardoner's body to the body of pilgrims supposedly authoring that discerning subject position—it is evident that the Host no more speaks *in proprio nomine* than does the Pardoner. For while the Pardoner's exaggerated gestures provoke even stronger policing efforts, the Host's extreme assertions of "authority" and "normality" attract notice as constructed acts. In expressing moral outrage at being asked to kiss the Pardoner's relics, the Host may be invoking the authoritative signs absent in the Pardoner's presentation of himself—"coillons," true relics, "the croys which that Seint Eleyne fond" (VI.951–53)—in order to be heard. Indeed, if Daniel Knapp is correct, the Host's allusion to kissing the Pardoner's breeches would call to mind the hair breeches of Thomas à Becket that probably hung above the saint's shrine for pilgrims to kiss and venerate.[47] But such substitutions of supposedly virile activity for the Pardoner's verbal effeminacy detract from the Host's attempts to establish his personal authority at the forefront of the pilgrimage. When the Host announces that he "wol no lenger pleye / With thee, ne with noon oother angry man" (VI.958–59), he silences his adversary, it appears, only to enshrine his own more profitable play with the other pilgrims. For the more the Pardoner can be maintained as an absence of potency, the more the Host can assert his own masculinity and moral authority and establish that he is no false copy but the real thing.

Moreover, if the Host can construct himself as moral physician to the pilgrimage, he will have a far greater warrant for speaking than he did in the "play" of the introduction to the *Pardoner's Tale*. He should thus solidify a previously contingent authority concerned only with material well-being and dependent on the agreement and goodwill of the other pilgrims. But to achieve this end, the Host must, like the Pardoner, rhetorically elide crucial differences between "pleye" and "ernest"; between London and Canterbury as end and center of this pilgrimage group; and among the Host, Knight, and Parson as leaders of the pilgrimage. This rhetorical grandstanding constructs the identity of the Host (as potent man, moral Christian) on the falseness of the Pardoner's body (that is, on the Host's own construction of what the Pardoner is). The Host's denunciation and warnings—such as his threat to cut off testicles, which it is implied, may not even be there—look suspiciously like the rhetorical ornamentation the Pardoner uses to disguise cupidity as righteousness. For the Host, by fostering his own desire to establish his virility and material success under the pretense of substituting the true Body of Christ for the Pardoner's false relics, is acting out exactly what the Pardoner stands accused of: representing the material and ephemeral as the true and eternal.

The kiss underscores that things do not end, as the Host would have us think they do, under the sign of satire and reformist indignation, with verbal castration uncovering, and being validated by, physical reality. Instead, the kiss aligns the Pardoner and his audience in ways that envelop and fold together the very categories and boundaries with which that audience has been seeking to define and distance him. For with both Pardoner and Host silenced as their mouths meet, who speaks and with what voice? Both Chaucer's text and the historical evidence are, of course, ambiguous about whether the public kiss of peace between Host and Pardoner would have to be a mouth-to-mouth kiss, nor would I want to make such a categorical statement. I choose instead to focus on what we can know: that the kiss—whether on the cheek *or* on the mouth—encourages an examination of the interpenetration of private and public, ideological and personal, occurring in such apparently transparent acts.

Throughout the Middle Ages, kisses on the mouth in all contexts—ceremonial and diplomatic kisses, kisses of fealty, and kisses of peace (between men and women *and* between men)—are frequent. While Nicholas J. Perella notes that in medieval pictorial imagery, "rather than a clear labial kiss of lovers one often finds something like a cheek-to-cheek representation," he adds: "Partly, however, the reason for this seems to have been the desire to portray the faces in a full or three-quarters view. This may be observed in the many scenes ... depicting the kiss of Judas or the theme of the Visitation, where again there is no question that a real kiss is intended, although in order to show as much of the faces as possible actual labial contact is hardly shown."[48] In literature, by contrast, references to labial kisses are numerous, even commonplace. Indeed, George Fenwick Jones notes that in German texts, "unless the contrary is stated, it may be assumed that all kisses are on the mouth," citing numerous examples of such kisses between men in rites of homage, in ceremonial and diplomatic greetings, and in contracts.[49] Closer to Chaucer is the moment in the *Roman de la Rose* when the Lover renders homage to the God of Love with a kiss on the mouth (translated without change in meaning two centuries later in the Middle English *Romaunt*):

> Fully, for thyn avauntage,
> Anoon to do me heere homage.
> And sithe kisse thou shalt my mouth,
> Which to no vilayn was never couth
> For to aproche it, ne for to touche.[50]

Clearly the kiss here marks the intimate within and through the public, maintaining social and gender boundaries even as it blurs them.

While the kiss on the mouth in such public occasions seems to be dying out by the end of the medieval period, it is by no means clear exactly when it died out or why. J. Russell Major points out that in France the kiss on the mouth survives as an integral part of the ceremony of feudal homage until the end of the fifteenth century. And the English records from 1429 and 1439 that he cites would indicate a similar pattern across the Channel. Moreover, later changes to the ceremony in France, rather than substituting a kiss on the cheek, remove the kiss altogether. Major suggests that it was growing anxiety about and regulation of homosexuality in the later medieval period that contributed to the gradual abandonment of the kiss on the mouth. But the feudal kiss, both as a marker of class solidarity and as a hierarchical division between lord and vassal, may also have become increasingly problematic and unwelcome with the greater social competition and mobility of the later Middle Ages.[51]

Thus, any attempt to decide the significance of Chaucer's kiss on the basis of supposedly objective, historical "facts" will, I think, prove as much of a red herring as similar attempts to stabilize the meaning of the Pardoner in terms of the biological "facts" of his body. Whether the Host literally kisses the Pardoner on the mouth or on the cheeks, my point remains the same. That which has been constructed as "naturally" and absolutely other is now reconstituted as a sign of sameness and contiguity because of the traditional signification of the kiss as a mark of equality or near equality. Certainly this kiss is and remains a very public act that resonates through a variety of social and theological contexts. But the way it is staged and performed here can help us see how private desire helps shape, and is in turn shaped by, such public performances.

However much the actions of the Knight may construct the Pardoner once again as a respectable member of the Body of Christ, there remains the uncomfortable image of the Host kissing the Pardoner, that is, doing exactly what he had so strenuously rejected doing earlier: kissing an impotent and worthless relic (or, worse, performing an act equivalent to the heretic's kissing of the Devil's anus). The Host's verbal abuse of the Pardoner has done little to reform the Pardoner either as man or as potent religious symbol: that the Pardoner constitutes a sexual, social, and moral solecism is now more immediately, even glaringly, evident than at any other time in his tale. Yet when the Host (and the pilgrimage group he represents) touches "Sire Pardoner" in a sign of reconciliation and equality, the kiss reincorporates the Pardoner as if he were a normal man. The form of address used here, however, is ambiguous and slippery. While the Knight calls both Host and Pardoner "Sire," he also addresses the Host three times by the more formal "yow" and "ye" and the Pardoner twice by the more familiar "thee." This distinction would suggest that the Knight seeks to contain the Pardoner even while opening the ranks of polite society enough to appear to admit him. But the more formal address used with the Host might indicate a similar double maneuver. The Knight's invocation of a larger social and moral order at the heart of the pilgrimage group also serves to contain the angry Host, warning him that he has gone beyond his licensed authority as host of the company and, in breaking decorum, has also threatened the stability of that larger order the pilgrimage is meant to represent. In any event, the very propriety of the active position the kiss of peace offers both Pardoner and Host depends on their bending their wills to another, superior one. Clearly the Pardoner must be constructed, in some form at least, as a worthy, normal male agent of the church; otherwise the kiss would become an overtly cynical act or, more disturbingly, a sodomitical embrace of unbridled carnality. But can we really laugh and play "as we diden" (VI.967) when this action marries the supposedly normal with the perverse in a way that the Host's attempts to speak *in proprio nomine* had intended to avoid?

If, as the Knight points out, the kiss is necessary to initiate movement, have we indeed, in turning away from the altercation between Host and Pardoner, propelled ourselves down the path of truth? For while the kiss may be intended to send us on our way to Canterbury again, it also perpetuates the play of storytelling and postpones the "final" word of the *Parson's Tale* and *Chaucer's Retraction*. While the Knight—like the Host—may be trying to redeem a chaotic moment by moving us away from the Pardoner and pointing us toward Canterbury and the heavenly Jerusalem, his attempt also holds us where we are for a moment longer, to touch that which we have just said cannot be touched. As a result, the kiss of peace stills the active masculine renunciation of the Host into a "speaking picture" in which a variety of voices—and no one voice—is heard. It is precisely the Knight's (and the other pilgrims') desire to laugh and play as they did before that produces this other ending for the *Pardoner's Tale,* allowing the Pardoner's body to linger perversely in the foreground in active, "masculine" play with the other pilgrims.

By stilling and deferring the attempt by the masculine gaze of the "redeemed" pilgrims to control what the Pardoner means, the kiss provides an instance in which the Pardoner's body can do more than simply deconstruct categories or gesture elsewhere for meaning. As much an aesthetic as a properly moral moment, the kiss stands as a point of crucial excess—beyond either the hegemonic control of earnest satire or the vacuous chaos of libertarian game. In this instant the Pardoner's destabilizing presence can provoke the kind of social and discursive dislocation that Dollimore calls "discoherence," that is, "an incongruity verging on a meaningful contradiction."[52] In facing the Pardoner's body, we touch our own desire. And in observing that moment of proximity with an other whom we understand to be like us, we can begin to see our own identity as constructed (and to recognize that the Pardoner we have made makes us in turn). In this way the kiss provides the Pardoner's presence with the kind of semantic impertinence that leads to innovation—the kind that, according to Paul Ricoeur, defines true metaphor:

> [A] way of responding in a creative fashion to a question presented by things. In a certain discourse situation, in a given social milieu and at a precise moment something seeks to be said that demands an operation of speech, speech working on language, that brings words and things face to face. The final outcome is a new description of the universe of representations . . . *between* the sentence and the word, *between* predication and naming.[53]

The body of pilgrims we see and hear in, with, and under the *Pardoner's Tale,* then, has as much in common with the supposedly depraved Pardoner as with the redeemed reader outlined by the *Retraction.* For if the Host, the Knight, and the other pilgrims are forced to construct the Pardoner as one of them in order to substitute their Christlike bodies for his defective, fragmented body, they have become the very kind of unreflective reader described by the Pardoner's "lewed folk" (VI.389–94). Writing their desire for absolute reassurance in language and signs through the immobilized body of the Pardoner makes him as much a "false relic" for them as his pig's bones are for his less sophisticated audiences.

In presenting the pilgrimage body as spectacle—neither completely feminized and passive nor totally masculine and active—the kiss exposes the limitations of the "identities" put into the discursive marketplace by the linguistic economy of this society. Patricia Eberle has pointed out the pervasiveness of commercial language and outlook in the *General Prologue,* emphasizing that the "official destination of the Canterbury pilgrimage is the shrine of Thomas à Becket, but its point of departure is the commercial world of Harry Bailly's tavern."[54] I would extend Eberle's argument to suggest that at this point Harry Bailly, like the Pardoner embodying an emergent discourse of late medieval capitalism, outlines a set of identifications (oriented around a series of mobile gender, social class, and sexual distinctions) every bit as important to "gentil" self-identification as the more traditional, confessional essences insisted on later by the Parson (see chapter 6, below). Appropriately, it is not the Parson but the Knight who steps in to stabilize an epistemologically fraught moment, once again proving his "worth" both in its "high" (clerical/aristocratic) and "low" (bourgeois) senses. The virile, material identity that the Host claims for himself by fixing an essential sexual identity for the Pardoner works as an articulation of an autonomous subject position only to the extent that it presents itself as part of a prevailing disciplinary orthodoxy. The Host's attempts to reduce the Pardoner to a rhetorical trope shows how the delineation of a private, personal self can work in tandem with and extend the impersonal, public, hegemonic discourses of power. The Host's success in establishing a personal, private, material position depends on his having already policed himself enough to appear to be an orthodox Christian furthering his religion's views about right behavior. The Parson-like intervention of the Knight (representative of the larger order of disciplinary care), instead of being at odds with the Host, simply "turns down the volume" enough so that the Host cannot be heard to utter that which must not be uttered, the "open secret" of this disciplinary pact: the apparent opposites private/public or material/spiritual are in fact necessary co-agents in maintaining a status quo.[55]

While the prevailing discourse of power in the *Pardoner's Tale* seeks everywhere to establish the Pardoner as (an)other self, culture's opposite, the "dangerousness" of the Pardoner is not that he represents *another* essentialist self (homosexual rather than heterosexual or eunuch rather than potent male) or that he is some symbolic black hole of absolute nonmeaning. What is transgressive about the Pardoner, what provokes the violent responses of his audience, is precisely the way that he is *not* other, most obviously the way that the cupidity his audience attempts to fix in him alone actually fuels the discursive economy of the dominant culture. The "non-centered or vagrant desire" of the Pardoner present in the kiss—in a way that has surprising parallels to that of the quintessentially queer modern subject, Oscar Wilde—thus becomes in Dollimore's words "both the impetus for a subversive inversion, and what is released by it." According to Dollimore, "From an essentialist point of view, Wilde's position might seem to rest on a confusion: how can the desire which culture outlaws itself be thoroughly cultural? In fact it is because and not in spite of this shared cultural dimension that Wilde can enact one of the most disturbing of all forms of transgression, namely that whereby the outlaw turns up as inlaw, and the other as proximate proves more disturbing than the other as absolute difference. That which society forbids, Wilde reinstates *through and within* some of its most cherished and central cultural categories."[56] We have seen how the kiss represents familiar binaries governing sexual and hermeneutical activity in inverted, transposed, and ultimately transvalued ways. But the Pardoner's embodiment of transgressive desire also suggests other ways of looking at the Canterbury project itself—both at the possibilities for personal and institutional reformation promised by indulgences and pilgrimage, and at the attempt by vernacular poetry to claim truth-value for itself over and against the traditional authority of Latinate scripturally derived public discourse.

Again and again the Pardoner's audiences—pilgrim and modern alike—have sought to maintain the purity of the Canterbury journey by dissociating themselves from the Pardoner, thereby locating falsity within his fake relics and inflated indulgences or within the superficial literalism of his "lewed" patrons. As I have suggested, the relationship the kiss represents between the Pardoner and his pilgrim audience indicates a far more fluid, transvaluing commerce between subordinate and dominant cultures. And a closer look at the politics of pardon in late medieval society finds similarly complex negotiations at work establishing the merit and meaning of relics and indulgences.[57] On the surface the truth-value of a relic or indulgence appeared fixed and readily apparent, guaranteed by the authority of the church. In practice, however, a relic could not maintain its status without continuing asseverations of its vigor and efficacy from its devotees. Its authenticity more often than not might depend on the loudness and frequency of its endorsements or the social prestige of its enthusiasts. Indeed, the spiritual substance of a relic was often gauged by the wealth of the shrine or the number and material worth of the miracles worked by the saint. The renewed fashionableness of pilgrimages and indulgences among the affluent and powerful in the fourteenth and fifteenth centuries, which gave a new lease on life to some older shrines, stemmed from just such a linkage between worldly advantages and formal spiritual observance:

> The religion of the laity was above all a religion of external observances, marked by a strong element of ritual. . . . It was an attitude which bred extreme conformity and a somewhat unhealthy view that the clothes make the man. Wearing a pilgrim's badge or the emblem of a confraternity became pious works in themselves.[58]

Thus, if belief in relics and pardons bolstered the institutional status quo, providing riches and prestige to the custodial monasteries and churches, such articulations of faith also provided a discursive space for popular desire to reach consciousness. The very "invention" in 1300 of a Roman jubilee that offered a plenary indulgence resulted from popular pressure, not from the premeditated venality of the papacy; and there followed in the next two centuries a remarkable increase in the availability and popularity of plenary indulgences that did not require recipients to go on pilgrimage.[59] The tremendous appetite for the benefits of indulgences and pilgrimages at all levels of the church and society in the later Middle Ages was fueled, at least in part, by the believers' deep and widespread desire for the greatest possible return with the least expenditure of time and money.

What is striking about the Canterbury enterprise is the extent to which this desire is both manifested and obscured by the insistence that this pilgrimage is the real thing. The high proportion of men and "gentils"—both lay and clerical—making up Chaucer's group is the most immediate sign of the stability and orthodoxy of their pursuit.[60] But there are other, less immediately apparent signals that this pilgrimage is indeed a journey to truth. Despite the popularity of easy indulgences, no one except the Pardoner mentions them as a possible goal of the pilgrimage. Nor has anyone in this group sought out the newer English shrines, such as those at Hailes and Walsingham, or the more ephemeral local shrines popular with women and the lowborn. What the narrator stresses in the *General Prologue* is the established preeminence of Canterbury as a pilgrimage destination (though it was more nearly a regional shrine for Londoners, since they could reach it relatively easily and inexpensively). Furthermore, Canterbury had the added prestige of being an English shrine with a reputation equal to that of major Continental shrines. And since Canterbury is the site most singled out by Lollard satire, a journey there was a clear sign of religious, as well as social, orthodoxy. Significantly, only the Wife of Bath and the Pardoner have any connection with foreign shrines, and the Wife's choices are all eminently respectable and established.[61]

Once again, it is only the Pardoner who appears to be clearly other. His papal pardons and his association with the rival shrine of Saint James of Compostella link him with the generally unpopular export of cash and wealth that foreign control of the pardon business would bring. Moreover, his customary ignorant audience implicates him in the popular, emotional side of pardon, with its "magical" relics and obvious fads in shrines and miracles. Thus his involvement in the business of pardon is one that the gentlefolk—nationalist and respectably restrained—would want to repudiate. Yet the comment in the *General Prologue* that the company is going the "hooly blisful martir for to seke, / That hem hath holpen whan that they were seeke" (I.17–18) suggests that everyone expects some real return from this pilgrimage, that its spiritual reward will be materially signified—whether by a physical cure or by release from time in purgatory. And the pilgrims' own actions manifest those aspects of the penance "industry" that were most popular in the period, those that kept money, time, and effort close to home and that maintained the power of the system while giving the individual maximum benefit and control. Far from defining the Pardoner as absolutely other to the "gentils," his association with the more ambiguous "cutting edge" of pilgrimages, relics, and indulgences is transgressive and dangerous precisely because it is congruent with the desires of the rest of the company.[62] Nor is this situation unique in the period:

> Everywhere the pardoners owed their success to the fact that they were always slightly in advance of official thinking on the subject of indulgences. They offered their clients on paper more than could be had at the great sanctuaries. As a result, people expected the same benefits from their pilgrimages and, after a decent interval, they usually got them. In 1312 the council of Vienne sternly condemned pardoners for pretending that their indulgences could release souls from purgatory; but within twenty years such indulgences were being offered at the Portiuncula chapel, and by the middle of the fifteenth century they were being granted by the popes.[63]

Once again, the Pardoner as "open secret" embodies the paradox that powers the discursive system of the dominant culture. At all costs, therefore, his fellow pilgrims must keep this secret below discursive consciousness; for to speak it aloud would violate and undermine the stability of the binaries—noble/base, essence/accident, public/private—on which the dominant culture depends for its hegemony.

In bringing us closer to the Pardoner, and thus to the truth of our own desire, the kiss perversely provides a more holistic way to reformation than does the straight path insisted on by the gentlefolk and the Host. Harry Bailly's simplistic attempt to reform the pilgrimage body by excising the Pardoner replicates the desire of relic worshippers to fetishize a part rather than a whole and thus to falsely appropriate the meaning of the relic as their own. The transgressive aesthetic developing out of the kiss suggests a far more complex interdependence between subject and object. We can be like Saint Francis, say, but only by first acknowledging our own difference from him and the need to change to become like him. Only by highlighting sameness and difference can a relic truly change what we desire so we can reincorporate ourselves within the Body of Christ. But because the relic is a material medium like metaphor, it helps us touch the other in a contingent and inherently unstable way and thus carries with it the potential to change how the holy is manifested and understood in material existence. In the perverse or transvaluing moment of the kiss, then, the Pardoner's body can become just such an empowering relic of our paradoxical desire.

Political negotiation and its denial constitute a double bind at the heart of the *Canterbury Tales,* embodying both Chaucer's attempt to maintain solidarity with a unitary Scripture-based idea of the book and the ambiguities inherent in medieval artistic production. Clearly the *Parson's Tale* and *Chaucer's Retraction* invoke a totalizing sense of the Word when they seek to "end" the pilgrimage and storytelling. Similarly, the reading strategies enforced by hegemonic discourse about the Pardoner must absolutely separate him from us (readers and pilgrims alike), for we are empowered as whole, active, and truthful only to the extent that we erase the Pardoner's fragmentation, passivity, and falseness. Such reading strategies encourage us to experience the kiss solely as a performative moment whose orality establishes true intersubjective communication and autonomy for the subject "I." As readers following this first trajectory of meaning, attempting to maintain the unity and stability of this performative "I," we tend to fetishize certain fragments of the whole story—delimiting "meaning" to the tale proper, or the exemplum, or the old man, for instance—instead of taking on the elision of boundaries that this fragment of the *Canterbury Tales* exposes. The transgressive power of the Pardoner's continuing presence, however, derails this linear "pilgrimage to Truth" to the extent that his self-consciously constructed performance underscores the human inability to go beyond language or to give up the materiality of life. The kiss as spectacle suggests another, more overtly textualized subject position, one participating in, but also forced to analyze, the construction of identity and meaning.

Fusing the Pardoner and his audience in a new equation, the kiss opens much-needed room for maneuver between the performative and the textualized subjects. More than any other Canterbury tale (with the possible exceptions of the *Nun's Priest's Tale* and the *Canon's Yeoman's Tale*), the *Pardoner's Tale* insists that a tale must have an essential meaning but makes the discovery of that inherent meaning impossible. The interactions of the Pardoner, the Host, and the "gentils," culminating in the kiss, surround and merge into the tale proper so that the pilgrims—indeed, the Canterbury fiction itself—are in a real sense part of the "abhomynable superfluytee" that we supposedly reject in the Pardoner and his tale. Where *does* the essence of the tale reside—in the scriptural quotation "cupiditas radix malorum est?" In some orthodox medieval sermon "moralitee" that exists independent of the actual preaching occasion? In the exemplum? In the sermon that the Pardoner delivers to unlettered audiences? In the portion labeled the *Pardoner's Tale* in modern editions? Or even in the whole of Fragment VI and those portions of the *General Prologue* and the *Wife of Bath's Prologue* that deal with the Pardoner? In its puzzling fusion of essence and accident, the tale reproduces the hermeneutical instabilities occasioned by the communal production of meaning in medieval vernacular literature (and life?): poet, scribe, and reader—"soth" and "fals"—freely mix, and the silencing voice of ultimate authority is endlessly deferred by the exigencies of the textual moment, however much the myth of "myn auctor" may be invoked.

Yet even though the kiss inscribes another, textualized subject viewing the pilgrimage frame's interaction with the *Pardoner's Tale,* such recourse to the private and individual in the form of a textualized reader is, arguably, licensed in much the same way as are the activities of the Host and the gentlefolk (or modern critics). By purporting to complete the policing, redeeming activity that the Pardoner's misapplications have made necessary, in various ways (each of them *the* right way) the textualized reader (in private) fulfills the impulse to right speech that public authority demands. Surely in making sense of the Pardoner and his tale, the reader will agree with right reason and Christian dogma—choosing Christ over the Pardoner and serving as the perfect mouthpiece for authority that the various pilgrims have tried to be. Such a textualized reader cannot but become the next link in a hermeneutical chain aimed at dispersing disciplinary power ever more broadly and systematically. The construction of the Pardoner as absolutely other functions, one might say, as the "closet" of the pilgrims' own construction of the myth of a secure and unified self. If the Pardoner really were to speak *his* self, he would also speak the self of the reading "I" in direct contradiction to the pact of silence the "I" has constructed with the ruling discourse of power. Such unlicensed speaking must be avoided if the "I" is to maintain a profitable, privileged place vis-à-vis authority. The kiss, however, by underscoring the unavoidability of such discursive impurity, perpetuates the transgressive desire the Pardoner gave voice to with his overweening concern for the self and its materiality. If the Pardoner dangerously inverts ruling binaries, the kiss makes his otherness proximate and thus brings to consciousness our implication in the politics of inversion and perversion. The spectacle of the kiss—making us see ourselves in the Pardoner we have defined as not us and forcing our awareness of individual desire and its ability to effect change—thus decenters the whole, unitary self sought by the Host, the Knight, and the gentlefolk. In doing so, it requires us to recognize that the impossibly libertarian desire the Pardoner stands accused of is also our desire as readers. For in postponing, however briefly, this final collapse of binaries (inside/outside, private/public) and in allowing a textualized reader to see that inevitable possibility, the text also speaks another "open secret"—the pilgrimage as a privileged place to desire otherwise, a place to linger in play and fantasize a private self.[64]

## INCREASE AND MULTIPLY

Although the Pardoner's at once overdetermined yet radically unknowable body is layered within authorized patterns of assimilation and social organization, as I have argued, the kiss between the Host and the Pardoner foregrounds the necessary and lingering proximity of the perverse being articulated through the other and thus being disavowed by the proper subjects voicing their essential difference from the Pardoner. The Pardoner elicits a more absolutist reaction from the other pilgrims than the Wife of Bath did perhaps because he appears to be so wildly destratifying the organism that the Canterbury pilgrimage has been carefully building up. Rather than reinforcing the pilgrims' own sense of identification with their act of pilgrimage as an erotics of transcendental desire—something the monks of Canterbury and the shrine of Beckett would have done—this Pardoner exposes to the pilgrims their covert identifications with that erotics of worldly desire we have been considering at work in the play of the Canterbury game. This, I think, is the point of the infamous crux near the "end" of the Pardoner's tale where he asks the pilgrims to buy his pardons:

> But, sires, o word forgat I in my tale . . .
> If any of yow wole, of devocion,
> Offren and han myn absolucion,
> Com forth anon, and kneleth here adoun,
> And mekely receyveth my pardoun. (VI.919, 923–26)

It is not that the Pardoner is so stupid as to think that his actual audience will be moved in the same way by his sales pitch as his usual "lewed" audience (although technically many are in fact "lewed," not "lered"), nor that he has finally reached a moment of self-realization and desires to repent his sins and confess to the pilgrims. Rather the moment underscores the similarities between how "the Pardoner's" and "the gentils'" identity and agency are secured.

The "gentils'" project of disavowal enacts a traditional medieval Christian hermeneutic equating the constitution of a universally true subject position with a project of ascesis motivated by an erotics of transcendental desire: thus the Pardoner's excessive "self"-ishness must be inscribed by a would-be proper audience as lack, and the erotics that underwrite his attempts to assert an autonomous self as sterility and death. Yet the very "perversity" that the Pardoner stands accused of, that is, the appropriation of church office for personal ends, looks uncomfortably similar to the kind of appropriation of clerically mediated modes of subject formation that the lay "gentils" attempt as they try to fashion a new "universal" subject position for themselves. This hegemonic identity that the "gentils" want to establish for themselves is necessarily partial—gendered, estate specific, "national" (in the sense of using "English" to designate the interests of a ruling class to a large extent based in the southeast and organized around the City of London and the Court of Westminster)—and designed more to designate those groups of people who are "outside" than to delineate the common characteristics of those who are "inside." Taking charge of a previously clerically controlled ascesis that warrants the truly universal subject thus allows these "gentils" to assert the partial as the whole.

Their othering of the Wife or the Pardoner, precisely at the points where the latter most explicitly brings into view the partiality of these new "gentil" subject positions, attempts to disguise the proximate as the foreign, labeling the Wife and the Pardoner as excessive and different in kind from the "gentils."[65] The Pardoner's desire must therefore be seen as perversely consuming both the material resources of the communities he "ministers" to and the symbolic capital that has accumulated within the church by means of the faithful witness of the saints. In this respect, the Pardoner's wayward body and performance register the obverse side of the surplus production of saintly lives that the relic, and indeed, the office of Pardoner itself, supposedly embodies. In turn, "the gentils"—from Host to Knight—are able to relabel the Pardoner's excess as lack, his desire as death, in a project of ascesis that paradoxically endows them with a surplus of symbolic capital as "proper subjects," as "gentils."

As I have argued, however, this project of ascesis occludes, and thus helps perpetuate, material and symbolic excess production whose benefits are individual and unequal for a variety of Canterbury pilgrims and for certain of the *Tales*' readers, because such excess is rendered via the Pardoner as "common profit." What I have argued about the Pardoner's emphasis on a queer performativity, a queerness "brought home" and foregrounded in the kiss that closes but cannot "end" the Pardoner and his tale, is that this kiss "ends" discussion, not by sending us on our way elsewhere to find true meaning, but by setting up the kind of transvaluing exchange between the narrating "I" and the reading "I" in which the "I" shaming "you" and "you" being "shamed" can never be absolutely separated. It reveals not only the textual inscription of the Pardoner in the *Tales* as, in Deleuze and Guattari's terms, a "body without organs,"[66] but also, in a crucial sense, the pilgrims' inscription of a "gentil" body as one that can never entirely or convincingly invoke the sure foundations necessary for full stratification. However much that same pilgrimage body may be open to and desirous of stratification (represented by the successful incorporation of a modernizing elite within traditional frameworks of organization, signification, and subjectification), nonetheless its various and often competing lines of flight work to provoke as well a contrary disarticulation of such hegemonic impulses. My point here is not that the *Pardoner* achieves some form of pure revolt, but rather that only within the larger context of the *Canterbury Tales* and its pilgrimage group can his performance emerge as "wildly destratifying," and then not so much to the Christian hermeneutic of ascesis or to the Church's mediation of that process of ascesis. After all, no Reformation or Lollard outburst ensues. Rather it is the organism of "*gentil*" self-definition in and through the Canterbury "game" that the Pardoner is in danger of "wildly demystifying," and it is that play of identification and identity on the part of the lay gentils that threatens to be most "wildly demystifying" to the organism of the church office.[67] Kissing the Pardoner, then, allows the sexual, social, and linguistic dissidence of the Pardoner's voice to continue to resonate. And despite the efforts of readers to put the kiss behind them, it still manages to register the Pardoner's erotics of desire, that "pleasure that cannot be divided without remainder into teleological sequence," as an integral part of the structuring/destructuring movement of the *Tales*.

Kissing the Pardoner also initiates and gestures toward a reading strategy that might "increase and multiply" in meaningful ways outside hierarchical models organized around sex/gender difference, heterosexual procreation, or celibate/lay distinctions. In "touching" the Pardoner's "body without organs" in this way, we encounter a body no longer simply emblematic of "lack" or "absence," but rather constituting a point of experimentation in touch with the real. Such a reading strategy is less likely to produce coherent subjects either "properly" hegemonic or "improperly" sodomitical. And for that reason, the extent to which readers can embrace as their own the Pardoner's inversions or perversions of apparently stable binaries may thus also mark the extent to which they can affirm different or alternative kinds of cultural re-formation. In doing so, however, such readers may also create much needed room for maneuver within such apparently closed and hierarchical binaries as written/oral, author/reader, earnest/game, masculine/feminine, straight/perverse—binaries that have been closed off as much by modern reading habits as by medieval ones. That model in turn suggests a complex relation of sameness and difference between the authoring and reading functions for the *Tales* as a whole. Kissing the Pardoner, then, can provide a means of embracing the full potential present in that discoherence of masculinity (and power and authority) taking place here and elsewhere in the *Tales*, of putting the desire for meaning back into "common" circulation, and of articulating (an)other empowering sense of play as the "end" of the Canterbury project. In the next chapter, therefore, I turn to consider how Fragment VII intensifies and disperses these possibilities for discoherence of hegemonic constructions of meaning by representing the Canterbury project as a similarly generative, nonheterosexual desiring machine.

# 5

# Desiring Machines

## Fragment VII as Machinic Assemblage

Fragment VII returns to a number of the issues we have been considering in the previous chapters. The *Melibee* and the *Shipman's Tale,* and to a lesser extent, the *Nun's Priest's Tale,* focus once again on the matter of woman and the relationship between conjugality and agency. As well, the *Melibee,* the *Monk's Tale,* and *Nun's Priest's Tale* take up issues relating to good government. Within the fragment, as with other moments in the *Tales,* an unpredictable dynamic is created as the competing desires contained within the social order fictionalized in the pilgrimage frame come into contact with each other, and with the external aesthetic and generic demands brought by the kinds of tales told by individual narrators. Yet despite the connections that develop between tales within Fragment VII, its relationship with other fragments in the *Canterbury Tales* remains ambiguous. The dizzying momentum that builds up within Fragment VII, as tale succeeds tale—sometimes with little framing mechanism (as with the movement from the *Shipman's Tale* to the *Prioress's Tale*), sometimes with an overdetermining sense of external organization (as in the Host's interventions in relation to the narrator's tales of Thopas and Melibee)—produces none of the push to teleology, even a teleology ultimately frustrated, of the so-called Marriage Group. Nonetheless, the lack of a clear organizing principle for Fragment VII, and the consequent difficulty in fitting it into a theory of structure for the *Tales* as a whole, has not caused readers to see in it the kind of opprobrious "floating" nature Howard ascribed to Fragment VI.

Fragment VII would seem instead to reconfigure that which might have been labeled "foreign," "other," or "sodomitical" in Fragment VI as something of "common profit" (just as merchant profit could be resignified as for the common good rather than as simply usurious, with usury's perversity pushed back onto Jewish bodies). However, this reconfiguration does not stratify into a heterosexual teleology like the *Franklin's Tale,* but in certain crucial ways remains intent on promoting that "pleasure that cannot be divided without remainder into teleological sequence." As a result, this fragment interrupts any logic of the "proper place" intent on organizing what the *Tales* might mean. What critics often respond to as *lack* of organization might instead be understood as the prevalence of rhizomatic as much as arborescent connections made possible by a different constitution of the text as "book." Fragment VII, then, shows more explicitly than the others the queer torsions of the *Canterbury Tales* as *machinic assemblage,* where "[o]ne side faces the strata, which doubtless make it a kind of organism, or signifying totality, or determination attributable to a subject; [another] side fac[es] a *body without organs,* which is continually dismantling the organism"[1] What we are encouraged to undertake as readers, then, is a process of mapping the interrelationships of our desire with the meaning systems we are forced to encounter, as well as the meaning systems we *want,* rather than the tracing of authorial intention in all its ideological manifestations (a "Canterbury" tale-teller owning his tale, a "modern" author originating the truth of his text, or a "medieval" transcendent Word manifesting itself in willful flesh). Fragment VII's dynamic play of meaning "homes" *between* the world and the book, signified and signifier, author and reader, the authentic and its ground. Its emphasis on "becoming" rather than "being" articulates a representational strategy that can "increase and multiply" without "ending" either in a vilified and unknowable sodomitical fragmentation or in a hegemonic and always already known proper wholeness.

It is probably easiest to see how the fragment works as such a desiring machine in its opening tales. Not surprisingly perhaps, given the threat of sodomitical nonmeaning that such desiring brings with it, the fragment's opening pairs the Shipman's mercantile fabliau with the Prioress's anti-Semitic Miracle of the Virgin. Put simply, the *Shipman's Tale* destabilizes whatever push toward the strata might be built into the fabliau genre (see our discussion of the *Miller's Tale* and its masculinist discipline in chapter 1, for example), while the *Prioress's Tale* attempts to stratify the Body without Organs present in the feminine "innocence" of the little clergeon and in the proximate position of Jewishness within the supposedly bounded body of Christendom. In particular, the antifoundationalism of the *Shipman's Tale* provides an especially appropriate beginning for Fragment VII.[2] Unlike other fabliaux in the *Canterbury Tales*, the *Shipman's Tale* has no framing social or generic structure to note its proper place in the hierarchy or to "justify" its fabliau (a)morality and low humor. And within the tale itself, the metonymic potential of a series of puns is exploited to bring about a queer contiguity between supposedly different conceptual fields, as in the perverse conflation of a money economy with wifely constancy made possible by the "tail/tallying" pun that ends the tale ("God us sende / Taillynge ynough unto oure lyves ende" [VII.433–34]).

Similarly, the plot works to "prove" that there is no "natural" foundation for identities articulated in the marketplace of social and linguistic commerce, no recourse available to some stable, secure point of origin. Although the merchant comes originally from a village imagined as a stable place where one can really know who people are—hence the monk "hym claymeth as for cosynage" because they were both born in the same village—the hoodwinking (i.e., "cozening") of the merchant by the monk would suggest otherwise.[3] The monk makes clear he is no true relative of the merchant and seeks his friendship in order to make love to his wife. Although the merchant may sit in his counting house onanistically counting his gold, he, himself, makes clear that there is no stable good he can count on, only success in business where a reputation—necessarily uncertain—is everything. Even the household, where he imagines his sense of self can be secured by a stable femininity in the person of his wife, is, in this tale, represented as a place where volatile desires circulate and where the merchant must labor as carefully as in the larger marketplace to maintain his "proper" place. The *Shipman's Tale* embraces the room for maneuver made possible by its structures of exchange to explore the performativity needed to deploy successfully the kinds of contingent identities necessary for personal advancement and the generation of surplus wealth in a "modern" environment.

## The *Melibee*

Less obviously part of this desiring machine, though, is the *Melibee,* which, like the *Prioress's Tale* earlier in the fragment, seems at first all about stratification of the most traditionally medieval theological and social kind. The *Prioress's Tale* stands in a certain ambivalent relationship to the general volatility of Fragment VII—expressed literally in the angry demand of the Host for another tale to replace the *Thopas* and more broadly in the almost random and frenetic generic variety of this fragment. In contrast, *Melibee*'s length, its egregious sententiousness, its status as allegory and prose translation, all work to emphasize a measured, even labored, high seriousness that would appear to fix it as the stable center amidst the dynamism of the rest of Fragment VII. Yet, as I will argue in the rest of this chapter, it is precisely the *Melibee* story's ability both to incite and to occlude the mechanisms of desire motoring the processes of subjectification for its "gentil" audiences that puts it at the center of Fragment VII's desiring machine.

One of only two tales told in the narrator's own voice, Chaucer's *Melibee* is an almost word-for-word translation of Reynaud de Louens's *Le Livre de Mellibee et Prudence* (c. 1336), itself a freer translation of Albertano of Brescia's *Liber consolationis et consilii,* written a century earlier.[4] In addition, the tale's narrative line is so emphatically uncomplicated that it can be summarized quite briefly, as Daniel Rubey has done:

> Melibee is a young man, rich and powerful. While he is away, three old enemies break into his house, beat his wife Prudence, and wound his daughter Sophie with five mortal wounds in five places (corresponding to the five senses). Melibee's followers, friends, and advisors urge war on his enemies; Prudence advises patience and peace. Through the course of a long debate buttressed on both sides by references to authority, Prudence tries to persuade her husband to turn from vengeance to mercy. At midpoint the debate turns overtly allegorical: the house becomes Melibee's body made vulnerable by sin and entered by his old enemies—the World, the Flesh, and the Devil—through the windows of his body, his five senses. In the end, Melibee accepts the guidance of his wife and forgives his enemies.

> A settlement is negotiated with her help, and harmony is restored.[5]

Yet Prudence's extensive (some would say interminable) citation of learned and proverbial authority in Chaucer's version of the tale means that the *Melibee* occupies nearly twenty-three pages of double-columned text in the *Riverside Chaucer.*

Not surprisingly, perhaps, the average reader of the *Melibee* today, approaching it with the aesthetic standards of modern literary production in mind, often decides that it is not much of a tale, nor very "Chaucerian," and opts simply "to turn the leaf" (or rather the twelve leaves).[6] Modern critics and editors have also had a hard time knowing what to do with *Melibee* because of its unrelenting didacticism and apparent lack of originality. Some have ignored the tale altogether. Baugh and Donaldson, for example, omit the *Melibee* (along with the *Parson's Tale*) from their editions and thus explicitly define the essential Chaucer as his *poetic* works. Others have viewed the tale's overt moralizing as the key to an underlying structure of the *Canterbury Tales* that is similarly both "medieval" and sententious.[7] And some, while acknowledging the moral earnestness of the *Melibee* itself, have sought to justify Chaucer's version as properly "literary" and "Chaucerian" by ironizing its relationship to its context in the *Tales*—either by seeing it as an elaborate "quiting" of the Host's demand for something from the narrator that won't waste his time or as Chaucer's use of the *Melibee* to undercut the very didactic tradition it exemplifies.[8] Despite the radically different conclusions such approaches reach concerning the tale, however, they begin with a common assumption of the tale's exemplary "medievalness."

What often gets lost, though, when we constitute the tale as straightforwardly medieval or allegorical in this way are the material specificities of the tale's form and narrative structure, as well as the complexities of its production/consumption by its diverse medieval audiences. I want instead to focus first on the *Melibee* story itself as a desiring machine intent on stratification, but attributable to a subject position in excess of the "medieval" theological or noble subject that the story's generic status as Christian allegory or mirror for princes might suggest. Here I return in part to the new conjugality discussed in chapter 2 and its location as a place of libidinal excitement in the social imaginary. In turn, the *Melibee* story's success in representing the fullness of possibility in late medieval structures of subjectification can account for the special relationship this story offered to that "modernizing elite" whose desire is represented in the *Tales* and for why its inclusion at this point of the Canterbury project might be especially appropriate. Then I will consider how the story of Melibee, recirculated as "Chaucer's" *Melibee* in the context of Fragment VII, also functions as part of a "body without organs" continually dismantling such attempts to stratify the "gentil" organism.

In the first instance, it would be overly reductive and shortsighted to dismiss the story's plot as irrelevant, and thereby to limit its allegorical power to a mindless imposition of traditional clerical authority. As Larry Scanlon has noted, if events seem dwarfed by authorities in the tale, it is the events that provide the essential precondition of their compilation; compilation is never an end in itself. Moreover, if the *Melibee* is short on "event," it is long on "agency," that "other, equally essential aspect" of plot.[9] And such an agential plot may, indeed, be at the heart of its attraction for a late medieval lay audience: *Melibee* "tells the story of taking counsel—of preparing to cause an event, of becoming an agent. If it seems to break the process into such incremental stages, like some interminable series of freeze-frames, so that it ceases to be intelligible as a coherent process, we would do well to remember that this too is part of the ideal of authority it promulgates. By presenting every step in the exercise of such power as enabled by the citation of authority, it demonstrates . . . that lay authority has a systematic textuality proper to it."[10] Scanlon is particularly interested in showing how the *Melibee* fulfills the aims of the *Fürstenspiegel,* or "mirror for princes," form of medieval allegorizing. But I would argue that the fluidity and openness of the *Melibee*'s form—a narrative dialogue framework into which one can add or subtract layers of citation of learned and proverbial authorities—lends itself to a wider variety of lay readers' personal intervention in the story and what and how it means.

Certainly, individual readers can and did add to the sententious material, abstract the story from the other tales, and reduce the narrative portion to its "core" of "sentence," all to adapt it to their own household needs.[11] As Seth Lerer has noted,

> *Melibee,* for its medieval readers, was appreciated as a *compilatio,* a florilegium of moral texts, instructive quotes, and valuable citations. The fifteenth-century scribes who transmitted it often

> filled in the margins with the names of the *auctores* cited, keying them by means of symbols or red highlights to the quotations within the text. Its status as a *compilatio* was also reinforced by the effect it had on later readers. Whether abstracted from the Canterbury frame or written in the complete manuscripts of the *Tales,* the *Melibee* appears unique in the many variations of its wording, its length, and its sheer weight of authorial citation. Part of this phenomenon, certainly, is due to the prose nature of the *Tale* and to the greater possibilities of scribal error when unconstrained by the patterns of verse and rhyme. But part of this phenomenon, I believe, is due to the very staging and narration of the *Melibee* itself: a work presented as but one version of familiar, inherited material, a work self-consciously announced as longer than the others—and, hence, subject either to scribal truncation or to further augmentation by those who would seem to follow Chaucer's model.[12]

This is an active engagement of lay reader and tale that is in keeping with Melibee's marriage to Prudence being viewed as a private, interactive dialogue crucial to identity formation. And it suggests why the story was appropriated by such a wide variety of readers, both noble and "middle" class, of the later Middle Ages.

The *Melibee* was, after all, one of the most frequently anthologized of the *Canterbury Tales* during the fifteenth and sixteenth centuries,[13] and Albertano's Latin text—from which Chaucer's tale ultimately derives—enjoyed an equal or greater vogue among the literate laity of the later Middle Ages.[14] Indeed, all three of Albertano of Brescia's works were widely disseminated throughout the later medieval period, with over three hundred manuscript copies noted by the text's modern editor.[15] David Wallace's provocative reading of Chaucer's *Melibee* provides an especially rich account both of the urban politics informing Albertano's work and the openness of this work to later appropriation for quite different political and social agendas. Reynaud de Louens's French translation, Wallace maintains, marks a moment when Albertano's urban tale, written in aid of "the survival of a struggling, emergent city-state culture," is assimilated to the northern European "mirror for princes" tradition, a genre more suited "to the particular circumstances of Louens's war-torn Burgundy in the 1330s." But such changes "cannot obscure the residual otherness of Albertano's invention. Reynaud's *Livre de Melibee et de Prudence* reads like a palimpsest; Albertano's text and Albertano's Brescia continue to peer through." And Albertano's Melibeus "seems peculiarly the product of urban culture [enduring] the social isolation of the *nouveau riche*.... He and his kind need, in short, Albertano, 'a sociologist of the medieval urban experience,' a 'new man' of the early Duecento."[16] The most striking feature of the Melibee story as story, then, may be not its supposedly stable reproduction of some high medieval *sentence,* but rather its continued accessibility to and serviceability for a large and varied late medieval and early modern audience that crossed a variety of class, linguistic, and national lines.

This suggests that Chaucer finds in the story of Melibee a complex medium in which to identify a new class of reader, one moving beyond the contract forming the high medieval ruling class of lay aristocracy and literate clerisy. Wallace's discussion of Albertano emphasizes his fundamentally rhetorical and professional, rather than religious, aims. Wallace notes that "reading a manuscript of Seneca's moral epistles, Albertano was moved to mark passages ripe for recycling into his own treatises with a striking series of mnemonic devices."[17] Similarly, Albertano's association with friars in the meetings of his professional body, the guild or confraternity of the Brescian *causidici* (i.e., legal advocates) provided an important means of authorizing his own profession: for "the development of the kind of urban culture envisioned by Albertano required both the formation of professional elites and the development of a city-centered, rather than rural-monastic, spirituality."[18] Wallace goes on to point out that "Chaucer is similarly concerned, in the *Canterbury Tales,* with defining and justifying his own profession of authorship....[H]e trusts that the *Melibee* in prose, especially when complemented by the prose of the *Parson's Tale,* will win him an authority that is both urbane and religious in its appeal; that will both anchor and license his poetic fictions....Chaucer, I believe, would have recognized Albertano's *Liber consolationis et consilii* (even through vernacular intermediaries) as a work of counsel authored not by a magnate but by someone (much like himself) confecting a social and authorial identity from divergent bases of authority: a 'new man.'"[19]

I would argue, then, that what stands out in the specific contours of the Melibee story itself is its success in outlining a newly sexualized and gendered individual identity. Although the story is certainly capable of being read as advice for princes and nobles, as it was clearly intended to be in a number of the extant versions of the story (including Reynaud de Louens's), Melibee as a character is marked far more as youthful husband and householder than as high aristocrat or prince. Equally, the tale's didacticism is dominated by Prudence rather than Wisdom, delivered by an allegorical wife rather than a heavenly grande dame, and clearly does not require distinctively clerical learning or expertise. The tale emphasizes that Melibee and his household are alone in the world, without extended family. The violence committed by his enemies consists in the breaking into his house and the wounding of his daughter, rather than the occupation of territory or usurpation or disinheritance. The story thus conspires to turn Melibee's and our attention inward—to his household, to his marriage relationship, to his own sense of interiority.

At the beginning of the tale, Melibee is singled out as simply "a yong man... myghty and riche" who "bigat upon his wyf, that called was Prudence, a doghter which that called was Sophie" (VII.967). And his enemies break into his "hous" by using ladders to enter through its windows while Melibee (in an echo of the *Wife of Bath's Prologue*) has gone "into the feeldes" for "his desport" (VII.968–70). In response to the crimes committed upon him and his household, Prudence advises Melibee to call upon his "trewe freendes alle and thy lynage which that been wise." This "greet congregacion of folk" is made up of "surgiens, phisiciens, olde folk and yonge," "somme of his olde enemys reconsiled as by hir semblaunt" and "somme of his neighebores that diden hym reverence moore for drede than for love" (VII.1002–5). What is emphasized here are the ties of affinity constituted by economic exchange and patronage that "bind" Melibee and his advisors, rather than shared bloodlines or other family affinities. Only near the end of the tale does the narrative "ennoble" Melibee by shifting registers to describe Melibee's "hous" as "the court of Melibee" and Melibee as "so greet a lord" (VII.1805, 1816). And this shift depends on Melibee's proper socialization at the hands of his wife, Prudence, his retreat from public disputation and public activity to private reading, personal discernment, and household secrecy. Indeed, it is not too farfetched to read Prudence's actions as reconfiguring the initial attack on Melibee's household primarily as a violation of Melibee's privacy. It is only by reframing the problem and its remedies in this way, and thus instructing Melibee on how to reconfigure how he thinks about who he is essentially, that Melibee comes to understand what is truly worth preserving and how to go about preserving it. Thus the trajectory of the narrative and its learning process is not toward "traditional" guarantors of power, like an inherent right to rule because of noble blood or knightly prowess. Instead Melibee's ultimate power and success come more from his discovery and rearticulation of a set of textual effects establishing his own depth of character.

The primary "producer" of such textual effects is, of course, Melibee's wife, Prudence, who succeeds in advising Melibee within the structures of household conjugality. It is noteworthy, therefore, that Prudence first takes advice *within herself* rather than seeking counselors (as did Melibee early in the tale), and that taking advice is turning to *her* experience of a textual tradition of authorities and to an oral tradition of putting such *conseil* into practice. In this regard, one should note Daniel Kempton's point that Prudence invokes contradictory authorities without there being a successful (or even, perhaps intended) attempt at synthesizing such doctrine through dialectic, as would happen in a scholastic Book of Sentences.[20] I would argue further that most instances of contradiction are simply left uninterrupted and thus undercut the success of the tale as pure scholarship. But the point of prudence, after all, is practical wisdom, not speculative science. The point here is not to make Prudence or Melibee convincing clerks, but to incorporate clerical authority into the process of lay maturation and the development of a properly agential "gentil" subject.

David Burnley has demonstrated that, by the later Middle Ages, prudence as the virtue that ensured "that a man's actions are rationally considered and are consonant with the will of God" was not only a desirable quality in a secular ruler, but also "the essential ability possessed by all men to select the path which will lead to spiritual salvation."[21] Burnley goes on to outline the widening of the concept of prudence as practical wisdom in the later Middle Ages that made it applicable to a far broader range of the everyday life of a variety of social groups than as a theological virtue or an essential attribute of the successful prince. In Reginald Pecock's definition, written a little more than fifty years after Chaucer's death, prudence is:

> a kunnyng or knowing wherbi we knowen treuthis longyng to oure gouernaunce, that is to seie, it is the knowing wherbi we knowen what is to be doon or to be left vndoon in oure

> governauncis, and in which maner, in which tyme, with what meenes, into what eend, and so forth with whiche othire circumstauncis it is to be do, or left to be vndo, and what is to be suffrid or not suffrid, and in which maner, tyme and place and meene it is to be suffrid or not suffrid; and so forth of othire circumstauncis.[22]

This leads Pecock "to see prudence at work in many more spheres than civil rule or individual salvation: 'Also as is kunnyng to knowe how we schule bere vs to plese oure maystris, oure lordis, oure fadris, how to chastise oure children and seruantis, how to lyue pesabli with oure neighboris, how to spende that we falle not into pouerte, and so forth of otheire lijk deedis and treuthis of hem perteynyng to oure gouernaunce.'"[23] Burnley notes that for Pecock here, prudence is not so much a virtue as an accomplishment, and that prudence for the period needs to be conceived as a kind of knowledge upon which actions are based. In short prudence is practical science (as opposed to speculative science), and "prudence can therefore be substituted in appropriate contexts for a knowledge of economics and estate management, secular or canon law, government, or commerce. Each is a manifestation of prudence."[24]

Although reminiscent of a long line of female givers of advice, Prudence is notably different from Dame Nature or Philosophy in that her authority derives from her essentialized and embodied position as woman, wife, and husbanded femininity. Carolyn P. Collette notes in this regard that, as prudence became a science of social relations (as described by Burnley above), "it became a female science of actions within human relations, particularly marriage, in order to attain desired goals, a science of patience and indirection, of self-effacement and strict control of emotion."[25] She points out, for example, that "in the culture that produced and told these stories [of advice to wives on how to behave prudently with their husbands], it is clear that prudence was a woman's way to physical safety and domestic harmony."[26] And Collette notes, in relation to the *Melibee,* that "It is not just what Prudence says that is the subject of the tale here, but the way she plans, prepares, waits, and finally acts.... In contrast to Griselda's quiet patience, we have Prudence's patient watching for opportunities to speak, to act rather than merely to react.... The story of Prudence and Melibee in late medieval culture seems to have been a guide for real women living complicated lives, trying to find a space for themselves and their voices. Finally, whatever else we may find to say about it, the fact of Prudence's femaleness lies at the heart of the tale."[27]

Herself incapable of knightly action or clerical disputation, Prudence instead works to mirror Melibee's essential self back to himself by highlighting her difference as woman. For example, near the beginning of the tale (VII.1054–1113), Melibee lists four reasons why he must refuse to work by Prudence's counsel: because it would be an essential folly to choose a woman's counsel over men's, because women are essentially wicked, because it would give a wife mastery over her husband, and because she advises keeping his counsel secret until the proper time to implement it. Prudence first asks "licence for to speke" from Melibee and then goes on to refute such charges by proving that the "trouthe of thynges and the profit been rather founden in fewe folk that been wise and ful of resoun than by greet multitude of folk ther every man crieth and clatereth what that hym liketh" (VII.1068). Moreover, her own past behavior proves that women, too, can be such "fewe folk" and that the antifeminist views expressed by Melibee are at odds with individual experience. In speaking thus, the formerly resistant Melibee now realizes, Prudence embodies Solomon's truth that "'words that been spoken discreetly by ordinaunce been honycombes, for they yeven swetnesse to the soule and hoolsomnesse to the body.' / And, wyf, by cause of thy sweete wordes, and eek for I have assayed and preved thy grete sapience and they grete trouthe, I wol governe me by thy conseil in all thyng" (VII.1112–13).

In accepting the value of his wife's discursive strategies of containment and reflection, Melibee, whose name we are later told means "a man that drynketh hony," learns how to drink a different honeyed truth about his essential nature than that occasioned by his past drunkenness with "so muchel hony of sweete temporeel richesses, and delices and honours of this world" (VII.1407–08).[28] This trajectory reaches its logical conclusion near the end of the tale when Melibee announces to Prudence: "Dame . . . dooth youre wil and youre likynge; / for I putte me hoolly in youre disposicioun and ordinaunce" (VII.1725). It is only at this moment, when Melibee has accepted his true nature as the bounded self mirrored back to him by Prudence's discursive strategies, that he is able to be reconciled with his enemies and discern his true friends and family. By means of her womanly advice and, crucially, the new form of masculine activity on Melibee's part that her advice provokes, the tale constitutes a positive valence for secrecy, interiority, personal experience, patience, the body—all categories that were rendered suspect earlier in the *Tales* by the *un*husbanded claim to autonomous feminine subjectivity on the part of the Wife of Bath. Melibee will succeed, the tale maintains, to the extent that he can recognize, establish, and care for the boundaries defining his essential self.

Rather than simply reproducing the system of representation undergirding high medieval feudalism, the *Melibee* story's emphasis on a general access to practical wisdom and an interactive form of textual reproduction open to a lay "middle" class would encourage us to see it in the vanguard of Foucault's modern disciplinary regime of sexuality. The *Tale of Melibee,* then, as its title suggests, is at bottom about the ability of an interiorized, autonomous self (autonomous *because* properly masculine and heterosexual) both to constitute its "self" *and* to assert that self in the world. As Prudence mirrors the truth about Melibee to Melibee, she lets his true self come into representable form. And the self-discipline and care of the self that follow ensure Melibee's social reproduction—both in the discovery of other true selves like Melibee (such as the good advisors that make up his true household and the enemies that are won over to his side), and in the restored (re-productive) body of Sophia. Moreover, this is a lesson eminently translatable onto a variety of linguistic and social terrains. While a king could learn from this allegory, one certainly need not be noble by birth to become a Melibee. Nor does one need a clerical class to mediate this message; after all, a woman serves as the truest advisor here.

Clearly the Melibee story—in its emphasis on domesticity, its agential allegorical structure and sententious style, and its interactive and flexible mode of production as a form—has much to offer an emergent class of lay readers, neither traditionally clerical nor aristocratic, in their attempts to delineate the "new man" of the later medieval/early modern period. For it charts how such a "new man" might be made. In breaking down counsel into its incremental stages so that individuals can enter at points that suit their needs, the Melibee story structures a kind of bildungsroman out of Melibee's maturation as a fully formed individual, one that readers themselves can literally make their own by active reading (that is, by the process of commissioning a translation, anthologizing the work themselves, or condensing or expanding their version of the work by adapting the prudential citation to their own needs). This labor of making new necessarily links together the public and private, and clearly constitutes its own kind of politics, as Albertano's own situation demonstrates. Albertano writes the *Liber consolationis et consilii* for his son, so that he may embody this "new man." But the work is also meant to address the need to produce a new "civic subject" that might replace outmoded feudal estates models, or rather "fulfill" their potential by amalgamating many of the best attributes of the knightly, clerical, and mercantile classes.

The story of Melibee, although often striking modern readers as simple "medieval" didacticism, actually constructs new sets of identifications, and with that, a sense of a new imagined community for an as-yet-to-be represented audience. It inscribes this "modern" audience even as it insists on an unbroken line of reproduction of authority from the past to the present. The allegorical structure of the story gives it a disarmingly traditional appearance. It invokes a familiar clerical and aristocratic authority and a universalizing medieval Christian time and space that would empty the allegorical scene of all extraneous "accidents" as it moves to a transcendental mode of signification. And certainly the Melibee story can "work" in such a mode. Chaucer's immediate French source clearly reads the story as a "mirror of princes," and Paul Strohm makes a persuasive case for the validity of a Christian allegoresis.[29] But as I have been arguing, the appearance of the "old" for many readers may also be a means of securing an "aura" of universality and truth for the story's embodiment of a quite different mode of production of a "new man." The story's emphasis on self-discipline learned through a controlled contact with the feminine by means of conjugal affection and within the private sphere of the individual household has obvious resonance with the lay concerns raised in the tales of the so-called marriage group. But the Melibee story's success in articulating a mode of production for a new lay, "gentil" subjectivity makes it especially appropriate to the politics of "gentil" self-representation we have been observing in earlier tales.

The Melibee story I have been describing, the one Wallace sees as Albertano's new urban invention peering through attempts to limit the tale's meaning to traditional transcendental ones, can also be seen as producing the kind of homogeneous, empty time and mechanical reproduction of civic subjects that Benedict Anderson postulates as the prerequisite for the modern nation-state. Anderson singles out the modern newspaper as a prime medium for the reproduction of civic subjects of the nation-state and its imagined communities. For in the newspaper, the arbitrariness of the various events included on any given day, as well as their juxtaposition on the page, derive from two obliquely related sources. The first is simply calendrical coincidence: "The date at the top of the newspaper, the single most important emblem on it, provides the essential connection—the steady onward clocking of homogeneous, empty time." The second source of imagined linkage "lies in the relationship between the newspaper, as a form of book, and the market." As a modern-style mass-produced industrial commodity, the newspaper makes possible the "mass ceremony" of its simultaneous consumption at predictable intervals by modern citizens: "What more vivid figure for the secular, historically clocked, imagined community can be envisioned? At the same time, the newspaper reader, observing exact replicas of his own paper being consumed by his subway, barbershop, or residential neighbors, is continually reassured that the imagined world is visibly rooted in everyday life"[30]

The Melibee story provides a similarly safe and reliable notation system for its imagined community, one that will reproduce a common "home" for the subjects of this new modernizing elite in the individual household and present this imagined location as the real thing. Such a new "gentil" identity is enunciated both privately (within the "safe" space of household conjugality and by means of the active reading required by Prudence's counsel) and publicly by the re-presentation of the translated self back into the world (in Melibee's new policy and in the reader's active translation of the *Melibee* into his or her own life circumstances). Prudence's engaged counsel asks Melibee to consider what kind of man he truly is; Melibee's own personal engagement with that counsel allows him to speak that man to the world. Equally, the *Melibee* as textual experience asks its readers to consider what kinds of men they are, for out of that engagement comes a new, empowering ability to speak the fact that "I" am like "You," that is, Melibee. It is this combination of the personal and the political, as well as the predictability and repeatability of its form, that makes the Melibee story a mechanical mode of production for both a new "civic subject" and an imagined community built on such subjects. The changes in modes of production taking place in late medieval manuscript culture—increasing lay literacy, a lay-dominated book trade with professional scribes and "mass" production of manuscripts—allow lay subjects to take on both scribe/author and reader positions. And a story like the *Melibee* increases and multiplies the different kinds of temporal and cultural settings in which meaning can be made and from which the same subject (both Melibee himself and the "new man" created by a right reading of the story) can be constructed.[31]

It is not so much that the allegory provides the means for individuals to strip away the accidentals of materiality and make manifest in the world the transcendent pattern for behavior already revealed by divine example. Instead, the Melibee as allegorical counsel allows individual difference (expressed by means of the specific ways in which each version of the story comes into textuality) to become the means by which a pattern of likeness as part of an imagined community can emerge, and by which that imagined community can be made material. The Melibee story offers a strategy of lay subjectification via a new project of ascesis organized around an erotics of worldly (rather than transcendent) desire, and thus provides a strategy far more clearly and fully controlled by lay "gentil" hands than manipulated by clerical or aristocratic interests. But the mode of reproduction cannot be as mechanical or controlled as it imagines—at the literal level, all husbands clearly are not Melibees, all wives not Prudences. And while such attempts to identify with the Melibee story push to stratify a newly made "universal man," a "gentil" subject whose lineaments are surprisingly similar at times to those of the modern heterosexual subject, the nature of Melibee's allegorical mode of production means that the production of such a subject is always grounded in a particular historicized location. Thus, while "universal" in one sense, these subjects are also locally organized, geographically and linguistically discrete, and they articulate something like proto-national communities as much as transnational, modernizing equivalents of a feudal aristocracy or clerisy.

## "What Man Artow?"

Any push that Chaucer's *Melibee* might have to stratification and serviceability for the *Tales'* modernizing elite must therefore also be situated in the specificities of its embodiment in Fragment VII: notably in the narrator's attempt to answer the Host's interrogatory "What man artow?" and in the narrator's discussion of translation and the *Melibee*. This context makes clear both the Melibee story's appropriability for "gentil" identity formation in the *Tales* and the destabilizing consequences of the desire for such an identity. The *Melibee*'s situation in Fragment VII arises at a vexed moment around questions of authenticity as they relate to stories, authors, and the reading practices of the Canterbury project, one that can tell us much about how this fragment more generally sketches out a disorganized middle ground within the binaristic push of hegemony to assign a proper centrality to certain tales and a marginal "floating" grotesquerie to others. Curiously, the moment in Fragment VII that invokes the kind of questions of value and hierarchy associated with the Pardoner in Fragment VI is the narrator's inscription as tale-teller. The frame for the *Thopas* sets up a scene remarkable for its telling similarities to and differences from how the Pardoner's audience attempted to manipulate, marginalize, and contain the Pardoner. The Host's initial "What man artow?" expresses a similar uncertainty about the nature of the narrator and whether and how he will fit into the pilgrimage body.[32] In Fragment VI the negative reaction of the Host and "gentils" insists on the absolute knowability of the Pardoner, only to have the subsequent dramatic moment of the *Pardoner's Tale* insist in turn on a crucial unknowability of the Pardoner and hence his capacity to initiate a profound category confusion. Here the Host's initial response is a question that focuses instead on a problematic undecidability factor with regard to the narrator. As Lee Patterson points out, "what is striking about this occasion is the comprehensiveness of his opening question, its utter lack of specificity: 'What man artow?' . . . Recognizable as a knight, a miller, a reeve, and so forth, the pilgrims are identified by their social functions. . . . But what work does the narrator perform? What is his social function? 'What man artow?'"[33] More recently, David Wallace has noted that

> [t]his is a different Chaucer from the figure who, in the *General Prologue*, boldly talked himself into the pilgrim *felaweshipe* through the art of conversation. . . . This Chaucer is a person who cannot hold a level gaze . . . whose passivity is said to invite physical handling, whose body is read as his social being. And this, too, is an author portrait: a portrait, specifically, of an author about to speak for himself. Such emphases upon physical vulnerability

> and social isolation suggest the impress of political pressures requiring a new explanatory framework.[34]

The physical details the Host focuses on—plump like the Host but, unlike the Host, "a popet in an arm t'enbrace / For any woman," small and fair of face, "elvyssh by his contenaunce" (VII.701–3)—also suggest a certain queerness in terms of the Host's sex/gender system. What kind of *man* are you? the Host implies. The narrator's performance with *Sir Thopas,* I would argue, escalates this kind of reaction from the Host, with its "in-your-face" undecidability in terms of the Host's kinds of categories. The "lesson" of the *Melibee,* as it is contextualized in this fragment, focuses our attention as audience on the undesirability of too easily or completely knowing what a thing is, and of the pleasures and even the thriftiness of certain kinds of deferral of meaning in terms of sex/gender systems or estate divisions.

The narrator's first attempt at tale-telling fails with the Host precisely because it intensifies rather than resolves this undecidability factor. The narrator's feminized body (at least as refracted through the Host's eyes) presents us with a gender undecidability that has strong echoes with the Pardoner. So, too, setting the origins of his hero in *Sir Thopas* "In Flaundres" (echoing the location of the *Pardoner's Tale*) emphasizes the puzzling, even perverse, "middling" status of the narrator's first tale. David Wallace has recently brilliantly outlined the complex and compelling ways that "Flaundres" anxiously signifies the proximately perverse to the Englishness of Chaucer's fictional world in the *Tales.* A nonnoble and urban environment, "urbanized space in Flanders serves the needs of merchants and artisans," and in 1302, at the battle of Courtrai, the craftsmen of Bruges had been the first urban infantry to defeat cavalry commanded by nobles. Yet these same Flemish urbanites were, like their English counterparts, avid consumers of French or French-derived chivalric adventures.[35] So, too, in the field of vernacular literature Flemish and English were "hybridized languages lying along the shifting borderline of Romance and Germanic tradition. In this sense, to write in English in the 1380s is broadly equivalent to writing 'in Flaundres'; by insisting that Flemish 'sounds funny,' the English can distance themselves from the realization that, to the rest of the world, it was difficult to distinguish Flemings from Englishmen."[36] Moreover, as an urban culture built on land recovered from the sea (hence an artificial culture created by the hand of man against nature) and uniquely resistant to the established supremacy of the nobility, Flanders, as the Flemish cities told their count in 1473 "*is* a sterile country, infertile in itself, completely founded on the fact and course of merchandise, densely populated with foreigners, merchants, and others."[37] *Sir Thopas,* then, originating in Flanders and presented as the quintessentially native English tail-rhyme romance, perversely mixes styles (English medium and French romance style, bourgeois and aristocratic content, feminine passivity and would-be masculine activity) and thereby engenders a potentially sodomitical category confusion whose proximity (present-day Flanders rather than an exotically distant East or remote past, as in the *Squire's Tale* or the *Franklin's Tale*) is especially threatening.

Reaching back for a "rym I heard a long time ago," the narrator invokes an orality and a native Englishness quite different from that created at the beginning of the pilgrimage when the Knight, too, reached into the storehouse of his memory. This is not a tale committed to memory because of its innate worth, nor is the narrator able to do anything else that would provide the textual effect of origins, of origin-ality. His tale is very much a present thing, the romance form brought into the proximate and ambiguous "romance" landscape of Flanders, and effectively unrimed and unromanced by its translation into a native English verse form. Indeed, the many verbal echoes of the *Prioress's Tale* and its attempts at genteel style emphasize the proximate in obvious and potentially parodic ways. By implication, perhaps, the tale makes the attempts at "gentil" self-definition its "subject matter." After all, the genre of English metrical romance that Thopas here perversely represents was tremendously popular precisely with such a would-be "gentry" audience.[38]

What Thopas does not do, however, is create a reality effect of stable origins for such a genre, out there in a real noble past. Rather than providing some useful "historial" thing, *translatio imperii,* or piece of Eastern exotica (as, for example, the *Knight's Tale,* the *Franklin's Tale,* and the *Squire's Tale* attempt to do), *Thopas* comes close to home in precisely the wrong way. As the Host so effectively summarizes, this tale's "drasty riming" is not worth a "turd," and its narrator is unthriftily wasting the pilgrims' time ("thoo doost noght elles but despendest tyme" [VII.930–31]). The narrator responds by foregrounding translation and genre in such a way as to appear to guarantee the kind of stable text through which the truth about oneself and the textual means to mirror that self back out into the world in meaningful ways can be made clear. Moreover, the *Melibee* as story provides just the sort of satisfyingly open yet authoritative structure needed to allow its subjects to "float" in productive ways between the often conflicting demands of "medieval" allegorical and "modern" bourgeois hermeneutical strategies.[39]

Without mentioning the dangerous and controversial question of translating the Bible into English, the narrator nonetheless manages to use the authority of scriptural example to resonate powerfully with his own situation and to forestall the kind of blame he incurred from his "betters" with his "translation" of Thopas. The narrator's emphasis on translation in the prologue to the *Melibee* promises the certainty of proper *translatio* that was not achieved in the limiting materiality of the narrator's own appearance earlier or in the awkward mixed style of his first tale. In this way the potentially feminizing is remasculinized by "properly" adopting another's authoritative voice, exactly the kind of transformative performance Prudence will accomplish for the female body in the *Melibee* itself. Materiality is thus given an acceptable formal identity by means of this act of translation, and fleshliness is reworked as a positive signifier. The narrator's request that the "lordynges alle" listening to him "Blameth me nat" (VII.953, 961) echoes the narratorial comments in the prologue to the *Miller's Tale*. But here, his audience is not told to turn the leaf, but rather to note his embodiment in the act of translation, to allow for the supposedly innocuous effect of such accidence on the substance of the text, and ultimately to note as well the possible added value such "fleshing out" of the text can bring. He cites as authoritative example the Evangelists and their gospels, where each "Ne seith nat alle thing as his felawe dooth" (VII.945). Yet, despite differences in accidentals—"For somme of hem seyn more, and somme seyn lesse, / Whan they his pitous passioun expresse" (VII.949–50)—all agree in their true, essential meaning: "doutelees hir sentence is al oon" (VII.952). So, too, with the narrator's activity translating the *Melibee:*

> Though that I telle somwhat moore
> Of proverbes than ye han herd bifoore
> Comprehended in this litel tretys heere,

To enforce with th'effect of my mateere;
And though I nat the same wordes seye
As ye han herd, yet to yow alle I preye
Blameth me nat; for, as in my sentence,
Shul ye nowher fynden difference
Fro the sentence of this tretys lyte. (VII.955–63)

Comparing the narrator's fraught situation here in relation to the Host with similar moments earlier—that of the Host and "gentils'" shaming of the Pardoner or that of the narrator "forced" as scribe to reproduce the churlish words and actions of the *Miller's Tale,* we can see fear that a similar moment of "shame on you" might occur balanced by a greater assurance that the narrator in this case can assume a certain degree of agency with and support from his audience. The activity of translating into the vernacular, or from a high-level vernacular to a relatively unauthorized one like English, is open to blame. But the narrator emphasizes that he is not translating the Bible; his use of the Evangelist analogy makes that clear. Such an analogy, however, along with the promise of a sententious story, does provide the effect of decidability that the Host found lacking in the previous tale.

Moreover, the narrator's specificity about accidentals and their necessity—that the narrator/translator might add more proverbs than are usually present in other versions of the treatise in order to make his point to this audience, or that he might have to use English words different from those in the treatise's source language—foregrounds *his* presence in the English text produced *and* the added value such presence brings to the treatise. It is, he maintains, *natural* for such a deformation to inhere in this kind of vernacular textual activity; it does not mark disruptive change, in fact, it ensures the continued value of the treatise's essential meaningfulness. The narrator thus draws attention to the labor of subjectification and its usefulness. His translation into the vernacular, and through the personal medium of narration and specific textual context, may produce noticeable differences from other versions, but nonetheless, the same truth-value is maintained. Thus, although some versions may take more time, in this case, unlike the Host's charge against the *Thopas,* the narrator will not "despendest tyme." Indeed, the variability of translation in such a context can add value.

Unlike his previous tale-telling, the narrator now participates not only in a translation situation where differences between Latinate stability and vernacular contingency blur, but also in an essentialized (because sufficiently flexible) moment of lay textuality:

> for, as in my sentence,
> Shul ye nowher fynden difference
> Fro the sentence of this tretys lyte
> After the which this murye tale I write. (VII.961–64)

Paradoxically, even as this model of narration/translation effaces the question of "original"—after all, if all versions contain the "sentence," the question of origins is removed from specific textual examples—it reinscribes it in relation to the textual "I"s it creates. The narrator/translator here, like the Wycliffite Bible translators defending vernacular biblical translation that was idiomatic rather than word for word, "not only acknowledge[s] the potential for surplus semantic value in language, the impossibility of exact linguistic exchange, but valorize[s] it as productive."[40] The narrator's tale may not only be larger in number of words, but the very fact of reproducing "sentence" in an English idiom and form that his audience can utilize thriftily increases value. Moreover, the kind of interactive mode of textuality envisaged in this kind of translation recurs in the very form of the story represented by the *Melibee,* as we shall see below; the "sentence" that is reproduced by this action is the textual effect of interiority that allows an authentic, "whole" self to discover itself and represent itself in the world.

Such an attention to the productivity of the textual interactions enabled by translation in the very framing of Chaucer's *Melibee* thus foregrounds the marketplace and its values in complex and unpredictable ways. As Kellie Robertson reminds us,

> The growing fourteenth-century recognition that meaning was neither essential nor God-given but was rather agreed upon in common by the users of the language parallels the growing recognition in the economic sphere that value is man-made, a product of "common judgment" expressed in a market price that naturally varied according to time and place. In translation, as in

> trade, there were no essences. Debates over linguistic economic exchange were not just over how one substitutes words in order to render an exact biblical meaning or money for commodities but about the very process of exchange that engenders conditions of relative value and substitutability.[41]

It is not that a horizontal axis of lay exchange is now superseding a vertical axis of clerical or aristocratic metaphoric transcendence. Rather, several systems of exchange overlap in the linguistic and social economy that the Melibee story charts. Moreover, this economy is not one that can be understood solely as a matter of production, as the Host's reactions to the *Tale of Thopas* (or earlier, the kind of controlling relationship that the pilgrims tried to establish with the Pardoner) would imply. The narrator's comments about translation, and particularly the Melibee story's interactive, dialogic mode of textual interaction, would maintain that understanding the complexities of this textual/representational marketplace demands attention to the importance of modes of consumption as much as to modes of production.

It is just such a productive condition of relative value and substitutability that the Host alerts us to in his joking transition from the *Melibee* to the Monk. Here, as so often in the *Tales,* the Host's vulgar comments at the end of *Melibee* bring to the surface the ideological work it has been attempting. For the Host's comments about his wife and social precedence act as a mirror image to the lessons of the *Melibee,* underscoring the latter's gendered and sexualized power structures, as well as the fact that the tale's emphasis on patience, interiority, secrecy, and control in *Melibee*'s identity formation is all about power in the world. Later, the Host's highly sexualized characterization of the Monk as "a tredefowel aright" (VII.1945) and his joking assertion that such a waste of potency is the cause of the world's problems, not its salvation—"for al the world is lorn! / Religioun hath take up al the corn / Of tredyng, and we borel men been shrympes" (VII.1954–55)—are not-so-sly indications that the Host has understood that the new identity posited by the *Melibee* will assert a new hegemony based on lay husbands and householders.

The Host's "game" depends in part on his "playful" assumption that his lay criteria (im)properly read the Monk in telling ways. That is, the Host implies that criteria such as birth, estate function, and physical potency actually can tell us something significant about the Monk and his kind; in this way, a traditionally hegemonic clerical view of the world is quietly acknowledged, and its replacement by a lay viewpoint effectively articulated. That celibate clergy have enfeebled human stock by withdrawing the best and most potent masculinity out of the gene pool is, of course, patently absurd. Yet the "charge" does substitute an alternative mode of reckoning potency—that is, lay marriage and reproduction—for the "natural" one—the celibate priest or monk as the most manly man. Similarly, the Host's joking wish that "Goodelief, my wyf" (VII.1894) had heard the *Tale of Melibee* (so that she would not trespass on his husbandly authority anymore) obviously reduces the tale's "sentence" to an absurd extreme. But the joke also comically underscores that deeper lesson of the tale that I have been outlining as its interactive role for a group of "middle"-class readers like Albertano: that is, the tale makes possible the articulation of a "personal" allegory and with that, agency as a man and husband, something the Host's more broadly "domestic" translation parodically rewrites in a way that reminds us that such a process of exchange places limits on who can and cannot substitute for the other. Somewhere in between the Host's domestic farce of Goodelief and the rarefied allegorizing of the monastic school lies the middle ground that the narrator's *Melibee* (and the *Nun's Priest's Tale*) so successfully articulates and that the Canterbury project itself traverses.

The Host's comments link presence with presentness in complex and mobile ways. It is perhaps not surprising that this should be a moment when the present "erupts" into the controlled game of the *Tales*, both in the form of the reference to "Rouchestre" which "stant heer faste by" (VII.1926) and the necessity for active intervention so that "oure game" be not broken. But it surfaces, too, in the difficult relationship established between the Monk and his present, one that echoes the problems the narrator of the *General Prologue* faced in his portrayal of present examples, especially in the uncertainty the Monk evinces about the proper place for the present examples in his tale of tragic men and in the Knight's angry interruption of such "greet disese" (VII.2770). At a more general level, Fragment VII as a whole seems unable or unwilling to resolve the problem of the present by means of a traditional essence/accidence model (as in the *Second Nun's Tale*) or a more modern progressive teleology on the lines of the *Franklin's Tale*. Instead, the fragment emphasizes those processes of exchange governing a fourteenth-century marketplace of language that, as Kellie Robertson puts it, "engenders conditions of relative value and substitutability." Thus the *Shipman's Tale* asks whether one tale-teller can be substituted for another, a man for a woman, a wife for her husband, "tail" (female pudenda)/tale (story) for tally. Or the *Monk's Tale* substitutes one tragedy for another without any clear teleology being established. Similarly, throughout the fragment one tale generates another apparently *ad infinitum*—the *Prioress's Tale* substitutes for the *Shipman's Tale, Thopas* for the *Prioress's Tale,* the *Melibee* for *Thopas,* the *Monk's Tale* for the *Melibee,* the *Nun's Priest's Tale* for the *Monk's Tale,* and so on. How in this kind of multiplication without clear stratification do we arrive at the "common judgment" that will decide use value?

This preoccupation with, and anxiety about, presentness underscores a search throughout the *Tales* to find models for the stable reproduction of hegemonic subject positions that will articulate a new "English nation." To do so, the pilgrims must make the present "their own" in ways not possible within an older model of Christian allegory and of universal subjects rising above accidentals of sex, race, and class. This new "nation" requires an erotics to be articulated as the "price" of its subjectification, and therefore desire must be explored as the power animating this exchange on the marketplace. The "Englishing" of the Melibee story within Fragment VII constitutes a complex elucidation of the dynamics of production and consumption necessary to produce and maintain identities and the erotic charge/desire animating this exchange. Rather than seeing Chaucer's *Melibee* as a stable marker of something either purely medieval or purely modern and thus capable of constituting a point of origin for a modernist history of supersession—a reiteration of history as ascetic renunciation—I am proposing a mapping of social relations in and around the *Melibee* that proliferate the pleasures of history as an "erogenous zone" (to adapt Fradenburg and Freccero's formulation)[42] by helping to understand its function for premodern and postmodern audiences as a mobilizing point of entry into a mapping of the multiple relations of the possible. While there are forces ready to "organize" this new body and its erogenous zones, Fragment VII's desiring machine also explores the more muddled present, where subjects can increase and multiply in meaningful ways within the fragmentation of human language and embodiment. That fragmentation is represented not as mere sterility (as older theological models of essences would maintain), but rather as a useful site for surplus production and its exchange.[43]

*Melibee*'s place within Fragment VII also works to foreground the absence of a stabilizing authenticity for the structures of identity that it proposes: thus Fragment VII's emphasis on "little things" rather than wholes; on children, unhusbanded women, and henpecked men, rather than masculinity fully formed; on ludic proliferation of incident rather than meaningful reproduction of authority.[44] To this extent, the *Melibee* (placed in the context of Fragment VII) brings to representation not just the cultural fantasy of hegemonic identity for a new "middle class," but also the full range of anxious and mobile identifications necessitated by its uncertain position, simultaneously placed in a position of subordination in one relation (with an entrenched aristocracy and clerisy) and a position of dominance in another (with those labeled "churls"). Such hybridity is present at every point in the fragment: in the Prioress's performance (so often resolved as irony or self-destructive satire) using an older form of absolute difference (a Miracle of the Virgin) to represent the complexities of subordination/domination that constitute her gender, class, and estate situation in the present; in the currency of exchange that dominates the *Shipman's Tale* and which circulates outside of traditional "medieval" gender and class hierarchies; or in the thoroughgoing category confusion of the *Nun's Priest's Tale*'s becoming animal.[45] Such a deterritorialization, even as it makes possible the ground for a new hegemony—in the organized body of *Melibee*'s newly disciplined subjectivity—also brings into view—in the pilgrimage representation of an English nation yet to be—a body without organs that is continually dismantling the organism. Only in this way can "things as they are" be deterritorialized to an extent sufficient to begin to represent "things that might be." Fragment VII, then, intensifies "things as they are" to the point where the usual patterns of differentiation dissolve, constituting a desiring machine whose multiplicity opposes the notion of unity or One.[46]

# 6

# Post-ality and the "End" of the *Canterbury Tales*

In this postscript to my discussion of the *Tales,* I want to turn briefly to the question of their ending, and more specifically, to the common belief that in the *Parson's Tale* and *Chaucer's Retraction* we find some kind of resolution to the Canterbury project itself. Certainly it seems fair to say that, despite the original tale-telling agreement the Host and pilgrims forged at the Tabard Inn—that each pilgrim "shal telle tales tweye /To Caunterbury-ward, . . . And homward he shal tellen othere two" (I.792–95)—the *Parson's Prologue and Tale* appear intent on radically reshaping the end of the Canterbury project. The Host himself now looks to conclude the pilgrims' "game" *before* reaching Canterbury when he calls upon the Parson to be the final tale-teller who will "knytte up wel a greet mateere":

> Lordynges everichoon,
> Now lakketh us no tales mo than oon.
> Fulfilled is my sentence and my decree;
> I trowe that we han herd of ech degree;
> Almoost fulfild is al myn ordinaunce.
> I pray to God, so yeve hym right good chaunce,
> That telleth this tale to us lustily.
> Sire preest . . . ne breke thou nat oure pley;
> For every man, save thou, hath toold his tale.
> Unbokele and shew us what is in thy male; . . .
> Telle us a fable anon, for cokkes bones! (X.15–22, 24–26, 29)[1]

Moreover, a series of temporal and spatial allusions provided by the narrator in the *Parson's Prologue*—suggestive of death's shadow and divine justice—hint at a deeper fulfillment of the promise of pilgrimage in the approaching end to the traveling day and the pilgrims' entry "at a thropes ende" (X.12). Thus the narrator reminds us that the time of day is 4:00 P.M. and evening—as opposed to 10:00 A.M. and morning for the opening for the pilgrimage storytelling in the *Man of Law's Prologue* (II.2ff)—and that the proportion of "my shadwe" (X.8) on the ground at this time of day is a ratio of eleven feet to six, six feet being the traditional length of a man's grave. Similarly, his reference to "the moones exaltacioun—/ I meene Libra [ascending]" (X.10–11) not only signals the sign of the fall equinox (as opposed to Aries and the spring equinox, which open the *General Prologue*) but may also symbolically evoke this image of the zodiacal sign of the scales, the scales of divine justice. It is, moreover, precisely such a need to attend to the ultimate "end" of the pilgrims' activity that the Parson's intervention so starkly insists upon.

Responding to the Host's "game," the Parson reconfigures the end of the Host's Canterbury project with a set of overtly spiritual and harshly essentialist teleologies. "Thou getest fable noon ytold for me" (X.31) the Parson tells the Host, only "moralitee and virtuous mateere" (X.38) suitable for a Canterbury pilgrimage that enacts that pilgrimage to the "Jerusalem celestial" (X.51) that should mark the life of every Christian. The Parson's choice of subject, an extended prose treatise on penance, also makes clear his intention to underscore the *true* journey the group should be headed on. Beginning his "tale" with a citation from Jeremiah (a passage also used in medieval sermons on penance)—"Stondeth upon the weyes, and seeth and axeth of olde pathes (that is to seyn, of olde sentences) which is the goode wey, / and walketh in that wey, and ye shall fynde refresshynge for youre soules"—the Parson thereby emphasizes that, of the many "weyes espirtuels that leden folk to oure Lord Jhesu Crist and to the regne of glorie," the "ful noble wey and a ful covenable, which may nat fayle to man ne to woman that thurgh synne hath mysgoon fro the righte wey of Jerusalem celestial; / . . . is cleped Penitence" (X.77–81).

Such a penitential template for the *Tales* is reasserted even more dramatically at the end of the *Parson's Tale* in the brief prose passage that has come to be known as *Chaucer's Retraction*. The *Retraction* occurs in almost all manuscripts that contain a complete *Parson's Tale,* and here, it appears, Chaucer as author finally speaks *in propria persona,* asking forgiveness "of my translacions and enditynges of worldly vanitees," revoking by means of this list of retractions, not only *Troilus* and the early love poems but also all "the tales of Caunterbury, thilke that sownen into synne." Only for the *Boece* and "othere bookes of legendes of seintes, and omelies, and moralitee, and devocioun" does he feel free to thank "oure Lord Jhesu Crist and his blissful Mooder, and all the seintes of hevene," whom he beseeches to send him "grace to biwayle my giltes and to studie to the salvacioun of my soule" and to grant him "grace of verray penitence, confessioun and satisfaccioun to doon in this present lyf... so that I may been oon of hem at the day of doom that shulle be saved" (X.1085–86, 1088–92).

What are we to make of these "endings" to the *Canterbury Tales?* Their initial effect, certainly, is to provide a sense of radical closure to, even abandonment of, the proliferative "game" we have experienced to date. The statements of Host, Parson, and "Chaucer" all presume in their different ways a kind of preemptive teleology, and with it authoritative patterns of ascesis and self-discipline, that would appear to take us in very different directions from the lines of flight, rhizomatic structures, and desiring machines we have discussed in the preceding chapters. That is, by imagining the *Tales'* end, by projecting "beyond" the present moment in the way they do, the Host, Parson, and "Chaucer" of the *Retraction* try to overdetermine the historicity of the Canterbury project by settling its true relationship to time and space. For the Host, the end to tale-telling is bound up not just with filling the stipulated terms of an idle game, but with manifesting the ordered web of social relations that such game playing represents—"we han herd of ech degree" (X.18). For the Parson (and the "Chaucer" of the *Retraction*) the literal end of story (or life) is nothing but the sign of the emptiness of all human endeavors, and hence, of the need to allow a divine plan to fill and guide it. These "ends" to the *Tales,* then, enact a kind of coercive historicism, demanding that we exceed the boundaries of the *Tales* as we know them in order to fantasize their "beyond" and in order to return to our present "at a thropes ende" in the fullness of such knowledge of the "future."

All too often, it seems, modern criticism perpetuates this kind of hegemonic historicism when it asks us to choose between the Host and Parson and their divergent "ends" to the *Tales,* and in the process to reproduce the kinds of stabilizing teleologies that both pilgrims insist on.

This critical binary is often expressed reductively as a choice between a medieval/medievalist or modernist historicism. For example, according to the Parson's *medieval* historicism, his confessional "beyond" subsumes the *Tales* within the medieval Christian imaginary, substituting for their "game" a totalizing transcendental signifier that annihilates time and space. But the Parson's turn to universal history is also continued by a modern *medievalist* historicism that views such a "beyond" as defining the essential premodern otherness of the *Tales*—in this case, the *real* Chaucer and his true intentions for the *Tales,* which emerge in the moralizing of the *Parson's Tale* and *Chaucer's Retraction.* In contrast, a *modernist* historicism often espouses a more sophisticated version of the Host's imagined autonomy for the secular narrative, that is, his Canterbury project as its own "beyond," constituting a kind of limit case for the autonomy of fictional truth, individual subjectification, and "Chaucer" as an emergent "modern" author figure working within the limitations of a premodern Christian hegemony.

Despite their apparent differences, both kinds of historicism fantasize an imagined "beyond" of the Canterbury project as its necessary point of completion, making, in the process, the *present* experience of the pilgrimage only a meaningful stage on the way to Canterbury and the knowable future it represents. Individual accidents of time and space in the present thus give way to the essential and universal categories that order all human experience. In thinking about the *Tales'* historicism in this way, I am, of course, drawing on Walter Benjamin's distinction between a hegemonic historicism—intent on giving the "eternal" image of the past that stands outside time and space—and a politically engaged historical materialism—intent on stopping the march of time to encounter the full presentness of the past and to recognize the complexity of the present's own unique experience of such a past.

> Universal history... musters a mass of data to fill the homogeneous, empty time. [In] materialistic historiography, on the other hand,... [t]hinking involves not only the flow of thoughts, but their arrest as well. Where thinking suddenly stops in a configuration pregnant with tensions, it gives that configuration a shock, by which it crystallizes into a monad. A historical materialist approaches a historical subject only where he encounters it as a monad. In this structure he recognizes the sign of a

> Messianic cessation of happening, or, put differently, a revolutionary chance in the fight for the oppressed past. He takes cognizance of it in order to blast a specific era out of the homogeneous course of history. . . . Thus he establishes a conception of the present as the "time of the now" which is shot through with chips of Messianic time.[2]

Inhabiting the "beyond" of the Canterbury project, as the Host and Parson attempt to do, constitutes the ultimate in Benjamin's hegemonic historicism, constructing in various ways a sense of universal history and coherent identity for the pilgrimage group, and in the process establishing the *Tales* as a socially useful document and Chaucer finally as a public, commodifiable author figure. In the Parson's case, of course, such a universalizing history has the weight of traditional clerical authority behind it. Even in the Host's case, however, experience of the pilgrimage and of its practice of everyday life, "though noon auctoritee," works to provide a certain hegemonic power to the pilgrims' collective utterance.

But do such attempts to place the *Canterbury Tales* in terms of universal history really fully engage with the "nowness" of the present moment given to us at the *Tales'* conclusion? If we stop mustering these end tales as "a mass of data to fill the homogeneous, empty time" of history, if we instead arrest such thinking in a "configuration pregnant with tensions," such a materialist historiography exposes the impurity and presentness of the Canterbury project at work in its own historicization. And we begin to see the ending of the *Tales* as an occasion where recourse to the beyond of a clerically defined medieval historicism remains imbricated with, indeed can actually be used to warrant and stabilize, another, newer, lay-authorizing historicism that has been at work throughout the *Tales*. Rather than sending us "back" to the Canterbury project as "medieval" transcendental signifier, or as some founding moment in the march of modernist history, the *Tales'* endings continue to look "forward" in the manner of the Canterbury project, that is, they continue its interruption of a productively "collusive sense of cultural contemporaneity" between London and Canterbury, between middle class and clerical orthodoxy, between national and penitential body at work in the *Tales*.[3] In such a case, we see the *Parson's Tale* not in hegemonic historicist terms as the substitution of the universalizing category of sinner for the accidental variety of the Canterbury pilgrim characters, but instead as "arresting" the flow of thought of the *Canterbury Tales,* giving that configuration a shock, crystallizing into a monad that *other,* dangerously new project of materialist historicism within the *Tales* (that is, the desire to constitute a new social body through the Canterbury pilgrimage and its attempt to go beyond, to exceed the barrier of the knowable and the representable).

I want to begin, then, by challenging the presumptiveness of how the *Parson's Tale* introduces confession and its Christian subject as the endpoint of the Canterbury project. For I will argue that the *Tale* operates according to its own "don't ask, don't tell" model of willful ignorance. By doing so, the *Parson's Tale* disguises the complexity of the material conditions under which the confessional model produces meaning and thereby presents a unified, official "knowledge" as the necessary outcome of confession. To understand why the "secret" of confession might be made public at this moment of the *Tales,* and along with that why the "death" of the lay subject so carefully built up during the *Tales* and Chaucer's career might be imagined, we need first to consider the sacrament's complex and at times contradictory relationship to pleasure. Recently Karma Lochrie, in a study that owes much to Foucault's brief but suggestive treatment of confession in the first volume of the *History of Sexuality* (while resisting Foucault's collapse of all things sinful into sexuality, and his nostalgia for a prediscursive, mystical sexual experience as the truly medieval), has argued that a perverse dynamic is at the heart of the hermeneutic established by private confession in the Middle Ages.[4] The complex relationship to pleasure that results not only accounts for why confession became a key cultural discourse in the Middle Ages, but also for how it provided a crucial technology in the construction of medieval lay subjectivities.

After the Fourth Lateran Council of 1215 made private confession an annual requirement for all Christians, discussions of the sacrament of confession developed a truth technology focused not only in general terms on the care of the self, but also more specifically on the care of the laity. Standardization of the sacrament's constituent parts and its mode of delivery took place first in the scholastic discussions of the sacrament in the century or so after the council, but most fully in the series of penitential manuals for confessors (like the *Parson's Tale*) that flourished up to the Reformation in England and other Protestant countries and after in those countries that remained Roman Catholic. Thus, next to the Eucharist, the sacrament of confession became one of the most powerful media for the dissemination of ecclesiastical authority and its version of the truth. At the same time, however, confession (and the educative process it demanded, which brought clerisy and laity into intimate relations with each other) was one of the first, and most pervasive, means by which lay subjects could gain access, in their own right, to new modes of subjectification. Because of the very ubiquity of the sacrament and the necessity for it to be *personally* meaningful, the possibility arose for a perverse dynamic to circulate within this supposedly unitary truth technology. Lochrie notes that "the objects of confessional disclosure were always less the secrets themselves than the ritualized telling and sacerdotal listening," so that "the medieval subject comes into being through her acts of disclosure, through the discovery of her secrets, and through the ritual discourse that enables such discoveries. The manifestations of these secrets and the sacrifice of the self that accompanies self-disclosure—these are the requirements of the new truth technology produced by Christian confession in the Middle Ages."[5] In addition to the perverse dynamic that Lochrie sees produced by the hermeneutic structures of the sacrament and its attempts to delineate a universalizing pattern of ascesis, it is also important to note the incoherences and contradictions resulting from the sacrament's performativity as a material practice. One trajectory of the confessional "dialogue" is certainly top down, making the sacrament a powerful mode for the ever wider dissemination of ecclesiastical control and its state apparatuses through every aspect of lay experience. But at the same time, in ways both intended and unforeseen by clerical authorities, because the lay person becomes the *subject* of such activity, the sacrament as a truth technology also works to activate and empower lay experience in new ways.

I would argue as well that confession achieves its status as dominant medieval truth technology precisely because of its own performative nature and the variety and complexity of material conditions by which the sacrament is made "universally" meaningful. Confessional manuals such as the *Parson's Tale* may strike many modern readers as abstractly theoretical, but their initial purpose was the very practical one of educating parish clergy to enable them better to minister to lay concerns in the confessional. Eamon Duffy cites St. John's College, Cambridge, MS S 35, a compilation assembled by two different priests, as evidence of the very practical, day-to-day use made of such manuals:

> In the section of inquiries about the deadly sins which forms the principal part of the compilation, the main text on each sin has a line drawn under it, below which the first compiler has jotted down a series of one-word headings which serve as a summary of the longer text and an *aide-mémoire* to himself in the course of hearing a confession. It is unmistakably a working book designed to help the owners to carry out their duties thoroughly and sympathetically.... The significance of the St. John's manuscript is not in any originality it contains, but in the evidence it provides of the actual employment of the theories and advice of the textbooks by working priests in their day-to-day practice.

Again at a practical level, Duffy reminds us that, while confession would have been a lengthy and harrowing business if it followed exactly the pattern prescribed in the textbooks, in practice it must have been much abbreviated:

> Confessors were sensibly advised to save their close enquiries for the sins particular people were likely to have committed—"as unto the people of the chirche of symonye... unto yonge people of temptacyons carnalles." For most people confessed once a year, in Lent, and often as not delayed coming till Holy Week. In any community with more than a hundred or so "houselling folk" a systematic confession of the sort envisaged by the manuals would have occupied the priest and his people for most of Lent.... For the majority of parishioners it remained a less subjective exercise, a time for practical reassessment, reconciliation with neighbors, and settling of spiritual accounts. It was, moreover, an exercise carried out with queues of waiting fellow-parishioners looming close behind, the mutter of their rosaries or their chatter plainly audible. Pastoral realism therefore demanded that the confession be kept within manageable dimensions; in a time-honored formula the penitent was to be brief, be brutal, be gone.[6]

On the other hand, another effect of the emphasis on accessibility to and education about confession is the trend through the late Middle Ages among pious and leisured laypeople both to seek out the best confessor, that is, the one best educated and most concerned with ministering to the specific spiritual needs of the confessing layperson, and to confess on a more regular basis than the basic annual requirement. This reconfiguration of confession as a form of spiritual direction thus becomes an important component in a general trend among a pious laity to take on to itself many of the spiritual aspects previously reserved to the clerisy.

In light of the perverse dynamic that Lochrie sees at the heart of confession's secrecy, as well as the renewed sense of lay communities as communities, and, in some cases, the new forms of subjectivity arising out of private introspection that Duffy describes as a result of the material practices of confession, the *way* that the Parson interpellates confession as simple ascesis—and as a kind of opposition to the Host's imagined community—becomes particularly interesting. Even as a call to spirituality (in opposition to the idle game of storytelling) the *Parson's Tale* seems slightly out of step with trends in lay piety and with ecclesiastical attempts to meet the spiritual needs of the laity. Recent work by cultural historians such as Duffy, Gail McMurray Gibson, and Caroline M. Barron has challenged any simplistic understanding of the traditional religion of the laity in the later Middle Ages as rote formalism or mindless acquiescence to clerical authority, and has instead called our attention to the dynamism, complexity, and creativity of lay religious practice in this period.[7] What stands out is both the variety of such practices and a common emphasis on individual self-articulation in the context of and in concert with the expression of community identity. Thus, while the Sunday Eucharist continues to be celebrated with the priest veiled by a rood screen, various moments in the service frame the display of the sacrament to the congregation. In addition, squint holes in the rood screen make possible individual viewing of the elevation at the communal Sunday mass, and weekday low masses at side chapels and chantry chapels allowed for more general and less sequestered lay participation in the rite at other times. Similarly, religious fraternities (often focused in terms of parish communities), an expectation that chantry priests would contribute to the communal life of the parish, rogationtide processions, and various kinds of public memorializations of the dead (including the annual reading of the bede roll of the parish, which included relatively modest contributors) all worked to emphasize the active intervention of the laity in the daily life of *their* communities.

The richness and diversity of these material frames through which medieval lay subjects came to understand clerical universals *as* universal are curiously absent from the Parson's retrospectively and hegemonically universal historicism. The *Parson's Tale* and *Chaucer's Retraction* are often viewed as two similar manifestations of the same confessional model. But in many ways the complexity of late medieval spirituality registers more in the *Retraction*'s emphasis on the kinds of things that typical lay piety focused on—a good death, a good funeral, appropriate means of memorialization after death—rather than in the Parson's abstract and dogmatic tracing of sin and penitence. Moreover, the *Retraction* constitutes Chaucer's writings as a kind of bede roll, memorializing his name and constructing the readers of the *Tales* (present and future, known and unknown) as a kind of imagined parish community given a substance and identity by such acts of communal memorialization. Thus, the *Tales* and *Retraction* might be seen as different registers in the same kind of imbrication of life and death, present and beyond, lay and clerical.

In the case of the *Parson's Tale,* confession provides a mode of emptying and homogenizing the time and space of the *Tales,* providing in Benjamin's terms, historicism's "eternal image of the past." What it tries to force us to do as participants in the Canterbury project is to acknowledge that the *Canterbury Tales* as secular productions cannot constitute the real journey that is the Canterbury pilgrimage. Mere empty fables, the *Tales* as tales simply "despend" time, and therefore the "I" they claim to utter cannot really represent the true "me." Only by such a shame-filled acknowledgment of the emptiness of the accidental and idle productions of the past can the certain subject of history be discerned. The Parson's evocation of Jeremiah tries to enact the prophetic stance that the biblical passage itself advocates: search out the old ways and we will make straight the ways of the present and be led to that heavenly Jerusalem that must be our present and future goal. Similarly, the scholastic taxonomies of the penitential manual that is the Parson's particular version of this journey work both to empty our past of obfuscatory identifications and to fill that emptiness with an arborescent structure for the new universal identity that will emerge from our journey through it. Penance is "likned unto a tree. / The roote of this tree is Contricioun, that hideth hym in the herte of hym that is verray repentaunt, right as the roote of a tree hydeth hym in the erthe. / Of the roote of Contricioun spryngeth a stalke that bereth braunches and leves of Confessioun, and fruyt of Satisfaccioun" (X.112–14). But then "Contricioun" is broken down into its four constituent elements—what it is, the causes that move someone to contrition, how one should be contrite, what contrition does for the soul. In turn the six causes of contrition are adumbrated, and so on. So, too, the seven deadly sins are each broken down into their constituent elements with different examples and then matched with their remedies. Not only is the overall effect one of complete mastery of a subject, such a mastery comes by faithfully tracing a completely knowable pattern onto what might seem the chaotic details of everyday experience. In the process, the relentless precision and endlessly reproducible methodology of division and subdivision appear to fill every nook and cranny of human experience, answering any possible question one might have about how to find the correct path to right behavior. No room, it appears, is left for dissent, confusion, or uncertainty. The Parson's choice of tale, and presentation within the tale of only one possible "choice" available to the confessing Christian subject, thus actively attempts to substitute the truth technology of confession for the Host's "idle" game. In doing so, the Parson also resists the identity as pilgrim that the Host proffers when he invites him to tell the last tale, that is, a private, individual identity as just another tale-teller. So, too, the *Parson's Tale* resists the efforts to authenticate individual autonomy and selfhood that the Host's Canterbury project has underwritten.

But the vehemence with which the Parson denounces the Host (and the pilgrimage fellowship and enterprise he has until now freely contracted to be part of) suggests that the *Parson's Tale* also acts in some ways as a kind of backward glance into a strangely distorting mirror. While he clearly speaks with the voice of traditional ecclesiastical authority, the standoff between the Host and the Parson cannot really be characterized as confessional dialogue, nor does it restore completely to this moment the power relations of sacerdotal confession (where the penitent is not allowed to keep his secrets from the priest and where only the priest is endowed with the knowledge, discretion, and power of absolution that will warrant the event as a true confession). It suggests that this moment in the *Canterbury Tales* constitutes something much more than the simple substitution of true ecclesiastical authority and eternal truth for false secular materiality and temporality. The Host's comments anticipate the fulfillment of the Canterbury project as its own kind of "truth technology," one that has in certain crucial ways lingered meaningfully in the pleasure of thinking about what the Parson will label as sin. In other words, the *Tales* have modeled their own kind of confessional technology, the kind of relationship between confession, storytelling, and technologies of the self that Foucault associates with modernity in the West: "pleasure in the truth of pleasure, the pleasure of knowing that truth, of discovering and exposing it, the fascination of seeing it and telling it, of captivating and capturing others by it, of confiding it in secret, of luring it out in the open—the specific pleasure of the true discourse on pleasure."[8] As Lochrie has emphasized, though, such a pleasure is also perversely present in the central truth technology of the medieval West: "The pleasure of thinking about a sin doubles the pleasure of its commission and compounds its seriousness. Interestingly, the process of confession necessitates just such a thinking, and, therefore, it always risks this secondary form of pleasure. . . . Confession necessarily ventured into this area of pleasure—of thinking about sin—through the act of verbalization, but this pleasure is one of the secrets and paradoxes of the confessional logic."[9]

The Host's articulation of an end to the pleasures of the Canterbury tale-telling project, then, outlines its own kind of historicist project, one founded on and arising out of the church's confessional truth technology. The Host's comments fulfill the fantasy articulated by the *General Prologue,* first of a homogeneous, empty time of the pilgrimage, then of the tales and their tellers becoming history as they muster a mass of data to fill that homogeneous, empty time. Like a confessor, the Host has elicited not just idle conversation that "despendest time," but rather acts of disclosure that ensure the truth of each subject coming into being: "Fulfilled is my sentence and my decree; / I trowe that we han herd of ech degree." In doing so, the Host points to the tale-telling project as its own technology of self-renunciation, self-examination, and verbalization. Thus, like the Ellesmere scribe, and countless readers since, the Host responds to and helps enact the powerful pleasures made possible by the *Tales'* "impersonated artistry." In other words, the Host identifies, by fantasizing its completion, a new universal secular subject who, paradoxically, "owns" his private selfhood by being able to "confess" it in the public arena. The Host's hailing of the Parson (as the last of many discrete tale-tellers rather than as the singular medium for a process of transcendental subjectification) thus is a threatening interpellation of the previously dominant institutional controlling subject (the priest) as now simply one more "gentil man" reproducible by and thus contained within this new technology of the self.

As I have tried to suggest in the previous chapters, one trajectory of this push to self-identification in the *Tales* is to move from the narrator's ambiguous sense of "a compaignye / Of sundry folk, by aventure yfalle / In felawhipe" (I.24–26) to a more empowering recognition in the Canterbury enterprise of a fraternity of like-minded "gentils." The opening "fiction" of the pilgrimage in the *General Prologue* established the promise of a "beyond" in which contradictions between social and theological, clerical and lay, medieval and proto-modern, past and future could fuse. Thus the courtly rhetoric of love and sexual reproduction that opens the *General Prologue* merges with the impulse to pilgrimage and the reproduction of the redeemed Christian subject. But what results is not a simple reproduction of older medieval systems of representation—such as the body of Christ, the three estates, or some other version of a hierarchized body where aristocrat and cleric share hegemony. Instead, a "new" group of English men and women is identified *as a group:* largely southern and metropolitan, a middling class neither aristocratic nor peasant, come together by chance association but gaining some sense of identity and community as the pilgrims of the *Canterbury Tales.*

If pilgrimage here continues to promise the "beyond" of typological fulfillment—an enacting of the pilgrimage of the life of man, it also in this context implies something more—the "beyond" of a unified body of "gentils": no longer defined simply as the body of the king or the body of Christ but as an emergent imagined community capable of articulating its own new "national" identity. This emergent imagined community can, of course, be connected with various kinds of contemporary examples, such as London religious fraternities, London parish communal life (especially the burgeoning parishes outside the City's walls), but none provide an exact "historical" model for this imagined community of the *Tales.* And I want to emphasize such an imagined community as something not yet known, and therefore separate from the kind of "English nation" defined a generation later by the fifteenth-century Lancastrian state apparatus. Subsequent early modern and modern attempts to define Chaucer as avatar of Englishness and an English literary tradition, and thus to root the *Tales* in various fantasies of the English nation, are later sedimentations of the kind of "beyond things as they are" that I am arguing is being imagined and given a temporality and topography in the *Tales*.

Of course the Host's "ending" presents this identity formation as if it were already realized by the tale-telling activity, already recognizable in the ordered, stable pilgrimage community constructed by the journey. I will consider below some of the many ways in which this kind of hegemonic historicism is qualified by the larger dynamic the end of the *Tales* inscribes. But nothing indicates the power of the Host's historicist project and the imagined community it fantasizes as already present so much as the repeated efforts of later fifteenth-century continuators to bring that "beyond" back into the present of the *Tales* and thus to see themselves and their present as naturally part of its imagined community. What is especially interesting about their interventions is that from their perspective the historicist project of the *Tales* has absolutely succeeded. The aims of a clerical and lay historicism are fused; the "beyond" is here. Lydgate in the Prologue to his *Siege of Thebes,* for example, by means of an elaborate astrological opening, conjures up a kind of contemporaneous "now" that occurs when Canterbury tales are performed, a time at once textual and historical yet also an imagined universal that Lydgate can enter as pilgrim and tale-teller:

> Whan bright Phebus passed was the Ram
> Myd of Aprille and into Bole cam,
>
> . . . . . . . . . . . . . . . . . . . . . . . . . . . . . . . .
>
> Whan that Flora, the noble mighty queen,
> The soyl hath clad in newe tendre grene
> With her floures craftily y-meynt,
> Braunch and bough with red and whit depeynt,
> Fletinge the bawme on hilles and on valys—
> The tyme in soth whan Canterbury talys
> Complet and told at many sondry stage
> Of estatis in the pilgrimage,
> Everich man lik to his degré
>
> . . . . . . . . . . . . . . . . . . . . . . . . . .
>
> As opynly the storie can yow lere,
> Word for word with every circumstaunce,

Echon y-write and put in remembraunce
By hym that was, yif I shal not feyne,
Floure of poetes thorghout al Breteyne,

. . . . . . . . . . . . . . . . . . . . . . . . . . . . . . . . . .

And this whil that the pilgrymes leye
At Canterbury, wel louged on and all,
I not in soth what I may it call—
Hap or Fortune—in conclusioun
That me byfil to entren into toun,
The holy seynt pleynly to visite
Aftere siknesse, my vowes to aquyte,

. . . . . . . . . . . . . . . . . . . . . . . . . . . . . . . . .

My man toforn with a voide male
Which of Fortune took myn inne anon
Where the pylgrymes were logged everichon.[10]

"Her governour, the Host, / Stonding in hall, ful of wynde and bost, / Lich to a man wonder sterne and fers,"[11] while still the bombastic performer encountered in the other *Tales*—and whose medicinal knowledge is here mocked slightly by the bookish monk, Lydgate—is nonetheless now someone whose self-controlled "game" has its "natural" place within the order of the pilgrimage and thus no longer needs the kind of extreme management by ecclesiastical authority that the Parson's moralizing intervention demanded. Instead, *moralitas* and fable, secular and religious, are represented as in productive rapprochement by Lydgate's prologue and act of tale-telling. Lydgate's description of the *Tales* as a temporal and spatial location that right-minded readers are assured access to emphasizes how Chaucer has created a special place where the full variety of the social can be sampled with impunity since all estates coexist in ordered harmony.

In "The Canterbury Interlude" that precedes another continuation, the *Tale of Beryn,* Chaucer's Canterbury pilgrims, now arrived at their destination, behave like a well-organized parish community or religious fraternity. On arrival, the first thing they do is to go as a group to the Cathedral and Becket's shrine to make their offerings. The *Beryn* poet notes in particular that when they arrive at "chirch dorr the curtesy gan to ryse, / Tyl the Knyght of gentilnes that knewe righte wele the guyse / Put forth the prelates, the Person and his fere," so that a Cathedral monk can sprinkle their heads with holy water, "Everich after other, righte as they were of states."[12] Once in the church, the churls may occasionally fall into churlish behavior, gawking at the stained glass windows and making a spectacle of themselves until the Host reminds them of good manners and directs them to go give their offering at the saint's shrine. Similarly, after lunch, the pilgrims of their own accord break into smaller groups appropriate to their social rank and engage in behavior "normal" to their estate. The Knight and Squire inspect the town's fortifications. The Clerk attempts to educate the Summoner in appropriately genteel behavior toward the Friar. The Monk takes the Parson and the Friar to visit a fellow monk. And perhaps most tellingly, the Wife of Bath, "so wery, she had no will to walk," invites the Prioress to spend time with her in the kitchen garden of the inn and afterward to rest with the innkeeper's wife in her parlor.[13] The project of tale-telling along the way to Canterbury, it seems, has not only produced an identifiable body of citizens, but a body that as fully as possible is now able to live up to its potential for social and cosmic harmony, each estate finally behaving as it should. London and Canterbury are thus connected by a knowable and reproducible highway of lay activity and literary production.[14] Notably, the Host as lay leader—with an authority given him by a Chaucerian mastery of high style—now properly orders both himself and the group. He had, we are told, "no spice of rage / But al thing wrought prudenciall, as sober man and wise."[15] In addition to encouraging good manners among the churls at the Cathedral, the Host—as a kind of marshal of the hall—also ensures that dining in the evening will be "yit as curtesy axeth." And when the drunken churls interrupt his and the Merchant's managing of accounts later in the evening, both, although "somewhat wroth . . . yit they preyd hem curteysly to rest for to wend."[16] Only the Pardoner, it seems, remains beyond redemption by the Canterbury experience. His lustful, effeminate behavior with Kit the Tapster, and bestial position—bruised and bloodied by his fight with Kit's boyfriend, and trapped for much of the night with the inn's mastiff—once again keep him physically and psychically separate from the ordered communal pleasures of the pilgrimage group.[17]

In imagining themselves as participants in a continuing Canterbury project, such later readers as the *Beryn* poet or Lydgate are, of course, taking their cue from Chaucer's own opening up of the Canterbury frame to admit the new arrival of the Canon's Yeoman and his tale. These later writers, however, may also be responding at a deeper level to the underlying historicist project of the *Tales,* its attempt to bring a new "English" nation into representability and to authorize that identity by claiming its interchangeability with an already established clerical model. Moreover, if they fulfill one trajectory of the *Tales,* that is, the pilgrims' attempts to produce a persuasive "collusive sense of cultural contemporaneity," these fifteenth-century "continuations" do so to an extent not actually achieved by the end of the *Canterbury Tales* itself. These continuators reimagine the *Tales'* "ending" as a present always available because perfectly historicized and commodified, filling homogeneous, empty time in productive uniformity. To that extent, they organize and overdetermine time and space in ways not managed even by the historicizing tendencies of Chaucer's endings. There is little of any "beyond"—in the sense of the unknowable, unrepresentable—left in these fifteenth-century Chaucerian "fictions." What happens in Canterbury is knowable from what one has experienced in London and along the way of Chaucer's pilgrimage route; and equally, the experience of fiction is the fullness of ideology naturalized and rendered invisible.

To turn to the tales immediately preceding the *Parson's Tale* after such fifteenth-century completions of the "beyond" of the Canterbury project is to encounter the materiality of a unique experience with the past. As Homi Bhabha has noted with regard to the postmodern attraction to post-ality, "'Beyond,' signifies spatial distance, marks progress, promises the future; but our intimations of exceeding the barrier or boundary—the very act of going *beyond*—are unknowable, unrepresentable, without a return to the 'present' which in the process of repetition, becomes disjunct and displaced."[18] The last set of tales, beginning with the *Second Nun's* and ending with the *Parson's Prologue,* interposes barriers and boundaries of temporal and social difference that interrupt the pilgrims' "collusive sense of cultural contemporaneity." We are brought back to the present whose beyond remains insistently unknowable and unrepresentable. These end tales are full of specific references to the position of the group on the pilgrimage route, but this is a route that is open to interruption and lines of flight unanticipated in Lydgate's or the *Beryn* poet's sense of pilgrimage—for example, when the Canon seeks to join the pilgrimage body midjourney and when his Yeoman is moved to tell a tale outside the protocols established by the Host, or when the Host's pushing around of the Cook as part of estates rivalry opens up the potential libel of the Manciple, or when the *Manciple's Tale* shows the openness of contracts to manipulation and abuse, as well as the fluidity and arbitrariness of apparently fixed identities.

Any attempt to finish the Canterbury project by some absolute move to the "beyond" is realizable only if we adopt a static, top-down model of "the medieval world view" or if one accepts, like Lydgate or the *Beryn* scribe, the English nation "as is." The fact that the future (in the sense of a "beyond"), while fantasized as ever closer, remains forever beyond the reach of this fiction's representability is crucial to the *Tales*' construction of that beyond, and at the same time throws into relief the differences that interrupt "our collusive sense of cultural contemporaneity." Unless a great deal of collective "forgetting" occurs, those hoped-for set identities remain forever slightly out of reach, and the present is instead represented as "an expanded and ex-centric site of experience and empowerment."[19] So these "end" tales, rather than simply telling us who we are by a process of historicizing tracing and causality, instead embody the restless and revisionary energy that circulates so intensely throughout the *Tales,* stimulating a materialist historiography and interest in the world as they map Chaucer's queer nation in "the time of the now."

Here I would like to turn to consider how the intrusion of the Canon and his Yeoman works to bring the "beyonds" of the Canterbury project, as represented by the Host and Parson, back to a present that becomes disjunct and displaced as a result. The juxtaposition of the *Canon's Yeoman's* and *Second Nun's Tales* could be seen as conclusively answering the perverse dynamic of Fragment VI's representational politics. In the *Second Nun's Tale,* chaste marriage and the series of metaphoric substitutions it makes possible provide a way both to acknowledge and to elide those differences between lay and clerical spheres, female and male bodies, past and present that proved so problematic for the *Physician's Tale.* Now the decapitated and desexed (female) body can speak the proper masculine will of the Father, knit together potentially fragmented and perverse subjects into the whole body of Christ, and communicate the urgency of the primitive church's experience of truth to a laxer, more sophisticated successor. In the process, the tale asserts its fantasy of past perfection in an act of hegemonic historicism over the present's difference. The many become one.

So, too, the relationships established between the Canon and the pilgrimage body mirror the earlier encounter with the Pardoner in Fragment

VI. The Canon joins the pilgrimage group not as a chance encounter, but after observing the group for some time at their previous inn. "[F]ul fayn" to ride with them "for his desport" and because "he loveth daliaunce" (VIII.591–92), the Canon now rushes to overtake them at Boughton-under-Blean (some five miles from Canterbury). The desire of the Canon thus mirrors in certain crucial ways that secular will to identity that we have been observing throughout the *Tales* and makes it recognizable through the intrusion of his own bodily presence into the pilgrimage group. But the Canon's interruption of the pilgrimage, his drawing attention to the constructions of identity at work in this community of tale-tellers, also elicits the gaze of the pilgrimage group and their consequent subjectification of him. The Canon as unknown quantity—here the mirror image of the supposedly absolutely knowable Pardoner—both elicits and validates the confessional mode of the *Tales* as truth technology. The narrator is first to try to figure out who and what the Canon is, recognizing him first as a canon by the kind of clothing he wears, but more importantly, in the imagery used to describe his sweating—"His forheed dropped as a stillatorie / Were ful of plantayne and of paritorie" (VIII.580–81)—underscoring that it is truly by means of his *body* that we will learn his true nature. So, too, the Host pushes such investigation further by means of a series of leading questions to the Canon's Yeoman. Thus, a combination of confessional tale-telling and the truth-telling ability of bodily presence allows us finally to learn the true nature of the Canon, a truth, moreover, that he would prefer remain secret.

This interactive process of subjectification provides an interesting parallel with the identification of the Pardoner's wayward presence earlier in the pilgrimage. There, "gentil" knowledge of the Pardoner is always already overdetermined at the level of signification, and the activity of the Pardoner reactively works to forestall and resist such overdetermination by foregrounding his status as open secret of the Canterbury project. Here, the Canon's true identity emerges as a secret that it seems the pilgrims' methodologies can thoroughly expose and know. The activity of the Canon's Yeoman in validating the truth of their reading of the Canon further validates the worth of such a presumptive knowledge system and thereby works to shut down other predicative possibilities. In this way, the *Canon's Yeoman's Tale* emphasizes that the Canon's alchemical activities are useless multiplication and idleness (as opposed to the Host and pilgrim's useful telling of secrets and establishing of powerful identities). In rejecting the Canon, the pilgrimage body tries to reject the metonymic "touch of the queer," along with the category confusion that the Canon's alchemical labor threatens to unleash, and they do so with a decisiveness that was not possible in their attempts to deal similarly with the Pardoner and the problems of metonymic perversion that he raised (where we do not know where one thing begins and another ends). The pilgrims' hermeneutic activity thus constructs a kind of hegemonic historicism, since their ability to uncover the Canon's secret forces him to withdraw abjectly from the pilgrimage body before he can infect it. Indeed, because the Canon cannot join them, the very fact of joining becomes a crucial marker of worthiness (and mimics the action of joining the One Body of Christendom that took place in the *Second Nun's Tale*).

Despite these attempts to reinforce an organic unity at the heart of the Canterbury project, the *Canon's Yeoman's Tale* also records the entry of the "alien"—in the chance encounter with the Canon and the incorporation of the Canon's Yeoman into the pilgrimage body—as a line of flight that contains within it the power to disturb the original historicist teleology of the Host's tale-telling game. The Canon, his Yeoman, and the *Canon's Yeoman's Tale* burst through the "real-life" pilgrimage frame to provide a story of a present life. The sweat of the horses, the blackened face of the Yeoman, the fervent desire of the Canon to attach himself to this pleasant company of pilgrims, all foreground the "work" that the *Second Nun's Tale* sought to disguise. The interruption of the Canon draws attention as well to the sense of community, not just association, that the *Tales* have been constructing through the pilgrims and their tales. For the Canon desires to join *this* pilgrimage group (and his deletion from the pilgrimage ensures its continued ability to fantasize its own imagined community). And the Canon's arrival, its own line of flight within the Host's ordered "game," also draws attention to the temporal and spatial gaps that exist between the "presents" of the two tales of Fragment VIII (Rome/England, primitive church/an almost post-church secularity, metaphor/metonymy) and by implication, perhaps, within the supposedly homogeneous present of the pilgrimage. Moreover, in the process of completing the pilgrims' examination of the Canon, the Canon's Yeoman makes the pilgrimage group itself the unwitting subject of his tale-telling. After all, the Canon's Yeoman occupies himself for nearly the first half of his tale with continuing the story of the actual Canon newly expelled from the pilgrimage group, that is, with material that had until now been part of the "real" of the pilgrimage frame. As with the Pardoner earlier, the line between real and fictional, prologue and tale, accidental and essential has blurred in disturbing ways. Therefore, even though the *Canon's Yeoman's Tale* explicitly argues against muliplicatory strategies by exposing the unthriftiness of the Canon's experiments, in a curious way it and the *Canterbury Tales* practice their own not-so-different multiplicatory strategies.

This interplay between ending and nonending, hegemonic historicism and materialist historiography, is, of course, exactly what we have seen played out in the final set of endings for the *Tales*. But it also underscores, perhaps, the ways in which the end of the Tales reiterates and subtly shifts the underlying dialogue between Pardoner and Parson that structures so much of the meaning system of the *Tales*. Mark Jordan has discussed the double bind of the sodomite in medieval clerical discussions, at once exiled from his homeland as unfit for citizenship, yet conceived by definition as a citizen of an ancient, enduring city, the city of Sodom.[20] On the surface the Pardoner and the landscape of his tale embody the sterility and fragmentation ascribed to this sodomitical identity and its nonteleological pleasures: hence the ease with which the Pardoner and his tale are so often cast as mirror image to the Parson and his tale, so that in the *Pardoner's Tale* material accidents are seen as inhibiting the kind of emptying of time and space demanded by the Parson, with the result that literal death triumphs. Yet as we have seen, pleasure without teleology is at the heart of the Canterbury project and its processes of subjectification. And attempts to "empty" the *Tales* of the Pardoner produce their own queer torsions for "gentil" self-identification. The various endings of the *Tales* pose these representational problems in ever more pressing ways. The binary between the body of Christ and the sodomite, as well as the model for the death of the self at the heart of the sacrament of confession, provides one kind of redemptive topography for the Canterbury project and "gentil" self-identification. But the end tales also return us to "the time of the now" that this pilgrimage imagines, and with that, to the work of materialist historiography that the gulf between such a redemptive symbolic landscape and the now of the pilgrimage makes space for.

Both the *Pardoner's Tale* and the *Parson's Tale* threaten death to the imagined community of the Canterbury project if they are read only as universalizing history. But if the Parson demands that we think "beyond" the limitations of the superficial moment, the activity of the *Tales* might in turn demand that we think "beyond" the limitations of the Parson. This is not to take us to some postmedieval secular space (that happens to look pretty much like modernity), but rather to bring us back to a medieval present that (to adapt Bhabha's formulation) "in the process of repetition, becomes disjunct and displaced." This is the kind of present that we find made possible in the laity's embrace of the late medieval machinery of the cult of death (with its chantry priests and chapels, "mechanical" indulgences, personalized piety), or in the importance of parish structures and local fraternities as locations for new and different modes of social organization and self-identification. It is precisely such productive middles that bring lay and clerical, men and women, together as a mobile and unpredictable "middle" class of "free agents." The dangerous novelty of this present, read through the Parson's universalizing hermeneutical lens, might be imagined (and contained) as some "no man's land" of death, nonmeaning, waste and sterility—as "Flaundres" in the *Pardoner's Tale* can so easily be allegorized.[21] But the unpredictable and liberating predicative possibilities of the present moment also mark the proximate, "middle" ground of the *Canterbury Tales* fictional journey.[22] Neither a completely allegorical universal nor a simply verisimilitudinous accident, that journey marks instead a present disjunct and displaced, traversing a nonteleologically *productive* topography of desire.

# NOTES

## INTRODUCTION

1. Michel Foucault, *The History of Sexuality,* vol. 1, *An Introduction,* trans. Robert Hurley (New York: Vintage, 1990); Jonathan Dollimore, *Sexual Dissidence: Augustine to Wilde, Freud to Foucault* (Oxford: Clarendon Press, 1991); Judith Butler, *Bodies That Matter: On the Discursive Limits of "Sex"* (New York: Routledge, 1993); and Eve Kosofsky Sedgwick, *Epistemology of the Closet* (Berkeley and Los Angeles: University of California Press, 1990).

2. See, for example, recent work by Carolyn Dinshaw, *Getting Medieval: Sexualities and Communities, Pre- and Postmodern* (Durham, N.C.: Duke University Press, 1999), and "Chaucer's Queer Touches/A Queer Touches Chaucer," *Exemplaria* 7, no. 1 (spring 1995): 75–92; Karma Lochrie, *Covert Operations: The Medieval Uses of Secrecy* (Philadelphia: University of Pennsylvania Press, 1999); the theoretical introductions and critical essays in Glenn Burger and Steven Kruger, eds., *Queering the Middle Ages* (Minneapolis: University of Minnesota Press, 2001); Louise Fradenburg and Carla Freccero, eds., *Premodern Sexualities* (New York: Routledge, 1996); and Gregory S. Hutcheson and Josiah Blackmore, *Queer Iberia: Sexualities, Cultures, and Crossing from the Middle Ages to the Renaissance* (Durham, N.C.: Duke University Press, 1999).

3. For a useful overview of queer theory, see Annamarie Jagose, *Queer Theory: An Introduction* (New York: New York University Press, 1996).

4. Ross Chambers, *Room for Maneuver: Reading (the) Oppositional (in) Narrative* (Chicago: University of Chicago Press, 1991), 10.

5. See Gilles Deleuze and Félix Guattari, *Anti-Oedipus: Capitalism and Schizophrenia,* trans. Robert Hurley, Mark Seem, and Helen R. Lane (Minneapolis: University of Minnesota Press, 1983); and especially *A Thousand Plateaus: Capitalism and Schizophrenia,* trans. Brian Massumi (Minneapolis: University of Minneapolis Press, 1987).

6. For a discussion of the gender implications of this tradition of Chaucer, "the great author," see Elaine Tuttle Hansen, *Chaucer and the Fictions of Gender,* (Berkeley and Los Angeles: University of California Press, 1992), especially 284–92.

7. See, e.g., Hansen, *Chaucer and the Fictions of Gender,* and Carolyn Dinshaw, *Chaucer's Sexual Poetics* (Madison: University of Wisconsin Press, 1989).

8. See, for example, David Aers, *Chaucer, Langland, and the Creative Imagination* (London: Routledge & Kegan Paul, 1980); Steven Justice, *Writing and Rebellion: England in 1381* (Berkeley and Los Angeles: University of California Press, 1994); Peggy Knapp, *Chaucer and the Social Contest* (New York: Routledge, 1990).

9. See, for example, Seth Lerer, *Chaucer and His Readers: Imagining the Author in Late-Medieval England* (Princeton: Princeton University Press, 1993); Lee Patterson, *Chaucer and the Subject of History* (Madison: University of Wisconsin Press, 1991); and Paul Strohm, *Social Chaucer* (Cambridge: Harvard University Press, 1989).

10. Carolyn Dinshaw, *Getting Medieval,* 100–43.

11. Sedgwick, *Epistemology of the Closet,* 51–52.

12. See Christopher Cannon, "Raptus in the Chaumpaigne Release and a Newly Discovered Document Concerning the Life of Geoffrey Chaucer," *Speculum* 68 (1993): 79–94.

13. For transgressive reinscription, a concept that emerges in the early 1990s in a number of locations, see Butler, *Bodies That Matter,* especially 223–42; and Dollimore, *Sexual Dissidence,* especially 279–325.

14. For the perverse dynamic, see Dollimore, *Sexual Dissidence,* especially 228–30.

15. Bruno Latour, *We Have Never Been Modern* (Cambridge: Harvard University Press, 1993), especially 46–48; see also chapter 1, below.

16. It will be clear from my discussion here and in chapter 1 that my sense of queer theory and queer medievalism, and what they can do as methods of historicization, differs radically from the containing and dismissive treatment recently given it by Allen Frantzen, *Before the Closet: Same-Sex Love from Beowulf to Angels in America* (Chicago: University of Chicago Press, 1998), especially 1–25.

17. Kathleen Biddick, *The Shock of Medievalism* (Durham: Duke University Press, 1998).

18. John Dryden, *Of Dramatic Poesy and Other Critical Essays,* ed. George Watson (London: J. M. Dent, 1962), 2:280, 284–85. See also E. Talbot Donaldson, *Speaking of Chaucer* (London: Athlone Press, 1967).

19. See, for example, John Bowers, "Chaucer after Smithfield: From Postcolonial Writer to Imperialist Author," in *The Postcolonial Middle Ages,* ed. Jeffrey Jerome Cohen (New York: St. Martin's Press, 2000), 53–66.

20. Homi Bhabha, introduction to *The Location of Culture* (London: Routledge, 1994), 4.

## 1. Shameful Pleasures

1. Hansen, *Chaucer and the Fictions of Gender,* 284–85.

2. Latour, *We Have Never Been Modern,* 40, 48.

3. Ibid., 40, 74.

4. Ibid., 75–76.

5. What follows in the first section of this chapter thus constitutes my own, albeit very differently framed, attempt at the kind of reevaluation of the role of affect in thinking about the past that Nicholas Watson has recently called for—an attempt to "devise historiographic models that are self-conscious about their incorporation of affect, rather than

seeking to exclude it." See Watson, "Desire for the Past," *Studies in the Age of Chaucer* 21 (1999): 72.

**6.** David Leavitt and Mark Mitchell, eds., *The Penguin Book of Gay Short Stories* (New York: Viking, 1994). John Preston, ed., *Flesh and the Word* (New York: Dutton, 1992).

**7.** Leavitt and Mitchell, *The Penguin Book of Gay Short Stories*, xx.

**8.** Ibid., xix.

**9.** Ibid., xxii.

**10.** Ibid., xx–xxi.

**11.** Ibid., xxviii.

**12.** Michel Foucault, "Sade, sergent du sexe," interview by Gérard Dupont, *Cinématographe* 16 (December 1975–January 1976): 5, in *The Passion of Michel Foucault*, trans. James Miller (New York: Doubleday, 1993), 278.

**13.** Fradenburg and Freccero, eds., preface to *Premodern Sexualities*, viii. See also Fradenburg, "'So That We May Speak of Them': Enjoying the Middle Ages," *New Literary History* 28 (1997): 205–30.

**14.** My thanks to Bruce Holsinger for reminding me of this connection.

**15.** John Preston, ed., *Flesh and the Word*, 1.

**16.** Michel de Certeau, *The Practice of Everyday Life*, trans. Steven Rendall (Berkeley and Los Angeles: University of California Press, 1984), 44. De Certeau continues: "In spite of the contradictory ideologies that may accompany it, the setting aside of the subject-object relation or of the discourse-object relation is the abstraction that generates an illusion of 'authorship.' It removes the traces of belonging to a network—traces that always compromise the author's rights. It camouflages the conditions of the production of discourse and its object. For this negated genealogy is substituted a drama combining the simulacrum of an object with the simulacrum of an author" (44).

**17.** Preston, ed., *Flesh and the Word*, 2–4.

**18.** Ibid., 5.

**19.** Ibid., 4.

**20.** Eve Kosofsky Sedgwick, "Queer Performativity: Henry James's *The Art of the Novel*," *GLQ* 1, no. 1 (1993): 3–4.

**21.** Ibid., 12.

**22.** Ibid., 4.

**23.** According to Sedgwick, for the American psychologist Silvan Tomkins, shame and interest are related affects: "[Tomkins] places shame, in fact, at one end of the affect polarity *shame-interest*, suggesting that the pulsations of cathexis around shame, of all things, are what either enable or disable so basic a function as the ability to be interested in the world" (Sedgwick, "Queer Performativity," 7). In Tomkins's own formulation: "Like disgust, [shame] operates only after interest or enjoyment has been activated, and inhibits one or the other or both. The innate activator of shame is the incomplete reduction of interest or joy. Hence any barrier to further exploration which partially reduces interest... will activate the lowering of the head and eyes in shame and reduce further exploration or self-exposure.... Such a barrier might be because one is suddenly looked at by one who is strange, or because one wishes to look at or commune with another person but suddenly cannot because he is strange, or one expected him to be familiar but he suddenly appears unfamiliar, or one started to smile but found one was smiling at a stranger" (Tomkins, *Affect Imagery Consciousness*, vol. 2, *The Negative Affects* [New York: Springer, 1963], 123; quoted in Sedgwick, "Queer Performativity," 7).

**24.** Sedgwick has theorized this political usefulness of shame's liminality in the following way: "Shame interests me politically, then, because it generates and legitimates the place of identity—the *question* of identity—at the origin of the impulse to the performative, but does so without giving that identity-space the standing of an essence. It constitutes it as to-be-constituted, which is also to say, as already there for the (necessary, productive) misconstrual and misrecognition. Shame—living, as it does, on and in the capillaries and muscles of the face—seems to be uniquely contagious from one person to another" (Sedgwick, "Queer Performativity," 14).

**25.** As Sedgwick puts it, "'Shame on you' is performatively efficacious because its grammar—admittedly somewhat enigmatic—*is* a transformational grammar: both at the level of pronoun positioning, as I've sketched, and at the level of the relational grammar of the affect shame itself.... [S]hame effaces itself; shame points and projects; shame turns itself skin side outside; shame and pride, shame and self-display, shame and exhibitionism are different interlinings of the same glove: shame, it might finally be said, transformational shame, *is performance*. I mean theatrical performance" ("Queer Performativity," 4–5).

**26.** Preston, *Flesh and the Word*, 4.

**27.** Ibid., 9.

**28.** Ibid., 11.

**29.** Ibid., 12.

**30.** "What distinguishes the map from the tracing is that it is entirely oriented toward an experimentation in contact with the real.... A map has multiple entryways, as opposed to the tracing, which always comes back to 'the same.' The map has to do with performance, whereas the tracing always involves an alleged 'competence.'... *The tracing should always be put back on the map*.... That is why the tracing is so dangerous. It injects redundancies and propagates them. What the tracing reproduces of the map or rhizome are only the impasses, blockages, incipient taproots, or points of structuration" (Deleuze and Guattari, *A Thousand Plateaus*, 12–13).

**31.** See Deleuze and Guattari's discussion of the book as rhizome rather than image of the world (11), and their later delineation of the rhizome as "middle": "A rhizome has no beginning or end; it is always in the middle, between things, interbeing, *intermezzo*. The tree is filiation, but the rhizome is alliance, uniquely alliance. The tree imposes the verb 'to be,' but the fabric of the rhizome is the conjunction, 'and... and... and....' This conjunction carries enough force to shake and uproot the verb 'to be.'... Making a clean slate, starting or beginning again from ground zero, seeking a beginning or a foundation—all imply a false conception of voyage and movement (a conception that is methodical, pedagogical, initiatory, symbolic...). But [there is] another way of traveling and moving: proceeding from the middle, through the middle, coming and going rather than starting and finishing.... The middle is by no means an average; on the contrary, it is where things pick up speed. *Between* things does not designate a localizable relation going from one thing to the other and back again, but a perpendicular direction, a transversal movement that sweeps one *and* the other away, a stream without beginning or end that undermines its banks and picks up speed in the middle" (*A Thousand Plateaus,* 25).

32. Sedgwick, "Queer Performativity," 3.

33. Deleuze and Guattari, *A Thousand Plateaus,* 3–4. See chapter 4 (notes 65 and 66) for their discussion of the "Body without Organs," and chapter 5 for a more particular discussion of how Fragment VII manifests the *Tales'* structure as a machinic assemblage. Deleuze and Guattari's discussion of text as machinic assemblage offers an especially useful model for queer attempts to think through questions of difference, hegemony, and pleasure without resorting to disciplinary/ascesis models organized around lack or models based on heterosexual filiation (or on utopian models of revolt and repression). In part this results from Deleuze and Guattari's resistance to Freudian models, a resistance parallel in certain ways to Irigaray's but without her anxiousness over homosexuality as *hommesexuality.* See Luce Irigaray, *This Sex Which Is Not One,* trans. Catherine Porter with Carolyn Burke (Ithaca, N.Y.: Cornell University Press, 1985).

34. These features of the *Tales* have led Carolyn Dinshaw to assert, somewhat tendentiously, that, if the opening lines of the *Tales* have come to signify "Literature" to the anglophone West, "it is perhaps because they may be the first in English to articulate with such clarity what we may call a sexuality—heterosexuality, taken to be one of the founding markers and guardians of the Western world.... An act of generative penetration inaugurates this work, an act which links humankind to the generative cycle of nature.... It's no surprise, then, that these are the best known of Chaucer's lines—Chaucer, who is himself revered for his generative powers, critically constructed as the father of English poesy. They establish a tradition of English literature consonant with larger heterosexualized literary structures.... It's no surprise, either, that critics have rather routinely interpreted the *Canterbury Tales* as being structured in a major way by marriage.... Since Chaucer himself has established such a norm in the opening lines, those heterosexual arrangements become a means of interpreting, a hermeneutic according to which events and characters are rendered intelligible or unintelligible. Kittredge is looking through the lens Chaucer has polished" ("Chaucer's Queer Touches," 80, 82–83; see also *Getting Medieval,* 117–18).

35. Patterson, *Chaucer and the Subject of History,* 40.

36. Geoffrey Chaucer, *The Canterbury Tales,* cited from *The Riverside Chaucer,* ed. Larry D. Benson (Boston: Houghton Mifflin, 1987), I.3167–81. All future references to the *Tales* will be to this edition and will be given parenthetically (fragment and line number) in my text.

37. See Paul Freedman, *Images of the Medieval Peasant* (Stanford: Stanford University Press, 1999), especially 133–76, for a full discussion of the longstanding links between peasants and a shaming, bestial materiality and bodiliness in the Middle Ages.

38. Patterson, *Chaucer and the Subject of History;* Strohm, *Social Chaucer;* David Wallace, *Chaucerian Polity: Absolutist Lineages and Associational Forms in England and Italy* (Stanford: Stanford University Press, 1997). For the ambiguities of Chaucer's position as an *esquire de servise,* deriving status and privileges from contractual service to the king rather than through aristocratic bloodlines and inheritance, see Strohm, *Social Chaucer,* especially 1–23. For the importance of guilds and other associational polities as forces of social change and models for Chaucer's "mixed" location in the power politics of his age and the

mobile identifications of the Canterbury project, see Wallace, *Chaucerian Polity,* especially 65–103.

**39.** Patterson, *Chaucer and the Subject of History,* 26.

**40.** I am grateful to Duncan Faherty for drawing my attention to this parallel.

**41.** As such it sounds uncannily like that "interstitial passage between fixed identifications" that Homi Bhabha sees in today's postcolonial, postfeminist, postmodern moment, one that "opens up the possibility of a cultural hybridity that entertains difference without an assumed or imposed hierarchy": "'Beyond' signifies spatial distance, marks progress, promises the future; but our intimations of exceeding the barrier or boundary—the very act of going *beyond*—are unknowable, unrepresentable, without a return to the 'present' which, in the process of repetition, becomes disjunct and displaced.... Unlike the dead hand of history that tells the beads of sequential time like a rosary, seeking to establish serial, causal connections, we are now confronted with what Walter Benjamin describes as the blasting of a monadic moment from the homogenous course of history, 'establishing a conception of the present as the "time of the now"'" (*The Location of Culture,* 4). Of course for Chaucer it would not be sequential time that is here interrupted, but the universalizing repetition of transcendent truth on the lines of the Parson's metaphoric substitutions at the end of the *Canterbury Tales.*

**42.** See, for example, Michael Camille's speculation about the kinds of dialogic reading provoked by bawdy or personal reference included in manuscript frames, a "feminine" frame, as it were, for "masculine" authority in the actual "text," in *Image on the Edge: The Margins of Medieval Art* (London: Reaktion Books, 1992).

**43.** See, for example, Carl Lindahl's reading of the *Canterbury Tales* in the light of its antecedents in medieval festivals and through the lens of Bakhtinian carnival in *Earnest Games: Folkloric Patterns in the Canterbury Tales* (Bloomington: Indiana University Press, 1987).

**44.** Carol Everest, in "Medicine, Aging, and Sexuality in Chaucer's 'Reeve's Prologue,' 'Merchant's Tale' and 'Miller's Tale'" (Ph.D. diss., University of Alberta, 1992), 160–208, argues persuasively for cauterization and against David Williams's suggestion, in "Radical Therapy in the Miller's Tale," *Chaucer Review* 15 (1981): 227–35, that Absalon's punishment of Nicholas involves anal penetration by a hot poker and consequently parodies the operation for *fistula in ano.* See also Edward C. Schweitzer, "The Misdirected Kiss and the Lover's Malady in Chaucer's *Miller's Tale,*" in *Chaucer in the Eighties,* ed. Julian N. Wasserman and Robert J. Blanch (Syracuse: Syracuse University Press, 1986), 223–34; Danielle Jacquart and Claude Thomasset, *Sexuality and Medicine in the Middle Ages* (Princeton: Princeton University Press, 1988); and Joan Cadden, *Meanings of Sex Difference in the Middle Ages: Medicine, Science, and Culture* (Cambridge: Cambridge University Press, 1993), especially 167–227.

**45.** Various critics have noted the relationship between the generic differences of the Knight's and Miller's tales and the representation of a social contest. For examples of this approach, see Knapp, *Chaucer and the Social Contest,* 15–44; Patterson, *Chaucer and the Subject of History,* 244–79; and Strohm, *Social Chaucer,* especially 130–82. Strohm points out, as well, the ways in which even narrative structuring of time and space in the two tales has a social dimension. The Knight works in symbolic "church time," advancing a long-standing sacralized notion of fixed social relationships, while the Miller works in quantifiable "merchant's time," inscribing the new contractual, communitarian relationships governing postfeudal medieval society (123–25).

**46.** Gilles Deleuze, *Sacher-Masoch: An Interpretation* (London: Faber, 1971), 21.

**47.** Deleuze, *Sacher-Masoch,* 33.

**48.** Ibid., 16 (Deleuze's italics). Deleuze here summarizes Bataille's discussion of Sade's language in *Erotism: Death and Sensuality,* trans. Mary Dalwood (San Francisco: City Lights Books, 1986), 187–88.

**49.** See also Dolores Warwick Frese, "The Homoerotic Underside in Chaucer's *Miller's Tale* and *Reeve's Tale,*" *Michigan Academician* 10 (1977): 144–50.

**50.** Deleuze, *Sacher-Masoch,* 18.

**51.** I am, of course, condensing what are complex, shifting, and at times contradictory discourses and images of the body as organic hierarchy. See Michael Camille, "The Image and the Self: Unwriting Late Medieval Bodies," in *Framing Medieval Bodies,* ed. Sarah Kay and Miri Rubin (Manchester: Manchester University Press, 1994), 62–99, for a useful introduction to this complex textual and visual history, especially plates 7–11.

**52.** Jeffrey Jerome Cohen and the Members of Interscripta, "Medieval Masculinities: Heroism, Sanctity, and Gender," available at http://www.georgetown.edu/labyrinth/e-center/interscripta/mm.html. See also Cadden's discussion of sex difference and the construction of gender in medieval medical texts in *Meanings of Sex Difference in the Middle Ages,* 167–227.

**53.** Foucault, "Sade, sergent du sexe," in Miller, *The Passion of Michel Foucault,* 278.

**54.** "Art and Scatology in the Miller's Tale," *Chaucer Review* 12 (1977): 92.

**55.** V. A. Kolve, *Chaucer and the Imagery of Narrative: The First Five Canterbury Tales* (Stanford: Stanford University Press, 1984), 191. For discussion of such marginalia in the context of the *Miller's Tale,* see Kolve, 191–97; and for speculation about the dialogic reading such marginalia might provoke or represent, see Camille, *Image on the Edge.*

**56.** Strohm, *Social Chaucer,* 11–13.

**57.** In a similar vein, Sarah Kay has argued "that changing attitudes towards the problem of knowledge between the twelfth and thirteenth centuries trouble the equations between femininity and carnality, and between masculinity and the mind or spirit, which are extensively invoked in classical and patristic writing to justify the subordination of women to men. The increasingly complex treatment of the mind-body dichotomy in this period [the twelfth and thirteenth centuries], and the growing emphasis (under the influence of new translations and adaptations of Aristotle) on the senses as a source of knowledge, lead to the body figuring in intellectual discourses other than those propounding moral or theological hierarchies, and pose the threat that the alleged physicality of the feminine implies not women's inferiority, but the possibility that they might enjoy more immediate access to knowledge than men" ("Women's Body of Knowledge: Epistemology and Misogyny in the *Romance of the Rose,*" in Kay and Rubin, *Framing Medieval Bodies,* 210). See also Camille, "The Image and the Self," 62–99, for a discussion of "the ways in which a host of competing notions of the body existed in the thirteenth and fourteenth centuries that were articulated, not through texts, but through images" (62).

**58.** Cf. Strohm's argument in *Social Chaucer* that "Chaucer preeminently occupied what Eagleton calls a 'dissentient conflictual position' within his own society, a position that throws the ideological faultlines of his literary production into high relief" (142). Thus, "Chaucer's generic and stylistic variation, and his multiplication of the different vocalities by which this variation is sustained, may be viewed as a mediated response to factionalism and contradiction within his own social experience.... Viewed in relation to this challenge, Chaucer's aesthetic enterprise of defining a literary space that permits free interaction of different forms and styles may be placed in reciprocal relation with the social enterprise of defining a public space hospitable to different social classes with diverse social impulses" (164).

**59.** Cf. Deleuze's comments that "[t]he sadist enjoys being whipped as much as he enjoys whipping others.... It would therefore be difficult to say that sadism turns into masochism and vice versa; what we have in each case is a paradoxical by-product, a kind of sadism being the humorous outcome of masochism, and a kind of masochism the ironical outcome of sadism" (*Sacher-Masoch*, 34–35).

**60.** For a recent discussion of the masochistic contract in French romance, see Jeffrey Jerome Cohen, "Masoch/Lancelotism," *New Literary History* 28 (1997): 231–60; and the similarly titled chapter in his book *Medieval Identity Machines* (forthcoming, University of Minnesota Press).

**61.** I am indebted here to Carolyn Dinshaw's attempts to distinguish what she has called "the touch of the queer," a critical category that might help resist the metaphoric, substitutive, colonizing power of the gaze: "I begin with this representation of a hand on a thigh, and I speak of the tactile—'the touch of the queer'—because I want to highlight the metonymic workings and corporeal impact of queerness on its surroundings. Queerness works by contiguity and displacement, knocking signifiers loose, ungrounding bodies, making them strange; it works in this way to provoke perceptual shifts and subsequent corporeal response to those touched" ("Chaucer's Queer Touches," 76).

**62.** For other medieval conflations of female vagina and ass, see E. Jane Burns, *Bodytalk: When Women Speak in Old French Literature* (Philadelphia: University of Pennsylvania Press, 1993), especially 31–47.

**63.** Foucault, "Sade," in Miller, *The Passion of Michel Foucault*, 278.

**64.** Leo Bersani, "Is the Rectum a Grave?" in *Reclaiming Sodom*, ed. Jonathan Goldberg (New York: Routledge, 1994), 256.

**65.** Lochrie, *Covert Operations*, 186. She also notes that "[o]nly sex in the proper vessels with the proper instruments in the proper positions with the appropriate procreative intentions in orderly ways and during times that are not otherwise excluded 'counts' as natural and normative in medieval theology, canon law, and penitentials. At the same time, most 'heterosexual' sex occupies the same unnatural category as sodomy, the main difference being that same-sex acts were placed under the interdiction of secrecy, while other unnatural sex acts were not" (199). See also James A. Brundage, *Law, Sex, and Christian Society* (Chicago: University of Chicago Press, 1987), 162. Both Pierre Payer, *The Bridling of Desire: Views of Sex in the Middle Ages* (Toronto: University of Toronto Press, 1993), 14; and Mark Jordan, *The Invention of Sodomy in Christian Theology* (Chicago: University of Chicago Press, 1997), especially 154–58, emphasize that discussions of sodomy frequently take place within the discourse of sin, rather than in anything approaching modern discussions of sex or sexuality. See also chapter 4 in this volume.

## 2. MEDIEVAL CONJUGALITY AND THE *CANTERBURY TALES*

1. George Lyman Kittredge, "Chaucer's Discussion of Marriage," *Modern Philology* 9 (1912): 435–67. See also Kittredge, *Chaucer and His Poetry* (Cambridge: Harvard University Press, 1915), 181–218, for a final discussion of the Marriage Group in tandem with a treatment of the Pardoner as the "most abandoned character among the Canterbury pilgrims" (211). Eleanor Prescott Hammond, in *Chaucer: A Bibliographic Manual* (New York: Macmillan, 1908), 256, was actually the first to single out this set of tales as the thematically unified Marriage Group.

2. Kittredge, "Chaucer's Discussion of Marriage," 467. Subsequent critics—for example, William W. Lawrence (*Chaucer and the Canterbury Tales* [New York: Columbia University Press, 1950], 131–33); Germaine Dempster ("A Period in the Development of the *Canterbury Tales* Marriage Group and of Blocks B2 and C," *PMLA* 68 [1953]: 1142–59); and Donald Howard ("The Conclusion of the Marriage Group: Chaucer and the Human Condition," *Modern Philology* 57 [1960], 223–32)—have added tales to Kittredge's Marriage Group: notably the *Squire's Tale*, the *Nun's Priest's Tale*, the *Tale of Melibee*, and the *Second Nun's Tale*. Howard, *The Idea of the Canterbury Tales* (Berkeley and Los Angeles: University of California Press, 1976), later changed his mind about the *Second Nun's Tale* ending the Marriage Group, but he still saw Fragments III, IV, and V, the "Tales of Domestic Conduct," as one of the five sequences of tales begun by headless junctures that formed the basic building blocks of the idea of the *Tales* (247–70). Although the critical focus in recent years has shifted from Kittredge's belief in a marriage *group* that dramatized an organized debate about marriage, the idea of marriage, and especially its ability to embody a proper balance between individual desire and social structure, retains a powerful attraction for Chaucer studies. See, for example, Kathryn Jacobs, "The Marriage Contract of the *Franklin's Tale:* The Remaking of Society," *Chaucer Review* 20 (1985): 132–43.

3. Kittredge, "Chaucer's Discussion of Marriage," 438.

4. Ibid., 450.

5. Ibid., 442.

6. Ibid., 466–67. Since Kittredge is following the Bradshaw shift and its order for the *Canterbury Tales* as laid out in Skeat's edition, the Franklin does provide one "end" to the *Tales;* only Fragments VIII, IX, and X would come after his tale—that is, the *Second Nun's Tale*, the *Canon Yeoman's Tale*, the *Manciple's Tale*, and the *Parson's Tale*.

7. Kittredge, "Chaucer's Discussion of Marriage," 460.

8. See, for example, Hansen's summary of feminist attempts to recuperate the Wife of Bath in *Chaucer and the Fictions of Gender*, 26–27, especially notes 2–4.

9. See, for example, Aers, *Chaucer, Langland, and the Creative Imagination;* Knapp, *Chaucer and the Social Contest;* Justice, *Writing and Rebellion: England in 1381;* Patterson, *Chaucer and the Subject of History;* and Paul Strohm, *Social Chaucer*.

**10.** See, for example, Dinshaw's account in *Chaucer's Sexual Poetics* of "reading like a man" / "reading like a woman," which inscribes male/female sex difference (or its absence in the eunuch hermeneutics of the Pardoner) as *the* crucial fact. Sexuality when it enters the picture remains, by default, heterosexuality as we know it. More recently, of course, Dinshaw has engaged directly with the question of sexuality and medieval texts, stressing "the touch of the queer" and "the metonymic workings and corporeal impact of queerness on its surroundings . . . knocking signifiers loose, ungrounding bodies, making them strange" ("Chaucer's Queer Touches/A Queer Touches Chaucer," 76). While this emphasis on articulating "not a determinate thing but a relation to existent structures of power" opens up space for the Wife of Bath's and Pardoner's queer presences in the *Tales,* when it comes to Chaucer, however, the touch of the queer is even more contained than the feminine was in *Chaucer's Sexual Poetics* by the essential heterosexuality of Chaucerian fictions and Chaucer's author function (77). As a result, the touch of the queer (in both its medieval and modern manifestations) remains curiously contained by an argument whose aim is to show how "the queer makes heterosexuality visible" (91). See also Dinshaw's partial revaluation of at least the Pardoner's queerness in *Getting Medieval,* 113–36, especially 136.

**11.** Deleuze and Guattari, *Thousand Plateaus,* 12–13.

**12.** Cf. Larry Scanlon's recent mapping of Kittredge and sexuality in the *Tales* in "Return of the Repressed: The Sequel," in Burger and Kruger, *Queering the Middle Ages,* 284–301. Scanlon examines an article by the youthful Kittredge in the *Harvard Advocate* ("At the Music Hall," *Harvard Advocate* 32, no. 10 [3 February 1882]: 111) describing, in the voice of a young girl, Oscar Wilde's lecture of 31 January 1882 at the Boston Music Hall. Scanlon writes that "[i]n this odd (not to say queer!) piece of juvenilia we can detect anticipations of a few of the fascinations that will make the mature Kittredge the founder of modern Chaucer studies and that will give his work a dominant force it retains even today. There is the keen interest in impersonation, which will issue in the 'dramatic principle': for Kittredge the Canterbury collection's fundamental rhetorical motive. But the connection between impersonation and sexual identity suggests a stronger link between this formal principle and two of his most influential thematic concerns than may be evident on the surface. These are the 'Marriage Group' and his reading of the Pardoner as the pilgrimage's one 'lost soul.' . . . It is now a commonplace of queer theory that the invention of the term 'homosexuality' in the last quarter of the nineteenth century enabled the subsequent coinage of 'heterosexuality' its binary opposite and undergirded modern regimes of the heteronormative. This philological argument helps explain in broad ideological terms why Kittredge juxtaposes the utter desolation of the sexually ambiguous Pardoner with his claims that the Canterbury collection's central quest is to resolve a marriage debate. But this remarkable Wildean moment in Kittredge's intellectual formation gives such an explanation biographical specificity—not necessarily because it gives us any window on Kittredge's own sexuality, but because it forcibly reminds us of the world he lived in. We are not accustomed to thinking of Kittredge and Oscar Wilde as occupying the same intellectual universe, but in fact they did, and here is the proof. Alan Sinfield calls this century 'The Wilde Century.' If Sinfield is right, then Kittredge's reading of Chaucer—whom he proclaimed 'the most modern of English poets'—should be viewed as substantially driven by emerging modern ideologies of gender and sexual identity. It seems there was something queer about modern Chaucer studies from its inception" (286–87). Dinshaw also discusses this early Kittredgian text in *Getting Medieval*, 121–26.

**13.** Judith Halberstam, *Female Masculinity* (Durham: Duke University Press, 1998), 53.

**14.** Michel Foucault, *Discipline and Punish: The Birth of the Prison*, trans. Alan Sheridan (New York: Routledge, 1994), 31; Sedgwick, *Epistemology of the Closet*, 44; and Halberstam, *Female Masculinity*, 54–55.

**15.** Sedgwick, *Epistemology of the Closet*, 48.

**16.** I use "conjugality" here to describe the individual, private relations that are bound up with the public face of such categories as husband, wife, or the sacrament of marriage. In addition, I want to distinguish conjugality from other approaches to marriage in the Middle Ages that would emphasize marriage in relation to a particular class identity or social function—noble or queen or dynasty—or "lay" only as an inferior ground to "clerical" or "chaste" (that is, marriage as an institution for those who would otherwise burn from their uncontrollable desire). Conjugality also allows us to acknowledge the usefulness of a sacramental view of marriage (and the emphasis on individual choice it supports) while at the same time allowing us to see the many ways in which lay conjugality might use ecclesiastical support to articulate identities surplus to an ecclesiastical ideology for laity and marriage. "Conjugality" as I am using it here obviously has parallels with the term "companionate marriage," which historians like Lawrence Stone, in *The Family, Sex and Marriage in England, 1500–1800* (New York: Harper and Row, 1977), have used to describe the pattern for bourgeois marriage in the early modern period. I have used a different term to avoid collapsing important distinctions between these different cultural and social moments and simply incorporating the late medieval into a modernist historiography that would see it as capable only of being absolutely other to, or the first stage, in the early modern.

**17.** Kathleen Biddick, "Genders, Bodies, Borders: Technologies of the Visible," in *Studying Medieval Women*, ed. Nancy F. Partner (Cambridge, Mass.: The Medieval Academy of America, 1993), 108 and 108 n. 46. Cf. also Brian Stock, *Implications of Literacy: Written Language and Models of Interpretation in the Eleventh and Twelfth Centuries* (Princeton, Princeton University Press, 1983), 241; and Miri Rubin, *Corpus Christi: The Eucharist in Late Medieval Culture* (Cambridge: Cambridge University Press, 1991), especially 348.

**18.** Robert J. C. Young, *Colonial Desire: Hybridity in Theory, Culture, and Race* (London: Routledge, 1995). Young presents a theoretical and historical discussion of the genesis of the term *hybridity* in eighteenth- and nineteenth-century discussions of eugenics, sex, and race; its current centrality for much postcolonial theory; and an argument for bringing Deleuze and Guattari's theories of desire to bear on such discussions.

**19.** Mikhail M. Bakhtin, *The Dialogic Imagination*, trans. Caryl Emerson and Michael Holquist (Austin: University of Texas Press, 1981), 358.

**20.** Ibid., 358–59.

**21.** "The image of a language conceived as an intentional hybrid is first of all a *conscious* hybrid (as distinct from a historical, organic, obscure language hybrid); an intentional hybrid is precisely the perception of one language by another language, its illumination by another linguistic consciousness. An image of language may be structured only from the point of view of another language, which is taken as the norm. What is more, an intentional and conscious hybrid is not a mixture of two *impersonal* language consciousnesses (the correlates of two languages) but rather a mixture of two *individualized* language consciousnesses (the correlates of two specific utterances, not merely two languages) and two individual language-intentions as well: the individual representing authorial consciousness and will, on the one hand, and the individualized linguistic consciousness and will of the character represented, on the other. For indeed, since concrete, isolated utterances are constructed in this represented language, it follows that the represented linguistic consciousness must necessarily be embodied in 'authors' of some sort who speak in the given language, who structure utterances in that language and who therefore introduce into the potentialities of language itself their own actualizing language-intention. Thus there are always two consciousnesses, two language-intentions, two *voices* and consequently two accents participating in an intentional and conscious artistic hybrid" (ibid., 359–60).

**22.** Ibid., 360.

**23.** H. Marshall Leicester Jr., *The Disenchanted Self: Representing the Subject in the "Canterbury Tales"* (Berkeley and Los Angeles: University of California Press, 1990), 4.

**24.** Young, *Colonial Desire,* 22.

**25.** Homi Bhabha, "Signs Taken for Wonders: Questions of Ambivalence and Authority under a Tree outside Delhi, May 1817," in *Location of Culture,* 112.

**26.** Young, 22.

**27.** Jill Mann, *Chaucer and Medieval Estates Satire* (Cambridge: Cambridge University Press, 1973), especially 1–16.

**28.** Patterson, *Chaucer and the Subject of History,* 27.

**29.** See, for example, Georges Duby, *The Three Orders: Feudal Society Imagined,* trans. Arthur Goldhammer (Chicago: University of Chicago Press, 1980).

**30.** Strohm, *Social Chaucer,* 67. Strohm adopts the term "middle strata" from Sylvia Thrupp, *The Merchant Class of Medieval London, 1300–1500* (Ann Arbor: University of Michigan Press, 1962), to evoke that recently emergent social grouping in late medieval English society "which includes such diverse and partially stratified ranks as knights, esquires, gentlepersons, merchants, citizens, burgesses, clerks, lawyers, and prosperous guildsmen" (*Social Chaucer,* 2 n. 2). Strohm cites Henry de Bracton, *De Legibus et Consuetudinibus Angliae,* ed. George Woodbine and Samuel E. Thorne, vol. 2 (Cambridge: Harvard University Press, 1968), as typical of ideologically conditioned social theory in presenting the system as self-evident, accepting the "three estates" model, and emphasizing a hierarchical ordering of society, and thus not particularly descriptive of the thirteenth- or fourteenth-century English state of affairs. In contrast, Strohm says, Bishop Thomas Brinton (*The Sermons of Thomas Brinton, Bishop of Rochester,* ed. M. A. Devlin, vol. 2, Camden Society, ser. 3, vol. 86 [London: Camden Society, 1954]), exemplifies a countertradition in contemporary social theory that "found value in the social activities of other, sometimes unlanded, social groupings" and thus follows "the fourteenth-century habit of recognizing a fourth social category, between the lords on the one hand and the peasants on the other." Strohm says, "We should immediately notice the considerable weight given by Brinton to the middle groups within society—especially in his characterization of knights as the right arm [of the body politic], merchants and faithful craftsmen as its left arm, and citizens and burgesses as its heart. This expansion is accomplished by two strategies distinctive to the later fourteenth century: a demotion of the knights and a promotion of certain categories of tradesman" (3–4). In addition, for his discussion of the complexity of late medieval social organization and Chaucer's place in it, Strohm draws on two documents that attempt to enumerate the estates of society in later fourteenth-century England: the Statute on Diet and Apparel (1363) and the Poll Tax of 1379.

**31.** Patricia Eberle, "Commercial Language and the Commercial Outlook in the *General Prologue*," *Chaucer Review* 18 (1982): 161–74. See, for example, the opening discussion of the Friar as having "a skill in finding and exploiting commercial opportunities which even the Merchant might envy" (161), or the examination of the Host's "keen eye for assessing commercial values" as it emerges in his attempts to learn who the Canon is by finding out what he does for a living (169).

**32.** Lindahl, *Earnest Games*, 24. See Lindahl's figure 1 for a listing of the pilgrims as they might have been ranked for dining in a fourteenth-century noble household.

**33.** Lindahl, *Earnest Games*, 25–31; and Wallace, *Chaucerian Polity*, especially 65–103.

**34.** Caroline M. Barron, "The Parish Fraternities of Medieval London," in *The Church in Pre-Reformation Society: Essays in Honour of F. R. H. Du Boulay*, ed. Caroline M. Barron and Christopher Harper-Bill (Woodbridge, Suffolk: Boydell, 1985), 14. See also Barbara Hanawalt "Keepers of the Lights: Late Medieval English Parish Guilds," *Journal of Medieval and Renaissance Studies* 14 (1984): 21–37.

**35.** Barron, "The Parish Fraternities," 23–24.

**36.** As Barron notes, "The inference to be drawn from the surviving London guild accounts is that only a very small proportion of the fraternity income was spent on works of charity and that the bulk of the money was spent on the stipends of the fraternity priest and the clerk and in payments to the tallow chandler" (ibid., 27).

**37.** Ibid., 30–31.

**38.** Ibid., 33.

**39.** Wallace, *Chaucerian Polity*, 2.

**40.** Judith Ferster, *Fictions of Advice: The Literature and Politics of Counsel in Late Medieval England* (Philadelphia: University of Pennsylvania Press, 1996), 18. Ferster also cites Bertie Wilkinson's observation that "[i]n England, the idea of liberty never became identified with local independence as it did in Germany or to a lesser extent in Italy and France," noting that, on the contrary, in medieval England liberty had to be preserved precisely through contact with the national government (*Constitutional History of Medieval England, 1216–1399*, vol. 3 of *The Development of the Constitution, 1216–1399* [London: Longmans, Green and Co., Ltd., 1958], 2). As Helen Cam notes, "It was the effective centralization of power under the Angevins that made possible the preservation and utilization of local institutions and local sentiment by the monarchy, which in its turn made possible the growth of the conception of the community of the realm" ("The Theory and Practice of Representation in Medieval England," in *Historical Studies of the English Parliament*, vol. 1, *Origins to 1399*, ed. E. B. Fryde and Edward Miller [Cambridge: Cambridge University Press, 1970], 277, quoted in Ferster, *Fictions of Advice*, 19).

**41.** Ferster, *Fictions of Advice*, 19.

**42.** According to Helen Cam, "Though the knights or gentlemen will undoubtedly take the lead in country doings, they will be working with freemen of ungentle blood, yeomen, *valetti,* who may represent the shire at parliaments if knights are not available" ("The Theory and Practice of Representation," 274, quoted in Ferster, *Fictions of Advice,* 19).

**43.** As Ferster notes, "According to George Sayles, by the thirteenth century there was widespread interest in parliament and well-established channels for disseminating information about it. 'There was no difficulty in acquiring information, for England was a much governed and busy country with a remarkable criss-cross of messengers, professional messengers, traveling regularly between London—or where the court, chancery, and the king's bench happened to be—and the local regions'" (Sayles, *The King's Parliament of England* [New York: W. W. Norton, 1974], 72, quoted in Ferster, *Fictions of Advice,* 22). The case is made even more strongly by Colin Richmond: "Not only are 'central' and 'local' meaningless terms within so small a country, which by the fifteenth century had been much and closely governed for five hundred years, the personnel at Westminster and in the localities overlapped, intermingled, interconnected. That is why and how information was conveyed to and fro so freely, so casually. Everyone, or almost everyone who was anyone, was in the know. This was open government" ("Hand and Mouth: Information Gathering and Use in England in the Later Middle Ages," *Journal of Historical Sociology* 1 [1988]: 243; quoted in Ferster, *Fictions of Advice,* 24).

**44.** See, for example, R. H. Hilton and T. H. Aston, eds., *The English Rising of 1381* (Cambridge: Cambridge University Press, 1994); Susan Crane, "The Writing Lesson of 1381," in *Chaucer's England: Literature in Historical Context,* ed. Barbara A. Hanawalt (Minneapolis: University of Minnesota Press, 1992), 20–21; and especially Steven Justice, *Writing and Rebellion.*

**45.** *Polychronicon Ranulphi Higden Monachi Cestrensis,* ed. Churchill Babington and J. R. Lumby (London: Rolls Series, 1865–86), 2:156–66.

**46.** Bowers, "Chaucer after Smithfield," 59. See also, John Fisher, "A Language Policy for Lancastrian England," *PMLA* 107 (1992): 1168–80, for the suggestion that the publication of Chaucer's poems and his enshrinement as the perfector of rhetoric in English were part of the deliberate policy of encouraging the English language (that is, the dialect of London) and an English national identity as a way of securing support for Henry V and the new Lancastrian line.

**47.** Bowers, "Chaucer after Smithfield," 59–61. See also David Wallace's discussion of London as the absent center of the *Canterbury Tales,* "Chaucer and the Absent City," in Hanawalt, *Chaucer's England,* 59–90. In "Diachronic Historicism," a paper presented at the MLA convention in Chicago in December 1999, Wallace also suggested that we should think of Chaucer as much as a regional poet as a national one, much as we have traditionally treated the *Gawain* poet or William Langland. He has also pointed out that for much of the fourteenth century, the road the pilgrims followed ended not at Canterbury but at Calais, and thus led *outward* to a nationalist and imperialist project in France (in "At Calais Gate," a paper presented at the New Chaucer Society Congress, London 2000, and in his forthcoming book, *Premodern Places,* which deals with Calais, Flanders, Somerset, Genoa, the Canary Islands, and Surinam).

**48.** Bowers suggests that "[t]he Pardoner—who represents the Spanish religious house of Roncesvalles, has recently come from Rome, and preaches 'in sundry landes' while belonging to none—becomes his [i.e., Chaucer's] true personification of an English multiculturalism that is as eclectic as it is eccentric" ("Chaucer after Smithfield," 56).

**49.** Strohm, *Social Chaucer,* 68. Thus, what Strohm says of Chaucer—that he "pre-eminently occupied what Eagleton calls a 'dissentient conflictual position' within his own society, a position that throws the ideological faultlines of his literary production into high relief" (142)—also in certain ways applies to these Canterbury pilgrims.

**50.** Patterson, *Chaucer and the Subject of History,* 35–37.

**51.** Ibid., 37–38; Patterson is citing Storey, "Gentlemen-bureaucrats," in *Profession, Vocation, and Culture in Later Medieval England,* ed. Cecil H. Clough (Liverpool: Liverpool University Press, 1982), 90–129.

**52.** Partha Chatterjee, *The Nation and Its Fragments* (Princeton: Princeton University Press, 1993), 36.

**53.** Ibid., 35–36.

**54.** Ibid., 36–37.

**55.** Ibid., 36.

**56.** The process I see at work relating conjugality and the formation of newly empowered and self-aware subjects has obvious parallels with Foucault's discussion of private confession as a crucial moment of transition in Western constructions of the self—in *The History of Sexuality,* vol. 1—and especially with Lochrie's recent discussion in *Covert Operations* of the perverse dynamic inherent in the sacrament's structures of secrecy. I will return to the importance of the confessional model in chapter 6.

**57.** Michael M. Sheehan, *Marriage, Family, and Law in Medieval Europe,* ed. James K. Farge (Toronto: University of Toronto Press, 1996), 90–91. For a general introduction to marriage in the Christian church, see Henri Crouzel, *L'Église primitive face au divorce du premier au cinquième siècle* (Paris: Beauchesne, 1971); and Korbinian Ritzer, *Le Mariage dans les églises chrétiennes du Ier au XIe siècle* (Paris: Editions du Cerf, 1970). As R. H. Helmholz, *Marriage Litigation in Medieval England* (Cambridge: Cambridge University Press, 1974), notes: "In Roman law, marriage was a relatively private matter. No special formula or ceremony was required to contract a valid marriage. There was no requirement of intervention by any sort of a public official, and there was no registration of marriages. Divorce was allowed without a decree by any court. There were, of course, laws which defined and regulated relations between husband and wife. But no action by a public officer was a necessary part of a formation and dissolution of the marriage bond. This was left open to the parties directly concerned" (5). For a detailed account of Roman law, see P. E. Corbett, *The Roman Law of Marriage* (Oxford: Clarendon Press, 1930).

**58.** Helmholz, *Marriage Litigation,* 4–5.

**59.** Michael M. Sheehan, *Marriage, Family, and Law in Medieval Europe,* 84.

**60.** Sheehan, *Marriage, Family, and Law,* 91–92.

**61.** Another focus of church regulation in this period was the problem of consanguinity and marriage. Not only did the church attempt actively and uniformly to enforce Roman law forbidding marriage within the fourth degree of consanguinity, for a time the forbidden degrees were expanded to seven. Jack Goody, *The Development of the Family and Marriage in Europe* (Cambridge: Cambridge University Press, 1983), has studied the relationship between the church's forbidding of consanguinity and the attempt of the post-Gregorian church to retain control over church property. Historians such as Georges Duby have emphasized the role that such regulations over consanguinity played in marking a turn from endogamous to exogamous kinship patterns, especially among northern European aristocratic families (*Medieval Marriage: Two Models from Twelfth-Century France*, trans. Elborg Forster [Baltimore: The Johns Hopkins University Press, 1978]). But evidence from late medieval England would indicate that by this period, consanguinity was not a major concern of ecclesiastical courts, or by implication, of married people and clerical administrators (see Helmholz, *Marriage Litigation in Medieval England*).

**62.** For the importance of the church's emphasis on individual consent as the basis for the sacrament of marriage, and hence of the significance of ecclesiastical courts, canon law, and theology in providing the medium for a changing understanding of the institution of marriage during the later medieval period, see Sheehan, *Marriage, Family, and Law;* John T. Noonan Jr., "Power to Choose," *Viator* 4 (1973): 419–34; Charles Donahue, "The Policy of Alexander III's Consent Theory of Marriage," in *Proceedings of the Fourth International Congress of Canon Law. Toronto, 21–25 August 1972*, ed. Stephan Kuttner, Monumenta Iuris Canonici, ser. C: Subsidia, vol. 5 (Vatican City: Biblioteca Apostolica Vaticana, 1976), 251–81; L. D'Avray and M. Tausche, "Marriage Sermons in *ad status* Collections of the Central Middle Ages," *Archives d'histoire doctrinale et littéraire du moyen age* 47 (1981): 71–119; Erik Kooper, "Loving the Unequal Equal: Medieval Theologians and Marital Affection," in *The Olde Daunce: Love, Friendship, Sex, and Marriage in the Medieval World*, ed. Robert R. Edwards and Stephen Spector (Albany: State University of New York Press, 1991), 44–56; Rüdiger Schnell, "The Discourse on Marriage in the Middle Ages," *Speculum* 73.3 (July 1998): 771–86.

**63.** While the words of present consent were all that were needed to make a marriage valid, Sheehan says, a *licit* marriage usually required the following procedures: "After financial arrangements had been made by the families concerned, the betrothal took place. This consisted of a promise to marry *(per verba de futuro)* and often was expressed as a form of words before witnesses. Next the banns were read in the parish church. If no objection to the marriage resulted, or if objections had been dealt with in a satisfactory way, the couple publicly solemnised their union by an exchange of consent *(per verba de presenti)* at the church door. This would be seen as the moment when the sacrament was given by the couple to each other. The ceremonies before witnesses included the endowment of the bride, her delivery by her father to the husband, and various rituals, including a form of words and the giving of a ring. Finally, the bridal party entered the church for the nuptial mass" (*Marriage, Family, and Law*, 48).

**64.** Because of the success in redefining marriage as a sacrament and thus under the jurisdiction of canon law, throughout the later Middle Ages (and in England, until the nineteenth century), legal disputes about marriage were decided largely by ecclesiastical, rather than secular, courts. See Sheehan, *Marriage, Family, and Law*, 38–76; Helmholz, *Marriage Litigation;* and Frederick Pedersen, *Marriage Disputes in Medieval England* (London: The Hambledon Press, 2000). Pedersen's study focuses on the records of the ecclesiastical court of York and thus provides a valuable addition to Sheehan and Helmholz, who focus more on the records of Ely. Helmholz notes that "matrimonial litigation in later medieval England was, above all else, litigation over the interpretation and enforcement of marriage contracts. The principal business of the Church courts was not determining whether an existing marriage could be dissolved: their main task was the settling of disputes about the initiation of the marriage relationship. . . . The records suggest that the cause of this characteristic lies in the conjunction of two things. First was the lack of a required formula by which marriage had to be contracted and the legal difficulties of interpreting the words used in practice [i.e., distinguishing between what constituted *present* versus *future* consent]. Second was the continued vitality of an older view of marriage as a private contract. What the law regarded as a complete and indissoluble marriage, many men regarded as a contract to marry" (72). Thus, the process by which the church instantiated its theoretical control over marriage was only begun by the definitive formulation of canon law in the twelfth century. It was not until the practice of a church ceremony and the publication of banns became more general and customary in the fifteenth and sixteenth centuries that such control was securely in place. Helmholz notes that, as a result, matrimonial suits occupy an increasingly smaller portion of the business of ecclesiastical courts in this later period; see especially 165–86.

**65.** Sheehan, *Marriage, Family, and Law,* 99.

**66.** Ibid., 102, and also 111–17, for an extended discussion of this process.

**67.** See especially D'Avray and Tausche, "Marriage Sermons"; and Kooper, "Loving the Unequal Equal." For general discussions of love in marriage, see Philippe Ariès, "L'Amour dans le mariage," *Communications* 35 (1982): 116–22; Johan Chydenius, *Love and the Medieval Tradition* (Helsinki: Societas scientiarum Fennica: Commentationes humanarum litterarum 58, 1977); Jean Leclercq, "The Development of a Topic in Medieval Studies in the Eighties: An Interdisciplinary Perspective on Love and Marriage," in *Literary and Historical Perspectives of the Middle Ages: Proceedings of the 1981 SEMA Meeting,* ed. Patricia W. Cummins, Patrick W. Conner, and Charles W. Connell (Morgantown: West Virginia University Press, 1982); and Willy Van Hoecke and Andries Welkenhuysen, eds., *Love and Marriage in the Twelfth Century,* Mediaevalia Lovaniensia, series 1, studia 8 (Leuvain: Leuven University Press, 1981). See also M. Teresa Tavormina, *Kindly Similitude: Marriage and Family in Piers Plowman* (Cambridge: D. S. Brewer, 1995), especially 187–90.

**68.** See Elizabeth M. Makowski, "The Conjugal Debt and Medieval Canon Law," *Journal of Medieval History* 3 (1977): 99–114. Thus, for example, Margery Kempe, despite her desire to lead a celibate life, continues to pay her marriage debt (and gives birth fourteen times) until she is able to secure her husband's agreement to lead separate, celibate lives (and only then by agreeing to pay his debts). See also the continental examples provided by Dyan Elliott, *Spiritual Marriage: Sexual Abstinence in Medieval Wedlock* (Princeton, N. J.: Princeton University Press, 1993), especially "The Conjugal Debt and Vows of Chastity: The Theoretical and Pastoral Discourse of the High and Later Middle Ages," 132–94.

**69.** Pedersen, *Marriage Disputes in Medieval England,* 156; see also 153–75 for a detailed discussion of the complexity of the terms used in the cases heard by the archbishop's court in York in the fourteenth century.

**70.** Sheehan, *Marriage, Family, and Law,* 270, 271. Although the Wife of Bath's style of argument with her husbands is interpreted by many of her listeners and readers as extreme, her arguments are in many respects similar to the canonists' regarding marital affection.

71. Cf. Pedersen, *Marriage Disputes in Medieval England:* "The word *affectio,* which was first used in Roman law to indicate the willingness to permit the transfer of property, in its combination with a word indicating marriage has continued to evolve in western European thought over the centuries to the point where, by some time after the fourteenth century, 'affection' lost its initial meaning of 'will' and became the word used to describe an internalized ongoing psychological process in the emotional involvement of one person in another" (174–75).

72. Ibid., 172.

73. Sheehan, *Marriage, Family, and Law,* 264.

74. Ibid., 265.

75. Hugh of St. Victor, *De sacramentis Christianae fidei,* 11.11.4, in *On the Sacraments of Christian Faith,* trans. Roy J. Deferrari (Cambridge, Mass.: The Medieval Academy of America, 1951), 329. Quoting this passage, Kooper notes that "Hugh places the equality of man and woman as human beings created in the image of God before their inequality, which belongs to the order of creation" ("Loving the Unequal Equal," 47). Kooper also suggests that Hugh here is influenced by Bernard of Clairvaux's sermons on the *Song of Songs,* where "Bernard expounds that the love between the mystical Bride and Groom leads to a harmony of will in which the inequality of the partners was no longer felt. . . . it is friendship and (near) equality which constitute the essence of the love of the Bride and the Groom and enable them to be joined not only in the flesh, but, in the spiritual marriage, also in one spirit" (46–47).

76. *Non est bonum hominem esse solum; faciamus ei adjutorium simile sibi.* . . . Dicit etiam *simile sibi;* quod est relativum aequiparantiae. In quo notatur quod mulier debet esse aequalis viro suo, sive socia, non sub viro, non supra virum. Item, mulier facta fuit de costa viri, non de inferiori parte vel de superiori, sed de media, ut per hoc significaretur quod mulier debet esse aequalis viro suo (Robert de Sorbon, *De Matrimonio,* in B. Hauréau, *Notices et extraits de quelques manuscrits latins de la Bibliothèque Nationale* [Paris: Librairie Klincksieck, 1890], 1:189 [English trans. Erik Kooper, "Loving the Unequal Equal," 45]). Kooper notes that Robert, in his sermon, "explicitly addresses himself to members of the monastic orders, which, as shown by his *exempla,* he puts on a level with the order of marriage *[ordo coniugii]:* if the orders of the black monks and of the Cistercians are to be called noble because of the saintliness of their founders, so much more noble ought to be the order of marriage which was established by God" (49). Kooper wants to fit Robert into a "monastic" mold on this subject established by such writers as Bernard of Clairvaux, Hugh of St. Victor, Aelred of Rievaulx, Thomas Aquinas, and such an argument for a textual tradition is persuasive. But equally noteworthy, perhaps, is Robert's own position as a canon regular, occupying a "secular" chair of theology, enjoying royal favor as a "clerc du roi" and possibly even as confessor to Louis the Pious, receiving rich gifts for his colleges from the king (Kooper, "Loving the Unequal Equal," 55). For what is especially interesting about this case is precisely the fact that the sacrament of *lay* marriage tops monastic nobility.

77. D'Avray and Tausche, "Marriage Sermons," 118; see also Kooper, "Loving the Unequal Equal"; and David D'Avray, "The Gospel of the Marriage Feast of Cana and Marriage Preaching in France," 207–24, in *The Bible and the Medieval World: Essays in Memory of Beryl Smalley,* ed. Katherine Walsh and Diana Wood (Oxford: Blackwell, 1985).

**78.** Andrew Galloway, "Marriage Sermons, Polemical Sermons, and *The Wife of Bath's Prologue:* A Generic Excursus," *Studies in the Age of Chaucer* 14 (1992): 6–7.

**79.** D'Avray and Tausche, "Marriage Sermons," 114; "Est etiam dilectio socialis, qua debent se coniuges diligere, quia pares sunt et socii" (BN lat. 15943, fol. 144va). D'Avray and Tausche note that Guibertus's use of the phrase "equal and partners" is remarkable because "pares" is left unqualified, whereas Jacques de Vitry, in another marriage sermon from early in the century, "says that a wife is not her husband's equal *tout court,* but only so far as the marriage debt is concerned" (114).

**80.** D'Avray and Tausche, "Marriage Sermons," 115, quoted in Kooper, "Loving the Unequal Equal," 53: "Ista autem dilectio formanda <est> ut sit in ea puritas intentionis, ut non diligent se coniuges nec matrimonialiter coniungantur proper emolimentum *(sic)* aliquod temporale vel pulcritudinem forme vel impetionem voluptatis libidinose, sed ut vivant simul iocunde et honeste, ut deus honoretur et fructus ad serviendum deo inde gignatur.... Quando enim pares sunt, tunc in pace vivunt, sed quando propter dotem vel aliquod temporale nupserunt, semper litigant. Unde si vis nubere, nube pari" (BN lat. 15943, fol. 144vb). See Kooper (54–55), for a discussion of the many echoes of Thomas Aquinas and Aelred of Rievaulx in the sermons of Guibert and for the likely links between Aquinas, Robert of Sorbon, and Guibert because of their close relationship at the University of Paris.

**81.** D'Avray, "The Gospel of the Marriage Feast of Cana," 216.

**82.** See Sister Prudence Allen, *The Concept of Woman: The Aristotelian Revolution, 759 B.C.–A.D. 1250* (Grand Rapids, Mich.: William B. Eerdmans, 1985).

**83.** "The period between the end of the thirteenth century and the Reformation in England, as in the Church generally, was not to see original legislation touching marriage, but the councils of the period were to return again and again to reinforce the proper reading of the banns and to prevent the use of an unacceptable solemnization of marriage to circumvent it" (Sheehan, *Marriage, Family, and Law,* 176).

**84.** Ibid., 176, 102.

**85.** Judith M. Bennett, *Women in the Medieval English Countryside: Gender and Household in Brigstock before the Plague* (Oxford: Clarendon Press, 1987). For a provocative discussion of marital property law and changing perceptions of bourgeois marriage relations in late medieval/early modern Douai, see Martha Howell, *The Marriage Exchange: Property, Social Place, and Gender in Cities of the Low Countries, 1300–1550* (Chicago: University of Chicago Press, 1998). She notes, for example, that the custom of late medieval Douai "defined wives as their husband's partners and widows as their substitutes," decidedly "not a representation of partners with identical social or legal capacities," but nonetheless a "kind of *economic* mutuality, a partnership made up of two members who provided roughly equal economic worth, and whose economic capacities were taken as utterly commensurate" (116).

**86.** Carruthers notes in addition,"[t]he extent to which parents who were set on a marriage would go in order to break the will of a reluctant daughter is chillingly attested by the experience of Elizabeth Paston when her mother had bound her to the dreadful Scrope: 'sche hath son Esterne [this letter was written 29 June] [th]e most part be betyn onys in [th]e weke or twyes, *and* som tyme tywes on o day, *and* hir hed brokin in to or thre places.'... After such treatment poor Elizabeth gave in and agreed to 'rewle hire to hym as sche awte to do' even though 'his persone is simple,' though for other reasons the marriage finally fell through" ("The Wife of Bath and the Painting of Lions," *PMLA* 94 [1979]: 213, 214).

**87.** Pedersen, *Marriage Disputes in Medieval England,* 120–21. Pedersen notes as well that, although force was used in a number of cases, a successful plea based only on the existence of force is rare.

**88.** *Paston Letters and Papers of the Fifteenth Century,* ed. Norman Davis (Oxford: Clarendon Press, 1971), vol. 1, no. 415, 662–63.

**89.** [E]o quod non diligent affectionem qua tenetur. Et ideo pro certo nuncquam intendo consentire in eam quod sit uxorem meam nec cum ea coha[bi]tare (Pedersen, *Marriage Disputes in Medieval England,* 155). Pedersen is citing from the evidence given by William Raynald, a witness for William Aungier.

**90.** Georgine E. Brereton and Janet M. Ferrier, eds., *Le Menagier de Paris* (Oxford: Clarendon Press, 1981); see also *The Goodman of Paris: A Treatise on Moral and Domestic Economy by a Citizen of Paris (c. 1393),* trans. Eileen Power (London, Routledge, 1928); Geoffroy de la Tour-Landry, *Le Livre du chevalier de La Tour Landry, pour l'enseignement de ses filles* (c. 1371; reprint, Paris: P. Jannet, 1854); *The Book of the Knight of the Tower,* ed. M. Y. Offord, trans. William Caxton, EETS SS No. 2 (c. 1484; reprint, Oxford: Oxford University Press, 1971). See also Carolyn P. Collette, "Heeding the Counsel of Prudence: A Context for the *Melibee," Chaucer Review* 29, no. 4 (1995): 416–33, for a discussion of these works in relation to the development of prudence as a female science of actions within human relations, particularly marriage.

**91.** See Andrew Galloway, "Marriage Sermons," 3–30, for a discussion of the uses made of the genre of marriage sermons in the *Wife of Bath's Tale* both to establish and to undermine her authority. Galloway then traces the widespread "professionalizing" of sermons in the period to justify one or another branch of the clerisy against each other: "The shifting forms and uses of preaching in the period aptly suggest the uncontrollably divisive professionalism of the period, as well as the equally uncontrollable drift of knowledge away from clerical constraints and into the lay world, and the Wife of Bath at once emphasizes and disassembles these social and professional markers, preventing her learning even from conferring final authority on herself. Women, excluded from learned culture even in the late Middle Ages, are well suited to speak to the desires for intellectual authority felt by the whole class of those traditionally excluded, the 'educated or half-educated laity' emerging in the late Middle Ages. That the Wife does not finally invert learned authority so much as display its elusiveness, its proliferation into a multitude of social meanings, constitutes her fullest demonstration of the resistance of such genres and such expertise to any firm professional or social control" (29).

**92.** Jo Ann McNamara, "The *Herrenfrage:* The Restructuring of the Gender System, 1050–1150," in *Medieval Masculinities: Regarding Men in the Middle Ages,* ed. Clare A. Lees (Minneapolis: University of Minnesota Press, 1994), 8.

**93.** "Proponents of the apostolic movement boasted that women proved themselves fit for the hardest ascetic practices and manual labor. . . . Groups of women, relatives, or simply pensioners formed an aureole of recluseries and women's communities around many, perhaps most, male monasteries.... In many cases, the women's community was made up largely of female relatives and separated wives of the monks (as at Vannes and Tart), opened to relieve the pressures of unplaced women. The power relations of recluses were less clear, but we have numerous examples of men who subjected themselves to the tutelage of women. Hermits living in rural solitude or even in urban areas looked to holy women as their mentors. Abbots of male communities drew spiritual sustenance from recluses clustered around their monasteries" (McNamara, "The *Herrenfrage*," 12–13). "A syneisactic society, where women and men mingle and relate to one another without reference to accepted sex roles, is deeply threatening to the conventional order. The socialization of gender identity, a person's own view of maleness or femaleness, assumes heterosexuality and indeed leaves no room for deviation of any sort from the polarized sex roles into which each individual can be fitted or forced during the vulnerable period of early childhood. A fluid relationship between women and men enabled women to take the lead when the normal variables of talent, age, experience, and social status made it appropriate.... Men and women worked alike and dressed alike. They might become indistinguishable if they really escaped sexuality and its procreative results. Indeed, if gender differences were reduced to the level of biology, sex itself might be changed" (14).

**94.** Thus, "[a]mong monks, safely segregated from women, perhaps the safest way to restore the gender system was to play both roles and, by implication, deny the need for women in any capacity" (McNamara, "The *Herrenfrage*," 20).

**95.** Ibid., 20–21. Cf. also Idung of Prufenung: "It is not expedient for that sex [woman] to enjoy the freedom of having its own governance because of its natural fickleness and also because of outside temptations which womanly weakness is not strong enough to resist" (ibid., 20).

**96.** Carruthers, "The Wife of Bath and the Painting of Lions," 221 n. 35.

**97.** Fiona Somerset, "'As just as is a squyre': The Politics of 'Lewed Translacion' in Chaucer's *Summoner's Tale*," *Studies in the Age of Chaucer* 21 (1999): 193.

**98.** Eberle, "Commercial Language and the Commercial Outlook," 161–74.

**99.** One can see this in a number of locations, and variously framed as crisis or as the anxieties generated by a pragmatic politics working outside of current representational models. The growing self-sufficiency of guild and parish life as a worthy model for lay community life (as opposed to the primacy of the monastic life in the twelfth century) means that lay people are increasingly able to secure for themselves in these locations a sense of successfully "real" religious piety (modeled on monastic communities, but now increasingly available to lay audiences on their terms). A similar movement, but expressing itself as "crisis," would be Lollard calls for reforms that would effectively wipe out the special status of the celibate clerisy. Increasingly in the public world, state bureaucracies (both those of the king and the great magnates) come to rely on a secular *affines* drawn from a wider meritocratic pool rather than from a celibate clerisy or kinship groupings. And there is an increasing intersection of interests and practices between traditionally different estates, as with the landowning feudal class and an urban merchant patriciate. Here again, such change can be expressed as crisis, as for example, when such a tendency—as with Richard II's tilt to tyranny in the 1390s—pits such new affinities grouped around individual power bases against traditional hegemonies, such as those of the great magnates (or when the scapegoating of Lollards in the fifteenth century makes possible a new accommodation between church and an upstart Lancastrian dynasty).

**100.** Of course, another manifestation of this gender crisis occurs around laywomen's bodies, where the claustration of woman effected by the clerical activity McNamara describes, is, in the later Middle Ages, resisted by combining the "freedom" of the lay female body (from monastic claustration) with activities associated with clerical masculinity (celibacy, ascetic practices) into a new hybrid form that redefines the feminine and the female body in newly empowering ways.

**101.** Emma Lipton has recently presented a similar reading of John Gower's privileging of a new masculine identity articulated through conjugality in his Anglo-Norman poem, "Traitié Pour Essampler Les Amants Marietz" (*The Complete Works of John Gower*, ed. G. C. Macaulay [Oxford: Clarendon Press, 1899], 1:378–92, 470–73): "Revising medieval clichés of female virtue and vice familiar from hagiography and clerical misogyny, the tales value marriage over chastity and shift moral responsibility for sexual practices from women to men. Gower replaces the three estates with the three grades of chastity and implies that anyone who is morally superior in marriage can be of the highest status" ("Public Voice, Private Life: Sexuality and Masculinity in Ricardian Poetry," paper presented at the New Chaucer Society Congress, London, July 2000). For example, the poem focuses not on the heroic exploits of Hercules but on his initial success in "taking a wife honorably" ("prist femme a son honour," part 7, stanza 1), and then on his failure in hating his wife and loving Iole: "He bore the retribution of his misdeed; / It is a great peril to break a marriage" ("De son mesfait porta le contretaille; / C'est grant peril de freindre l'espousaile," part 7, stanza 3). This message is later summarized thus:

Of the three estates, the most blessed is the second
Which submits itself to marriage according to proper love
And whoever brings this order to ruin by foolish pleasure
Has much to fear if he does not get himself back on the right track
Therefore everyone should take care to
Love in such a way that his faith not be injured:
He is no lover who misguides his love. (part 18, stanza 2)

Des trios estatz benoitz c'est le seconde,
Q'au marriage en droit amour se ploie
Et qui cell ordre en foldelit confonde
Trop poet doubter, s'il ne se reconvoie
Pource bon est qe chascun se pourvoie
D'amer ensi, qu'il n'ait sa foi blemie:
N'est pas amant qui son amour mesguie.

Moreover, as Lipton points out, "While presented as a classless secular model of male moral virtue, with the prologue addressed to 'everyone in general' (a tout le monde en general) and envoy 'to the community of the whole world' (Al université de tout le monde'), in fact, the ballads of the 'Traitié' participate in a new ideology for the emergent upper middle strata of society and reveal the roots of the public voice of Ricardian poetry in a new masculinized vision of private life."

**102.** As Helmholz, *Marriage Contracts,* points out, when Pope Alexander III adopted the substance of Peter Lombard's position, so that "a contract by words of present consent constituted, without more, the marriage bond itself," the *verba de presenti* were, "in J. L. Austin's terminology, performative words, themselves creating the bond of marriage" (27). Cf. Austin, *How to Do Things with Words* (Oxford: Clarendon Press, 1962). Austin's discussion, of course, forms the basis for Sedgwick's rethinking of (queer) performativity.

## 3. Modernity and Marriage in the *Canterbury Tales*

**1.** Both the *Knight's Tale* and the *Man of Law's Tale* also have conflicted temporal relations that attempt to reform an unstable present and bring it into alignment with a supposedly set past.

**2.** See Steven F. Kruger, *Dreaming in the Middle Ages* (Cambridge: Cambridge University Press, 1992), for a richly nuanced discussion of the doubleness and middleness of dreams in the Middle Ages.

**3.** Halberstam, *Female Masculinity,* 1. See especially the introduction, "Masculinity without Men," 1–44, and the discussion of "perverse presentism," 50–59. Halberstam is particularly interested in female masculinity as it queers our understanding of women's relationships with women and her perverse presentism provides a way of reaching back into modern history without automatically reproducing modern lesbianism as the only "alternative" to compulsory heterosexuality for women or excising queer eroticism from early modern women's relationships. My own historicization of the Wife's sex/gender politics suggests a parallel strategy in her self-representation of male/female relationships. What becomes clearer, as well, when translating Halberstam's methodological resistance to modernist historiography of gender and sexuality in the modern period is the dynamic relationship that a term like "perverse presentism" might imply. Clearly what is happening here is not simply reading present practice backward so that only the present can explain the past, but rather such a perverse presentism opens up the past in such a way that it, too, can insistently and perversely read the present in challenging and disruptive ways. We might think of such a methodology as perverse historicism as much as perverse presentism.

**4.** Perhaps the only other such moment occurs with the Pardoner, in part because of a similarly confessional prologue but perhaps more importantly because a similar emphasis on his sexualized body plays a crucial role in grounding the essentializing hermeneutic that his audience uses in their disavowal of him. Curiously, a similar dynamic is constructed (in a very different way) around the tales of Chaucer; here the supposed absolute difference between the tale-teller constructed and the *real* Chaucer, between these utterly "conventional" tales and the "originality" of the real Chaucer oeuvre, work to naturalize the achievement of the "great author."

5. A modernist historiography, on the other hand, could view the Wife as "modern" by reading her as an example of the liberal self *avant la lettre* or of the unrepresented reality of a medieval woman's life. Even feminist readings of the tale, in their attempts to resist masculinist medieval (and modern) reading patterns, have sometimes constructed their own version of this medieval/modern dichotomy: as a character, the Wife of Bath may emerge within the shaming discursive framework of a clerical tradition of citation and proper imitation of authority as the nightmarish virago or monstrous feminine of antifeminist satire. Or she may be bound within a hierarchized gender binary, the female/feminine/woman as ground to male/masculine/patriarchy. Previous critics reading her tale as opening the Marriage Group may have reproduced this masculinist framework to the extent that they characterized the Wife and her view of marriage as a deformation requiring the reformative work of the other tales in this group. But these "medieval" hegemonic constructions are historical repressions of another's experience that can be resisted and changed. Thus modern feminist readings of the poem can find a point of resistance to dominant masculinity because of, in spite of, or in excess of this controlling framework of the prologue and tale.

6. The too easy linkage that the characterization of the Wife encourages between authenticity (her emphasis on a biological and social presence in the supposed "here and now" of the pilgrimage frame) and stable identity also installs a false consciousness around medieval and modern universals and the sense of history they depend on. Such a modern "masculinist" reading will rejoice in the "liveliness" of the Wife's characterization and in the process of accepting her as "woman" perpetuate a sense of the transhistorical "humanity" of Chaucer as great author and a universal liberal subject whose historic maleness remains unexamined. Similarly, such a modern "feminist" reading might reach out to the Wife as an early modern "woman's voice" finding its own mode of expression in spite of a masculinist hegemony ranged against such a subject position. In both cases but in different ways, a modernist history of (hetero)sexuality is reinscribed through such a linkage of presence and identity. The reality effect created by the Wife, then, rather than providing the sure foundation for the kind of strong intervention that will change the way things are, actually produces a set of binaries that are surprisingly stabilizing in their temporal and representational effects. First, because the Wife's liveliness sets her up to be read in certain crucial ways as "modern," it also, paradoxically, often works to ensure that she remains marginal to "normal" medieval modes of understanding, both for her medieval and modern audiences. Second, this marginality emerges out of mutually constitutive masculinist and feminist hermeneutic strategies that together structure the relationships between past, present, and future in knowable ways.

7. See Dinshaw, *Chaucer's Sexual Poetics*, 3–27, 113–31, for a discussion of the relationships between the female body (clothed and stripped) and the text in medieval clerical hermeneutics; also, Laura Hodges, *Chaucer and Costume: The Secular Pilgrims in the General Prologue* (Cambridge: D. S. Brewer, 2000), 161–86. Hodges notes that "collectively and paradoxically dame Aly's garments accurately evoke her social class, economic prosperity and possible responsibility, her vain pride, and her knowledgable practicality" (186).

8. John Hajnal, "European Marriage Patterns in Perspective," in *Population in History: Essays in Historical Demography*, ed. D. V. Glass and D. E. C. Eversley (Chicago: Aldine,

1965), 101–43. Hajnal's thesis about European marriage patterns and household formation has been accepted by a variety of scholars working on these issues in the late medieval and early modern periods. See, for example, Richard M. Smith, "Some Reflections on the Evidence for the Origins of the 'European Marriage Pattern' in England," in *The Sociology of the Family: New Directions in Britain,* ed. Chris Harris (Totowa, N.J.: Rowman and Littlefield, 1979), 74–112; Alan MacFarlane, *Marriage and Love in England 1300–1840* (Oxford: Blackwell, 1986); L. R. Poos, *A Rural Society after the Black Death: Essex 1350–1525* (Cambridge: Cambridge University Press, 1991); P. J. P. Goldberg, *Women, Work, and Life Cycle in a Medieval Economy: Women in York and Yorkshire, c. 1300–1520* (Oxford: Clarendon Press, 1992); Jan de Vries, "Population," in *Handbook of European History 1400–1600,* ed. Thomas A Brady, Heiko A. Oberman, and James D. Tracy (Grand Rapids, Mich.: Eerdmans, 1994), 1:36–40; Maryanne Kowaleski, "Singlewomen in Medieval and Early Modern Europe: The Demographic Perspective," in *Singlewomen in the European Past, 1250–1800,* ed. Judith M. Bennett and Amy M. Froide (Philadelphia: University of Pennsylvania Press, 1999).

**9.** Kowaleski, "Singlewomen in Medieval and Early Modern Europe," 44 nn. 30, 31, and 60. The young aristocratic (or quasi-aristocratic, mercantile) bride comes endowed with the "natural" surplus of good name, lineage, and dowry lands, a female body absolutely delineating the sign of the father. Far from signifying the product of individual labor, the female body here marks the "natural" surplus that characterizes a class and its innate right to rule.

**10.** Direct evidence for the age at which women married in late medieval northwestern Europe is scarce and problematic. Jeremy Goldberg, *Women, Work, and Life Cycle,* 225–32, although working with relatively few cases ranging over more than two hundred years from 1303 to 1520, suggests that rural women married in their late teens and early twenties, but urban women waited until their early to mid-twenties. Kowaleski, reviewing the demographic evidence accumulated since Hajnal's work in the sixties, suggests that "during the early modern period (and probably in the late Middle Ages as well), women in most parts of northwestern Europe (British Isles, Low Countries, northern France, Germany, and western Scandinavia) married in their mid- to late-twenties" ("Singlewomen in Medieval and Early Modern Europe," 40).

**11.** "Variations in the timing of marriage also reflected different life experiences. Women who waited until age 25 to marry, for instance, had generally enjoyed a period of independence while they earned wages and lived outside their parents' home; this independence, in turn, also gave them a greater voice in selecting a marriage partner, a choice perhaps evident in their tendency to marry men only a few years older than themselves. In contrast, women who married at the age of 18 or younger usually went straight from their parents' household to their husband's, thereby experiencing little independence in their short time as an adult singlewoman, while also being subject to more parental influence in their choice of a marriage partner" (Kowaleski, "Singlewomen in Medieval and Early Modern Europe," 40).

**12.** See Lochrie, *Covert Operations,* 146, and Judith Bennett, "Medieval Women, Modern Women: Across the Great Divide," in *Culture and History, 1350–1600: Essays on English Communities, Identities and Writing,* ed. David Aers (Detroit: Wayne State University Press), 155, for a discussion of how, even in those restricted cases of married women gaining the right to function in public as a *femme sole,* this option did not necessarily constitute a real female public agency. Lochrie goes on to note that the realm of privacy around married women's household identities and activities that coverture established did not produce the kind of entitlement that modern privacy promises—that is, "controlled access to one's person and freedom from public scrutiny"—but "was a privacy that signified dependence, lack of personal responsibility, and public disability. In this way coverture not only distinguished the experiences of marriage for men and women, it structured social relationships along the axis of private women and public men" (149).

**13.** Kowaleski, "Singlewomen in Medieval and Early Modern Europe," 46; cf. 46 n. 39. See also, Caroline Fenwick, "The English Poll Taxes of 1377, 1379, and 1381: A Critical Examination of the Returns" (Ph.D. diss., University of London, 1983).

**14.** Sharon Farmer, "'It Is Not Good That [Wo]man Should Be Alone': Elite Responses to Singlewomen in High Medieval Paris," in Bennett and Froide, *Singlewomen in the European Past,* 87.

**15.** For widows, see Sue Sheridan Walker, ed., *Wife and Widow in Medieval England* (Ann Arbor: University of Michigan Press, 1993); Christiane Klapisch-Zuber, *Women, Family, and Ritual in Renaissance Italy* (Chicago: University of Chicago Press, 1985); Louise Mirrer, ed., *Upon My Husband's Death: Widows in the Literature and Histories of Medieval Europe* (Ann Arbor: University of Michigan Press, 1992); Caroline M. Barron and Anne F. Sutton, eds., *Medieval London Widows, 1300–1500* (London: Hambledon Press, 1994). See also Ruth Mazo Karras, "Sex and the Singlewoman," in Bennett and Froide, *Singlewomen in the European Past,* 132, for a discussion of how the widow was not as sexually anomalous or problematic as the single woman.

**16.** Karma Lochrie's is the most recent and most provocative exploration of this "open secret" that the *femme covert* makes possible: "A woman who is *covert de baron* is not simply a woman who has surrendered her independent, single status as *femme sole* to join her husband in marriage: she is a woman who is no longer. She is a woman in disguise, or if you will, a baron with a secret. Her subjectivity evacuated, her identity merges—or submerges—into that of her husband. The marital union thereby created elides the woman entirely and substitutes for her the secret she must become. The medieval married woman cannot be defined simply as a secret, however, for she has no power over coverture: she is always someone else's secret. If *lieu covert* referred to a 'hiding place' in medieval French, marriage could be said to be that hiding place, at least for women, where the *femme covert,* by analogy, referred to the 'hidden' (not hiding) woman. . . . [A]s an open secret, the married woman is marked and qualified by her concealment and by her husband's possession. In turn, the husband's legal power is increased by his wife's conversion into his secret: not only is he the sole possessor and articulator of her person and property, but he is the virtual guarantor of her very existence. In fact, there is no real designation of the wife apart from her husband's possession of her as a secret. The name for wife and husband is, curiously, one and the same: a baron with a secret. A secret without a baron is nothing at all" (*Covert Operations,* 144).

**17.** There is another form that the Wife's female masculinity takes: her attempts at glossing and her engagement with "scole-matere." Dinshaw, in *Chaucer's Sexual Politics,* situates this within the antifeminist clerical tradition represented by Jerome and Tertullian, where the (masculine) glossator necessarily does violence to the (feminine) literal text in his attempts to strip the text of its superfluous literal meaning to reveal the naked text, its spiritual core and meaning. But could we think about the Wife's glossing as mimicking not so much clerical antifeminism as clerical approaches to marriage, which were not always misogynist and antifeminist, where the differences between men and women (supposed dominant and unequal) are open to a more associational polity?

**18.** Lochrie has recently drawn attention to the status of women's work in the *Book of Margery Kempe,* especially the ways that the conversion narrative rejects women's work outside the parameters of the household economy as instances of pride: "As long as she serves in the capacity of carder or spinner of wool—two traditionally female occupations that were regarded as low-skilled and low-status in the trade of cloth-making—Kempe would be regarded as suitably performing both her roles as worker and as wife. Although brewing was also traditionally a woman's occupation, Kempe's experimentation with it and milling is characterized by the desire for public approbation and power. It is this desire that defies the laws of the household economy because it threatens to define a woman's work outside of her marriage and in a public way.... [T]he laws and customs governing the work of women in the medieval household were likewise restrictive. Kempe's business endeavors violate one of the principal customs of the household economy, namely, that the husband's work was the defining work of the household, with the wife's work being either secondary to his or supplementary to it.... Kempe's business ventures recklessly disregard her husband's role in the economy and her own obligations to him. In fact, we never even learn from her narrative what work her husband does. In an interesting reversal of the submergence of women's work in the male-identified household economy of poll tax records, Kempe features her own work as the defining enterprise of her household" (151–52).

**19.** As Halberstam has noted in *Female Masculinity,* "To understand such a process, we would need to do more than map psychic and physical journeys between male and female and within queer and straight space; we would need, in fact, to think in fractal terms about gender geometries" (21). "If what we call 'dominant masculinity' appears to be a natural relation between maleness and power, then it makes little sense to examine men for the contours of that masculinity's social construction.... [Masculinity] becomes legible as masculinity where and when it leaves the white middle-class body" (2). The *Wife of Bath's Tale* does more than simply show the anxieties of a changing male population's access to dominant masculinity, although it does do that. And if it is not able to represent an autonomous female voice, it still manages a liberatory exploration of the complexity of gender politics.

**20.** "She makes audible precisely what patriarchal discourse performs. Speaking as the excluded Other, she explicitly and affirmatively assumes the place that patriarchal discourse accords the feminine. Far from being trapped within the 'prison house' of antifeminist discourse, the Wife of Bath, I argue, 'convert[s] a form of subordination into an affirmation,' to adapt Luce Irigaray's words here; she *mimics* the operations of patriarchal discourse.... Through the Wife, then, Chaucer imagines the possibility of a masculine reading that is not antifeminist, that does acknowledge, in good faith, feminine desire; and further, he represents the struggle and violence to the feminine that accompany the articulation of this fantasy" (Dinshaw, *Chaucer's Sexual Poetics,* 115, 117).

**21.** Patterson, for example, says: "What the Wife champions, as perhaps we should expect from a male author, is less the rights of her sex, much less those of her class, than the rights of selfhood. It is subjectivity per se that she promotes, a subjectivity that Chaucer, by no means uniquely, here associates with women. Throughout the Middle Ages women were denied social conceptualization, even existence as social—and historical—beings.... In the estate lists by which medieval society imagined itself, lay women are categorized not by economic, social, or political function but either by social status as determined by their male relatives or by marital status.... But perhaps this exclusion also carried with it (or so men thought) a sense of freedom, a liberation from the constraints of a highly regulatory system. If women were denied social definition, did this not mean that the realm of the *asocial*—of the internal, the individual, the subjective—was peculiarly theirs? Men, as befitted historical beings, had social responsibilities; women, as befitted the socially invisible, had private lives. Men had careers; women had characters.... What Chaucer's Wife wants is not political or social change; on the contrary, the traditional order is quite capable of providing the marital happiness she desires. To be sure, to acknowledge that the basic unit of social life is a socially undetermined selfhood entails important consequences that themselves carry the possibility (although by no means the necessity) of political changes. And to see that the bearers of this message are women is also a political statement. But the implications of the politics of individualism are very different from the class-determined dissent articulated by the Miller: the selfhood privileged by individualism is by definition already common property. Thus the Wife avoids the kind of antagonistic political issues invoked by the Miller and offers in their place a less activist, more congenial message" (*Chaucer and the Subject of History*, 281–83). Cf. Susan Crane's very different reading of the Wife's politics in the light of 1381: "Incoherence itself bears a message in the *Wife of Bath's Prologue*. Here again I differ from Patterson's analysis of the *Miller's Tale* in relation to the rising of 1381 and the Wife of Bath.... The Wife of Bath attempts to speak against an established discourse, and in so doing moves beyond cultural paradigms toward positions unprecedented in medieval literature. In staging the impossibility of speaking beyond literate paradigms, Chaucer makes the voicelessness of suppressed groups a subject rather than an unconsidered condition of his writing" ("The Writing Lesson of 1381," 217).

**22.** See Wallace, *Chaucerian Polity*, especially 9–64. For a view of late medieval/early modern marriage that depends on the binary, see Steven Ozment, *When Fathers Ruled: Family Life in Reformation Europe* (Cambridge: Harvard University Press, 1983).

**23.** Mary Carruthers, "The Wife of Bath and the Painting of Lions," 210; see also 219 nn. 11, 12. Carruthers cites Theodore F. T. Plucknett, *A Concise History of the Common Law*, 5th ed. (London: Butterworth, 1956): "The common law was the custom of the King's Court, and an outgrowth of feudal conditions which applied particularly to the larger landowners; for the upper classes of society its rules were no doubt appropriate, but it is only in the local customs of numerous cities, towns, and villages that we can see how different the life of the ordinary people was. In these customs, for example, we find that the position of the married woman was very different from that which the common law assigned her, the complete merging of her personality being obviously out of harmony with bourgeois habits. Local customs frequently keep the woman's property free from her husband's control, accord her liberty of contract (which was denied at common law), and even allow her to trade separately upon her own account" (313).

**24.** Carruthers notes that "[b]y the late fourteenth century, the English wool trade had become as much a trade in finished cloth as it was in the raw wool itself, and the clothmaking industry had entered the export markets, in addition to supplying domestic needs.... The English cloth makers, thanks to protective legislation, were able to underprice their European competitors, to the point of contributing to a severe depression in Flanders, and thus to surpass the Flemish product in quantity as well as in quality" ("The Wife of Bath and the Painting of Lions," 209–10). According to Eileen Power (*The Wool Trade in English Medieval History* [London: Oxford University Press, 1941], 37), in the first decade of the fourteenth century virtually all English wool exports were raw wool; whereas by the mid-fifteenth century, half of English exports were in the form of finished cloth. And E. M. Carus (*Medieval Merchant Venturers,* 2d ed. [London: Methuen, 1967]), indicates that cloth and wool exports were equal for the first time in the last decade of the fourteenth century. Carus also points out that by the time of Richard II, royal cloth purchases were virtually all from English clothiers dealing in English cloth, as opposed to the earlier domination of Flemish cloth (242 n. 3).

**25.** Julia Bolton Holloway, Joan Bechtold, and Constance Wright, eds., *Equally in God's Image: Women in the Middle Ages* (New York: Peter Lang, 1990), 27, citing W. C. Shickle, ed., *Ancient Deeds Belonging to the Corporation of Bath, Thirteenth–Sixteenth Centuries* (Bath: Bath Records Society, 1921).

**26.** D. W. Robertson Jr., "'And For My Land Thus Hastow Mordred Me?': Land Tenure, the Cloth Industry, and the Wife of Bath," *Chaucer Review* 14 (1980): 409–10. Robertson cites R. E. Glasscock in H. C. Darby, *A New Historical Geography of England before 1600* (Cambridge: Cambridge University Press, 1973), 113–14. See also Edward Miller, "The Fortunes of the English Textile Industry during the Thirteenth Century," *Economic History Review,* 2d ser., 18 (1965): 64–82.

**27.** Robertson Jr., "'And For My Land,'" 413–14. Stewart Justman ("Trade as Pudendum: Chaucer's Wife of Bath," *Chaucer Review* 28 [1994]), on the other hand, has argued that the Wife's association with the spirit of commerce links her indelibly to the town: "It was in the town that medieval people found the 'freedom of movement and contract' conducive to trade, freedoms that have meaning for Alice of Bath, who likes to go places and regards the sexual act itself in the light of an exchange—her very bed is a Rialto. There attaches to the Wife of Bath not only the ill fame of the traditional figure of the wanton woman, but the aggressiveness of the bourgeois way of life as seen by traditional eyes. Animated with the spirit of bourgeois life, she dramatizes the novelty, at once tempting and repulsive, which as Jacques Le Goff reminds us distinguished the towns. The vigor of the towns, their commercial character, their challenge to traditional relations: all this is legible in the Wife" (345–46).

**28.** Beryl Rowland, "Chaucer's Working Wife: The Unraveling of a Yarn Spinner," in *Chaucer in the Eighties,* ed. Julian N. Wasserman and Robert J. Blanch (Syracuse: Syracuse University Press, 1986), 137–49.

**29.** Heather Swanson, *Medieval Artisans: An Urban Class in Late Medieval England* (Oxford: Basil Blackwell, 1989), 1–8; see also her detailed discussion of the textile industry (26–44).

**30.** Carruthers, "The Wife of Bath and the Painting of Lions," 218 n. 2.

**31.** There is a difference here, for however much the Wife may present woman's estate as open and mobile (and thereby paralleling the real increase in mobility and activity within the middle ranks of the third estate—i.e., those who labor), the historical evidence would suggest that the parameters of woman's estate were becoming more and more fixed during the late medieval and early modern period. See Lochrie's discussion of "When Work Disappears," in *Covert Operations,* 149–64.

**32.** One way this might be tracked is by means of the Wife of Bath's complex manipulation of the concept of marital affection—as intention to marry and transfer property, as the proper concern for a spouse's well-being manifested in the material conditions appropriate to her class (e.g., clothing), or as the loving concern for a spouse's emotional well-being and contentment. See the discussion of *affectio maritalis* in chapter 2.

**33.** McNamara, "The *Herrenfrage,*" 21.

**34.** But I would also want to suggest how the examples of Margery Kempe (*The Book of Margery Kempe,* ed. Lynn Staley [Kalamazoo: Western Michigan University and TEAMS, 1996]); and—in a different register—Christine de Pisan (*The Book of the City of Ladies,* rev. ed., trans. Earl Jeffrey Richards [New York: Persea Books, 1998]), suggest the difficulties in realizing agency in the world from such attempts to reform or rehabilitate the representational force of the feminine. See also Karma Lochrie, *Margery Kempe and Translations of the Flesh* (Philadelphia: University of Pennsylvania Press, 1991); and Maureen Quilligan, *The Allegory of Female Authority: Christine de Pizan's 'Cité des dames'*" (Ithaca, N.Y.: Cornell University Press, 1991). It requires a very particular set of personal and momentary circumstances, and perhaps a large dose of luck, to be able to use the feminine in this way. See Caroline Walker Bynum's influential and provocative examination of such a use of the feminine by late medieval women mystics in *Holy Feast and Holy Fast: The Religious Significance of Food to Medieval Women* (Berkeley and Los Angeles: University of California Press, 1987).

**35.** Although it is primarily the "personal" tale in the *Wife of Bath's Prologue*—that is, the intrusion of the marginal frame as tale proper—that provokes other pilgrims and is the most explicitly disturbing element in her play, the Wife's appropriation of romance in the tale itself (like the appropriation of "glosing" in the prologue) has parallels with what Steven Justice terms the "insurgent literacy" that characterizes the actions of so-called peasants in the Rising of 1381: their selective destruction of Latin charters and other archival material relevant to seigneurial rights and privileges, the appropriation of the eucharistic and Corpus Christi festivals, and the "translation" of oppressive documents from the sphere of monastic or seigneurial privacy to the more malleable public arena. Thus, according to Justice, what often seemed like senseless, churlish violence and destruction, or what was retrospectively read in such a dismissive mode by contemporary chroniclers, actually could constitute a strong and informed political and hermeneutical engagement by social "inferiors" that showed their power to "read" foreign discourses even while supposedly "illiterate." See *Writing and Rebellion: England in 1381* (Berkeley and Los Angeles:

University of California Press, 1994), especially chapter 4, "The Idiom of Rural Politics," 140–92. Justice's analysis of Walsingham's account of the revolt at St. Albans is particularly interesting in this regard. When the rebels broke into the cloister, they invaded a parlor where handmills had been placed as paving stones, as a document and memorial of an old dispute between the villeins and the monastery. These rebels then broke up the stones and distributed the fragments among themselves. According to Justice, the rebels' systematic destruction of the parlor floor "was just a special case of what they did to documents of the parchment kind: they removed them from a place of private reservation, displayed them publicly, and destroyed them. In appropriating the millstone 'documents,' however, they also appropriated eucharistic sacramentality (distributing the pieces like the bread at mass) and displayed the structural similarity between documents and sacraments: two forms of clerical privilege, each of which, though formally matters of public concern, had been withheld from the community to which they rightly belonged. The rebels generalized their complaint about documentary culture—its reservation of record and command to a self-perpetuating clerisy—into a complaint about culture as such, about clerical control of the central expressions of common existence and belief" (168).

**36.** This might be expressed in terms of the Wife's interruption of a variety of "natural" teleologies: the move to celibacy and predominance of clerisy, to the male body/husband in marriage, to procreation for woman and marriage, to the primacy of a past example and a known future, to the primacy of literacy (in the sense of Latinate clerical culture).

**37.** This is a female embodiment more "substantial" and complex than the "hole" that Alison presents in the *Miller's Tale,* a voice with its own vocabulary and syntax, albeit one often discredited for "solipsism."

**38.** Benson, *The Riverside Chaucer,* 885.

**39.** Kittredge, *Chaucer and His Poetry,* 201–3; J. S. P. Tatlock, "Chaucer's *Merchant's Tale,*" *Modern Philology* 33 (1936): 367–81; G. G. Sedgewick, "The Structure of *The Merchant's Tale,*" *University of Toronto Quarterly* 17 (1948): 337–45; Donaldson, *Speaking of Chaucer,* 30–45; Norman T. Harrington, "Chaucer's Merchant's Tale: Another Swing of the Pendulum," *PMLA* 86 (1971): 25–31.

**40.** For a survey of critical opinion, see Donald R. Benson, "The Marriage 'Encomium' in the *Merchant's Tale:* A Chaucerian Crux," *Chaucer Review* 13 (1979): 48–60.

**41.** See, for example, Bertrand Bronson, *In Search of Chaucer* (Toronto: University of Toronto Press, 1960), and "Afterthoughts on the *Merchant's Tale,*" *Studies in Philology* 58 (1961): 583–96; Robert M. Jordan, "The Non-Dramatic Disunity of the *Merchant's Tale,*" *PMLA* 78 (1963): 293–99; T. W. Craik, *The Comic Tales of Chaucer* (London: Methuen, 1967), 133–53; and Martin Stevens, "'And Venus Laugheth': An Interpretation of the *Merchant's Tale,*" *Chaucer Review* 7 (1972): 118–29. For a survey of the critical debate, see Emerson Brown Jr., "Chaucer, the Merchant, and Their Tale: Getting Beyond Old Controversies," *Chaucer Review* 13 (1978–79): 141–56, 247–62; and C. David Benson, *Chaucer's Drama of Style* (Chapel Hill: University of North Carolina Press), 14–16, 116–30.

**42.** The ambiguities and contradictions made apparent by the gender dynamics of the *Merchant's Tale* (and the relationship between male narrator and author and tale) have provided another very useful route for critics to think beyond simple autobiographical or generic explanations for the tale's ironic structure. See, for example, the very different views taken by Mann, *Geoffrey Chaucer* (Atlantic Highlands, N.J.: Humanities Press International, 1991), 55–70, and Hansen, *Chaucer and the Fictions of Gender,* 245–66.

**43.** Patterson, *Chaucer and the Subject of History,* 337.

**44.** Ibid., 338.

**45.** Therefore he reiterates the Wife's presentism as a way of multiplying possibilities in the present (hence the emphasis in his tale on a variety of forms and on different perspectives on the same action), but with the multiplication here intent on creating room for maneuver—a place in the garden, as it were—while maintaining the privileged exclusivity of the garden and its key. Masculinity thus becomes a crucial representational category and marriage the ground on which to write it—hence the curious fusion of foreign (Italian) and present (mercantilism) with past (noble) in the character of January.

**46.** The tale's Italian setting also connects it with the *Clerk's Tale* (and its story of male tyranny) and distinguishes it from the fabliaux that precede (the *Miller's Tale,* the *Reeve's Tale,* and the *Cook's Tale,* all given very specifically English settings) and follow it (the *Shipman's Tale,* with its French setting). My thanks to Larry Scanlon for pointing this out to me.

**47.** See, for example, Patterson's discussion of late medieval chivalric identity and why, in the late fourteenth century, chivalric identity might be starting to appear inadequate, even to the governing class. Patterson contends that medieval warfare provided the necessary arena for a knightly class whose social status and financial well-being most depended on it: "The term 'honor' became its own verbal symbol, a shorthand for motives that would not bear further inspection. . . . By defining its values almost entirely in terms of personal worth, chivalry tended to privatize all historical action. . . . It was committed to codes of behavior not as programs of action but techniques of self-fashioning: the chivalric life was its own goal. Becoming ever more elaborate in its self-articulation, chivalry sought to create a form of life that was autonomous and self-sustaining, complete in itself and requiring no authentication from outside. Acknowledging no goal other than its own enactment, chivalry justified itself by the very absolutism of its self-commitment and the intricacy and elegance of its performance; and by understanding itself only in its own terms, it preempted the critical thought that a more strategically self-aware engagement with the world might have prompted. Hence the insistence throughout chivalric writing on the simplicity of chivalric selfhood. Chivalric heroes are represented as driven by a single, all-compelling desire. Peter of Cyprus is inspired by a youthful vision to found the Order of the Sword, 'and this was the goal of all his efforts.' Geoffroi de Charny, a preeminent chevalier who died defending his king's *oriflamme* at Poitiers, tells us in his authoritative *Livre de Chevalerie* that the youths who will become successful soldiers are those who have haunted the *mestier d'armes* from their earliest days and are driven solely by the desire 'to have the high honor of prowess.' All other interests are weaknesses. . . . The question is not only whether the ideals of chivalry conformed to the military reality of the later Middle Ages. Rather, it is what was entailed, psychologically as well as socially, by this self-definition, and also what was left out. Insofar as the nobleman restricted his self-understanding to a chivalric identity, to that extent he excluded from his view the economic, social, and political forces that were challenging his dominances" (*Chaucer and the Subject of History,* 173–78).

**48.** Such an identification perhaps accounts for why the description of January's lovemaking on his wedding night is presented from May's point of view, thereby forcing us to experience from underneath, as it were, January's "thikke brustles of his berd unsofte, / Lyk to the skyn of houndfyssh, sharp as brere" rubbing May's "tender face" (IV.1823–24, 1826), and "slake skyn" that "about his nekke shaketh / Whil that he sang" (IV.1849–50).

**49.** It is useful to think through the satire of January in terms of "common profit." January fails to add to the common profit, not because he is not engaged in capitalism because he's a knight, but because of the subject positions he inherits from such older models—his lack of self-control and his effeminizing selfishness. Neither January's conspicuous consumption (of May's youth, of his own vital heat, of his goods), nor Damian and May's conspicuous production produces the valuable surplus that would add to the common profit.

**50.** This is akin to the lot of the early modern courtier, or the state subject under the new despotic regime that Wallace describes in *Chaucerian Polity* (see especially 261–98).

**51.** For a consideration of the performative nature of ends that has been influential for my thinking here, see Steven F. Kruger, "Medieval/Post-Modern: HIV/AIDS and the Temporality of Crisis," in Burger and Krueger, *Queering the Middle Ages,* 252–83. Kruger notes that Jacques Derrida "has suggested that declarations of ends operate not as constative but as performative speech acts, wishfully attempting to call into being the situations they claim to describe. This is a powerful way to read the apocalyptic language that has circulated throughout the AIDS crisis—as declaring the 'end of queerness' (gayness, injecting drug use, African heterosexuality, etc.) through the agency of a so-called plague" (271). In an obviously very different context, I am arguing that the *Franklin's Tale*—especially in its opening representation of marriage, but also in the later representation of a succession of "fre" subjects made possible by that marriage relationship—explores the "I do" of such moments more as a performative speech act, an ending in the Derridian sense of "wishfully attempting to call into being the situations they claim to describe."

**52.** There is a play here on gentility as cultural capital, restrained femininity as cultural capital, and a freedom generated by labor as *new* cultural capital.

**53.** Similarly, Dorigen's laments in response to Aurelius's demand that she fulfill her promise to return his love if he removes the black rocks, based as they are on female suicide as the only noble response to loss of virtue, expose how the clerical texts available to her to cite and rhetorically color her "ful sorweful cheere" (V.1353) do not readily allow for the *inventio* she needs to represent the complexity of her situation as Arveragus's wife.

## 4. Queer Performativity in Fragment VI

**1.** Howard, *Idea of the Canterbury Tales,* 334, 338.

**2.** The placement of the *Second Nun's Tale* after the so-called Marriage Group, for example, might suggest how such a tale of chaste marriage could be intended as a fitting culmination to the marriage debate, cathecting in its vision of chaste marriage and the speaking power of the virginal female body both an influential form of contemporary lay desire and the deep structures of traditional medieval clerical identity. That many of the other tales about marriage also lack a fixed place in early orderings of the tales might reflect both a scribal recognition of their centrality to the Canterbury project and an uncertainty about the exact teleology for such a debate conducted according to "new" and not always predictable rules (a situation analogous perhaps to the multiple organizing principles that the narrator is forced into as he attempts to organize the portraits in the *General Prologue*). Similarly, the place of the Wife and her tale, while not absolutely stable, is clearly central to any teleology arising out of a marriage debate. Thus, however problematic she and her tale may be for the other pilgrims (or early scribes and readers), neither can be pigeonholed simply as grotesque and peripheral in the way that Howard sees happening to the Pardoner and his tale.

3. Fragment VI is notable for its foregrounding of the pilgrimage frame: giving 286 lines to the *Physician's Tale* proper, 176 lines to the link between the *Physician's Tale* and the *Pardoner's Tale* and to the *Pardoner's Prologue,* 442 lines for the *Pardoner's Tale* itself, and 64 lines to the Pardoner's address to the pilgrimage group and altercation with the Host. Only the *Wife of Bath's Prologue* focuses as much or more attention on the fictional frame of the *Canterbury Tales.*

4. Hansen, *Chaucer and the Fictions of Gender,* 288.

5. In what follows I am attempting to make a similar point concerning the different relationships between sex, gender, and sexuality in the Middle Ages to that made by Karma Lochrie when she recently asserted that sodomy in the Middle Ages was primarily conceived of as a gender disorder: "[W]hen theologians turned to sodomy, they located its sinfulness and its horror in its most deeply conflicted gender attributes: its passivity and unrestrained desire, an 'abominable' state that could not be named without danger of contamination and corruption" (*Covert Operations,* 191). As a result, Lochrie challenges analyses that would impose a modern sexuality binary of sodomy/heterosexuality on a medieval preoccuption that was primarily organized around sex/gender distinctions. In turn, this leads her to question whether terms such as "heterosexual" or "heternormative" are applicable in a medieval context where most sodomitical acts involve "heterosexual" couplings: "[E]ven sex between married people is, for the most part, unnatural, too. The band of 'heterosexual' sex that is natural, and therefore normative, is so narrow as to be almost meaningless. Only sex in the proper vessels with the proper instruments in the proper positions with the appropriate procreative intentions in orderly ways and during times that are not otherwise excluded 'counts' as natural and normative in medieval theology, canon law, and penitentials" (199).

6. Sedgwick, *Epistemology of the Closet,* 184, 185.

7. See Jordan, *Invention of Sodomy,* especially chapters 2 ("The Discovery of Sodomy," 29–44) and 3 ("Peter Damian: Books in Gomorrah," 45–66), as well as "A Postlude after St. Ambrose: The Responsibilities of a Theology of Sodomy" (159–76).

8. Ibid., 175. Is it really so surprising, then, that sodomitical panic emerges so vehemently and virulently in Fragment VI and around the body of the Pardoner, given the earlier attention to the erotics of "gentil" desire that could be expressed through the married estate, and the submerged anxiety represented as sodomitical panic that it brought out in the *Merchant's Tale?*

9. Noting the oscillation in Thomas Aquinas's discussion of the category of sodomitic vice, "by which it swings from a middling sin of *luxuria* to the eponymous sin against natural theology," Jordan attributes such oscillation to a paradox in medieval clerics' notions of unnatural pleasure—"a paradox glimpsed in the category of *luxuria* but observed most strikingly in the persistent fact that some people derive pleasure from unteleological copulation." He continues: "For Thomas, true pleasure is the effect of natural completion, of the fulfillment of natural teleology. The Sodomitic vice radically disrupts the most obvious continuities of animal nature. Yet the cause of this violently antinatural sin is the intensity of pleasure it yields—a pleasure so intense that it 'dissolves the soul.' But it is not only the intensity that is troubling: Thomas here confronts a kind of pleasure that cannot be divided without remainder into teleological sequences. He confronts a pleasure without end. He names the possibility of this pleasure the antithesis of nature. . . . [T]he fact of Sodomitic pleasures threatens to assert that a large group of moral arguments from natural teleology is specious" (154, 155–56).

10. See especially, *Invention of Sodomy* (161ff), where Jordan distinguishes *homosexuality,* "a term from late nineteenth-century forensic medicine" from *sodomy,* a term coined in medieval theology by derivation or deduction from a previous term, the term *Sodomite.*

11. Ibid., 163.

12. James Miller, "Dante on Fire Island: Reinventing Heaven in the AIDS Elegy," in *Writing AIDS: Gay Literature, Language, and Analysis,* ed. Timothy F. Murphy and Suzanne Poirier (New York: Columbia University Press, 1993), 265–305.

13. Jonathan Dollimore makes a similar distinction in his discussion of the early modern sodomite: "[I]t is not true that prior to the nineteenth century (or eighteenth, depending on when the change was said to occur) sexual deviance was conceptualized only as a form of behavior. I suggest that in early modern England the sodomite, though not an identity in the modern sense, could and did denote subject positions or types; 'he' precisely *characterized* deviant subject positions as well as denoting the behavior of individuals. Sodomy was not thought to originate in a pathological subjectivity (the modern pervert); rather the sexual deviant was the vehicle of a confusion never only sexual, and sexual in a way different from the sexological and psychoanalytic accounts. As such the deviant was the point of entry into civilization for the unnatural, the aberrant, and the abhorrent, the wilderness of disorder which beleaguered all civilization; a disorder in part, but rarely only ever, sexual" (*Sexual Dissidence,* 239). Dollimore also notes that "[i]maged in such terms, the sodomite indeed became the supreme instance of the demonized other. But so extreme was the sodomite's construction that most of those actually engaging in 'homo/sexuality' did not identify themselves with it; not only did they not have our modern categories, but the prevailing categories were so far removed from how they saw themselves, that apparently the connection was not made" (238).

14. Sedgwick, *Epistemology of the Closet,* 185.

15. Jordan, *Invention of Sodomy,* 156.

16. Cf. Karma Lochrie's discussion of "Sodom's Women, or Women on Top" (*Covert Operations,* 192–99), where she argues that in the relevant medieval clerical discourses sodomy was represented as a vice that afflicted women as well as men and suggests, citing

Margaret Hunt and Thomas Laqueur, that the far greater attention paid to male sodomy might have resulted from the fact that well-established mechanisms for regulating women's sexuality and gender roles already existed in ways that did not for men, and that since gender, not sexuality, is the real issue, male sodomy was perceived as more threatening because of the cultural power and prestige associated with masculinity.

**17.** Lee Edelman, *Homographesis: Essays in Gay Literary and Cultural Theory* (New York: Routledge, 1994), 10.

**18.** Ibid.

**19.** Cadden, *Meanings of Sex Difference;* Thomas Laqueur, *Making Sex: Body and Gender from the Greeks to Freud* (Cambridge: Harvard University Press, 1990). Cadden's book is particularly useful in complicating Laqueur's overdependence on Aristotle and a one-sex model as *the* model for sex difference in the premodern and early modern periods. See also, Jacquart and Thomasset, *Sexuality and Medicine in the Middle Ages;* Carol Clover, "Regardless of Sex: Men, Women, and Power in Early Northern Europe," in *Studying Medieval Women,* ed. Partner, 61–87; and Camille, "The Image and the Self."

**20.** Laqueur, *Making Sex,* 61–62.

**21.** See the useful discussions of the ideological import of the relationship between margin and text in medieval and early modern manuscripts and printed books by Michael Camille, *Image on the Edge;* and Evelyn B. Tribble, *Margins and Marginality: The Printed Page in Early Modern England* (Charlottesville: University Press of Virginia, 1993), especially chapter 1, "Authority, Control, Community: The English Printed Bible Page from Tyndale to the Authorized Version," 11–56.

**22.** See Hansen, *Chaucer and the Fictions of Gender,* 284–92, for a discussion of how constructions of Chaucer—as the "first" English author and the "father" of an English literary tradition—have worked to establish and maintain just such a foundational moment.

**23.** This is, of course, at bottom, a largely *clerical* model, and as such, one that arises out of the ideological needs of a celibate clerisy and the ruling hegemony of a clerically dominated church bureaucracy. Thus there are important differences from the representational practices and desires of medical discourse (deriving from earlier pre-Christian classical models of what is "natural") and of the laity (for whom, as earlier chapters have discussed, marriage and social relationships founded on its models had become "good to think with").

**24.** Clearly here I'm not talking about "real" women's bodies, i.e., about biological sex per se, but about a representational phantasmatic of "the real." Furthermore, as phantasm it may have considerable ideological force, but at the same time it does not completely describe the complex ways in which individual bodies take on and resist such gendered identities (as my discussion of Fragment VI below tries to demonstrate). See Kathleen Biddick, "Genders, Bodies, Borders: Technologies of the Visible," for discussion of a similar phantasmatic relationship between the eucharistic body of Christ and the common body of Christendom. I also want to emphasize the ways in which this medieval inscription of gender difference as *the* crucial difference (rather than race, sex, or sexuality today) brings male/female, Christian/non-Christian bodies into relationship in ways different from (although also similar to) modern representational practices. Misogyny, queer bashing, racism, and colonialism may take place under both regimes, but the ways in which power circulates differs.

**25.** Hansen, *Chaucer and the Fictions of Gender,* 286–87.

**26.** Laqueur, *Making Sex,* 59–60.

**27.** According to Dollimore, "The perverse dynamic is not an identity, a logic, or an economy, so much as an anti-teleological dialectic producing knowledge in opposition to destiny.... So the perverse dynamic transvalues sameness, abandoning self-identity for the unstably proximate; it discloses not an underlying unity in the name of which social division can be transcended, but a radical interconnectedness which has been and remains the unstable ground of both repression and liberation; the ground from which division and discrimination are both produced and contested. So we are not all the same. We are differences which radically proximate.... The perverse dynamic challenges not by collapsing order but through a reordering less tolerable, more disturbing, than chaos. Its difference is never the absolutely unfamiliar, but the reordering of the already known, a disclosure of a radical interconnectedness which *is* the social, but which present cultures can rarely afford to acknowledge and must instead disavow" (*Sexual Dissidence,* 229–30).

**28.** Cf. Dollimore's discussion of the perverse dynamic and transgressive reinscription: "If perversion subverts it is not as a unitary, pre-social libido, or an original plenitude, but as a transgressive agency inseparable from a dynamic intrinsic to social process. Provisionally then, this concept of the perverse dynamic denotes certain instabilities and contradictions within dominant structures which exist by virtue of exactly what those structures simultaneously contain and exclude. The displacements which constitute certain repressive discriminations are partly enabled via a proximity which, though disavowed, remains to enable a perverse return, an undoing, a transformation" (*Sexual Dissidence,* 33).

**29.** "If queer is a politically potent term, which it is, that's because, far from being capable of being detached from the childhood scene of shame, it cleaves to that scene as a near-inexhaustible source of transformational energy" (Sedgwick, "Queer Performativity," 4).

**30.** Butler, *Bodies that Matter,* 241.

**31.** Kittredge, *Chaucer and His Poetry,* 211. Cf. Carolyn Dinshaw (*Getting Medieval,* 121ff) for a discussion of Kittredge's analysis as suggesting a "forbidden yet fascinating sexual experience rendered homophobically." For a useful survey of issues of gender and sexuality and the Pardoner's body, see Robert S. Sturges, *Chaucer's Pardoner and Gender Theory: Bodies of Discourse* (New York: St. Martin's Press, 2000).

**32.** Walter Clyde Curry, "The Secret of Chaucer's Pardoner," *Journal of English and Germanic Philology* 18 (1919): 593–606. See also Robert P. Miller, "Chaucer's Pardoner, the Scriptural Eunuch, and the Pardoner's Tale," *Speculum* 30 (1955): 180–99; and Carolyn Dinshaw, "Eunuch Hermeneutics," *Chaucer's Sexual Poetics,* 156–86.

**33.** McAlpine, "The Pardoner's Homosexuality and How It Matters," *PMLA* 95 (1980): 8–22; Rowland "Animal Imagery and the Pardoner's Abnormality," *Neophilologus* 48 (1964): 56–60; Stockton, "The Deadliest Sin in the Pardoner's Tale," *Tennessee Studies in Literature* 6 (1961): 47–59. Cf. also Rita Copeland, "The Pardoner's Body and the Disciplining of Rhetoric," in Kay and Rubin, *Framing Medieval Bodies,* 148–59; and Michael A. Calabrese,

"'Make a Mark That Shows': Orphean Song, Orphean Sexuality, and the Exile of Chaucer's Pardoner," *Viator* 24 (1993): 29–86.

**34.** Green, "The Sexual Normalcy of Chaucer's Pardoner," *Medievalia* 8 (1985): 351–57. See also Green, "The Pardoner's Pants (and Why They Matter)," *Studies in the Age of Chaucer* 15 (1993): 131–45; and Helen Cooper, *Oxford Guides to Chaucer: The "Canterbury Tales"* (Oxford: Clarendon Press, 1989), 59.

**35.** Melvin Storm, "The Pardoner's Invitation: Quaestor's Bag or Becket's Shrine?" *PMLA* 97 (1982): 813.

**36.** R. Howard Bloch, *Etymologies and Genealogies: A Literary Anthropology of the French Middle Ages* (Chicago: University of Chicago Press, 1983), 133. Bloch goes on to quote, and to translate, Alain's *De planctu naturae,* prose 5: "Incudum etiam nobiles officinas ejusdem artificio deputavi, praecipiens ut eisdem eosdem malleos adaptando rerum effigiationi fideliter indulgeret, ne ab incudibus malleos aliqua exorbitatione peregrinari permitteret. Ad officium etiam scripturae calamum praepotentem eisdem fueram elargita; ut in competentibus schedules ejusdem calami scripturam poscentibus, quarum meae largitionis beneficio fuerat compotita juxta meae orthographiae normulam, rerum genera figuraret, ne a propriae descriptionis semita in falsigraphiae devia eundem devagari minime sustineret. Sed cum ipsa genialis concubitus regula, ordinates complexionibus, res diversorum sexuum oppositione dissimiles ad exequendam rerum propaginem connectere teneretur" (*Satirical Poets of the Twelfth Century,* ed. T. Wright [London: Longman, 1872], 475). (Also, I [Nature] appointed for her work anvils, noble instruments, with a command that she [Venus] would apply these same hammers to them, and faithfully give herself up to the forming of things, not permitting the hammers to become strangers to the anvils. For the office of writing I provided her with an especially potent reed-pen, in order that, on suitable leaves that desire the writing of the pen and that she had taken possession of thanks to my generosity, she might, according to the rules of my orthography, trace the nature of things, and might not suffer the pen to stray at all in the trackless diversion of false style away from the path of proper description. But since for the production of progeny the rule of marital coition, with its lawful embraces, was to connect things unlike in their opposition of the sexes.) For recent queer readings of the *De Planctu,* see Jordan, *Invention of Sodomy,* 67–91; Elizabeth Pittinger, "Explicit Ink," in Fradenburg and Freccero, *Premodern Sexualities,* 223–42; Susan Schibanoff, "Sodomy's Mark: Alan of Lille, Jean de Meun, and the Medieval Theory of Authorship," in Burger and Kruger, *Queering the Middle Ages,* 28–56.

**37.** Eugene Vance, "Chaucer's Pardoner: Relics, Discourse, and Frames of Propriety," *New Literary History* 20 (1988–89): 741–43.

**38.** Vance ("Chaucer's Pardoner," 738, 742) is quoting from Augustine's sermon on the circumcision (*Tractatus in Iohannis Evangelium* 30.5).

**39.** Cf. the feminist readings of Leicester, *Disenchanted Self,* and Dinshaw, *Chaucer's Sexual Poetics.* According to Leicester, the Pardoner remains bound by an identification with the "masculine" imagination—"a commitment, even in the mode of negation, to the fundamental assumptions of the status quo" (193). Because the Pardoner's imagination is so utterly masculine, limited to viewing things typologically as black or white, he can signify only absence and nothingness. In contrast to Leicester, Dinshaw focuses on the unknowability of the Pardoner's body and on his absolute resistance to categorization and control. Although the Pardoner's literalizing "eunuch hermeneutics" deepens a critique of patriarchal discourse developed in the *Wife of Bath's Tale* and the *Clerk's Tale,* in the end, according to Dinshaw, it goes too far by bodily enacting what has been imaginative speculation before (for example, in the Clerk's "reading like a woman"). And while the Pardoner's "unclassifiable body" may signal the need for something "beyond gender as we know it in androcentric culture" (182), only the Parson—or the Chaucer of the Retraction—can actually begin to fill this need.

**40.** Howard, *Idea of the Canterbury Tales,* 344–45. C. David Benson ("Chaucer's Pardoner: His Sexuality and Modern Critics," *Medievalia* 8 [1985]: 337–46) argues against what he sees as a tendency in modern critics to read the Pardoner as a "real" character that is based on insufficient textual evidence. However, the effect of Benson's argument is to downplay the effects of sexuality altogether in a way that implicitly asserts its own presumptive heterosexuality.

**41.** Kruger, "Claiming the Pardoner: Toward a Gay Reading of Chaucer's *Pardoner's Tale,*" *Exemplaria* 6, no. 1 (spring 1994): 115–40.

**42.** For a provocative reading of the Pardoner as a "deleuzoguattarian" "pervert" who is characterized by his lack of lack and who parodies the exchange of material goods for spiritual gain constituting the late medieval ecclesiastical system, see Alan Frantzen, "*The Pardoner's Tale,* the Pervert, and the Price of Order in Chaucer's World," in *Class and Gender in Early English Literature: Intersections,* ed. Britton J. Harwood and Gillian R. Overing (Bloomington: Indiana University Press, 1994), 131–48: "Harry, I submit, is the neurotic, as many of the Canterbury pilgrims are, trapped like him by the territorialities and the confines of ecclesiastical and financial networks. But the Pardoner, the pervert, is not. He creates his own networks and strategies for confining—for reterritorializing—others. He shows the pilgrims the operations of the system with complete clarity and, unforgivably, suggests that their privileged place in society is in part an illusion. They are not duped by *his* machinations, of course, for he has exposed his techniques; but the true believers among them may suspect that they are duped by the larger machinations of the system that remains hidden from view" (143–44). While I share Frantzen's belief that the Pardoner's perversity makes him "integral, not marginal," as I will show below, I think this is true not simply because his *tale* "leads us to the heart of medieval Christianity" (145), but because the Pardoner's perversity continues to resonate in productive ways throughout the Canterbury project.

**43.** See Nicholas J. Perella, *The Kiss, Sacred and Profane: An Interpretive History of Kiss Symbolism and Related Religio-erotic Themes* (Berkeley and Los Angeles: University of California Press, 1969), for a survey of these traditions. See also George Fenwick Jones, "The Kiss in Middle High German Literature," *Studia Neophilologica* 38 (1966): 195–210; J. Russell Major, "'Bastard Feudalism' and the Kiss: Changing Social Mores in Late Medieval and Early Modern France," *Journal of Interdisciplinary History* 17 (1987): 509–35; and Lewis E. Nicholson, "Chaucer's 'Com Pa Me': A Famous Crux Reexamined," *English Language Notes* 19 (1981): 98–102.

**44.** See Rubin, *Corpus Christi,* 74–77; Dom Gregory Dix, *The Shape of the Liturgy* (London: Dacre, 1945), 105–10; and Josef A. Jungmann, *Public Worship,* trans. Clifford Howell (Collegeville, Minnesota: Liturgical, 1957), 142–43.

**45.** See John Bossy, "Blood and Baptism: Kinship, Community and Christianity in Western Europe from the Fourteenth to the Seventeenth Centuries," in *Sanctity and Secularity: The Church and the World,* Studies in Church History, vol. 10, ed. Derek Baker (Oxford: Blackwell, 1973), 129–43; Bossy, "The Mass as a Social Institution, 1200–1700," *Past and Present* 100 (1983): 29–61; Colin Richmond, "Religion and the Fifteenth-Century English Gentleman," in *The Church, Politics, and Patronage in the Fifteenth Century,* ed. Barrie Dobson (New York: St. Martin's, 1984), 193–208; and R. G. K. A. Mertes, "The Household as a Religious Community," in *People, Politics, and Community in the Later Middle Ages,* ed. Joel Rosenthal and Colin Richmond (New York: St. Martin's, 1987), 123–39.

**46.** See Perella, *The Kiss,* 29–33, 154; Dante, *Inferno,* 5, and *Purgatorio,* 26; and Sander L. Gilman, *Sexuality: An Illustrated History* (New York: Wiley, 1989), 89–97 (where a medieval illustration of the *Purgatorio* passage is reproduced).

**47.** Daniel Knapp, "The Relyk of a Seint: A Gloss on Chaucer's Pilgrimage," *ELH* 39 (1972): 1–26, especially 5–14.

**48.** Perella, *The Kiss,* 74.

**49.** Jones, "The Kiss in Middle High German Literature," 200.

**50.** Chaucer, *The Romaunt of the Rose,* in Benson, *Riverside Chaucer,* 1997–2001.

**51.** Major, "'Bastard Feudalism' and the Kiss," 509–35.

**52.** Dollimore, *Sexual Dissidence,* 87. The full context is as follows: "In highlighting the contingency of the social, the critique of ideology may also intensify its internal instabilities, doing so in part by disarticulating or disaligning existing ideological configurations. [The result is] not so much an incoherence as a *dis*coherence—an incongruity verging on a meaningful contradiction. In the process of being made to discohere, meanings are returned to circulation, thereby becoming the more vulnerable to appropriation, transformation, and reincorporation in new configurations. Such in part are the processes whereby the social is unmade and remade, disarticulated and rearticulated."

**53.** Paul Ricoeur, *The Rule of Metaphor: Multi-disciplinary Studies of the Creation of Meaning in Language,* trans. Robert Czerny and Kathleen McLaughlin (Toronto: University of Toronto Press, 1977), 125.

**54.** Eberle, "Commercial Language and Outlook," 170–71. See also Eugene Vance, "Chrétien's *Yvain* and the Ideologies of Change and Exchange," *Yale French Studies* 70 (1986): 43–62; R. Howard Bloch, "Silence and Holes: The *Roman de silence* and the Art of the Trouvère," *Yale French Studies* 70 (1986): 81–99; and Sheila Delany, "Sexual Economics, Chaucer's Wife of Bath, and *The Book of Margery Kempe,*" in Delany, *Writing Woman: Women Writers and Women in Literature, Medieval to Modern* (New York: Schocken, 1983), 76–92.

**55.** See D. A. Miller, "Secret Subjects, Open Secrets," in *The Novel and the Police* (Berkeley and Los Angeles: University of California Press, 1988), 192–220. As Miller notes: "[I]n a world where the explicit exposure of the subject would manifest how thoroughly he has been inscribed within a socially given totality, secrecy would be the spiritual exercise by which the subject is allowed to conceive of himself as a resistance: a friction in the smooth functioning of the social order, a margin to which its far-reaching discourse does not reach. Secrecy would thus be the subjective practice in which the oppositions of private/public, inside/outside, subject/object are established, and the sanctity of their first term kept inviolate. And the phenomenon of the 'open secret' does not, as one might think, bring about the collapse of these binarisms and their ideological effects, but rather attests to their fantasmatic recovery. In a mechanism reminiscent of Freudian disavowal, we know perfectly well that the secret is known, but nonetheless we must persist, however, ineptly, in guarding it. The paradox of the open secret registers the subject's accommodation to a totalizing system that has obliterated the difference he would make—the difference he does make, in the imaginary denial of the system 'even so'" (207). See also Sedgwick's provocative discussion of an epistemology of the closet, especially *Epistemology of the Closet,* 213–51. Miller's term *open secret* has also been adapted by both Bruce R. Smith, *Homosexual Desire in Shakespeare's England: A Cultural Poetics* (Chicago: University of Chicago Press, 1991), 31–78; and Jonathan Goldberg, "Colin to Hobbinol: Spenser's Familiar Letter," *South Atlantic Quarterly* 88 (1989): 107–26, to describe the discursive presence-absence of homosexual desire in early modern England.

**56.** Dollimore, *Sexual Dissidence,* 14–15. Dollimore's discussion of Oscar Wilde's transgressive desire, especially its ability to "transvalue" traditional categories through perversion and inversion, provides a useful model for understanding the similarly transgressive power of the Pardoner's body. The substitution of characteristic X, normally assigned to the subordinate culture, for term Y, normally associated with the dominant culture, that Dollimore attributes to Wilde is something we have seen the Pardoner accused of by the other pilgrims and by many modern critics. And the X examples that Dollimore cites are remarkably similar to the characteristics often associated with the Pardoner:

| X | Y |
|---|---|
| surface | depth |
| lying | truth |
| change | stasis |
| difference | essence |
| persona/role | essential self |
| abnormal | normal |
| insincerity | sincerity |
| style/artifice | authenticity |
| facetious | serious |
| narcissism | maturity |

**57.** Peter Brown, *The Cult of the Saints: Its Rise and Function in Latin Christianity* (Chicago: University of Chicago Press, 1991), discusses the origins of relics in early Christianity. Patrick J. Geary, *Furta Sacra: Thefts of Relics in the Central Middle Ages* (Princeton: Princeton University Press, 1978); and Benedicta Ward, *Miracles and the Medieval Mind: Theory, Record, and Event, 1000–1215* (Philadelphia: University of Pennsylvania Press, 1982), describe the growing popularity of relics in the early and high Middle Ages. Ronald C. Finucane's analysis (*Miracles and Pilgrims: Popular Beliefs in Medieval England* [London: Dent, 1977]) of the social composition of pilgrims attracted to the various English shrines is especially useful. Jonathan Sumption, *Pilgrimage: An Image of Mediaeval Religion* (London: Faber, 1975), still provides one of the best overviews of the social and political factors involved in the altered status of relics and indulgences in the late medieval culture. Ben Nilson, *Cathedral Shrines of Medieval England* (Woodbridge, Suffolk: Boydell, 1998) is an invaluable resource for the material contexts of actual shrines such as Canterbury, including details of the shrine's architectural setting, pilgrim numbers and patterns, and pilgrims' offering and shrine accounts.

**58.** Sumption, *Pilgrimage,* 268. See Eamon Duffy, *The Stripping of the Altars: Traditional Religion in England 1400–1580* (New Haven, Conn.: Yale University Press, 1992), for a richly provocative consideration of the complex agency to be expressed through such a "religion of external observance."

**59.** "In the autumn of 1299 a notion spontaneously arose that the year 1300 would be a year of Jubilee in which pilgrims to St. Peter's would win huge remission.... That this seminal event should have occurred unprompted and unplanned was altogether characteristic of the religion of the late middle ages. Far from provoking this display of enthusiasm, the pope, Boniface VIII, was taken aback by it.... Nothing could be found in the writings of the fathers about Jubilees,... [the cardinals] concluded, however, that a tradition so general ought to be respected. The time was ripe to spread the fame of St. Peter, and to encourage the faithful to pay tribute to the prince of the apostles in his own basilica. It was decided that the aspirations of the crowd should be given authoritative support" (Sumption, *Pilgrimage,* 231–32).

"Indulgences, once a valuable stimulus to pilgrimage, had become an alternative. Collecting them was an object in itself, and by the close of the Middle Ages, few pilgrimages could prosper without them.... Less direct but equally damaging was the practice of offering indulgences *ad instar,* that is, of offering the indulgences of major shrines to minor ones. This again began in the fourteenth century with the marketing of the Roman Jubilee indulgence of 1390 at churches within a few miles of their homes" (ibid., 291–92).

**60.** Finucane, *Miracles and Pilgrims,* shows a high correlation between the number of male and upper-class pilgrims and the prestige of a saint and his or her shrine (see especially 130–72).

**61.** The example of Margery Kempe, another well-traveled Englishwoman, provides an illuminating counterpoint to Chaucer's bourgeois pilgrims, especially the Wife of Bath. Kempe, too, went to Compostella and the Holy Land, but she was shunned by her fellow pilgrims for her refusal to eat meat, her insistence on talking about the Gospel at meals, and her excessive weeping. See *The Book of Margery Kempe,* ed. Lynn Staley (Kalamazoo: Western Michigan University and TEAMS, 1996), 71–80; and *The Book of Margery Kempe,* trans. Barry Windeatt (Harmondsworth, England: Penguin, 1985), 99–109. Kempe also visited Hailes, Walsingham, the Portiuncula chapel in Assisi, and Wilsnack in Poland, and even established her own pilgrimage sites. For example, at the command of Christ in a vision, Kempe went to the grave of the vicar of Saint Stephen's, Norwich, to ask his intercession in the recovery of a favorite priest. In similar ways countless local, spontaneous, and unauthorized cults arose in the Middle Ages. Kempe's "excessive" behavior here, as elsewhere, met with strong disapproval from her neighbors.

**62.** See William Kamowski, "'Coillions,' Relics, Skepticism and Faith on Chaucer's Road to Canterbury: An Observation on the Pardoner's and the Host's Confrontation," *English Language Notes* 28 (1991): 5–7.

**63.** Sumption, *Pilgrimage,* 294.

**64.** Cf. Larry Scanlon's richly suggestive discussion of the discursive energy of the Pardoner, *Narrative, Authority, and Power: The Medieval Exemplum and the Chaucerian Tradition* (Cambridge: Cambridge University Press, 1994), 192–205. Scanlon focuses on the laicist politics bound up in Chaucer's equation of the inherent authority of narrative (over against sermon exemplum) with "precisely the capacity of narrative the Pardoner so memorably embodies: its generation of subject positions" (194). Moreover, the *Tale* also provides "a model narrative which is authoritative precisely because it is collective. As the textual form appropriate to the vernacular and the secular, narrative provides the collective means whereby its audience can affirm access to cultural authority on its own terms" (204).

**65.** Cf. Karma Lochrie's recent parallel observation of the underlying similarities between the two characters: "In fact, the Wife of Bath may be closer to the Pardoner than most scholars have realized so far. While the Wife's irrepressible spirit distinguishes her in character from the angry and self-destructive Pardoner, by the standards of medieval sexual ideology the two are companions in perversion. The unnatural sexualities so volubly defended and elaborated in the one case in the Wife's treatise of a Prologue and so venomously exposed in the Pardoner's self-disclosure are part of the same condition of gender pathology, the Wife's being expressed chiefly through a rampant and unchastened appetite and the Pardoner's through his feminized body, his spiritual depravity, and his invidious lust for money" (*Covert Operations,* 203). Carolyn Dinshaw also brings the two characters into productive contiguity in *Getting Medieval,* especially 126–36.

**66.** See, for example, Deleuze and Guattari, *A Thousand Plateaus:* "The B[ody] w[ithout] O[rgans] is the *field of immanence* of desire, the *plane of consistency* specific to desire (with desire defined as a process of production without reference to any exterior agency, whether it be a lack that hollows it out or a pleasure that fills it).... We come to the gradual realization that the BwO is not at all the opposite of the organs. The organs are not its enemies. The enemy is the organism. The BwO is opposed not to the organs but to that organization of the organs called the organism.... The organism is not at all the body, the BwO; rather, it is a stratum on the BwO, in other words, a phenomenon of accumulation, coagulation, and sedimentation that, in order to extract useful labor from the BwO, imposes upon it forms, functions, bonds, dominant and hierarchized organizations, organized transcendences.... But who is this we that is not me, for the subject no less than the organism belongs to and depends on a stratum? Now we have the answer: the BwO is that glacial reality where the alluvions, sedimentations, coagulations, foldings, and recoilings that compose an organism—and also a signification and a subject—occur.... The judgment of God uproots it from its immanence and makes it an organism, a signification, a subject. It is the BwO that is stratified. It swings between two poles, the surfaces of stratification into which it is recoiled, on which it submits to the judgment, and the plane of consistency in which it unfurls and opens to experimentation" (154, 159).

**67.** Cf. Deleuze and Guattari, *Thousand Plateaus:* "You have to keep enough of the organism for it to reform each dawn; and you have to keep small supplies of significance and subjectification, if only to turn them against their own systems when the circumstances demand it, when things, persons, even situations, force you to; and you have to keep small rations of subjectivity in sufficient quantity to enable you to respond to the dominant reality. Mimic the strata. You don't reach the BwO, and its plane of consistency, by wildly destratifying. That is why we encountered the paradox of those emptied and dreary bodies at the very beginning: *they had emptied themselves of their organs* instead of looking for the point at which they could patiently and momentarily dismantle the organization of the organs we call the organism. . . . Staying stratified—organized, signified, subjected—is not the worst that can happen; the worst that can happen is if you throw the strata into demented or suicidal collapse, which brings them back down on us heavier than ever. This is how it should be done: Lodge yourself on a stratum, experiment with the opportunities it offers, find an advantageous place on, find potential movements of deterritorialization, possible lines of flight, experience them, produce flow conjunctions here and there, try out continuums of intensities segment by segment, have a small plot of new land at all times. . . . We are in a social formation; first see how it is stratified for us and in us and at the place where we are; then descend from the strata to the deeper assemblage within which we are held; gently tip the assemblage, making it pass over to the side of the plane of consistency. It is only there that the BwO reveals itself for what it is: connection of desires, conjunction of flows, continuum of intensities. You have constructed your own little machine, ready when needed to be plugged into other collective machines" (160–61).

## 5. Desiring Machines

1. Deleuze and Guattari, *Thousand Plateaus*, 3–4. See also chapter 1 for an earlier discussion of machinic assemblage, and chapter 4 (notes 66 and 67) for the Body without Organs.

2. This extends to the tale-teller himself. Certainly we have little of the impersonated artistry—to use Leicester's apt phrase describing the complex reality effects created by the pilgrimage frame (*Disenchanted Self*, 1–13)—provided by other tales' sense of appropriateness to their tale-teller, nor any action in the pilgrimage frame to situate the tale (as is the case with the *Miller's Tale*, the *Reeve's Tale*, or the *Summoner's Tale*). Perhaps the clearest proof of this lack of secure foundation for the tale in the body and personality of a teller is the fact that a number of critics have suggested that the tale was originally intended for the Wife of Bath, in part because the teller of the tale seems sometimes to speak as a woman.

3. See Gerhard Joseph, "Chaucer's Coinage: Foreign Exchange and the Puns of the *Shipman's Tale*," *Chaucer Review* 17 (1983): 351–52, for a discussion of why such a pun might be read into the tale, despite the fact that the earliest known use of "cosin" to mean "fraud" or "trickery" cited by the OED and MED is 1453, and the verb "to cozen" in its modern sense of "to cheat" does not appear in English until the sixteenth century. Joseph speculates that "the standard lexical authorities are wrong: it is here at the end of the fourteenth century in the *Shipman's Tale* that we encounter the earliest English use of 'cosynage' as 'cheating' or 'deceiving.' Chaucer has himself coined, has 'fallen' into that sense of the word in the process of narration: just as the tale's circulation of money has created sexual commerce among the wife, monk, and merchant and a thousand-frank profit for the merchant, so the free and easy use of a word, 'cosynage,' has produced a linguistic increment, the production of a new signification" (352). See also Thomas Hahn, "Money,

Sexuality, Wordplay, and Context in the *Shipman's Tale,*" in Wasserman and Blanch, *Chaucer in the Eighties,* 235–49.

4. Reynaud de Louens, *Le Livre de Mellibee et Prudence,* ed. J. Burke Severs, in *Sources and Analogues of Chaucer's Canterbury Tales,* ed. W. F. Bryan and G. Dempster (Chicago: Chicago University Press, 1941), 568–614; Albertano of Brescia, *Liber consolationis,* ed. Thor Sundby, Chaucer Society, 2d series, vol. 8 (London: Trübner, 1873).

5. Daniel Rubey, "The Five Wounds of Melibee's Daughter: Transforming Masculinities," in *Masculinities in Chaucer,* ed. Peter G. Beidler, Chaucer Studies 25 (Cambridge: Boydell and Brewer, 1998), 157–71, quotation on 157.

6. Indeed, many potential modern readers do not even have this option since the *Melibee* is often omitted from the course syllabi of college Chaucer courses.

7. The *locus classicus* for the tale as proof of Chaucer's allegorizing moral intentions for the *Tales* is, of course, D. W. Robertson Jr.'s *Preface to Chaucer: Studies in Medieval Perspectives* (Princeton: Princeton University Press, 1962): "Chaucer tells us that the Melibee, although it differs verbally from the other tales the audience has heard from the 'sondry folk' who proceed toward Canterbury, and contains more proverbs than any of the others, after which it is now placed, it does not differ from them in *sentence.* But all this is a rather indirect and poetic way of saying something else: pay attention to the *sentence* of the Melibee because it affords a clue to the *sentence* of all the other tales which come before it" (369). But a similar tendency to read the *Melibee* straight also dominates other less programmatic approaches. Although antithetical to Robertson in his understanding of "the idea of the *Canterbury Tales,*" Donald Howard also sees the *Melibee* as a moment in which Chaucer "appears before us in good earnest" and thus underscores the tale as "the focal point of an 'address to the court' which runs throughout *The Canterbury Tales*" (*Idea of the Canterbury Tales,* 315).

8. See, for example, Dolores Palamo, "What Chaucer Really Did to *Le Livre de Mellibee,*" *Philological Quarterly* 53 (1974): 304–20; Alan Gaylord, "Sentence and Solaas in Fragment VII of the *Canterbury Tales:* Harry Bailly as Horseback Editor," *PMLA* 82 (1967): 221–35; Ruth Waterhouse and Gwen Griffiths, "'Sweete Wordes' of Non-sense: The Deconstruction of the Moral *Melibee,* (Part 1)," *Chaucer Review* 23 (1989): 338–61, and "(Part II)," *Chaucer Review* (1989): 53–63.

9. The fact that allegorizing in the tale arises from the activity of Prudence translating authorities and applying them to Melibee's situation is an important reason for this emphasis on agency. Consider the very different relationship of the reader to narrative if the allegory were delivered in fable/allegorical commentary mode. Lloyd J. Matthews notes in this regard that while Melibee's name gets allegorical treatment, Prudence's does not: "Prudence remains essentially a fictional, as opposed to an allegorical, character." In *Troilus and Criseyde,* on the other hand, Prudence is allegorized in traditional terms as a lady with three eyes ("The Date of Chaucer's *Melibee* and the Stages of the *Tale*'s Incorporation in the *Canterbury Tales,*" *Chaucer Review* 20 [1986]: 221–34).

10. Scanlon, *Narrative, Authority, and Power,* 210.

11. Lerer cites the example of Huntington Library MS HM 144, where the tale appears without its author's name or reference to the *Canterbury Tales* and is headed simply "Prouerbis" (*Chaucer and His Readers,* 95ff.). He also notes how the owner's annotations

to the Helmingham manuscript of the *Canterbury Tales* (now in the Princeton University Library, MS Princeton 100) show the uses made of *Melibee* in educating youthful members of the household.

**12.** Seth Lerer, "'Now holde youre mouth': The Romance of Orality in the *Thopas-Melibee* Section of the *Canterbury Tales*," in *Oral Poetics in Middle English Poetry*, ed. M. C. Amodio (New York: Garland, 1994), 195.

**13.** John M. Manley and Edith Rickert (*The Text of the Canterbury Tales, Studied on the Basis of All Known Manuscripts*, 8 vols. [Chicago: University of Chicago Press, 1940]) note that the *Melibee* has survived in seventy-eight of eighty-two manuscripts of the *Canterbury Tales* and surmise that "obviously the tale was popular" (2:371–72).

**14.** For fifteenth-century anthologizations of *Melibee*, see Daniel S. Sylvia, "Some Fifteenth-Century Manuscripts of the *Canterbury Tales*," in *Chaucer and Middle English Studies in Honor of Rossell Hope Robbins*, ed. Beryl Rowland (London: George Allen and Unwin, 1974), 153–63. See also Lerer, *Chaucer and His Readers*, 95ff.

**15.** See Albertano of Brescia, *De amore et dilectione Dei et proximi et aliarum rerum et de forma vitae. An Edition*, ed. Sharon Hiltz (Ph.D. diss., University of Pennsylvania, 1980), 290–325. See also, James M. Powell, *Albertanus of Brescia: The Pursuit of Happiness in the Early Thirteenth Century* (Philadelphia: University of Pennsylvania Press, 1992), 14, and David Wallace, *Chaucerian Polity*, 214–21.

**16.** Wallace, *Chaucerian Polity*, 217.

**17.** Ibid., 218.

**18.** Ibid., 219.

**19.** Ibid., 220.

**20.** Daniel Kempton, "Chaucer's Tale of Melibee: 'A litel thing in prose,'" *Genre* 21 (1988): 263–78.

**21.** J. D. Burnley, *Chaucer's Language and the Philosophers' Tradition* (Cambridge: D. S. Brewer, 1979), 51–52.

**22.** Reginald Pecock, *The Folewer to the Donet*, ed. Elsie Vaughan Hitchcock, Early English Text Society, Original Services no. 164 (London: Oxford University Press, 1924), 52; Burnley, *Chaucer's Language*, 53.

**23.** Ibid.

**24.** Burnley, *Chaucer's Language*, 55.

**25.** Collette, "Heeding the Counsel of Prudence," 421.

**26.** Ibid., 423–24.

**27.** Ibid., 427, 429.

**28.** Cf. Prudence's later instruction to Melibee, quoting Solomon, that "right as the herte of a man deliteth in savour that is soote, right so the conseil of trewe freendes yeveth swetnesse to the soule" (VII.1157).

**29.** Paul Strohm, "The Allegory of the *Tale of Melibee*," *Chaucer Review* 2 (1967): 32–42.

**30.** Benedict Anderson, *Imagined Communities: Reflections on the Origin and Spread of Nationalism*, rev. ed. (New York: Verso, 1991), 33–36.

**31.** In many ways, then, the *Melibee* restructures these relationships in a way that fantasizes the evacuation of the mechanisms of shame I have been arguing as crucial to the construction of "gentil" identity in the *Tales*, so that it no longer seems necessary to choose between the sadism of disciplinary control and the masochistic contract.

**32.** Of course, the Melibee story itself poses such a question (via Prudence) and resolves it (via Prudence's good counsel and Melibee's subsequent maturation).

**33.** Lee Patterson, "'What Man Artow?': Authorial Self-Definition in the *Tale of Sir Thopas* and the *Tale of Melibee*," *Studies in the Age of Chaucer* 11 (1989): 117–18.

**34.** Wallace, *Chaucerian Polity*, 212–13.

**35.** David Wallace, "In Flaundres," *Studies in the Age of Chaucer* 19 (1997): 74–75.

**36.** Ibid., 76.

**37.** Cited by Wallace, "In Flaundres," 84.

**38.** Harriet E. Hudson notes that "Middle English popular romances reached a diverse audience, depending on the occasion of their reading or recitation, and were produced in diverse milieux. However, they are particularly associated with the gentry" ("Class, Family, and Gender in Some Middle English Popular Romances," in *Class and Gender in Early English Literature: Intersections*, ed. Britton J. Harwood and Gillian R. Overing [Bloomington: University of Indiana Press, 1994] 76–94, quotation on 77). Cf. also Derek Pearsall, "The Audiences of the Middle English Romances," in *Historical and Editorial Studies in Medieval and Early Modern English for Johan Gerritsen*, ed. Mary-Jo Arn and Hanneke Wirtjes (Groningen: Wolters-Noordhoff, 1985), 37–47.

**39.** Interestingly, the *Melibee* manages this mobility without resorting to the dream vision form and its kind of middle experience. Instead, *Melibee* remains mundane, "in the world," and yet *as allegory* in a "becoming" rather than strictly referential relationship to the mundane.

**40.** Kellie Robertson, "Common Language and Common Profit," in *The Postcolonial Middle Ages*, ed. Jeffrey Jerome Cohen (New York: St. Martin's Press, 2000), 218.

**41.** Ibid., 210. For a full and richly suggestive discussion of the changes that a growing acknowledgment of the burgeoning market economy had on late medieval philosophy, canon law, and the general culture, see Joel Kaye, *Economy and Nature in the Fourteenth Century: Money, Market Exchange, and the Emergence of Scientific Thought* (New York: Cambridge University Press, 1998).

**42.** Fradenburg and Freccero, *Premodern Sexualities*, viii.

**43.** For example, the *Nun's Priest's Tale* does not work in terms of a simple referentiality back to "real life" or some symbolic "Real" of allegorical signification, but instead "dreams" the present in all its potentiality.

**44.** See Patterson's discussion of childhood, childishness, and immaturity in the fragment (and Chaucer's work more generally), and Chaucer's use of childhood to stage a problematic central to the act of writing, in "'What Man Artow,'" 162–75.

**45.** For a provocative discussion of masculinity in Fragment VII as an economy of flows, see Jeffrey Jerome Cohen, "Diminishing Masculinity in Chaucer's *Tale of Sir Thopas*," in *Masculinities in Chaucer*, ed. Peter Beidler (Minneapolis: University of Minnesota Press, 1999), 143–56. Cohen notes: "The six narratives of Fragment VII and their dramatic bridges explore how masculinity represents itself as bigger than life, like a giant, a *universal*. Yet masculinity in practice turns out to be a phenomenon of little things: merchant bodies, elvish authors, tiny clergeons, infantalized knights, self-inflated monks, farmhouse fowls" (*Masculinities in Chaucer,* 144).

**46.** "The only assemblages are machinic assemblages of desire and collective assemblages of enunciation.... There is no longer a tripartite division between a field of reality (the world) and a field of representation (the book) and a field of subjectivity (the author). Rather, an assemblage establishes connections between certain multiplicities drawn from each of these orders, so that a book has no sequel nor the world as its object nor one or several authors as its subject.... How can the book find an adequate outside with which to assemble in heterogeneity, rather than a world to reproduce? The cultural book is necessarily a tracing: a tracing of other books however different they may be, an endless tracing of established concepts and words, a tracing of the world present, past, and future. Even the anticultural book may still be burdened by too heavy a cultural load: but it will use it actively, for forgetting instead of remembering, for underdevelopment instead of progress toward development, in nomadism rather than sedentarity, to make a map instead of a tracing.... *Between* things does not designate a localizable relation going from one thing to the other and back again, but a perpendicular direction, a transversal movement that sweeps one *and* the other away, a stream without beginning or end that undermines its banks and picks up speed in the middle" (Deleuze and Guattari, *Thousand Plateaus,* 22–25).

## 6. Post-ality and the "End" of the *Canterbury Tales*

**1.** I would like to bracket for a moment the questions raised by the Host's comments. Clearly all the pilgrims have not yet told a tale, at least according to any of the extant manuscripts of the *Tales* that we have. Nor is it clear whether the Host means the Parson to "knytte up" the storytelling contest for the trip *to* Canterbury, with more tales to follow on the return journey, or whether the Host's comments mark a change of heart on Chaucer's part for the Canterbury project that was not incorporated into a revised *General Prologue* (which suggests four tales from each pilgrim—two on the journey to Canterbury and two on the return journey to London—I.792–95). See Charles A. Owen Jr., *Pilgrimage and Storytelling in the Canterbury Tales: The Dialectic of "Ernest" and "Game"* (Norman: University of Oklahoma Press, 1977), for an argument that this latter plan still held true and that the *Tales* as we have them are massively unfinished; and Donald Howard, *Idea of the Canterbury Tales* (especially 1–20, 210–332) for the alternative view that the *Tales* are "unfinished but complete" (1). Clearly later readers such as Lydgate and the Beryn scribe felt free to incorporate more tales into the return journey. Nonetheless, as I will make clear in this chapter, I am concerned with larger questions of closure and historicist teleologies that inhabit the structure of the *Tales,* whether they "end" with the Parson or not.

**2.** Walter Benjamin, "Theses on the Philosophy of History," in *Illuminations,* trans. Hannah Arendt (New York: Schocken Books, 1986), 262–63.

**3.** Bhabha, *Location of Culture,* 4.

**4.** See Lochrie, *Covert Operations*, 15–24, for her discussion of Foucault and confession.

**5.** Ibid., 32, 41. Lochrie notes that this production of the self via confession, along with the pleasure associated with such labor, despite Foucault's attempts to distinguish such activity as a quintessentially modern invention, is medieval. Nor was such pleasure confined to the subject of sex and sexuality as Foucault thought. Sexuality was "only one aspect of a system devoted to the surveillance of the individual, and it was not always the most verbose" (41).

**6.** Duffy, *Stripping of the Altars*, 59–60.

**7.** Duffy, *Stripping of the Altars;* Gail McMurray Gibson, *The Theater of Devotion: East Anglian Drama and Society in the Late Middle Ages* (Chicago: University of Chicago Press, 1989); Caroline M. Barron, "The Parish Fraternities of Medieval London," 13–37.

**8.** Foucault, *History of Sexuality*, vol. 1, 71, quoted in Lochrie, *Covert Operations*, 40.

**9.** Lochrie, *Covert Operations*, 40.

**10.** John Lydgate, "Prologue to the *Siege of Thebes*," ll. 1–2, 13–21, 36–40, 66–72, 76–78, in *The Canterbury Tales: Fifteenth-Century Continuations and Additions*, ed. John M. Bowers (Kalamazoo: TEAMS, 1992), 13–15.

**11.** Ibid., ll. 79–81.

**12.** *The Canterbury Interlude and Merchant's Tale of Beryn*, ll. 135–37, 140, in Bowers, *The Canterbury Tales*, 63–64.

**13.** Ibid., ll. 281–94.

**14.** The fifteenth-century tale assigned to the Ploughman also provides an interesting case in point. Late fourteenth- and early fifteenth-century associations of ploughmen with dissident social and theological views such as Lollardy, as John Bowers points out, meant that by the mid-fifteenth century, "the agents responsible for organizing the Christ Church manuscript of *The Canterbury Tales* apparently felt that even a mute Plowman was not altogether desirable. This collection, which also includes the *Siege of Thebes*, gave the Plowman a tale and positioned it fourth from the end, between the Squire and the Second Nun. Provided with a makeshift prologue fitting the work into the pilgrimage narrative, this rhyme-royal Miracle of the Virgin originally written by Thomas Hoccleve (d. c. 1426) was placed in the mouth of the Plowman as a story of unimpeachable orthodoxy. In fact, the exemplum of a young monk rewarded by the Virgin for praying his Latin *Pater Noster* was implicitly anti-Lollard, since Wycliffites had insisted that it was better to say the prayer 'Our Father' in English without Mary's mediation. The subversive potential of the Plowman as a spokesman for radical change was fully realized during the Protestant Reformation of the next century. An anti-fraternal work, most of which was composed about 1400 and kept alive in the Lollard literary underground throughout the fifteenth century, surfaced to be printed with official sanction about 1536. The piece was then inserted as The Plowman's Tale immediately after the Parson's Tale, the two brothers side by side as they had been in the General Prologue in William Thynne's 1542 edition of *The Canterbury Tales* dedicated to Henry VIII" (*The Canterbury Tales: Fifteenth-Century Continuations and Additions*, 23–24).

**15.** *The Canterbury Interlude*, ll. 380–81, in Bowers, *The Canterbury Tales*, 70.

**16.** Ibid., ll. 420–21, in Bowers, *The Canterbury Tales,* 71.

**17.** The story makes up a major portion of the Interlude; see especially ll. 619–74.

**18.** Bhabha, *Location of Culture,* 4.

**19.** Ibid.

**20.** Jordan, *Invention of Sodomy,* 161.

**21.** See Wallace, "In Flaundres," 79–87, for a discussion of how the tale's Flemish setting resonates with the Pardoner's supposed counterfeiting of nature, his sterility, and his modernity.

**22.** The "figural possibility" that Scanlon has argued is made possible by the focus on death in the *Pardoner's Tale* has, I think, some telling correspondences with what I am arguing is happening with the various "deaths" threatened by the end of the *Tales:* "Death operates throughout the *Pardoner's Tale* as a product of figuration, as the result of the imposition on the world of discursive and ideological values. The death that comes to the three rioters is a death which they produce, albeit not under conditions entirely of their own choosing. From the moment of the oath onwards the death that comes to them depends on their efforts, and in particular on their manipulations of the discursive framework they all share. If this permeability between death and human forms of collectivity provides the tale with the vantage point from which it can gesture beyond itself, it also provides a model of narrative which is authoritative precisely because it is collective. . . . Chaucer's dependence on the figure of Death for access to such authority clearly bespeaks a profound conviction in the reality of Christian redemption. But it also bespeaks an equally strong belief in the performative power of narrative figuration. . . . [T]he death which authorizes the narrative of the *Pardoner's Tale* is not a terminal boundary, but a figural possibility which underwrites the narrative from start to finish, framing its logic and providing an essential element of its motivation. Moreover, what it figures is not the actual limit of narrative, but narrative's capacity to figure such limits. . . . [for] human death is never purely biological. It is also irreducibly social, and not just when it comes to the form of execution or battle fatality.

"The *Pardoner's Prologue* and *Tale* insists on this collective aspect, which it grounds in Christian redemption, but which it articulates against clerical tradition in the name of the vernacular" (*Narrative, Authority, and Power,* 204–5).

# Index

# MEDIEVAL CULTURES

**Volume 31**
L. O. Aranye Fradenburg
*Sacrifice Your Love: Psychoanalysis, Historicism, Chaucer*

**Volume 30**
Stephanie Trigg
*Congenial Souls: Reading Chaucer from Medieval to Postmodern*

**Volume 29**
Edited by Kathleen Ashley and Robert L. A. Clark
*Medieval Conduct*

**Volume 28**
D. Vance Smith
*The Book of the Incipit: Beginnings in the Fourteenth Century*

**Volume 27**
Edited by Glenn Burger and Steven F. Kruger
*Queering the Middle Ages*

**Volume 26**
Paul Strohm
*Theory and the Premodern Text*

**Volume 25**
David Rollo
*Glamorous Sorcery: Magic and Literacy in the High Middle Ages*

**Volume 24**
Steve Ellis
*Chaucer at Large: The Poet in the Modern Imagination*

**Volume 23**
Edited by Barbara Hanawalt and Michal Kobialka
*Medieval Practices of Space*

**Volume 22**
Michelle R. Warren
*History on the Edge: Excalibur and the Borders of Britain, 1100–1300*

**Volume 21**
Olivia Holmes
*Assembling the Lyric Self: Authorship from Troubadour Song to Italian Poetry Book*

**Volume 20**
Karen Sullivan
*The Interrogation of Joan of Arc*

**Volume 19**
Clare A. Lees
*Tradition and Belief: Religious Writing in Late Anglo-Saxon England*

**Volume 18**
David Matthews
*The Making of Middle English, 1765–1910*

**Volume 17**
Jeffrey Jerome Cohen
*Of Giants: Sex, Monsters, and the Middle Ages*

**Volume 16**
Edited by Barbara A. Hanawalt and David Wallace
*Medieval Crime and Social Control*

**Volume 15**
Kathryn Kerby-Fulton and Denise L. Despres
*Iconography and the Professional Reader: The Politics of Book Production in the Douce "Piers Plowman"*

**Volume 14**
Edited by Marilynn Desmond
*Christine de Pizan and the Categories of Difference*

**Volume 13**
Alfred Thomas
*Anne's Bohemia: Czech Literature and Society, 1310–1420*

**Volume 12**
Edited by F. R. P. Akehurst and Stephanie Cain Van D'Elden
*The Stranger in Medieval Society*

**Volume 11**
Edited by Karma Lochrie, Peggy McCracken, and James A. Schultz
*Constructing Medieval Sexuality*

**Volume 10**
Claire Sponsler
*Drama and Resistance: Bodies, Goods, and Theatricality in Late Medieval England*

**Volume 9**
Edited by Barbara A. Hanawalt and David Wallace
*Bodies and Disciplines: Intersections of Literature and History in Fifteenth-Century England*

**Volume 8**
Marilynn Desmond
*Reading Dido: Gender, Textuality, and the Medieval "Aeneid"*

**Volume 7**
Edited by Clare A. Lees
*Medieval Masculinities: Regarding Men in the Middle Ages*

**Volume 6**
Edited by Barbara A. Hanawalt and Kathryn L. Reyerson
*City and Spectacle in Medieval Europe*

**Volume 5**
Edited by Calvin B. Kendall and Peter S. Wells
*Voyage to the Other World: The Legacy of Sutton Hoo*

**Volume 4**
Edited by Barbara A. Hanawalt
*Chaucer's England: Literature in Historical Context*

**Volume 3**
Edited by Marilyn J. Chiat and Kathryn L. Reyerson
*The Medieval Mediterranean: Cross-Cultural Contacts*

**Volume 2**
Edited by Andrew MacLeish
*The Medieval Monastery*

**Volume 1**
Edited by Kathryn L. Reyerson and Faye Powe
*The Medieval Castle*

**Glenn Burger** is associate professor of English at Queens College and the Graduate Center, City University of New York. He is the editor of Hetoum's *A Lytell Cronycle: Richard Pynson's Translation c. 1520 of "La Fleur des histoires de la terre d'Orient" c. 1307*, and coeditor, with Steven Kruger, of *Queering the Middle Ages* (Minnesota, 2001). He has published widely on Chaucer, queer theory, and postcolonial medieval studies.